Larry Semon,
Daredevil Comedian
of the Silent Screen

Larry Semon, Daredevil Comedian of the Silent Screen

A Biography and Filmography

CLAUDIA SASSEN

Foreword by NORBERT APING

McFarland & Company, Inc., Publishers
Jefferson, North Carolina

Frontispiece: Collage of Larry Semon's artwork for the *New York Evening Telegram*, 1910–1911 (courtesy Fulton History, composed by Claudia Sassen).

Library of Congress Cataloguing-in-Publication data [new form]

Names: Sassen, Claudia.
Title: Larry Semon, daredevil comedian of the silent screen : a biography and filmography / Claudia Sassen.
Description: Jefferson, North Carolina : McFarland & Company, Inc., Publishers, 2015. | Includes bibliographical references and index. | Includes filmography.
Identifiers: LCCN 2015038046| ISBN 9780786498222 (softcover : acid free paper) | ISBN 9781476620275 (ebook)
Subjects: LCSH: Semon, Larry, 1889–1928. | Actors—United States—Biography. | Motion picture producers and directors—United States—Biography. | Screenwriters—United States—Biography.
Classification: LCC PN2287.S349 S37 2015 | DDC 791.4302/8092—dc23
LC record available at http://lccn.loc.gov/2015038046

British Library cataloguing data are available

© 2015 Claudia Sassen. All rights reserved

No part of this book may be reproduced or transmitted in any form or by any means, electronic or mechanical, including photocopying or recording, or by any information storage and retrieval system, without permission in writing from the publisher.

Front cover: Larry Semon (photograph by Albert Witzel); back cover illustration by Steve Rydzewski © 2015

Printed in the United States of America

McFarland & Company, Inc., Publishers
Box 611, Jefferson, North Carolina 28640
www.mcfarlandpub.com

To my research assistants Chris, Steve and Patrick
(in order of appearance)

Table of Contents

Acknowledgments ix
Foreword by Norbert Aping 1
Preface 3

1. Roots and Settings 7
2. On the Road 18
3. Paperland 28
4. Early Directions 53
5. Growing Success 71
6. Womenfolk 94
7. The Flawmill 114
8. Image Change 133
9. The Perfect Frown 152
10. From Broke to Breakdown 172
11. Slow Motion 176
12. Fade out 184

Appendix: "Magic, Past and Present, Exposed" 191
Filmography by Patrick Skacel and Claudia Sassen 193
Chapter Notes 229
Bibliography 239
Index 247

Acknowledgments

Over the past twenty years, Steve Rydzewski, who gave my manuscript the once-over, has so generously supplied me with finds and further help that I always wanted to have him co-author this book. He was the first to make me feel confident with my writing on Semon and through his friendship always encouraged me to continue. He was also the one to inspire me to do some deeper digging into Semon's untimely death, be it fake or not, but worth considering.

Eagle-eyed film collector, scholar and Semon filmography co-author Patrick Skacel supplied me with many rare prints from his long-time film collection. These films helped me evaluate Larry Semon's work from a different perspective as well as compile our filmography. He has also located hundreds of Larry's cartoons and illustrations which are deserving of a book on their own.

Chris Seguin has been there since the beginning of my Larry Semon endeavor and has helped with many finds over the years. We have shared numerous intensive discussions and he has been one of my strongest supporters and biggest motivators.

For their vital help I would also like to thank the following people: Bob Dickson for critical advice and combing through the microfilm at Special Collections-URL, UCLA, when a find was not a mouse-click away; Stewart Ng of Special Collections-URL, UCLA for Vitagraph release synopses; Lynne Whitcopf, Reuben Matzkin, Joan Berschler, Jessie Salmon, and Shirley Lagasse for private photos and information; Ned Comstock at USC for material, Glenn Mitchell for discussion, rare films and research material; Sam Gill for photos and quotations; Jürgen Krzistetzko for advice when there seemed no possible way; Camillo Moscati for kindly opening his large film archive; Andreas Koller for his generosity and keeping the "Larry-Semon-Stiftung" going; Scott Hayden for photos and memories; Simon Myers for films and systematic information; David Wyatt for films; Jordan Young and George Katchmer for research material and discussion; Rob Stone for sharing his notes from his book *Laurel or Hardy*; Marc Wanamaker of Bison Archives, Bob Correia and Dr. Robert Kiss for photographs; Tom Tryniski for his abundant online archive; Karin Hartwich for making available the German *Klamottenkiste* series; Davide Turconi for his fundamental Semon filmography; Kevin Brownlow for letting me quote from his interviews; Adam Čwiklak for restoring Semon films; Dr. Norbert Aping for granting me access to the files of Heinz Caloué and the German

Board of Censors; Lyman Hardeman of Old Cardboard Magazine, Chris Carmen, Elif Rongen-Kaynakcı (EYE Film Institute, Amsterdam), Andy Bertore, Ned Thanhouser, Carlos Paz Molina, Marilyn Slater, Bill Oates, Anthony Slide, Tommie Hicks, Dorit Stayne, James Neibaur, Jean-Jacques Couderc, Juan Gabriel Tharrats, Karel Čáslavský, Cole Johnson, Coy Watson, Alberto Del Fabro, Medardo Amor, Petr Král, Gian-Luca Farinelli, Zsuzsa Perjési, Michael Hanisch, Romina Marks, Sven-Lars Kludig, Judy Hall, Anna Lüders-Cavaliere, Bruce Long, Sylvia Nasaroff, and Lawrence Martin Semon.

I would like to thank Sid Goldin for discovering Larry Semon, and film pioneer James Stuart Blackton for signing him to Vitagraph, and Thomas Alva Edison for talking James Stuart Blackton into buying one of those Vitascopes. Without you, Larry Semon and this book would never have been possible. More thanks go out to Google Street View, whose recently updated version allowed me to follow Larry's trip to many different locations, saving me the pleasure of my own trip to the States.

Thank you, Mother, for proofreading, thank you, Father, for listening.

Patrick wishes to thank Tom Stathes and Gerry Orlando. And our sincere apologies to anyone we may have omitted or failed to credit, but thank you.

Last but not least, we wish to thank all the film dupers out there who made sure that Larry Semon's pictures continued to circulate.

Foreword

by Norbert Aping

In late 1964 I saw my first Larry Semon film on *Es darf gelacht werden* (*You Are Allowed to Laugh*), the pioneering German TV series which introduced us to American slapstick comedy. Werner Schwier, a film expounder from the silent era, presented to his audience movie havoc accompanied by a piano and a solo violinist. This series gave exposure to many other comedians, among them, naturally, Chaplin, Buster Keaton, Laurel and Hardy and Harold Lloyd. But Semon's *Holzhackereien*, as *The Sawmill* was known in Germany, was an eminently wild spectacle, quite unprecedented—and soon it was the talk of my classmates and myself. Most of us had become slapstick fans thanks to *Es Darf Gelacht Werden*. The cinema, however, fell short of Larry Semon, the clown of the white face, wide-flapping too-short trousers and incredible stunts. The era of silent slapstick films was long gone by then and the first two compilations by Robert Youngson, *The Golden Age of Comedy* (1959) and *When Comedy Was King* (1960), did not offer any trace of Larry Semon.

The question was where to find more Larry Semon films. The sobering response was: nowhere! Then two fragments emerged in Bob Monkhouse's *Mad Movies*. A larger number of Semon clips was available only some years later, from the German TV series *Männer ohne Nerven* (*Gentlemen of Nerve*) and *Klamottenkiste* (*Ragbag*). These meant no cinematic presentations, though. The films were padded with newly created funny comments which did not necessarily coincide with their original intertitles. Nevertheless, the remainders had not lost their breathtaking quality. Larry Semon and his foils were masters of their art. It was a pleasure to witness their frolicking which was shot in a way that gave the impression that their players never had an opportunity to pause for breath. Larry Semon was—by far—not a product of days long gone that could randomly have been assigned to anyone else. He was unique. But where could you learn something about him in the early 1980s? The mere attempt at tracking down Kalton C. Lahue and Sam Gill's book *Clown Princes and Court Jesters* in a library was a decided drag.

When I began researching the German history of Laurel and Hardy, Semon naturally played a role. Approximately 50 of his films had made it to the box office of the Weimar Republic in the 1920s. The censorship documents of German releases had not been passed on to coming generations in their entirety. They would have offered information on the films' intertitles which in turn would have meant a chance at identifying their original titles. Sometimes German intertitles were so random that hardly any conclusions could be drawn to their original counterparts. And then there were titles from German exhibitors lacking additional information. They matched too broad a selection of films so that identification appeared futile.

In the course of my research I bumped into Claudia Sassen at the end of the 1990s. To my surprise she was quite familiar with Larry Semon. Not only did she help me with my search, but also whetted my appetite for this neglected artist. She was fulfilling her desire to write a biography on his life and work. And finally there is certainty: Claudia Sassen has closed a gap within the history of classical American slapstick film and impressively gives evidence that Larry Semon was surely no clown in the "also ran" class. Rather he was a most important artist who gave blockbuster star Charles Chaplin serious competition. Up to now only rumors had been floating about this.

He who has tried to locate biographical data about artists and their families will know how much toil is owed to each piece of information. Semon's family tree and curriculum vitae are now enhanced by suchlike data. Of an equivalent importance it is to understand the interaction of Semon the cartoonist and Semon the mirthmaker. It seems that Semon's tentatively spoken, turbulent and much too short life outside films somehow finds its match in them. Claudia Sassen's biography paints a clearly different picture of photoplayer Semon who, perpetually, was widely reduced to being jealous of Stan Laurel and to his thoughtless overspending on the film set. Another asset is the most detailed filmography of Semon I have ever seen. It was co-written by dedicated film collector Patrick Skacel. It is a tremendous achievement considering that the filmography is focused on titles from an era when hardly anything was archived, let alone systematically documented. You will only go to pains like this when you love what you do, and this is obviously what Claudia Sassen has done.

Judge, district court director and avid film buff Norbert Aping is a recognized authority on Laurel and Hardy and author of three books on the duo, including The Final Film of Laurel and Hardy *(McFarland, 2008), and two on Chaplin.*

Preface

Larry Semon, whose surname by the way does not rhyme with "lemon," was an outstanding character, with strange, nonetheless appealing looks, eccentric behavior and many talents. His talents allowed him to adjust to a rough life and start three if not four different careers. He became a Hollywood star and was celebrated all over the world as Ridolini, Zigoto, Agapito, Bigorno, Jester, Jaimito, Tomasín, Narizotas or simply Larry. Rarely had there been a comedian who created such a strong bond with his audience and who conveyed a feeling of high spirit and a lust for life as convincingly as Larry Semon did.

In the midst of stardom, Semon's films were marvelous, nicely composed and crammed with originality. Consider the two-reelers filmed in 1919 such as *Traps and Tangles* and *Scamps and Scandals*; the gags develop from the situations. The plot is in a natural flow. Freeze-frame those films wherever you want; every frame will make a tremendous impact. Larry's inventiveness seemed to suffer in late 1919, soon after he had signed his $3.6 million contract with Vitagraph. That sum today would amount to an estimated $32.4 million. But something apparently inexplicable had happened. By around 1921, Larry's films, although still worth watching, had lost much of their novelty, character, and innocence. They were polished and that did not do them any good. Gag recycling was typical, and in the end, Semon's films were nothing but routine work, as if he had lost his interest in them and considered them a burden. This development may be attributed to Larry's desire to free himself from Vitagraph, a film company that did not give him the artistic freedom he had hoped for. They also kept him often in court.

It may be explained by a personal mishap, since Larry was having an ill-fated love affair with his leading lady Lucille Carlisle, for whom he had left his wife and child. Leaving Vitagraph, Semon thought that he was on his way into a velvety future. However, with his new contracts, he found himself on a downhill path resulting in his financial and physical breakdown.

That only Semon's later work is easily available may explain why he has been underrated over the recent decades. Walter Kerr in *The Silent Clowns* spends a complete chapter explaining why one better *not* like Larry Semon and why just *everybody* else must be better.[1] He supports his view with *The Wizard of Oz* (1925) and *The Stunt Man* (1927), undeniably poor films, but would that not be the same as judging Buster Keaton by

What, No Beer? (1933)? Kerr must have been familiar with Semon's masterpieces, yet he ignored them. Many others just touch upon Semon's biography and try to prove that Semon's main goal in life was to sabotage Stan Laurel's talent.

So, what is the objective of this book?

To acknowledge and document the long-forgotten contribution and life of Larry Semon.

To be fair, there *has* been some serious interest in Larry Semon. Author Petr Král dedicated several philosophical essays to him,[2] as did Jean-Jacques Couderc.[3] Camillo Moscati celebrated Larry through a compilation of memorabilia, contemporary Italian articles, and frame enlargements that help every archivist identify Semon's films currently extant.[4] Phil Hall and Rory Aronsky gave Semon a chapter in their book *What If They Lived?* along with other prematurely deceased Hollywood stars such as Jean Harlow and River Phoenix, to name but a few.[5] Author Rob Stone discussed Semon's oeuvre in *Laurel or Hardy*.[6] Richard M. Roberts devoted a tripartite article to Semon's life and work.[7] Apart from Král, writers Sam Gill, Kalton C. Lahue[8] and Anthony Slide[9] were probably the first post-war authors to try to save Semon from complete obscurity. Finally, some retrospectives have been staged, some on Semon's behalf, some not. Nonetheless, it leaves a bitter taste that Semon is today best remembered for his association with Laurel and Hardy. In this vein, his original work has steadily been undermined because different labels are being assigned to Larry Semon films. Now they are called Stan Laurel films—or Oliver Hardy films.

So, what else is the objective of this book?

I intend this book as the first comprehensive biography and filmography of Larry Semon for which I began to compile research in 1985 at the age of fourteen. The filmography, composed with co-writer Patrick Skacel, is the most complete we could achieve with our current research facilities. You will for example learn that Semon had a pre–Vitagraph "career" in films and that several projects were never realized. We have added reviews and, whenever possible, details on their production.

Other aspects I have focused on: Larry's roots as they help in understanding his later motion picture work, a re-evaluation of his illustrations before the background of a recently retrieved wealth of instantiations, since he has largely been identified as "never more than an itinerant penman."[10] I also looked at Semon as an egotistical madman, an alleged trait that reportedly led him to notorious overspending. Then I compiled the conspiracy theories that emerged on the evidence of Semon's death and inconsistencies in the documentation of his final days. I also concentrated on Semon the man to the greatest possible extent. What he was like. What made him move—into the movies.

To talk about Semon *the man* was one of the most difficult tasks of the book. I never met him, as I was born too late. When I realized that there were silent movies and wanted to know about them, the last of Semon's contemporaries had departed. When Larry died, a book was closed. Hardly anyone cared to remember him. While the memory of others was kept alive, Semon was just mentioned in passing, maybe one or two sentences dedicated to him. If he deserved to be forgotten, why do people still laugh at his movies? I had to rely on primary sources, the artwork, and the films I could track down, his family, and Lucille Carlisle's family. It is a sad fact that hardly any of the Semon descendants remembered anything about Larry. What is more, his family-in-law who never accepted him and finally expelled him from their circles made sure to destroy everything reminiscent of Larry.

Regarding Larry's earliest published cartoons, they were printed on acidic paper and not many of the *North American* volumes could be preserved. Another copy of a quarterly volume might have been lost—this time to water damage—had I not arrived home early one day. I kept the *North American* under my sofa and my upstairs neighbor filled his bathtub and left for work. When I entered my flat, floods of water were pouring down the walls and had crept towards the volume. It was just inches away from being destroyed.

· 1 ·

Roots and Settings

Larry Semon belonged to a family of celebrities and represented the third generation of European immigrants of notable success. He believed the name Semon to be of French origin, although from both sides he came from Quaker stock. Larry's grandfather Emanuel Semon was born in Amsterdam, the Netherlands, in 1798, and became interested in magic art. About 1820 he followed renowned magician Hermann the Great on his tour of the United States. Emanuel decided to stay in Philadelphia, filing his first papers in 1835 and obtaining U.S. citizenship five years later. Like other Dutch Jews, he made Richmond, Virginia, his home and worked as a customs collector.[1] He was one of the most prominent Masons and Tylers of the Grand Lodge of Virginia for a period of twenty-five years. His wife Mary Bailey (circa 1814–1871) was an American-born Quaker who acted as steward. Emanuel and Mary had sixteen children, many of whom lived well into their seventies. One sad exception was their son Benjamin who died at seventeen at the hand of one of his brothers who accidentally fired a pistol at him. Popular Benjamin passed away "without a murmur, saying he was not afraid to die and acquitted everyone of any blame."[2]

A photographic portrait of Emanuel taken during the Civil

Emanuel Semon, member of the Richmond Light Infantry Blues unit in Richmond, Virginia, 1860s (courtesy Virginia Historical Society, Richmond).

War displays a good-looking, vibrant man of sixty-seven years with a heart-shaped face, fair wavy hair, protruding ears, and full lips, who could not hide a certain waggish smile. One expects Emanuel to wink from his portrait at any moment. Trying to find the genealogical link between Larry and his parents by determining any facial resemblances from photos is difficult, although they did belong to the same bloodline. Emanuel more easily makes the short list of candidates that handed down looks and appeal to on-screen Larry. The only overt facial features that father Zera turned over to his son was his large curved nose—something Larry was proudest of—and the utterly serious expression he wore in private life.

Emanuel nurtured a knack for drawing, proven by a card on which he drew a portrait of a bearded man in pen and ink. With light fluent strokes, the portrait had been scribbled on the spot.

During the war, Emanuel operated a newsstand. As pocket change became scarce, he and other merchants decided to issue currency of their own in fractional amounts. He had printed about $100 worth of these "shin-plasters" of five and ten cents each with a text certifying that Semon would pay to its bearer five or ten cents, when presented in sums of one or more dollars. Signed by him, the notes passed as cash among all merchants. Before the war ended, many thousands of dollars were redeemed and Emanuel made sure he gathered all of his issue. Yet there was perhaps a million dollars' worth of them still outstanding that would never be claimed. When the homemade currency grew to an alarming extent, the State of Virginia was forced to put a stop to it, issued their own scrip and arrested Emanuel. A bill introduced by the Legislature of Virginia in late 1861 was perceived by many people as distasteful and had its most bitter opponents in the *Richmond Dispatch*. It editorially denounced the bill as being as worthless as "Semon's trash." Ever since, this assertion rankled in the breast of his son, Jacob.[3]

A sketch in pencil, pen and ink by Emanuel Semon, 1820 (author's collection).

Emanuel's death in Philadelphia on July 9, 1871, was unexpected and without any prior illness, although one might fancy that he died of a broken heart. His wife's passing the previous month, after a long illness, and the loss of all their belongings after Union soldiers had brought down the city of Richmond during the Civil War contributed to his demise at the age of 73.

One of Larry Semon's uncles, Judah C. Semon (born c. 1849), followed in Emanuel's footsteps with regard to media. He opened a book and newspaper shop at 805 Broad Street in the city center of Richmond, much to the delight of the crowds roaming the place every day. His enterprise was a welcome update to the old periodical stand of his predecessor: Citizens were supplied with a vast range of books, periodicals and fancy goods, with the option to subscribe to brand new issues of foreign and domestic magazines.[4] At Christmas time, Judah turned his shop into a children's highlight with Kris Kringle emerging from the shop's chimney.[5] In 1880, he was brought to the Philadelphia Insane Asylum. Five years later he died.

Born in Richmond, Uncle Jacob "Jake" S. Semon (1838–1923) started out as a manager in a tobacco factory, worked as a sales agent for Northern and European newspapers and later took charge of the telegraph system of Virginia. He was Jefferson Davis' private messenger from the telegraph office during the war. It was a responsible position, as some decisions about life and death passed through Jacob's hands. When all set to leave the telegraphic office on a cold and stormy Christmas Eve night for home, the operator advised the irritated Jacob that an important message was coming for the president. In this message, a soldier, sentenced to death for desertion, was begging for pardon, as he saw the lives of his wife and seven children jeopardized. Jacob dashed to Davis' house, but was referred to relentless Adjutant General Cooper. It was thanks to Jacob's persistence and the presence of a flock of compassionate young women at Cooper's house that the soldier was reprieved.[6]

Jacob greatly resembled John Wilkes Booth, the slayer of Presi-

A sketch in pen and ink by Emanuel Semon, 1820 (author's collection).

dent Lincoln. He and Booth had their pictures taken together when they were young men. In the old-fashioned daguerreotype it was difficult to tell them apart.[7] In 1865, shortly after Lincoln's assassination, Jacob moved to Philadelphia. On his arrival, he was taken as a suspect in the manhunt for Booth, roughly handled by a mob, and had to twice explain he was not the assassin. What helped him out were friends and newspapermen who identified him.

Soon after, Jacob became a popular figure in the city and his tobacco store in the Merchants' Hotel opposite the State House was a rendezvous for many prominent men. He later moved to Chestnut Street, where the theater was located.

Jacob married Anna Bailey, who died one year later. They had a son, Joseph E. Semon. He succumbed at one month old to debility. Not before too long, Jacob married the daughter of Thomas Jackson, a well-known newspaperman. An animal lover, he supplied the Zoological Garden in Philadelphia with rare species of owls and possums. He tamed forlorn kittens, babying them as if they were his offsprings.

Determined to rehabilitate the name of his father, whose reputation had been damaged owing to his "shin-plasters," thirty years later Jacob advertised in Richmond papers that he would redeem every dollar of his father's issue of currency and pay thirty years interest on it. People flocked to his sister's house where Jacob had installed himself and presented him with the notes; *none* had been issued by his father. The holders had believed that all their old scrip was to be made good. Those who still held the genuine notes did not want them to be cancelled for old associations. Today, a good collection of Emanuel Semon's notes are housed by the Virginia Historical Society.

In the 1890s, Jacob Semon was unfavorably involved in a suit brought against him and his associates by executors of the late millionaire Richard Wistar and the Secretary of the Treasury Edward W. Ayres. Wistar was the property owner at Philadelphia's Broad and Cherry streets on which the U.S. government had instituted a condemnation proceeding, as they considered the site suitable for a mint. Wistar did not wish to part with the property and entrusted upon Semon's advice Ayres with preventing condemnation. For his help, Ayres was to receive $25,000 as agreed in a contract. Indeed, he succeeded in making the government abandon the site. A fifth of the sum was to be paid on account and given by Wistar to Jacob Semon, who was to take the money to Washington and deliver it to Ayres. The money allegedly never reached Ayres, but was reportedly pocketed by Semon and associates. A letter written by Semon to Wistar spoke of Ayres as being in the position where "now he must be prepared to pay the inside workers,"[8] which made Wistar withdraw from the whole business and never pay the balance of $20,000. After more than four years of hearing witnesses and surveyors testifying that Wistar was unfit to plead during his last days, Philadelphia's Orphan's Court rejected Ayres' claim. As they saw it, there had been no performance of the contract by the claimant. In addition, methods had been used that were not approved by law so that there could be no recovery.

Another Richmond-born member of the Semon family was Larry's father Zerubabel "Zera" Semon (1845–1901). Zera and Larry were constantly traveling for over twelve years, which made them share success and failure in a most intensive manner. Due to their close bond, Zera had an enormous influence on Larry's education, behavior and professional career. Zera became a traveling ventriloquist and magician, as at an early age, he showed ability and fondness for the magical art which he had inherited from his father Emanuel. When Zera was still a boy, Emanuel induced Hermann the Great to return to the United States to teach Zera all he knew of the Black Art.[9]

Zera's magic art may be best understood when taking into account his master—and friend—Robert-Houdin (1805–1871), also known as the Father of Modern Magic. Once a clockmaker, Robert-Houdin was knowledgeable about electricity and mechanics, an asset he later improved at Papa Roujoul's magic store. Proficient in sleight-of-hand, Houdin began constructing his own automatons and introduced a new era of conjuring. He became famous for a vast range of mechanical tricks. To the unsuspecting public it seemed as if he had created everything by his own hands. He operated marvelous cork-rooted orange trees which blossomed and grew fruits before the eyes of audiences and he enthused contemporaries with an illusion in which he allowed an Arab to shoot at him with a marked bullet. Instead of dropping dead, Houdin removed the bullet from between his teeth. At one point, Houdin was coerced to expose his tricks to authorities in order to avoid persecution for witchery. In patient study, Zera had spent years abroad in Paris as Houdin's assistant and favorite disciple[10]—his persistence being a striking feature that he would hand down to Larry. Having graduated at Heidelberg, Germany, Zera was at home "in the deep labyrinths of electricity"[11] which equipped him with the requisites to enter Houdin's realm of magic inventions. He picked up his master's tricks, staged them himself and developed new ones. At twenty-three, Zera's achievements on stage were so outstanding that Napoleon III and his wife Eugenie came to witness his show.

A consciousness and pronounced feel for automaton-rooted trickery is visible in Larry Semon's film work along with the obsession for a perfective performance. Larry's stop motion routines were executed in an extremely fine-ground manner, with a result devoid of any rocky movements, such as the walking egg in *The Counter Jumper* (1921), or lightning bolts that stalk everyone within reach in *Lightning Love* (1922). Other well-planned routines were beer-like liquids traveling parallel to the floor from glass to glass in *Huns and Hyphens* (1918) and motorbikes that take shortcuts by passing underneath parked vehicles with the bikers sitting upright as in *Horseshoes* (1923). Colleagues

Professor Zera Semon, newspaper advertisement, 1894 (author's collection).

in filmland would always gasp in awe at Semon's cinematographic achievements. Larry's propensity for new developments was without doubt foreshadowed by his father. Among the profession, Larry Semon's studio was regarded as a place where anything mysterious and uncanny was liable to happen during a production. The whole place was full of trick doors, rooms, secret panels, buttons and mechanical devices. Many of these were Larry's own inventions. His early training with his father's vaudeville troupe had taught him how to make sleight-of-hand devices. In the 1970s, critics reproached Larry of the mechanical appeal of his comedy. That he only picked up the zeitgeist in his comedies had been forgotten by then.

Zera prompted at least one competitor, Frank C. Osborne, to plagiarize the name Zera or Professor Zera for advertising his own business. Osborne toured the country with his wife as Prof. and Madam Zera, forcing Semon to change his playbills. For the sake of quality control, he insisted that he be called Zera Semon from the early 1880s on. At one point their Southern routes partly overlapped. Osborne, without doubt a professional, though on a much smaller scale, concentrated on sleight-of-hand tricks and specialized in psychology and phrenology, while another act of his company supplied ventriloquism and trained doves.[12] In the end, Osborne would survive Semon and continue touring, whereas Semon was meant to lose everything to a violent storm at the turn of the century.

Over the years, Zera Semon had developed into the proverbial universal genius. Apart from presenting the usual effective tricks in the vein of a prestidigitator, he was an old school conversationalist, excelled in ventriloquism and puppeteering, and he demonstrated his skills as a vocalist, mimic, comedian and gymnast. Zera also gained fame as a pianist, playing in the dewdroppy style that had made Louis Moreau Gottschalk famous,[13] and was known as a composer. His "Sweetwater Waltz" was widely distributed by American and French publishers and enjoyed extensive sales.[14] During his final years, Zera devoted all his time to bringing his ventriloquial art to perfection, no movement of his lips or his larynx being observable. Within this framework, he invented the Talking Hand: He dressed his hand as a prima donna and held it in a fashion that the opening and closing of his first finger and thumb emulated lips. This feat was revived years later by Spanish ventriloquist Senor Wences.

A principal activity that Zera pursued through his professional life was marketing, which he sometimes paired with humor and sometimes also with imposture. He did not shy away from billing himself as a Corsican Conjurer to make his appearance more exotic.[15] The painstaking creation of an image was a leitmotif that anticipates photoplayer Larry Semon mutating into an advertising blockbuster in the late teens and early twenties.

Magic shows without marketing meant no audience, and no audience meant no success. The best publicity for a magician was a reputation for tricks that could not be explained. However, only too frequently, magic stunts did not live up to their marketing stunts. Zera, in response, was busy stressing in advance advertising that his show meant neither humbug nor charlatanry and that he was a sincere person. It is titillating to learn that Zera made a specialty in victimizing trades people such as printers in Herkimer, New York.[16] After playing two nights and a matinee he skipped the town of Grand Rapids, Michigan, beating the place for $500.[17] Newspaper notes of Zera swindling others out of bills were not rare, owing to the terrible financial difficulties he had to face on a daily basis. Even if business was good (more than a thousand attendees) and although evenings resulted in hundreds of dollars producing ravishing reviews, the early shows did not pay.

Zera's wife Irene was playing tricks on him when she and his male assistant ran away with all his money and apparatus after a show in Scranton, Pennsylvania, in May 1880.[18] Zera and Irene reconciled, but there was a considerable gap in tour dates for nearly half a year.

Along with conjurers such as Robert Heller and Zera's disciple Joseph Hartz,[19] Zera had entered the business of magic gift shows the way they were popular in America during the nineteenth century. Gifts created a furor among audiences and left them with the certainty that their tickets were worth double the money. Yet another marketing tool to ensure packed houses everywhere: Zera gave out prize objects of high quality and usefulness and he insisted that tickets were sold at reasonable prices. The major prizes were hams and small sacks of flour or other food items, on down to brass jewelry and toiletry items. By that, Zera made sure that everyone went home with something. The range of his gifts made him stock up opera locations and music academies equal to that of a wholesale grocery store—a setting that would heavily influence Larry.

About 500 reviews of Zera Semon's shows were available for research, the majority praising the artist. It is striking, though, that tone and contents frequently tended towards a rehash of prefabricated press releases which Zera and his manager were issuing before entering the locations ahead. Apart from the occasional recommendation that he ought to reorganize his orchestra, one independent reviewer seemed quite reluctant about Zera's abilities and appearance:

> There was one thing about Zera Semon's show that took well. That was the presents. We have not a doubt that the crowd would have stayed all night if the presents had not run short. In this department of the show the utmost satisfaction was given to all—who didn't hold blanks. The ladies who went to see the real Zera Semon expecting to find the handsome face pictured on the show bills, had their dreams rudely shattered. The juggler and his photographs are about as much alike as an Esquimaux belle and a creole beauty.[20]

Larry Semon remembered his father as a tall, smooth-shaven and imposing-looking man, but it seems that the two of them shared a sunken face and skin with a tendency to develop wrinkles at an early age.

The local press commonly avoided mentioning the bitter outcome of stints. Even though the Semon troupe used to present a well-balanced program with high-quality acts that would play 90 minutes or two hours, people would be dissatisfied. There were usually three acts on the bill, Irene and Zera being the principal one. Should a team fall short of doing a double act, the show would have folded at about quarter past nine and the customers might have started a riot—which often happened anyway.[21] A clash of Zera and West Virginia's *Wheeling Intelligencer* in 1876 was well documented and symbolized the tip of the iceberg in the Semons' world of show business. Zera detested bad press for anything he was associated with, but did little to remedy his troupe's reputation. For the show at Hamilton's Opera House that would make him fall out of favor with the newspaper people, Zera had booked and announced the Cawthorne Boys, a group of juvenile mimics and character artists. *The Wheeling Recorder* commended the boys' achievements on the stage, contrary to the *Wheeling Intelligencer* that downgraded the "Cowthorne Boys" as fill-ins. Any gamin picked up on the street could be drilled in a few hours to entertain an audience in better style, the paper mourned, with the effect that Professor "Zera, Zero or Zebra," inflamed with rage, paid local editor, the Reverend Halsted, an unforgettable visit the next day. Reverend Halsted reported,

> As he came in the door everyone in the editorial room saw he was a showman. There was that irrepressible look about him obtained only from the reflection of the footlights, and a brilliant shabbiness, such as stage clothes ever will possess. "Is the local editor in?" he inquired in a most condescending manner, which made one really sorry to think such greatness could drop to the homely level of every-day etiquette. The reporter who was busy at his desk dropped his work and looked up with pleasure. Still nobody said anything, and His Excellency with almost annihilating dignity, repeated his interrogation.
> "Local editor?" says the visitor. A frightened nod was the only response, and his Lordship's nose, which really would have looked better had it been pulled out straight, curled up with elegant disgust. "Did you write that notice of the Cawthorne Boys?" he asked. Then spoke the showman: "This is an insult, sir; after traveling this wide world over, and by working up the press succeeding in getting the boys favorable notices, I come to this insignificant town to be told the truth. I'll give you a fearful deal on the stage tonight; I'll—"
> The walking gentleman at this juncture, seeing that not the slightest attention was paid to his remarks, and feeling satisfied that he had reduced the garrison to the last brink of despair, took himself away. We all breathe easier.[22]

Zera was accompanied by an enraged Mrs. Cawthorne and an equally upset Semon company. That same evening, during his nightly performance, Zera publicly gave vent to what he thought about the *Intelligencer*'s criticism and made a few remarks at the expense of their reporter then present. *The Intelligencer* concluded that his little speech was pervaded by a peculiar solemnity, which rendered him "even more ridiculous than his language. But," the paper continued, "Zera's licks are not dangerous, for he strikes as with bladders filled with wind."[23]

Semon's attacks were complemented by mother Cawthorne, who had installed herself near the entrance and dared the reporter in a very loud and coarse voice to savage her boys again. John Frew, one of the *Intelligencer*'s owners, showed up at the St. James the next morning in order to attend the matinee. With him were the two children of another editor. At the door, there seemed to be some difficulty about the tickets and a discussion between Frew and Zera developed. When one of the children was bending down to grab a program, Zera misread this as an attempt to steal some tickets. This made Frew angry. The interaction of the two became rather sultry and it looked as though they might end up in a fight, but then interrupted and quieted them. The scene was continued at the Police Court the same afternoon, as Frew accused Zera of using abusive language, while Zera had a warrant issued for the arrest of Frew. Both cases were dismissed and the war was officially ended. Instantaneously, *Wilkes' Spirit of the Times*, the leading dramatic paper of the country, ranted that gift "Fakir" Professor Zera succeeded in disgusting a large audience as he took umbrage at some adverse criticisms on his entertainment, denouncing the press from the stage. He had not only insulted his audience, but stamped himself "a mere mountebank."[24] It was part of Zera's stage philosophy that newcomers should be given a chance to probe themselves, knowing only too well no one was born a master. Playing the Odd Fellow at British Columbia's Nelson with

Little Larry in 1896, he granted young minstrels their act although the press qualified them as evident amateurs of pronounced stage fright, yet Zera recognized their ability to provide first-rate entertainment.

Though the police had decreed peace among the theater and newspaper folks, some days later the *Wheeling Intelligencer* snapped with pleasure in their *Amusement Notes*:

> Zera and his party will leave town this morning at 4 o'clock for Springfield, Ohio, where they will play three nights. The Cawthorne children, who unwittingly jumped into a little notoriety here, were discharged on Saturday morning, and left the same day for Boston, in company with their gentle mamma.[25]

On this occasion, Zera's show effects were confiscated for debt and sold at auction in front of Washington Hall. Superintendent Cummings bought his egg trick, and someone else bought his complete collection of dancing babies for 25 cents. Sales amounted to a scanty six dollars.[26] The Semon troupe paid Wheeling another visit exactly two years later, this time playing to small audiences on Washington Hall stage, a fact again gleefully observed by Zera's old pal, the *Intelligencer*. To the very few people who had come, Zera this time bitterly denounced bill-poster Davis as a swindler. Davis had obtained money from Zera under false pretenses and not been seen for days. Numerous parties were in *pursuit* of him.[27]

Zera had virtually encircled the globe. After great success in Europe, he was more widely known in the Dominion of Canada, Nova Scotia, and Newfoundland. His popularity equaled that of the best performers in the United States and won him a line in the poem "Skating Carnival" by Nova Scotian poet Hefferman. Zera's heyday must be placed in the 1870s and 1880s when his persona and acts were celebrated as novelties and many socialites and emperors came to see his show. In later years, his performing qualities were still at a high standard, but his sensational appeal had declined. Addicted to hard work, he had continuously been touring for over thirty years, from an estimated 1868 until early 1901. In America he gave more than 15,000 performances—an incredible achievement.

Zera's favor did not only originate from his magic skill, but was intensified by his unrestrained generosity in aiding people in need. In several Canadian mine disasters and elsewhere, he gave freely of his money and always showed sympathy for the working classes. In 1900, a year before his death, Zera devoted the entire proceeds of a packed house to the Transvaal War Fund. Without his permanent acts of charity he would have accumulated a large fortune. As it was, he died poor.

On April 7, 1901, Zera succumbed to acute or chronic nephritis at the home of his daughter in Philadelphia. Despite his fame and contributions to the art of magic, he has yet to make the list of the Hall of Fame of the Society of American Magicians.

The Semon family was known for having brought forth quite a number of liberated women, among them fearless Rachael Semon. On April 3, 1865, Richmond, Virginia, fell into the hands of Union soldiers and would end up in complete devastation. While the troops were approaching Emanuel Semon's house at Main Street, daughter Rachael opened a window and waved a self-embroidered Union flag—much to the horror of her father and her husband. Against all odds, the soldiers drew up and cheered, Major Stephens came into the house, thanked Rachael and left a guard to care for the Semon residence. More than thirty years later, Rachael, now dance instructor Madame L. Louis, sold the flag to the owner of the war museum in Richmond for $200. The flag was in a deplorable condition, yellowish-gray, moth-eaten and worthless, but still enough to stand as a witness of a fearless cry for protection.[28]

Rachael and her sisters Emma and Rebecca were liberated enough to make their own rules. During wartime, they visited Libby Prison, moved close to the gratings and swore at the convicts in order to disguise their charity actions. In fact, Rachael and her sisters reached beneath their coats and gave the convicts something reasonable to eat.

That women in the Semon family enjoyed a high status certainly had an effect on Larry's upbringing. The concept of emancipated females making intelligent decisions was a constant in Larry Semon films, no matter whether in the category of beauty or activity. Unabashed, they show off their bare legs in the self-explanatory *Bathing Beauties and Big Boobs* (1918), they let hair cascade down to their hips in *The Suitor* (1921) and they take pride in wearing overalls in *The Simple Life* (1919). Larry's leading ladies make a successful living from inventing gas masks as in *Frauds and Frenzies* (1918) in order to brave the German enemy and head gangs of crooks in *Oh, What a Man!* (1927). They often know more about engineering than men and outwit them in relentless car chases as in *Pluck and Plotters* (1918), while betraying their husbands in *A Jealous Guy* (1916).

When asked about Irene Semon, Larry Semon's mother, one of Zera's managers painted a picture of her that makes one fancy the souls of three Brooklyn truck drivers caught in one shapely body:

> I thought [Zera] was under my management but soon found out that I was under his wife's management. She was an attractive woman and ruled the roost with great vigor, and the way

Zera and Irene Semon with their sensational Bell's Marionettes that could be operated in a life-like manner, ca. 1882 (author's collection).

in which she bossed the outfit was a dream in generalship. And say, that girl could cuss and swear to make your soul rejoice. I have never heard her equal among the male sex in constant and competent cussing."[29]

Like Larry's sister Elizabeth May, Irene was on the stage where she acted as Zera's principal support. She was part of their original spiritualistic canopy act, an improvement on the one introduced by Robert Heller. Born Irene E. Rea in Lancaster, Pennsylvania, circa 1852, she was presumably Amish. Her parents were Jane Elizabeth (1828–1908), a housekeeper, and Samuel M. Rea (circa 1827–1902), a stone mason. They had a servant and were living in Philadelphia. In the 1870 census, eighteen-year-old and single Irene is listed as having no occupation. She and Zera were married at the Asbury Methodist Episcopal Church in Philadelphia on April 2, 1874.

Irene helped with the sleight-of-hand tricks and she was one operator with Zera's famous full stage set of life-size marionettes in a complete minstrel scene, the Bell's Royal Marionettes. They were named for Gus Bell, business manager of the Semon-Marionette combination, and proved to be a hit in the U.S., as Zera was the only one to offer an act like this. The marionettes, automatons from the Crystal Palace in London, England, were operated in a kind of Punch and Judy fashion. Apart from minstrel, they gave a Humpty Dumpty pantomime and could be "made to sing and dance in a truly lifelike manner."[30]

Elizabeth May Semon was born in Philadelphia around 1877. She started out as a child actress in her parents' show and was soon popular with audiences. May was a child wonder, "beautiful, vivacious and precocious beyond her years."[31] May did not pursue a career on stage as an adult because her parents did not encourage her to. In 1902, she married Howell Chestnut Cunningham, who also had Philadelphian roots. Howell was later made chairman of the board of the Crucible Steel Casting Co. in 1952, and held various positions since joining in 1905, including secretary, officer, treasurer and vice-president. He was also a member of the Lansdowne Lodge 711, F. & A.M. of the Aronimink Golf Club and the Egypt Mills Club. In September 1903, May and Howell's first child, Howell C., Jr., was stillborn. In about 1908, May gave birth to their daughter Elizabeth M. "Bettie" Cunningham. May (Semon) Cunningham died on December 6, 1941, in Philadelphia, survived by her husband and daughter.

Irene had given birth to two additional boys. They would have been Larry's elder brothers, but for both death came in infancy. William Zera Semon died at four years of age during a tour in Reading, Pennsylvania, from convulsions on April 10, 1880, when father Zera was playing the Grand Opera House. Only two days earlier, a "Mrs. Prof. Zera" had advertised in the *Reading Times* that she wanted a middle-aged woman to travel as a child's nurse and take charge of two children, a girl and a boy.[32] The other boy, Zera Jr., passed away on April 4, 1883, in Philadelphia of malignant scarlatina or scarlet fever. He was buried the next day. Baby Zera was born when Irene and Zera were touring the South, in Georgia, in mid–November 1881.

· 2 ·

On the Road

While Zera and Irene Semon were touring the South in the late 1880s, they registered with their company at the Henley House, Commerce Street, in West Point, Mississippi, a small town with cotton plantations. The Henley, a two-story brick building, was once the largest mansion in town. That Larry Semon would see the light of day at this residence was by far not on the bills. As measured by overwork, endless journeys and homeless life, bad roads, disastrous trains and undernourishment, there was no chance for Irene to carry a child to term. Though pregnant, she was constantly involved in the everyday circus life.

A week after Larry's birth, the whole company with its animals and actors left the town. The Semon family took the train northeast toward Philadelphia so that they could allow Larry some peace. The hiatus was longer than those after the two little Zeras had arrived as Irene and Zera Sr. had learned from their early losses. Larry recalled that the break lasted for several months[1]; this, however, is belied by tour dates. Despite the care, Larry was a tender, scrawny child who could pass for a few years his junior, something on which the Semon troupe capitalized when advertising his performances. For Larry there was no leisure either. By the time of his physical examination in 1917, Larry had developed into a size assessed "medium," although in all of his films he appears anorexic though brawny.

The exact date of Larry's birth remains unconfirmed, as no document testifying to his arrival could be tracked down. Most books cite a July 16, 1889, birth for no obvious reason. In 1916's *Motion Picture News Studio Directory*, February 6, 1889, is given. Other sources list February 16 of the same year. On Larry's death certificate, yet another date can be found, July 16, 1890. In the 1900 Philadelphia census, there is an entry that very probably relates to Larry and gives his date of birth as August 1887 and his place of birth as Georgia. Though no first name is given for Larry, the person's age and the entry "vaudeville" for the column "profession" makes a link to him most likely. The source of information was obviously Rebecca (Semon) Bowman. Maybe she was ill at the time, affecting her memory for dates, places, and names and confusing Larry's place of birth with that of the late Zera, Jr. Rebecca died two years later at age 63. On the birth certificate of his only child, Virginia, Larry claimed to be 25 years of age, setting the year of his birth in 1886 or 1887. An 1894 playbill advertises Larry as a "six-year-old,"[2] and on an 1895 playbill as an "eight-year-old."[3] Attempts to trace Zera's tour route in order to track down Larry's date of birth are still being scrutinized. Provided a route could be reconstructed that included West Point or a neighboring town with a subsequent halt of business for a few days, the date might at least be narrowed down. Citizens of West Point have told the author on request that the local papers of 1888, 1889 and 1890 make no mention of Larry's birth. Currently, it seems as if the Semon troupe was only touring Mississippi in 1886 and 1887 (cf. vaudeville tour paper[4,5]). They did give performances in Jackson and Vicksburg, Mississippi, the latter about three hours southwest of West Point. Another hint that Larry was born before July 1889 is a newspaper clipping listing Lawrence Semon among a large group of little dancers at the Atlantic Hotel, Philadelphia, in early August 1889.[6] Even the most talented child would not be able to take up terpsichorean moves a fortnight after birth. An instance of the remotest credibility seems the New York State Census of 1915. Here Larry Semon's age is given as thirty-two, suggesting his year of birth as 1883.

Larry believed that no one in the motion picture profession had more to overcome than he. Larry's young life was indeed packed with shattering experiences, hunger and the furthest thing from luxury. He once stated that he never knew what it meant to have enough to eat regularly until he was about fourteen. Quite frequently Zera's troupe would arrive in a town and be forced to build their own stage in a poorly lighted, scantily furnished hall that reminded one of a huge barn. Larry was used to roughing it, for often everyone was obliged to sleep on benches in some hall, or their bed consisted of a couple of boards in a cold loft or the theater floor, while all members of the company had to rustle up their own victuals. Al Fostell of the musical act Fostell and Emmett put lie to what Larry Semon said, maybe because he hit the Semon circus when they were better off and Larry was too young to remember. It simply adds to the impression that Zera Semon experienced a rollercoaster ride of success. Fostell and Emmett traveled with the Semon Novelty Gift Show in the early 1890s; Fostell wrote,

Little Larry Semon as a child actor, photographed in Halifax, ca. 1894 (courtesy Sam Gill). The reverse bears an inscription by Semon himself stating that he was six years old here.

Prof. Semon was one of the finest and squarest men that I ever met during my whole stage career extending over a period of forty-six years. No tourist ever travelled under better conditions than we did. It was one continual round of pleasure from start to finish. We had first-class travelling accommodations; and every Sunday morning after breakfast, we were paid in full regardless of the fact that we worked one night or six.[7]

At the time of Larry's birth, Zera owned and managed the Pepper Pot at the maritime Halifax, believed to be America's pioneer cabaret restaurant. Afterwards he established several cabarets (all patterned after the Pepper Pot) throughout the east of Canada. Larry made his stage debut in the famous portfolio act that Zera had adapted from Robert-Houdin to fit his needs: From a flat portfolio he drew a picture of a birdcage. After showing it to the audience, he took the drawing and magically produced an actual birdcage. Zera continued with these actions to the grand finale: He drew from it a picture of a baby just old enough to toddle, and then magically the actual baby itself—Larry.

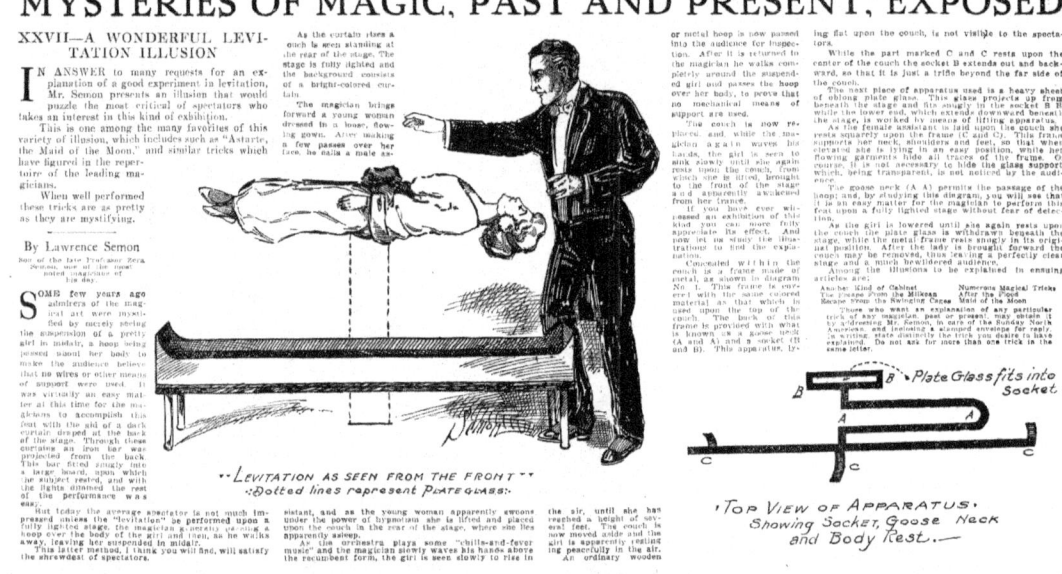

The aerial suspense or levitation illusion was one of the stunts that Larry Semon performed in his parents' show. On January 23, 1910, Semon exposed this trick along with an illustration to the readers of the *North American* (author's collection).

Being bright and talented, Larry soon followed in the footsteps of sister May when she had outgrown her role of a child actor. This meant that Larry was nightly beheaded and dismembered, and pressed into service as an aerial suspense: He was hypnotized with one of his hands being mounted on an iron stake set in the stage and then raised until he floated in the air at right angles with the iron. Larry accordingly rested in a metal network with springs, joints and clasps, so that he could walk, but was rigid when he was placed in the horizontal position. A robe of silk prevented the audience from noticing any of the mechanical work. The hardest part of the performance was handled by Larry, who had to be trained to hold himself perfectly rigid throughout the entire time he was suspended. In *Between the Acts* (1919), boobish stagehand Larry would uncover the trick, although displaying a simpler mechanic that consisted of an angular steel construction with shoes at both ends.

Larry received practical education from his father and fellow actors, listened to them recite their lines and recount their travels. He learned to train animals, leap in the air and land on his feet. He knew what timing meant and what made people laugh, backed by a good knowledge of pantomime. Eventually he replaced his mother and assisted his father, whose Southern accent he had picked up, in his most complicated stunts, notably Bell's Marionettes. To audiences and reporters it seemed impossible for Zera, his son and one assistant to manage the automatons all at once, but they mastered it.

Since the Zera Semon troupe housed singers, contortionists, dancers, acrobats and shadowists, Larry had the opportunity to study the artistic and the grotesque. Acts of other troupes playing the same houses meant even more inspiration, foremost "Human Shadow" Edward A. Needling, 1899's principal attraction. Larry and Needling met when both were appearing at Austin and Stone's in Boston where Zera operated a Punch and Judy show. The place had a curio hall at the back and a vaudeville show at the left as one went in through an entrance full of oil paintings of world-famous freaks. Needling was of such a unique nature that he could have played the curio hall *and* the vaudeville show. He was so thin that one could read newspaper advertisements through him with the help of Roentgen Rays (being x-rayed was a popular fairground attraction back then). He stood six feet high and his management was reluctant to announce his weight for fear of being charged with exaggeration.[8] A strange acrobatic act that came with the Semon troupe was Hungarian juggler Karoly Ordley, who balanced a dove on a structure of clay pipes while firing a revolver.[9] Another juggler who made an impression on Larry was Edgar Nelton Bradford alias (Nino) Nelton or Nelson, who had been touring the states since his childhood days, mostly with P.T. Barnum. Zera's onetime marketing consultant Kit Clarke acted as Nelton's manager. Nelton was an on-and-off ally with the Semon troupe from 1889 until 1897. In his lamp act he placed a large lit table lamp on a stick and installed the stick on a string. This combination he would balance by his hands at each end.[10]

For some time, popular comedians Murray and Mack were attached to the Semon show. Charlie Murray would later appear with Semon in *The Girl in the Limousine* (1924) and *The Wizard of Oz* (1925).[11]

One of Larry's most striking talents, his marvelous soprano voice along with his talent for comedy, was featured between the regular acts of the show. He either accompanied the scene shifting or beautified slide shows such as views of U.S. battleships and photographic portraits of the latest celebrities. Zera, a good singer himself, knew how to use his natural and assumed voice and had Larry train his vocal chords starting at an early age. By 1894, Larry had made a name for himself and received billing on the posters below his father's name as the "World's Most Powerful Boy Soprano." Indeed he could have blown down the walls of Jericho with his young lungs, which received a prize at the Casino Theater on Broadway.[12] Larry's repertory embraced contemporary popular songs such as "And the Band Played On," the ballad "Break the News to Mother" and the sheet music million-seller "After the Ball." Reporters took a liking to Larry and always made sure to reserve a few benevolent lines in their reviews for him. On the evidence of Larry being encored umpteen times, the *Wilmington Messenger* wrote in 1894,

> The audience was captivated by Master Laurence who takes a turn at singing a parody on "The Man in the Moon" and another comic song. He sings and conducts himself with the abandon of a professional, and the audience was full of both amusement and wonder at the cute and excellent manner in which he gets off his part.[13]
>
> The audience was "much taken" with him, and greeted him with the most unbounded appreciation and the heartiest of applause. He is certainly a cute little fellow and Professor Semon should be proud of him.[14]

The press emphasized Larry's chic, manly and vivacious appearance and realized that his old-school grotesque methods and facial expressions as far ahead of his age. While his drollness made people laugh in Canada, the pathos with which he presented his songs brought audiences to tears in Newfoundland.

From time to time, Larry decided he did not need the footlights to be successful. When in Havre, Montana, a violent storm had afflicted the town on December 20, 1899, the night of their show. The next morning, all the roads were obstructed and no one cared for the troupe. Giving another performance was beyond reason, as everyone in the small town had already seen their show. The proceeds vanished and the company could not move on.

"Turkey for Christmas?" Larry asked, since he had let go any hope for presents. He was determined to do something and secretly snuck out to the lobby of the town's largest hotel, where a crowd had formed. "Hey—lookout!" he shouted. Securing the undivided attention of everybody, he continued with his song-and-dance specialty, with no music, but a desperate little humming supplied by himself.

Finally, Larry passed his woolly cap, collected quite a number of coins and decided: "Turkey for Christmas!" He had indeed provided dinner for the troupe.

"Better do something about the storm, sonny," they bantered him on his return, but the same night the weather cleared and the troupe could travel again.[15]

After extensive tours through the South and the British provinces, the Semon company made their first trip to the West Coast in January 1897. To Larry it seemed as if they would never get there. After a short stint in Oakland and San Francisco, business proved so poor that Zera and Irene decided against May's stage career and sent her to boarding school. She later worked as a teacher. The troupe went hungry and the comforts of home were conspicuous by their total absence. Larry years later recalled: "Had anyone told me then that I would again appear on the stage in California, I would have laughed at him, or tried to—as laughs were scarce in those days."[16] Irene also gave up work to be near her daughter and left behind a Zera who was hurt to be separated from his women. So he kept Larry with him.

They next played in Elwood, Indiana.[17] Tour dates between mid–February and early May 1897 are a blank, because Zera was anxious to recuperate for the losses in production and lined up with affairs beyond the stage of which he nourished quite a number: They were stretching from artistry and cartooning to business in the fish industry. When inventor and stagecraft innovator Loïe Fuller went into film production with her serpentine dance at Thomas Edison's, she asked Zera for aid. The Semon troupe had just fulfilled a joint engagement with Fuller's sister Ida in Oakland during their hapless winter season, so the contact to Loïe was made.[18]

Fuller was renowned for creating her own stage lighting system. Experimenting with fluorescent gels based on the relicts from pitchblende, she was responsible for revolutionary changes of the stage world and employed about 40 technicians for her shows.[19] In order to capture the charm of her performance for the screen, she needed experienced engineers to help her with the secure wiring and effective illumination on a stage that consisted of an empty room decorated in deepest black. So this was actually the moment when Zera came in with his education in electricity. It must have been quite a challenge to light Fuller to a degree that reproduced on orthochromatic emulsions. Zera brought Larry with him to the studio and by this sparked his passion for cinema. He encouraged him to try and study film, seeing a great future in it. Zera's affinity to film reached farther back, to the primary principles of this art. He was interested in flip-books, little photopackets, which gave the effect of moving images when the pages were riffled. Zera experimented with the flip-books and partnered with a company that manufactured them. Later he concentrated on mutoscopes that operated with a crank to make the pictures move. Larry reflected Zera's doings in the upper corners of his Latin grammar book, a volume he kept from the days when his parents were managing his education. He had drawn a cartoon image into every corner so that by flicking through the pages one could follow a round of boxing.

In early May of 1897, the troupe resumed their trip to the West Coast. In Alameda, near San Francisco, they had just concluded a three-day engagement at the Opera House with all their effects and properties packed up ready for transport. Maybe a leaky gas jet or some greasy rags used for cleaning wheels in the cyclery started a fire—the whole building went up in flames. The delay in getting water on the fire was caused by a hose that could at first not be attached to the hydrant and then had to be removed in order to give way to the fire engine. Some of the packing became messed and it took a while to remove it. Meanwhile the fire was quickly spreading.

Nothing was saved; even the troupe's clothes went up in flames. Zera had been many years in making his collection of sleight-of-hand machinery and other gadgets. He estimated his loss at more than $3,000 although he was aware that much of it could not be replaced. Theater owner J.C. Linderman discarded plans for rebuilding. It was insured for $5,000 and Linderman's total loss was estimated at about three times the sum.

One week later, the company played the Occidental Pavilion in Eureka, California, with an entirely new outfit. Still in Eureka, Zera's manager D.G. Waldron, who travelled with them, died at night in his hotel bed. The remainder of the engagement was cancelled. Until June, the Semon Company remains untraceable. Then in June–July, a "Zera Seeman," at times "Lemon," identified as a "female prestidigitateur" with "Larence, a boy singing comedian," re-emerged at the Chutes Amusement Park in San Francisco. Much accounts to the theory that Zera had separated from his troupe and taken Larry and descriptive vocalist John Spickett with him. They were back to entertaining people with their Royal Marionettes, scarcely heralded in advance, and getting scant, yet favorable, mention in the papers.[20]

Larry participated in a singing contest while in San Francisco and was close to winning a gold medal. Yet he never received it as he suddenly stopped chanting and nothing in the world could make him continue.[21] But one thing was certain, Larry loved music so well that he wanted to become an opera singer. He was able to play almost any instrument made.[22] Regardless of his son's affinity for music and the stage, Zera asked him regularly to quit show business. He did not want him to have the same hard life and thought it better for Larry to be guaranteed a daily warm meal. After observing him always sketching, in particular his roster and audience members, Zera, a fine illustrator himself, decided to cultivate his son's knack for cartooning as he foresaw him as a newspaperman and intended to send him off to an art school to perfect his talent. Yet for the time being, he had Larry re-draw the playbills of the company.

Back then, Larry did not attend school, as it was futile owing to his changing places in too quick a succession. Nevertheless he was made to study hard. Zera always carried a pile of schoolbooks along with him. He and Irene instructed their son in a great variety of disciplines. Zera taught Larry whatever he knew about physics and electricity, about engineering and math, since he wanted him to have a successful future. Larry always fondly remembered his father and his splendid training and knew that he owed his stellar career to him. It was not always easy to be Zera's son, in particular when performances went the other way, which is what happened in St. John's, Newfoundland. A hundred children or more could not get seating accommodation and another two hundred were obliged to return home due to the full house. Confections made by Zera were distributed among the children. Needless to say, there was not enough to go around and that dozens of children returned home disappointed, enough for one father to write the *Evening Telegram* to complain.[23] Larry, in those days, was advised to remain with the troupe and not go out as the children might have taken out their frustrations on him.

After the tour to San Francisco and a rest for more than six months, Zera built a new company and traveled to Manitoba, Winnipeg. Back on the bill was juggler Nino Nelton, whom Zera now fabricated as a member of the Semon family tree—another son. Manitoba felt like a reimbursement for the hardships suffered in California. The new success was overwhelming. When Larry recalled some of his days as "having had everything," he was referring to their tours to the Northeast. Here, Larry was treated like a little star with endless ovations from the audience. The lightheartedness of this time was enhanced by involuntary comical situations of Zera's gift show: One audience member had won the first prize, a pet pig supplied by a citizen. The lucky winner placed the screaming pig under his arm and started off down the hall when it escaped from him and dashed around the hall with a string of laughing men and boys in pursuit.[24]

Larry experienced the introduction of many novelties that would later become classics in magic shows. He remembered the excitement when his father brought the Trunk Trick to the Lyceum Opera House of the rather sleepy Halifax. The troupe announced in papers and on playbills that on a certain night in late December 1898 they would give $100 to any person who could lock and tie up a trunk in such a way that Zera's assistant was not able to get into it within three minutes. The whole town was worked up, Larry mixing with the crowd. On the face of it, the offer was a fool one. The "wise folks" thought the magician must be crazy. But the idea that none of Halifax's sailors could tie up a trunk seemed preposterous. When the big night arrived, the house was packed to the doors and the wise ones had a smart-aleck "I told you so" look in their eyes as they flashed towards Professor Semon. Three English sailors, the most accomplished stars of the town, got ready. Larry remembered that the way they went at that trunk set the audience wild. Having snapped a full set of padlocks where they thought they would do the most good, the fun began in earnest. The sailors got busy with a tarred rope, hitched and hauled and tied and knotted until the trunk looked like a pile of tarred rope. For almost three quarters of an hour they had amused themselves by tying all sorts of knots guaranteed not to slip. As a finishing touch they sealed those knots which they considered most important with wax. Halifax had made up its mind that the thing could not be done. The assistant gave in at the mere sight of it told Zera so in a woebegone manner. Not having any time to lose, Zera pushed him to one side, removed his coat, stepped to the trunk and gave a signal whereupon the cabinet was placed around him and the trunk. The orchestra began to play, all had their watches out, and as the hands travelled around to the three-minute mark everyone shared the same thought: that it could not be done. Of course, exactly on the second of the three minutes, Zera had accomplished just what he had set out to do: He was found inside the trunk and for the sake of the show his collar was ripped off, his shirt and trousers torn and in all he was a very sorry-looking spectacle. What later became the talk of the country for a long time could be de-mystified in several ways. Zera's version, for one, involved the presence of a trap-door. The trunk's bottom was split into two sections, one of them said trap-door provided with airholes. As Zera slid down a section of the cover he placed a round key in one of the holes and the trap immediately opened. He got in, replaced the cover in position and pulled the trap-door up. In order to reinstall the trunk in its natural position he used a long gimlet which he placed in one of the airholes, pushed it through the canvas and raised the trunk on its bottom.[25]

On the same tour, young Larry excelled in the historical Black Art act. Dressed in dazzling white on a stage of stygian darkness, Larry made beautiful women and household items appear and disappear with the help of an assistant in black and the elimination of reflection. Likewise, the objects presented were covered with black fabric which was removed to make them visible.[26] The bigger acts were left to Zera. Later in life, Larry became a member of the Los Angeles Society of Magicians (L.A.S.M.). His desire to maintain his skills was made impossible by his time-consuming film work.

Larry had travelled so many places in his youth that it was difficult for him to later recall the details. This explains why he erroneously determined San Francisco as setting an end to his juvenile stage career. A newspaper clipping from the *Atlanta Constitution* sheds more light. On September 28, 1900, the paper noted in its section for Savannah:

> Tagged and addressed, so that he could not get lost, a boy of about ten years reached the city yesterday. He was Master Lawrence Semon and the tag sewed to his coat bore the address of Mr. Lewis Lippman, 23 Jones Street, west. The boy is a nephew of Mrs. Lippmann. His mother is dead and his father recently met with a serious reverse of fortune during the storm in Newfoundland. For these reasons Mrs. Lippman decided to take young Lawrence and bring him up. Accordingly he was tagged and shipped from Newfoundland to Savannah, making his way without any difficulty.[27]

Larry's move to Savannah was necessary, since the troupe had been caught in a disastrous cyclone at sea in an attempt to bring their equipment to the next place. On September 12 and 13, 1900, it had devastated large parts of the cotton metropole, Galveston,

Texas, to claim more than 6,000 lives. Within a few days it fought its way to the Southern states, up to the large seas, then to the Canadian maritime provinces and Newfoundland, before dissipating into the Atlantic Ocean. Large parts of the circus were destroyed so that Zera saw no other way out but to have Larry entrusted to the care of someone who could give him a safe home: his wealthy sister, Emma Lippman. The Lippman family was headed by 59-year-old drug salesman Lewis Lippman; their middle-aged son Leonard worked as a traveling salesman; daughter Marie and the family servant Bessie Heywood, were both in their early twenties. Larry must have been underway for more than ten days before he arrived in Savannah, with the most difficult part of the itinerary in Newfoundland, as its infrastructure left much to be desired. It is inexplicable, though, why the gazette wrote that Irene had already died. The census of Philadelphia for June 1900 might however hint at a disruption in the family as Larry stayed for some time with Aunt Rebecca and not with his mother. Throughout his career Larry clung to the story of a contemporaneous death of his parents, although Irene survived Zera by five years. Then a 56-year-old housewife, she died from pneumonia at Philadelphia's Presbyterian Hospital on July 14, 1906. The contributing cause of her death was chronic poisoning through the constant consumption of headache powder suggests some suicidal tendencies.

The Lippmans accorded with Zera's and Irene's wish that Larry be sent to school, while he was trying hard to find employment with another traveling troupe. There was no place for him and he proved too young to go staging around the country on his own. In sum, he attended school for five years and finished high school. When his teacher wanted him to describe a historic personality, Larry always asked to be allowed go to the blackboard to draw a portrait of the person in question. This meant entertainment for the whole class, yet no threat to his grades.[28] He studied art and blended his education with different jobs. Art school in Savannah was a relict of the wealthy era of the Southern states. Here Larry was being equipped with what his teachers had learned at the Düsseldorfer Malerschule in Germany, the leading art academy of its time. Nearly every famous pictorial and graphic artist of the United States had been trained in Düsseldorf or drawn on this tradition. Part of it was the integration and reproduction of every possible era, something Larry's later work would show.

A football or baseball game allegedly cost Larry his singing voice. He suffered an injury to his neck, causing an abnormal development. His hopes of becoming an opera singer were once and for all destroyed. In a 1923 interview with *Cine Mundial*, Semon took the tragedy out of this story and simply attributed the loss of his singing voice to puberty vocal change.[29] Larry remained a singer by habit, until someone in the 1920s noticed his rich baritone voice and induced him to record some comic songs for a phonograph manufacturer.[30]

Despite the care of the Lippmans, Larry labeled his youth in Savannah an unhappy one and went even so far as to tell journalists that his parents' death left him "stranded, friendless, jobless and with hardly a nickel to his name."[31] What kept him going was his faith in his artistic skills. As long as he had some talent for drawing it would secure him a career. Larry passed time playing successful little gigs for the high society of the town and excelled as a dancer, puppeteer and prestidigitator. The laudatory comment of the *Atlanta Constitution*, though, leaves some room on top. Maybe the commentator was not aware that Larry had toured more than 13 years with his father and that he had appeared on stage as a professional:

> A very happy circle of young people gathered Wednesday evening in Mrs. Joseph Hull's drawing room to enjoy a "Punch and Judy" show. Miss Mary Blue Hull was the hostess. The room had been converted into a mimic theater, and at one end was erected a real stage. Here, to the great delight of the children, stood little Master Lawrence Semon and performed his wonderful sleight of hand tricks, with considerable skill and all the air of a professional magician. This was followed by the immortal comedy of Punch and Judy, which won much hearty laughter.[32]

· 3 ·

Paperland

Finishing school in Savannah in about late 1904, Larry headed to Philadelphia with the burning desire to become a successful artist. He moved in with Uncle Jake and Aunt Rosa Belle, but surely not with his sister. He was alienated from her as a result of a 1908 court case of his brother-in-law.[1] In center city, at 932 Chestnut Street, Larry became an entrepreneur, opening the Lawrence Semon Company and included in the phone book the intriguing plural "artists." Larry's shop was a few blocks from Jake's cigar store, where Larry still frequently helped out. Soon he found freelance jobs as a card writer and sign painter for Snellenburg's,[2] a Philadelphia-based middle-class department store and wholesale clothing manufacturer that sold directly from the workroom to the wearer, allowing for lower prices.

With some gentle prodding by his uncle or by people he met in his cigar shop, Larry allegedly interspersed his activity for Snellenburg's with occasional jobs as an illustrator. Around the same time, Larry landed a job as general handyman in the art department of the *North American*, one of Philadelphia's earliest and most renowned papers. In no time at all the editorial staff found Larry could really draw and soon he was doing odd bits of cartooning and spot drawings that appeared in the paper. He illustrated news stories and expanded on this through more artistic work that put the output of other papers such as the *Philadelphia Inquirer* in the shade: From spring 1909 until 1910 Larry's contributions to the children's section of the *North American*'s Sunday supplement grew into a syndicated series of caricatured, cut-out paper toys. In the style of the *Deutsche Kaiserzeit*, they covered a wide range of characters, jumping jacks or more elaborate jiggers with rotating heads and pendulum eyes, as well as illustrated scenes of a close to realistic type on foreign cultures. In order to give his toys a special twist, Semon re-interpreted the comic strip characters of his famous colleagues that usually occupied the upper half of the page he drew for. Hays and Wiedersheim's *Kaptin Kiddo* or Grif's awkward heroine seen in *It's Only Ethelinda* were revisited and Larry's colleagues were turned into paper toys as well. Co-worker Bradford, responsible for the *Enoch Pickelweight* strip and soon a cut-out jigger, once received an open apology from Semon because of an insulting extra-large nose.

It is easier to judge Larry's talent by his cut-out toys than by some of the syndicated work he would later deliver for New York newspapers. His toy characters have life; they radiate lightness and maturity combined with humor. The gentle onlooker will notice

The North American Building at Broad and Sansom streets, Philadelphia, when Larry Semon worked there on the editorial staff, ca. 1909 (author's collection).

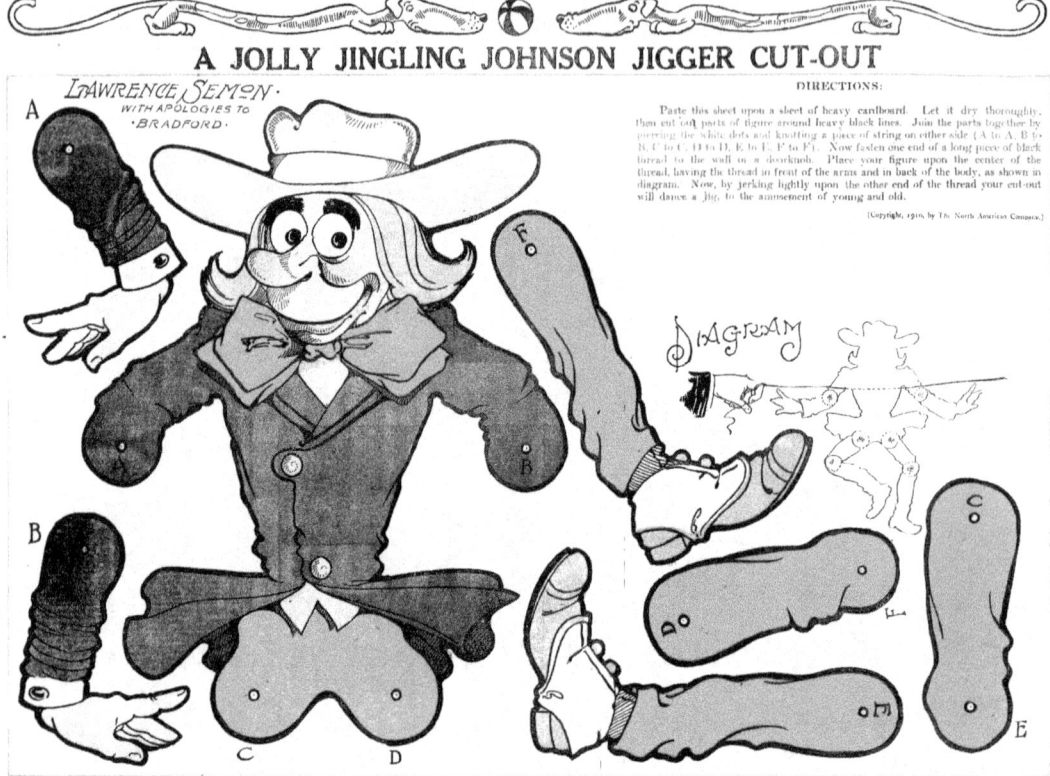

"With apologies to Bradford": Semon turning his cartoon colleague into a cut-out, the *North American*, January 30, 1910 (author's collection).

that his drawing talent was clearly better than average. The precision of his pen and ink strokes are impressive, the overall composition is well balanced—even more so when considering that Semon was still in his early twenties. He would never reach the heights of a Winsor McCay, who developed a realm of deeply insightful fancy figures in lunatic settings that never seemed to run dry. Nevertheless, Semon's work shows a solidity and presence that stands the test of time.

Playful Larry had the strange habit of changing his signature a little bit with every new item he submitted. Using serifs with one item, he abandoned them for the next, mingling initial letters with the following and melting all letters into one underlining stroke. While his artistic style stands for consistency, here we find him still in an experimental phase he would interestingly never drop. A handwritten document of 1924 proves that even the letters of Larry's casual script and print were ever changing.

On a darker side, and surely to the chagrin of magicians everywhere, Larry devilishly took advantage of his father's secrets. On July 18, 1909, Larry began a weekly series, *Mysteries of Magic, Past and Present, Exposed*, in the *North American* Sunday supplement. With a time offset of a week, the articles appeared nationwide. Usually occupying three or four columns, Larry authored and explained popular illusions to a tee and illustrated his articles with pen and ink. The tricks came straight from father Zera's treasure trove or that of Hermann the Great and covered big acts such as levitation and cabinets or smaller sleight-of-hand mysteries. As Larry was frequently enough part of the performance, his articles have autobiographical details. He encouraged readers to write him should they have further questions on any stage trick with the limitation that they should only ask for one trick per letter. As if giving himself permission to deprive professional magicians of their jobs, Larry called himself in the headline Professor Zera Semon's offspring and explained that his father had been one of the most noted magicians of his day. His articles would really expose and not be mere outlines of a few simple stock tricks, such as had often appeared under the guise of revelations. In a later interview, Semon glossed over the atrocity of this series. In his eyes it was necessary to preserve a great repertoire of magic knowledge against the future. The old magicians were gone and they had been too careful about their secrets so that in most cases those secrets had died with them. Thus a weekly series of exposure came in useful. Besides, Semon had given amateurs a simplified version of his tricks, making it easy for them to restage them at church fairs and school concerts. As the tricks back then still really left people awestruck, Semon assured his readers that the infamous decapitation illusion in fact just deceived the eyes and encouraged the amateur to go for it as it was safe. The series ended in late March 1910 after 35 episodes. This date intersects with Semon taking up work on the staff of the *New York Evening Telegram*. Father Zera back then had made it a habit right before each evening's final curtain to let his audience in on the *Davenports' Spiritistic Canopy Act* because he saw it as his duty to prevent people from believing in ghosts, but here

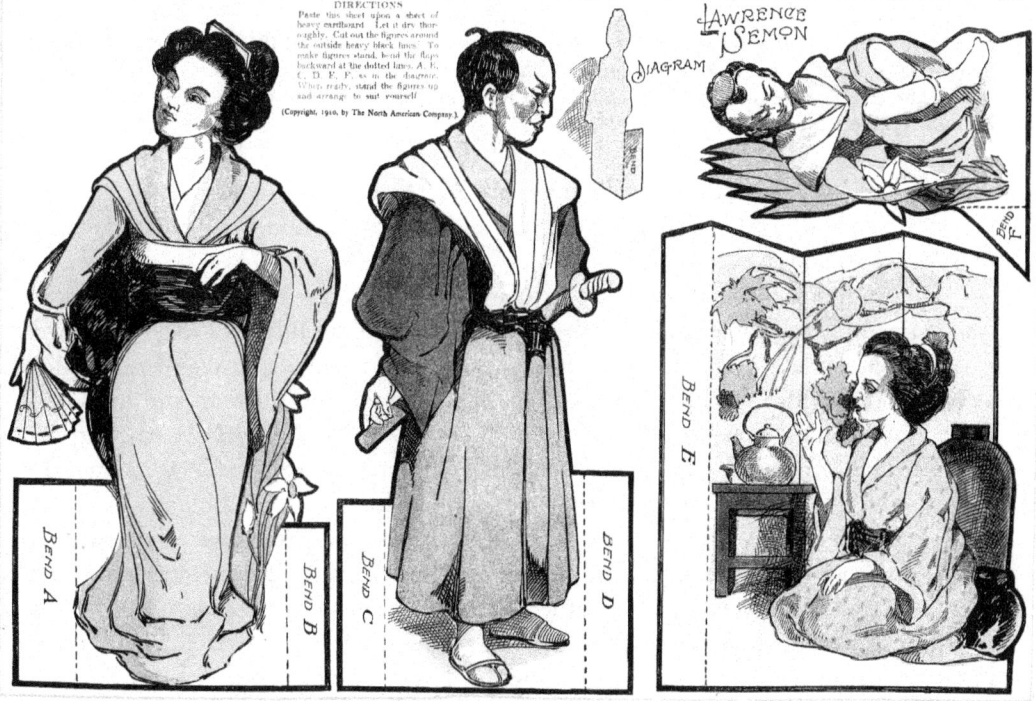

An educational cut-out by Semon, published on March 6, 1910, in the *North American* (author's collection).

Paper toy cut-out by Larry Semon for the *North American*, January 16, 1910 (author's collection). Semon used this kind of toy to entertain French waitress Madelon in *Spuds* (1927). For the film he turned the characters into Charlie Chaplin and Kewpie Morgan. Having become famous, Semon would often be referred to as "Simple Semon."

he stopped. Nonetheless, Zera had been more liberal with tricks in his early days, not necessarily to everybody's delight. Only later did it occur to him that people preferred to be deceived and to remain so.[3]

Larry Semon did not receive more than a weekly $18 for his contributions to the *North American*,[4] but for sure he needed the money, since on July 28, 1909, he had wed Augusta "Gussie" Rosenbaum (1880–1960). The two were married in West Philadelphia at 622 South 52nd Street, the home of Gussie's parents, tailor Nathan and housewife Ethel Rosenbaum.[5] The Rosenbaum family was of German-Austrian decent, and had emigrated in 1875. They had ten children, eight daughters and two sons, all very attractive people. The oldest was George Rosenbaum, Philadelphia's first radiologist, who had studied the science in Germany. The youngest, Bill, a salesman, was always remembered for his gentle and kind character. The oldest girl was married to a manufacturer of shirts.

Larry and Augusta met at one of the amateur theater circles of the city where Larry eagerly took part in order to expand on his stage experience. He received further training in the theatrical sense with the Motion Picture Theater Company of the city. Then he teamed up with the later famous Ed Wynn and other members of Philadelphia's Balbazoo Club that was part of the theater section of the Young Men's Hebrew Association (YMHA), mainly made up of German-rooted members. Founded in 1901, the Balbazoo produced periodic skits, usually in drag with all feminine parts being taken by the boys. Every year their activities were held at the Mercantile Hall, eliciting rave reviews resulting in a nationwide reputation. Papers lauded Larry's contribution to the cast for their 1908 production *The Merry Kiddo* in which he impersonated Miss Angelina Fitt, and he also performed for *Madame Flutterby*.[6] Larry was found to be a real clown and able to arouse laughter at will with his innocent deadpan face. One year later he took over the director's role for the Balbazoo's musical comedy *Pickles and Peanuts*, a show he had written himself. In January, the *Philadelphia Inquirer* informed its readers that Larry was preoccupied with coaching his players, as the spectacle in three acts was due on February 8, 1909. Expectations were high that Semon's show would surpass the previous year's.[7] Then reports disappear. There is no review nor a cancellation notice for the later production.

Larry also became associated with Philadelphia's highly popular Mask and Wig Club. His cartooned views of the principals of the 1909 season were printed as a centerfold in *Stageland and Society*, a weekly magazine published at Keith's Theater Building. These cartoons give us an idea of what would become a Semon trademark in pen and ink. Each character sported Larry's expressive eyes which made every figure he created look splendid. This feature prompted President William Howard Taft to send for Larry and to ask him to draw his caricature for the next election campaign in 1912.[8]

It is shrouded in mystery why Larry and Augusta were married. Certainly short-

Semon's view of Grif's comic strip, Semon's last paper toy for the *North American*, March 27, 1910, before he began working at the *New York Evening Telegram* (author's collection).

Mysteries of Magic, Past and Present, Exposed

XXXIV—THE MILKCAN MYSTERY
By Lawrence Semon
Son of the late Professor Zera Semon, one of the most noted magicians of his day.

THE escape from a milkcan is another one of those very puzzling feats which generally keep an audience guessing.

The performer, dressed in a bathing suit, exhibits for inspection an extra large size milkcan, such as is used to deliver large quantities of milk and is often seen at dairies or railroad stations.

Upon inspecting the can, the committee finds it to be perfectly solid and apparently unprepared. All the joints and parts are put together with heavy rivets. The top is provided with a neck, over which the cover fits snugly.

The cover has four or six metal arms, which reach downward and fit over metal hooks in the top of the can, as in the diagram. The performer now produces a pair of regulation handcuffs, which he shows for inspection. Assistants bring forward several large pails of water and, after the cover has been removed, fill the can more than three-quarters full.

One of the committee securely fastens a pair of handcuffs around the wrists of the performer and, if necessary, a second pair or a pair of shackles around his feet.

The performer now announces that it is his intention to be locked within the milkcan and escape from the same within a couple of minutes from the time that the cover is shut down. He is now assisted into the milkcan, holding his head above the water just long enough to take a deep breath. At a given signal he sinks beneath the surface, and two or more buckets of water are then thrown in to completely fill the can. The cover is shut down and locked in place by padlocks, which may be brought by any member of the audience.

When everything is secure, the can is rolled behind a screen and an assistant stands nearby with a sharp hatchet, ready to cut the can in case of an emergency. No doubt you realize the great excitement caused by this seemingly dangerous undertaking. But, usually in a minute's time, the screen is thrown aside and there stands the performer, dripping wet and holding the handcuffs in either hand, while the can is seen to be locked as securely as when last viewed by the audience.

Of course, the effect is doubly mysterious, because the performer has first to escape from the handcuffs and then from the can; but in this case the handcuffs are a simple matter if they are prepared as follows:

Take a pair of ordinary regulation handcuffs, and after putting the key into the lock, turn the same so that the spring bolts are left half open. Now, holding the handcuffs one at a time over a gas flame, allow them to be thoroughly heated at about the point where the spring is concealed. After they are heated in this manner, lay them away to cool off. By repeating this operation once or twice, you will find that nearly all of the temper is taken out of the spring bolts and that, after the handcuffs are locked, they may be easily opened by hitting sharply upon a hard surface.

Now let us refer to the diagram, and you will see that I have explained two entirely different methods of escape. The first is shown in diagram No. 1 and No. 2. There you will notice that the can is made double, practically a can within a can. The outside portion has no top, while the inside can has no bottom. The outside can is composed of a circular wall and bottom, while the inside can is composed of a circular wall and top. One fits snugly within the other, as shown in diagram No. 1.

The top rim of the outside can is cleverly hidden under a small projecting ridge, which runs entirely

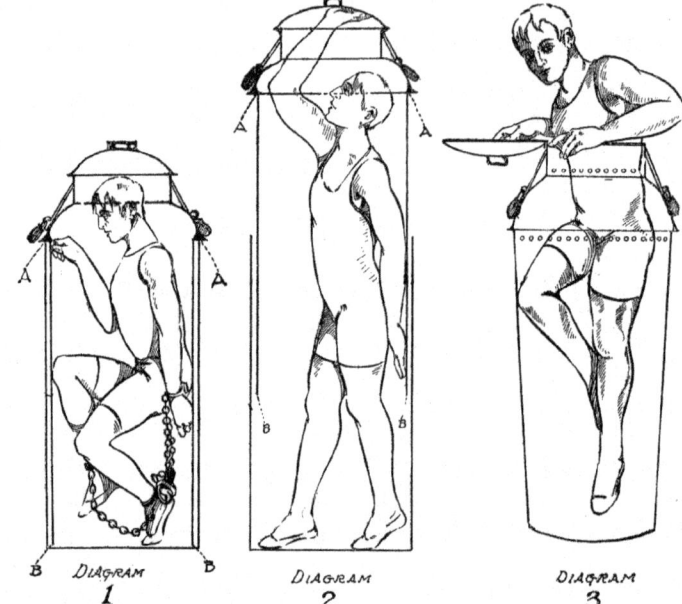

around the inside can at the points marked A, while the bottom rim of the inside can rests snugly upon the bottom of the outside can at the points marked B.

The cans are held securely together by means of one or more movable rivets or a tiny spring hinge, which cannot be seen unless one takes his place upon the inside of a can.

Diagram No. 1 shows the performer in the act of removing the concealed rivet after he has made his escape from the handcuffs.

By studying diagram No. 2, you will see that the inside can out of its position. Then calmly stepping out of the outside can, which, in the meantime, holds the water, he again replaces the inner can, which is caught and held in place by means of the tiny spring hinge described above. Of course, a small quantity of water is at first purposely spilled about the stage, and this seeming carelessness acts as a safeguard in case the performer should spill any water while making

his escape.

Diagram No. 3 shows you another type of milkcan, with a far simpler method of escape. In this case the curved upper part of the cover, while apparently riveted securely in place, is merely fastened at one point on either side. As before, a tiny spring hinge is used on one side, while an ordinary hinge is used on the other.

The apparently solid rivets are merely fakes—that is, the top parts of the rivets are soldered upon the outside of the can, while the lower parts are soldered upon the inside.

Now, as you will see, the outer curved part of the cover is merely a cleverly concealed trapdoor which may be opened from the inside. After releasing himself from the handcuffs, the performer merely reaches up and moves aside one of the fake rivets, which releases the spring hinge.

So you see that it is an easy matter for the performer to make his escape as shown in diagram No. 3.

The Milkcan Mystery: The thirty-fourth episode of Larry Semon exposing his father's tricks to the amateur in the *North American*, March 13, 1910 (author's collection).

statured Augusta, with her pure white skin, fair complexion, dark hair and hazel eyes, was an attractive woman from a wealthy family. Yet people described her as an unkind woman who was always miserable and highly manipulative. She loved to play people off against each other. Womanizer Larry for his part smiled his shy smile, rather with his lips closed as one of his front teeth had turned dark, and won people over by his great wit, his energetic appearance and talent to entertain. But the two did not match. Augusta was looking for a life at home, with the desire to comply with her nuptial duties and to raise children. Larry, by contrast, was always on the run and did not have much sense for returning home early—if at all. He was constantly looking for public approval and never skipped any opportunity to prove his prowess, not to mention his eagerness to find and develop new things. The Rosenbaum clan made the mismatch perfect. They did not like Larry. The family moved in different social circles and this young man was like any Tom, Dick or Harry. And he was from entertainment, too, the ultimate criterion for exclusion; show biz people were considered untrustworthy and most volatile. Gussie's family thought he was not good enough for Augusta, and unless someone was college-educated and headed toward a proper profession, he was considered worthless. A photograph that has survived

"Merely a Monarch": How Larry Semon saw the protagonists of Philadelphia's famous Mask and Wig Club in their 1909 production, *Stageland and Society*, 1909 (author's collection).

shows Larry in an oversized suit joining his new family. The Rosenbaums did not group around their new member Larry, but rather shifted him off to the picture's margin. He was not one of them and never would be. The only reasonable motivation for Augusta and Larry's marriage seems their expectation of a child. They did not want the scandal of an illegitimate child; however Augusta's first pregnancy ended in a miscarriage.

Only a few months after their word of consent, Larry began to show signs of the big town itch as he fancied that more was to come and he had plenty to offer. Aware that he was not a complete nobody thanks to his syndicated work, he sought the biggest market and went to New York City. In early 1910, Larry hopped a train to New York, not ready to take his portfolio.

> It was an awfully cold day and there was a big snowstorm in full blast—not a very encouraging prospect for a bright young cartoonist trying to pry off a job in New York. When I went out on the street after leaving the train I took one look at that storm and decided that maybe I'd better go back to Philly and get another job, for I had already given up mine on the *North American*.
>
> Then I thought that would be kind of silly—as long as I was in New York I might as well try a couple of places. A "newsy" came along and I asked him the way to the nearest newspaper office. He directed me to the office of the *Evening Telegram*, while I bought a copy of the "*Telly*" from him. The next move was to get installed in a cheap hotel, which I did, and read the *Telegram* up in my room. It struck me that they were a bit weak on sporting cartoons, so I put on my coat again and walked over to their office.
>
> The sporting editor finally saw me and, oddly enough, asked me for a sample of my work. I asked him to wait a few minutes and to give me an option on a job until I could get back with a sample. He agreed and I tore back to the room, batted out a sport cartoon and ran back

to the "*Telly*" with it. I guess he liked it because he let me on the staff at thirty-five dollars per [week]. I was tickled to death to get it. I felt like a prince. And from that day on things began to look up.[9]

Within a record-setting twenty minutes, Semon had secured a contract on a local newspaper in *the* metropole for cartoonists. In an attempt at dating Semon's trip to New York, he arrived during the notorious blizzard of January 13–15, 1910, that brought 14 inches of blinding snow and put the city on hold. Ten people died, trains crashed and thousands of men later cleared the snow off the streets. Philadelphia had just escaped its whitewash blizzard during the holidays of December 1909 and Semon's train was chasing it. After securing his *Telly* position, Semon returned to Philadelphia to organize his new residence in New York. There was no rush as the *North American* had paid him an advance on the art and articles they had put in reserve, but Semon was ambitious to climb the career ladder.

The Rosenbaum family, ca. 1909. From back row to front row, left to right: Max Peiken, William Rosenbaum, Lillian (*née* Rosenbaum) Peiken, Dorothy Roomberg, Nathan Roomberg, Simon Marcus, Edythe Marcus, Rebecca (*née* Rosenbaum) Marcus, Hannah (*née* Rosenbaum) Roomberg, Rebecca Rosenbaum, Dr. George Rosenbaum, Augusta "Gussie" Rosenbaum, Lawrence Semon; unidentified, unidentified, unidentified, Nathan Rosenbaum, Ethel Rosenbaum; unidentified, Matilda Rosenbaum, Florence Rosenbaum, Evelyn Peiken (courtesy Lynne Whitcopf).

3. Paperland

The Evening Telegram was owned by the *New York Herald* and had its headquarters at the self-titled Herald Square. Semon kicked off on its staff on March 30, 1910, with a baseball cartoon for the wordy *Up-to-Date News, Gossip and Comment on Sports of All Kinds* column. He drew a three-panel cartoon of the New York Giants' fans getting ready for the next baseball season. It includes a schoolboy that lists the current diseases within his family—without excepting himself—in order to dash off to attend their match.

Semon contributed daily black and white one-panel sports cartoons, alternating them with comic strips. Within a few weeks, the *Telly* gave him more opportunities with the society and theatrical pages and let him periodically handle the caricatures of New York authorities such as Mayor Gaynor, Charles Evans Hughes and Charley Murphy. They also turned him into a sports journalist. While his articles remain anonymous, he recognizably spoofed himself in a short-lived comic strip named *Mr. Wood B. Sport* that appeared from December 1910 until January 1911. Halfwit Wood B. Sport mixes with all kinds of athletics and is always getting severely hurt. The strip is intriguing as we see

A test run for motion pictures: "Mr. Wood B. Sport Is Introduced to Bowls." Larry Semon putting himself into a cartooned character, having had his first adverse encounters with bowling in real life, *New York Evening Telegram*, December 19, 1910 (courtesy Fulton History).

"Mr. Wood B. Sport Takes Advantage of the Cold Snap." Larry Semon's cartoon likeness boasting his athletic skills on the ice rink, *New York Evening Telegram*, December 24, 1910 (courtesy Fulton History).

a first sketch of Semon's later celluloid character, inept, ever-eager and always at the center of a riot. In the December issues he tries weightlifting, crashing through floors and landing in the arms of his neighbors. In another strip he flirts with the fairer sex at an ice rink only to get struck by the skid of a skate. Another reason the strip is worth considering: It shows Larry how he looked in daily life—in long shot. A large black slouch hat covers his bespectacled sunken face while he drowns in a dark tent-like coat that barely hides his spindly-legged, undernourished body. From time to time Larry pops up in other cartoon contexts and although it is wise to keep a work of art and its creator apart, it is just too tempting to fancy some kind of self-therapy when he comments on the fads of women. One cartoon sports a hysteric and stout Gussie-like character who decided to put black-eyed Larry in the trash after a beating with a rolling pin. Nuptial bliss in the Semon household was evidently an illusion.

Semon loved to play to the gallery and used his likeness for a variety of cartoons. A pied piper, eyes wide, marching towards the reader is like another test run for his later film appearances. The friendly stare into the camera from half-profile that would at once create a solid bond with his onlooker is already there. And so was the pace. In

Semon's cartoons there is hardly a standstill. His characters, preferably livestock and baseball players, often escalate into a thrill of speed with their arms and legs in convulsions. Elephants literally take their heels, well-studied muscle movement included. The image of a racer on his bicycle surging past and feathering into condensation trails is a perfect conversion of sports photography into pen and ink. Speed is often concomitant with desperate situations and their immediate resolution: Baseball legend Jeff of the Dodgers is saving himself from "being carried over the fall" by blowing and indeed we see Jeff in a boat on the edge of a waterfall as he kneels down with his lips pursed. Larry Semon generated flexible and tolerant universes on paper and on film. The option of manifest solutions to predicaments was passed down to his comedies. In *The Battler* (1916), a boxing champ uses gas bombs to his advantage, sending a whole crowd of competitors into oblivion. Only those remaining wizened fighters had enough forethought to seal their noses with a clothes pin.

If Larry desired to escape and take a shortcut, he would go through walls (*Whistles and Windows*, 1918). If he wanted his enemy's gun not to fire, he would simply lick his thumb and plug it into its barrel and be safe (*The Fly Cop*, 1920). If he wanted to be faster than policemen on motorbikes (*The Rent Collector*, 1921), he would pick a conven-

"Women Don't Agree That They Need a Whipping Occasionally." Henpecked Larry Semon in a trash can with a character maybe inspired by his wife Gussie, *New York Evening Telegram*, July 10, 1911 (courtesy Fulton History).

Jeffries of the Dodgers saves himself from being carried over the fall in this cartoon by Larry Semon, *New York Evening Telegram*, May 5, 1910 (courtesy Fulton History).

tional bicycle. Considering this, there is absolutely no reason why Semon should have resolved quite a number of his film scenarios in a dream. There was no logic to his universe, so his hero would have had every other opportunity for an ending despite coming back to reality. But, possibly he bowed to his cartoon colleague Winsor McCay and his *Dream of a Rarebit Fiend*.[10]

The playful use of shapes adds to the variety of Semon's artwork. The optical illusion of classics such as "The Window of Three Hares" in the cathedral of Paderborn, Germany, is re-implemented by Semon in the form of three men that share four legs, although each one stands on his own feet. In Paderborn every hare ended up with a complete set of ears despite all three having only three ears at their disposal. Another instance is a fantasy on a Canadian Maple Leaf and an ex–Canadian Half Moon fighting a thrilling ice hockey game. The Maple Leaf gave Semon another opportunity to incarnate his enormously curved nose in yet another cartoon. Kind behavior and high spirit are represented in animal studies such as taciturn turkeys and fashionable horses of ardor and racing mules, usually sporting a most enviable set of teeth.

Semon's cartoons also leave room for a microcosm of coincidental bystanders that pop up, never to be used again. Mr. Hercules Half Smoke, somewhat on in years, is one of them. He is a cigar and has never missed a race. Certainly he would make a character on his own. Absurd nightmarish situations that re-appear in movies such as *Spuds* (1927) were preceded by other bystanders of spiralized necks as they dared follow racers around. Character studies of sports buffs meant to Semon depicting spectators "in the balcony" from their soles that had been mended more than once.

Since Philadelphia and New York City are about 100 miles apart, Larry soon had

> THE DEACON, LARRY AND CY ARE IN OUR MIDST.

"The Cleveland Spirit of 1910." **Cartoon by Larry Semon for the** *New York Evening Telegram*, **May 19, 1910 (courtesy Fulton History).**

to find himself a place in the metropole where he could stay. Eventually Augusta joined him. On a visit to her family in Philadelphia, she gave birth to their only child, daughter Virginia, on May 29, 1912.

The young family's life bore some bohemian features: They moved a lot and too frequently they had to borrow money to raise their child and rent an apartment they could afford. One of Larry's co-workers at the *Telegram* recalled that he was so short of money that he did not have a collar button. One took it even further and stated, "If Semon found himself in possession of a round of 'third rail' in Perry's he would mistake it for the Fourth of July."[11]

Rents in Harlem were low. Until a few years previous, mostly German Jews had shaped this district, but they had moved on. With the economic lull in 1910, many owners began to sell their houses to Afro-American people that came from the South. Larry's earliest entry in New York's phone directory can be dated back to 1912 when the family lived at 352 W. 118th Street, a narrow red house with a front flight of stairs, arched windows, lying in the direct neighborhood of stately mansions, with Morningside Park right around the corner. The same year, the Semons moved to 220 W. 111th Street.[12] Early in 1912 Larry had been lured away from the *Telegram* and worked for the *New York Morning Telegraph* and soon after for the *New York Evening Sun*. This was a revelation to him, as his former employer regarded him as a second-class artist who was haplessly struggling for a place in the sun. Larry later explained that he felt exploited by him, which triggered his urge to satirize newspaper guys in his one-reelers. Now regularly employed on the

"The Window of Three Hares": a classic counterpart to Semon's "Cleveland Spirit of 1910" as often found in sacred sites, preeminently in the cathedral of Paderborn, Germany (courtesy Andreas Sassen).

Evening Sun, Larry contributed daily by straight reporting, writing feature stories and by adding baseball player portraits to its sporting sheet. He even ran a column in the same section called "Ho Fans!" and originated a funny character which he called "Mr. Everybody"—a good-natured fool always in everybody's way. The strip meant an elaboration on "Mr. Would-Be Sport" since Larry caricatured his own likeness in it with an update in costume: high-waisted trousers.[13]

With more than four years of experience in the business, Semon had a good idea about printing, reproduction and negatives. In the *Sun*'s darkroom, Semon invented or rather re-engineered a way of counterfeiting; in other words a color photograph scheme for making bogus $100 bills.

This find was highly welcomed by the producers of the detective comedy *The Argyle Case* that conquered Broadway in 1912 and featured Robert Hilliard, one of the handsomest and best leading men of his era. The comedy was a tremendous success in that it gave audiences new sensations: one of them, Larry's method of bleaching new one dollar bills with a combination of acids completely clean so that nothing but the blank fiber remained. When the $1 bills were blank, then cleaned and dried, he coated them

A quite Semonesque pied piper cartoon for the *New York Evening Telegram*, April 27, 1910 (courtesy Fulton History).

with a photographer's darkroom photo-sensitive emulsion and exposed the positive image of a $100 bill from a negative. It sounds time-consuming, unlike the method by which metal plates are inked and bills mass-produced the way newspapers are printed on a printing press, but a hundred dollars went a long way back in the day. The bleaching process was faked for stage purposes and accomplished in full view of everybody in the audience. The way it worked proved so startling that it gave audiences a fresh thrill.[14] Once a bunch of perfectly good one-dollar bills was destroyed every evening, Semon shifted into the focus of the local police.

The year 1913 brought a change. Larry made a return to vaudeville, for $175 a week, until William Randolph Hearst ended the whole thing because he wanted the cartoonists to do their work instead of giving descriptive lectures. Larry's first night on November 8, 1913, was not exactly a success. He was the last in a row of cartoonists who created their sporting toons live on stage. People had grown tired of them and Semon did not present anything new in his twelve-minute act so he met with a cold reception. A reviewer who saw Semon on Fifth Avenue wrote:

> With all due respect to Lawrence Semon's ability and cleverness to entertain with the chalk and crayon and incidentally make the gift of drawing pay, a sigh of relief will go up when all of the New York newspaper artists have made their debut on the local vaudeville stage. A likable chap, with a pleasing voice, Semon is able to make himself heard without tripping up any of the footlights. In this "act" he makes only heads of diamond heroes best known to New York fans. Semon will receive attention wherever they know baseball.[15]

"Where Everybody Tries to Be Busy": The Athletics' elephant speeds its members to the top, *New York Evening Telegram*, May 28, 1910 (courtesy Fulton History). Note at the bottom the doodle of boxing champion "Lil Artha," a favorite among Semon's cartoon characters.

"Good talker" Larry listened, and continued drawing rapid-fire sketches of baseball greats and changed something about his act that gave him a unique selling angle among cartoonists: He did stand-up. People loved his neat way, they saw that he was good at expressions and praised his ability to keep houses in good humor. *Variety* concluded that Semon got away from the established routine and that his sketches of baseball stars came nearer to artistic excellence than most of the work seen in this sort of vaudeville offering.[16]

A year into his return to vaudeville, Larry was still performing on stage. He was billed for Keith's, Proctor's and even the Palace, the epitome of every vaudeville career. Since Larry often did Jewish characterizations on the stage, a lot of people, notably fans in their letters, imagined that he was Jewish. It did not hold true, as he used to stress, but on the other hand he was quite liberal about it. Exhibitor Sam Bernstein recited a cute little story in which he visited Los Angeles and met Semon at Vitagraph. Semon introduced him to the making of films and showed him sensations such as a dozen companies working in one studio at the same time: "Semon saw I was having trouble in expressing myself in English when I got excited about the things he told me and showed me, so he said: 'Speak Yiddish, Bernstein. I'm a little Jewish myself.'"[17]

Semon actually kept silent about the religion he chose to be his. Yet by the time of his death, a Christian Science reader was responsible for his funeral services.

At the Palace, Larry once again became involved with mechanics on the stage. Yet instead of minstrel marionettes, "Coleman's Baseball Player" was presented in a twelve-

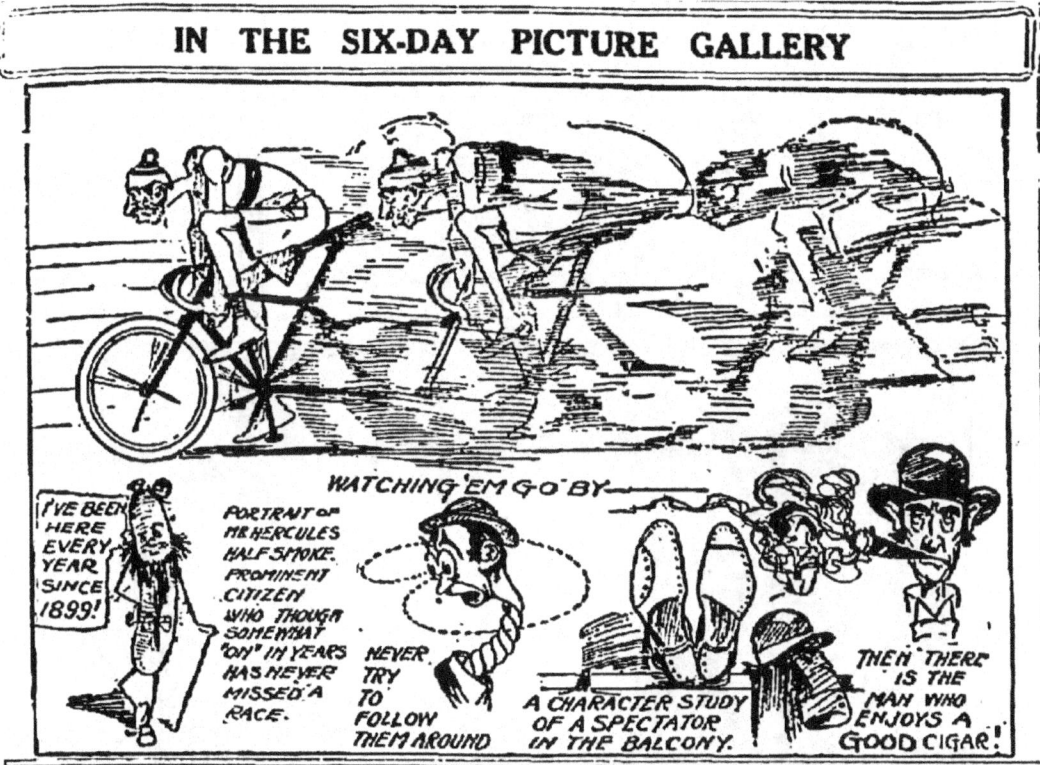

"In the Six-Day Picture Gallery," a full-speed cartoon and some microcosm by Larry Semon for the *New York Evening Telegram*, December 8, 1910 (courtesy Fulton History).

"The Annual Round Up," one of Semon's countless horse characters, *New York Evening Telegram*, September 9, 1910 (courtesy Fulton History).

"Billy Penn Divides Thanksgiving Affections": A taciturn turkey and jocose football meet in a cartoon by Semon, *New York Evening Telegram*, November 24, 1910 (courtesy Fulton History).

minute act in which Semon gave a lengthy talk. A critic mourned that it did not help the act much, as the trick behind this gimmick was easy to configure. Said invention was to give an exact reproduction of the game as played on the field with moving pictures of the players, though completely different from a motion picture, because it was operated without a machine. The players' actions were not in a flow, but rather done jerkily as if a series of lights was mechanically ignited to mark their movements. The machine-free zone turned out to be a fraud, nevertheless the best one available to replicate a ballgame.[18]

Larry drew cartoons on a daily basis and was headlining with *The Sun*'s Sunday supplement. He was associated with the baseball stars of the Major League team, including the New York Giants, many of whom are honored in the Baseball Hall of Fame. A complete series of 21 portraits has survived for which Larry illustrated the players "from life." In order to accelerate the process, he might have outlined or traced their faces using photos, yet the result is a fine work of pen and ink and confirms how aptly he could

Cartoon by Larry Semon, *New York Evening Telegram*, January 10, 1911 (courtesy Fulton History).

Semon makes fun of women and fashion, *New York Evening Telegram*, July 24, 1911 (courtesy Fulton History).

Semon's sidekick on women getting stout, *New York Evening Telegram*, July 1911 (courtesy Fulton History).

render faces. Today's price of postcards of other famous heads have rocketed sky-high at auctions, amounting to hundreds if not a thousand dollars. To the present day, many movie aficionados are unaware of Semon's accomplished baseball artwork. Conversely, while vintage baseball card collectors are aware of a rare series of 1914 postcards or other baseball-themed artwork that Semon crafted, hardly any of them knows of Semon's movie career.[19] Larry's own passion for baseball was a great one. In 1920 he paid $500 for a bat and ball autographed by Babe Ruth at a fundraising event at the hotel Alexandria in Los Angeles.

A portrait of Giants baseball star Al Demaree by Larry Semon, the *Evening Sun*'s Gallery of Famous Baseball Players, ca. 1915 (courtesy Lyman Hardeman).

There has been some discussion whether Larry's newspaper work was noteworthy at all. He has been judged as but an itinerant penman, perhaps because of a lack of reference. Semon surely knew to play the whole gamut of techniques, ranging from insightful portraits to "primitive." Given that he had only seven years to nurture his talent for the papers, the outcome is worth considering. Chief linguist Tad Dorgan thought otherwise and once stated that Semon was no good. Dorgan qualifies as an "associated" member of the *Telly*'s "I Knew Him When Club" that spontaneously formed on the occasion of Larry's $3.6 million movie contract with Vitagraph in 1919. The club shared their views on their former colleague and let the world know how poor a cartoonist Semon proved. Journalists were roused to take a deeper peek at his past and determined that he was some effeminate son who used to work in his father's company being badly in need of his paternal resources. The club continued remembering their former associate Semon as a conscientious objector to work and sensationally unfunny. Every week Larry would appear at the cashier's window with his hangdog expression, harassed by his permanent worry that instead of his $35 he would be sent away empty-handed.

Cornelius McGillicuddy (Connie Mack), baseball player, manager and team owner as part of a nowadays pricey postcard series, ca. 1915 (courtesy Lyman Hardeman).

One city editor acted as an "eye-opener" when he took Larry aside and suggested, man to man, that he'd better get out of that business as he would never be destined to greater success.[20] The oldest member of the "I Knew Him When Club," by contrast, believed that Larry climbed that high on the ladder of success as he was such a "persistent cuss."[21] He took Semon out on afternoons to a bowling alley, and at first Larry was the worst player his colleague ever saw. Larry stuck to it and eventually got to be a whiz. Semon later used his initial bowling experience in the one-reeler *Big Bluff and Bowling Balls* (1917).

Semon had found another good fellow, Louis Calhern, a cartoonist for the Newspaper Feature Syndicate on Park Row, who soon played leads at the Lois Weber Studios. The two enjoyed a little French restaurant on Nassau Street, near Fulton, downstairs, where lawyer Daniel Webster had his office. The place was notorious for its cointreaus, cafecognacs and benedictines. When Semon and Calhern bumped into each other again on Hollywood Boulevard, they were longing for the old days before Prohibition, but knew where to go to in Hollywood to continue with the hootch hunt.[22]

In 1915, Larry and his family moved to 119 West 47th Street. He now lived within walking distance from the Diamond District, the Broadway theaters and *The Sun* at Times Square. Semon's work was in demand, as was that of his colleagues Tad Dorgan, Winsor McCay and Rube Goldberg, all of them young men about thirty who were already earning more than most bankers.[23] Semon's fame as a cartoonist is perhaps best demonstrated in an extensive ad campaign in which Tuxedo tobacco was advertised. Interestingly, the same ad campaign did not only encompass endorsements from him and his fellow cartoonists, but also of several leading baseball players, musicians, and politicians. In September 1915, Semon was featured along with his comic strip "Marcus the Boarding House Goat," a character that borrowed Goldberg's drawing style at the expense of Semon's own recognizable style. A portrait of the cartoonist clad in a tuxedo and focusing on the paper under his pen did unfortunately not show much, except a bunch of diligently parted hair, pince-nez glasses and a large nose. From today's perspective, the advertisement's bottom line, actually signed by the artist, offered a most naive if not massively embar-

Announcement of the New York Giants' eighth annual ball in 1915 by Larry Semon (courtesy Lyman Hardeman). Note the dancing couple being reminiscent of Larry Semon and a pre–Lucille type.

rassing endorsement: "Tuxedo is great! Ideas come more easily and my pen moves more smoothly when I have a pipe of good old Tux between my teeth!"[24]

Rising in salary and importance, Semon was assigned a copy boy, James Cagney by name, who himself had a sensational film career in his future.[25] And in order to add yet another name that would become great in motion picture business, Semon was on the same staff as his buddy, Harry Charles Witwer, brilliant short story author and cartoonist.

Opposite: Photographic portraits of top cartoonists Tad Dorgan, Lawrence Semon, and Rube Goldberg trying their talents on the baseball diamond, unidentified magazine, ca. 1912 (author's collection).

Some Well-known Cartoonists as

"Tad" Dorgan, New York Evening Journal

Laurence Semon, New York Evening Sun

Reub Goldberg, New York Evening Mail

Photo by Paul Thompson

The two worked alongside soon-to-be Hollywood director Leon Lee, who entered motion pictures at practically the same time Semon did and later was involved in his independent pictures.[26] Although Semon now hobnobbed with the most popular sports journalists and cartoonists in the country, the situation with his in-laws did not improve. They did not approve. Semon's career kept him too busy to find time for Gussie. He was documenting the action of the baseball stars and followed them everywhere including Marlin, Texas, during training. When he worked out with the Giants for inspiration and material, it did not turn out too well for him: One day a fly ball he was pursuing in the outfield hit him on top of the head and knocked him loopy for some time.[27]

The winter seasons of 1914–15 and 1915–16 came along with the Newspapermen's Pocket Billiard Tournament for the sporting writers and artists of the various local papers. The candidates met in Doyle's Forty-Second Street Academy and clashed, surrounded by the press and everyone else willing to look on. More than 100 contestants were on the list and some of them prided themselves on their power to attract a big gallery whenever they stepped up to the tables. In the first season, Semon was in the also-ran class, but with the second, he shocked his audience. By a score of 83 to 68 he beat sports writer Sid Mercer, who was at that time considered invincible. Most of the players were relieved when Mercer fell. Although he would not make it among the finalists, Semon deservedly won that day, as he played remarkably.[28] Earlier that season Semon had defeated Harry Cross, a success that was not only owed to his technique, but also to the fact that he had completely out-talked him.[29]

· 4 ·

Early Directions

Larry's billiard tournament was overlapping with the first traceable film production that featured him as a star. He had always been focused on the greatest game in the world, as he used to call it, and this was his chance with Novelty, a small company that released through the large Mutual Film Corporation. *The Fiddler*, a one-reeler, hit theaters nationwide on December 20, 1915, and exhibited until September 1916. The only verifiable reference to this film that Larry made was in an interview with the French periodical *Cinémagazine*. He was asked about his first motion picture which was translated as *The Violinist*.[1] Larry took the lead as ravenously hungry Hans, who gets kicked out of a German band and ends up at the party of a rich family. He is mistaken for a well-known musician, enjoying all the conveniences of his false fame until the real fiddler turns up. In a nutshell, Semon caricaturing Germans foreshadowed his later anti-hun propaganda work. *The Fiddler* included sausage eating and other eccentric happenings so that one reviewer bemoaned the absence of refinement in this "rather slapstick sort of thing."[2] Semon was advertised as a well-known comedian, suggesting that he had proven his risibility in public before. But most probably his regional fame that covered the New York area was inflated to countrywide popularity for marketing purposes. B.H. Mills, since 1914 turning out one-reel comedies for Mutual, prided himself on having sold this first Larry Semon comedy.[3]

Since 1912, Semon had been trying hard to gain ground in the motion picture industry. His first attempts were so luckless that friends advised him to stay with the newspapers. Before being given his first chance, he had written countless comedy scripts which he distributed among the regional film companies; all were rejected. He had made the same mistake as many others, thinking that scenario writing was easy and could be done without intensive study of the requirements of the relatively new film medium. That Semon was used to typing newspaper articles did not suffice. Even authors of the greatest skill had to discover that a thousand words of description could be duplicated in a few seconds on the screen and that they had to learn to write action, not merely words. Papers were full of interviews with film producers that bewailed the many aspirants who thought their talent was enough to go places in motion pictures. Larry's rocky road to the movies proved good training and later made him always consider proposals from amateur writers for his scenarios.

Director Sidney Goldin (1878–1937) was the man who finally "discovered" Larry Semon[4] in about 1914 and put him on the payroll for one-reelers at the Universal Film Manufacturing Company. Russian-born Goldin was a kind-faced man with a black-rimmed monocle, a highly respected screen veteran who got his first experience as an actor in Chicago at Selig and Essanay. He soon gave up acting for directing and became known as one of America's first independent directors. Later he signed with Universal for a series of features and specialized in Jewish pictures and underworld films.[5] After his chance with Universal, Larry moved on. In late June 1915, Palace Players Film Corporation went into production and with them, director and scenarist Lawrence Semon. At this writing no credits could be determined for his work. In the Studio Directory section of *Motion Picture News* 1915/1916, Palace's office location at 2003 Times Building is listed as Semon's current contact address along with his affiliation with the *New York Sun*.[6] Palace's films were made in the company's own studio, the Victor, on West 43rd Street near Broadway. Semon was drawing cartoons for *The Sun* in the mornings and afternoons and making films at night, as Palace Players rented their studio out to other moving picture companies during the day. The company was supervised by director-general C.M. Ackerman, former scenario writer and actor. He constantly advertised for new photoplayers, demanding a good wardrobe and charging an extra fee for screen tests. At the turn of the year, "Ackie" appeared with co-star Suzanne Westford in farce comedies directed by Edward Warren. Possibly Larry was responsible for the writing.[7] He also worked for the Mittenthal Brothers in Yonkers, New York, as Jimmy Aubrey vividly remembered in an April 17, 1976, interview with film historians Sam Gill and Jordan Young. On making his own extrance at Mittenthal's Aubrey said:

> I was working on stage evenings when the Mittenthal brothers approached me, and wanted me to make comedies during the day. They signed me to play in their "Heinie and Louie" comedies, to replace "Heinie" who hadn't worked out....

Aubrey was referring to a series of comedies made under the brand name *Starlight Comedies*, released through Pathé and produced by the Mittenthal Brothers. The "Louie" was played at one time by Walter Kendig, who was soon fired and was replaced by another comedian. Aubrey continued:

> Mittenthal Brothers. I liked them, and they played straight. I tell you someone else who came over there at the time—Larry Semon—a cartoonist the Mittenthals said would be good. So he came over. God, he didn't know anything about film. He cut the picture in the camera. It came out short. It was okay, but short. Later I ran into Larry at Vitagraph.

The moviemaking Mittenthal Brothers were active from 1913 to 1917 with their greatest output in 1915. Semon probably stayed with them from 1914 to 1915. He might already have met his later stock company member Oliver Hardy there; Hardy starred in the Mittenthals' *Fatty's Fatal Fun* (1915).[8] Parallel to his doings in Yonkers and at Novelty's, Larry was flirting with the idea of entering the premises of Vitagraph.

One day in 1915, former newspaperman and current Vitagraph official James Stuart Blackton visited *The Sun* because he wanted to offer the stupefied Larry an opportunity to collaborate with him. On the evidence of some scripts Larry had penned and sent over, Blackton was sure he had found a promising comedy director in Semon, deploring

Playbill for an early and most successful comedy team: Flora Finch and John Bunny and two unidentified actors in *Bunny's Suicide*, Vitagraph, 1912 (author's collection).

the failed efforts of those he presently hired. Another reason to short-list Larry was his artist portfolio, reflecting a good sense of humor that spoke for itself. After his initial pratfalls he now bore strong opinions on how to write a comedy script and how to put it into production. Laughter would not be provoked by acrobatic antics alone but by well-studied pantomime. Things could not have turned out any better for Larry Semon: Founded by Blackton and one-time conjurer Albert Edward Smith in 1896, Vitagraph had developed into the most important of the early production companies. It might well be considered the MGM of the teens. It established the star system, built up a roster of players, gathered the finest technical staff available and placed them under contract. Vitagraph perfected the studio system of film production and devised an almost perfect distribution set-up.[9]

Like other producers, Blackton was courting New York's cartoonists in need of new directors, since he believed they could easily supervise the making of comedies. Vitagraph had dozens of dramatic companies at work and wanted farce directors. Two of them would turn out to be particularly adept, British-born C. Graham Baker of *The Times* and Lawrence Semon. Another reason for Blackton's recruitment campaign was the loss of John Bunny. On April 26, 1915, Vitagraph's top act had unexpectedly succumbed, leaving the company a huge void to fill. Frank Daniels was hired and debuted in the photoplay *Crooky Scruggs* in mid–July 1915. Semon undertook uncredited steps at directing the Daniels comedies as assistant to Blackton or C. Jay Williams. *The Motion Picture Directory* is the only reliable source to reference Semon's involvement with these comedies. As Larry honed his directorial skill under Blackton's tutelage, he also underwent a training that prepared him for acting for the camera. His theatrical experience was a basic one to guide people, but Semon still had to learn about the angles an actor would take before the lens to make it distinct from the legitimate stage. Blackton had grown fond of this young and clever disciple with his plaid newsboy cap and a haircut that made his high forehead appear even higher. Nurturing Semon, Blackton also saw his chances to retire from Vitagraph with the option to follow up on his own motion picture endeavors which he briefly did from 1917 on. Semon now divided his time between *The Sun* and Vitagraph with a short stint as a gag writer at Elm Avenue, before moving to their new studio in Flatbush.[10]

Vitagraph's plant in Flatbush was on Locust Avenue, on the outskirts of Brooklyn, from where a short trip by car placed the various companies in picturesque country locations. The studio's presence had stimulated trade among the small merchants of the neighborhood and triggered a little colony of restaurants, bakeries and ice cream soda fountains to spring up around its entrance. The liberal patrons within the gates did their very best to make the colony's existence flourish. Leaving the little brick station of the Brighton Line, one ran perchance into a pot-bellied tavern keeper of the period of Henry de Navarre smoking a cigarette with a Roman soldier and standing in the path which led across a meadow to the studio.

One of the first people to welcome Lawrence Semon was studio correspondent Ethel Pennington, who often left her work to conduct a tour of the Vitagraph building. Adjoining the main office—later to become a place Larry would be called to more than it pleased him—was a special suite for the officials with a private dining room attached. Here President Albert E. Smith, the financial brain of the company, studio manager

VITAGRAPH

BE THE FIRST
In your neighborhood to
BOOK THIS SERIES
of the cleanest, funniest and most profitable single reel motion picture fun makers enacted by
THE WORLD RENOWNED COMEDY KING

FRANK DANIELS

The one and only popular comedian who has been able to be really funny in the motion picture. The complete series of the twelve

"ESCAPADES of MR. JACK"
include the following
MR. JACK
A Hall Room Hero
Wins a Double Cross
Ducks The Alimony
The Hash Magnate
Trifles
Inspects Paris
A Doctor by Proxy
Mr. Jack's Hat and The Cat
Mr. Jack's Artistic Sense
Goes Into Business
Hires a Stenographer
His Dukeship, Mr. Jack

This series of superlative single reelers
Released through the V. L. S. E.

The VITAGRAPH COMPANY of America
EXECUTIVE OFFICES
EAST 15th ST. and LOCUST AVE., BROOKLYN, N.Y.
NEW YORK · CHICAGO · LONDON · PARIS

An advertisement for Vitagraph's star comedian Frank Daniels, for whom Larry Semon worked as an uncredited assistant director, 1916 (author's collection).

Frank Loomis, J. Stuart Blackton and other officials divided their time when not in the other administration offices at 1600 Broadway. Next was the wardrobe department with a staff of sewing women supervised by costume designer Jane Lewis. They turned out nearly all the outfits used in Vitagraph's productions. Soon they would be producing a growing stock of trick trousers with an Empress Josephine waistline and a derby that would so gracefully rest on someone's ears. At the other end of the building, Miss Dixon acted as the studio matron. She was better known simply as "Mother," since she had an interest in the well-being of the hundreds of teenage girls drifting in and out of the place. The new studio was at right angles to the first building and ran the entire length of the block, equipped with back lighting and every possible mechanical device. Much to Semon's delight, there was ample scope for experiments along every mechanical line and for some time he would jealously watch the doings there, as in his early days he would have to content himself with an older part of the Vitagraph lot. In the new studio's yard, hundreds of hopeful male extras and would-be extras had assembled. Occasionally the casting director appeared at an upstairs window, picked a suitable type and hired him.

The third side of the building was filled mainly with property rooms and a large carpenter shop where all the furniture used in the sets was constructed. Experts in period decoration manufactured furniture according to the sets' requirements.

Across the halls from the property rooms, Miss Levering supervised a section of all-white enamel and tiling: the company infirmary, Semon's future and frequent home. Miss Levering also provided each automobile going out with a complete emergency kit. The building completing the square was the old studio, namely Studio No. 3, Larry's new place of work.[11] It now housed the production of one- and two-reel comedies, leaving the larger portion of the studio free for five-reel productions. In one corner was a special makeup room with its walls covered with shelves of greasepaint, powder and wigs of every conceivable hue and texture. Larry was instructed by head Victor Steurt, who applied makeup to an average of 75 faces a day and was constantly experimenting with paints and bronze coverings said to give the desired effect without injuring the skin. He was keen to find an answer to the shortcomings of orthochromatic film, and tried out all flavors of greasepaint that usually came in a greenish shade in order to conceal blemishes and reddenings.

Considering the adjoining office of A. Roosevelt, production manager, it was paramount that its head had an eye on system and efficiency. Supervising every detail of the work without leaving his desk, Roosevelt could ascertain the exact location of any given company at any hour and phase of the film on which they were working. His office window commanded a view of the court framed by the buildings, which was used for exterior sets that did not require great perspective.

Much of the scenario work was done in the Broadway offices, but some of Vitagraph's writers had a secluded and quiet office on the top floor of the old building.

All in all, Semon entered pictures when Vitagraph was a full-fledged plant. By contrast, when comedian Ben Turpin and his foils were preparing to film a comedy on housekeeping and paperhanging some eight years before, it was a far cry from comfortable. Everybody brought what they could find at home or pick up on their way to the studio. When the strange-looking aggregation, loaded down like packhorses, boarded the Chicago public transportation, they had already incurred the conductor's wrath. Poor Ben was the most pitiable of them all: a stepladder, rolls of wallpaper and a large brush under one arm, in the hand of the same arm a big bucket of paste. Under the other arm he had several small rolled rugs of painted canvas and around his neck several coils of rope. It would have sufficed to put up a camera on site instead of resorting to a studio and direction.[12]

Young fledgling director Semon showed great aptitude for photoplays and was soon developing new ideas. Before long, Blackton asked him to write a script, pick a cast, and conceive a new style of comedy. *The Vitagraph Bulletin* of January 1916 made Semon's arrival on the company's lot official, introducing him as their "latest acquisition to the staff of directors."[13] Semon started out directing Adele de Garde, the vaudeville team of Bert and George Binns and star comedian Hugh R. McGowan, nicknamed Hughie Mack. Mack was the offspring of a long Irish line. Back in his youth, when he was not attending school, he sold newspapers and made people's days brighter with his naturally happy disposition, soon propelling him to the position of most successful newsboy in his district. At 16 he became interested in amateur theatricals and was appointed chief comedian within these circles. At a club supper, Vitagraph discovered Mack and promoted him to scenario writer and comedian in his own "Fatty" series, first appearing on the screen in the early teens.

Semon co-authored productions with C. Graham Baker. Both inaugurated farces built upon mirth, havoc and the frequent use of gags. One of their first collaborations (and Semon's first credited Vitagraph) was *Tubby Turns the Tables* (1916), whose plot still reads fresh: Hughie Mack has some trouble with a vacuum cleaner, inflames two crooks' anger and is chased over the tops of several office buildings. Semon went high and dizzy at least three years before Harold Lloyd would climb roofs and scale facades. Although Semon made his protagonists fear the heights, sometimes he had their behavior twisted. In *The Man from Egypt* (1916), he let them take a diagonal flight from a roof straight to a window across the yard. The flights were executed in such a convincing manner that still after a hundred years the effect is astounding. The picture was filmed on the roof of the Times Building, Semon drawing on his contacts with Palace Players.

The next release was an adaptation of George McManus's huge comic strip *Bringing Up Father*. There has been some confusion why neither any copyright synopsis nor any prints exist of this title. Some believe the film to be ill-documented and lost. Rather it is reasonable to think that Semon produced more than one film that covered McManus's daily comic strip and simply did not use the title *Bringing Up Father*. In this context, McManus is listed as in charge for the story of *Terry's Tea Party* and *Out Again, In Again*.

The Semon-Baker joint ventures became a success. What tickled audiences was everybody moving so fast that soon the plot was left behind. This is not to say that the comedies were simplistic, they just ended in big riots. Synopses suggest how complex some of the earliest Semon-Baker comedies were and that it was up to Larry to turn the chaos into a ballet. A representative example is *Out Again, In Again* (1916) that elaborates on several people depriving one another of their clothes so that everybody can conceal his misdeeds to third parties. In summer 1916, the Hughie Mack adventures generally ranked as the foremost rough and tumble comedies available.[14]

With *Terry's Tea Party* (1916), Larry continued to appear onscreen, in the major role of a janitor. Larry was on a regular one-reel-a-week schedule, filming during the day and editing at night. After refraining for the next three months from taking leads, he resurfaced for a short time as protagonist in *A Jealous Guy* (1916): A line in the Vitagraph press release reads that Hughie Mack was accompanied by some "well-known actor Billy Baxter,"[15] overtly nothing sensational, yet this name flagged Lawrence Semon himself. The comedy may have been a rage with contemporary audiences, but does not transmit the vivacity and freshness of the Larry Semon comedies to come. Clad in tuxedo without much makeup or high-key mannerisms, Semon still had to develop a distinctive character. The success of the picture was evidently owed to his direction and, above all, Mack's performance.

Although Larry was still maintaining his position as a famed writer and cartoonist, he allowed his career with *The Evening Sun* to end in order to stick with pictures exclusively. To him, newspaper business was a great deal like marriage: Those who were not in it wanted to join the bunch inside and the folks already in it wanted to get out.[16] His job as a scenario writer did not earn him much as yet (he was receiving $50 per manuscript). The monetary amount he earned for directing films is lost to time. His salary on the *Sun* was still incomparably higher at $1,000 a week,[17] so his step to leave the newspaper business behind must have been fueled by the strong belief that he was destined to achieve even more in motion pictures. There was, however, a second hidden reason for Larry Semon to forsake the papers, making his success in film come in quite handy: It was owed to a most unflattering and undignified cartoon of "Alderman So-and-So," as the *Lincoln Evening Journal* reported, who was choking a widow to death and grinding his heel into the face of an infant. It bore Larry Semon's signature at its bottom. That politician became upset at what his eyes beheld and swore to kill the artist on sight.[18]

Larry had put his earnings from *The Sun* aside so that he could use them as a foundation for a motion picture career, since he soon acted as a sub-producer to Vitagraph. *Out Again, In Again*, released on May 12, 1916, was the first comedy he financed on his own; he would continue to do so for his bulk of films during the next six months until *Shanks and Chivalry* and pocketing part of the revenues. Some restructuring processes in the Vitagraph Company, one of them expanding on their distributor V-L-S-E, might have changed Semon's situation and made him more money as writer-director so that he dropped his producing activity.

The troupe that regularly supported Larry was known as Semon's Sea Lions. It consisted of Hughie Mack, Frank Brule, Ed "Needles" Dunn, John O'Hara, leading woman, dancer and trick swimmer Patsy De Forest, "Doc" Donohue, cameraman Leonard "Len" Smith, and assistant directors Joe Basil, Bill Shea, and Joe Rock, then still using his birth name Joe Simberg. Commonly, Semon's cast consisted of trained acrobats and dancers, his leading women being small, slender and athletic. They drove cars, played tennis and knew how to ride horses. Often Semon was looking for further additions and preferred celebrities. Before Patsy De Forest took the female lead, Semon worked with Jewell Hunt, the Dancing Girl of the Movies, who created a sensation with a wide range of exotic dances on the screen, but took the dive after a few films.[19] Patsy De Forest was a household name for eccentricities, such as driving cars until their tanks were empty,

Opposite: "Semon's Sea Lions" in October 1916. Top row, left to right: Frank Brule, Ed Dunn. Center row, left to right: John O'Hara, Lawrence Semon, Patsy De Forest, Hughie Mack, "Doc" Donohue, cameraman Leonard Smith. Bottom row, left to right: Earl Montgomery, assistant director Joe Basil, Bill Shea, Joe Simberg (also known as Joe Rock (courtesy Media History Digital Library).

4. Early Directions

The Greater VITAGRAPH

Complete Program Now Available Through Vitagraph—V-L-S-E

GREATER Vitagraph aims not only to provide offerings that will outstrip the general output of the field, but, also, to supply exhibitors with a type of service which will make it easier and more profitable for them to operate their businesses.

As one of the preliminary steps in this direction, Vitagraph announces the release, through V-L-S-E of

THE BIG "V" COMEDIES

These are mints of merriment of one reel, featuring the famous Hughie Mack and his company of money-getting, crowd-winning cohorts, as well as other comedy stars of like drawing power—each film fully worthy of the Greater Vitagraph name.

The first of these releases, "Walls and Wallops," will be available on November 13, to be followed by one each week.

The release of these comedies through V-L-S-E now makes it possible for exhibitors to book through this organization, a complete program each week, including:

A Blue Ribbon Feature in Five or More Parts
A Super Serial in Two Parts
A Big "V" Comedy in One Part

Other short subjects will be added to this program, to the end that exhibitors may obtain with a *single* effort, an *entire program of equal standard*—that standard representing the apotheosis of photoplay production in all its phases.

leaving her wondering why they would not move. Important was her fatefully fragile relation to material stuff, as she made a specialty in losing purses and jewels backstage.[20] For *The Battler* (1916), Semon hired boxing champion Joe Cox and the retired Tommy Murphy. In September 1917, A.B. "Conky" Conkwright was signed; he was a former fashion model from the Meyer Both Company, Chicago, that also fostered the careers of Alice Joyce and Madge Kennedy. Now he was a well-known dancing master on Broadway. Conkwright was also famous for starting the auto-ped craze: He was one of the first to drive through New York by means of an early form of scooter[21] produced in the city from 1915 to 1921 and expected to be a magic carpet soon to replace the function of walking.

During the filming of *Walls and Wallops* (1916), *Picture-Play* magazine writer Robert C. Duncan followed Semon around while he was directing Hughie Mack in the old and smaller studios that could be reached through a long cool corridor between stone walls. Duncan described the outfit of the scene as roofless, quite common in the studios then, with a staircase ending in thin air at the top of the ceilingless walls. At the bottom, a corridor, a lamp on a stand and an open door led into some structure not continued farther than a foot from the door. There was just enough of it for the camera's eye to see what was apparently part of a real room through the three-quarter-open door. At the top of the staircase a group of actors had convened; magnificently rotund and perspiring profusely under the arc lamps, thespian Hughie Mack was among them. Clustered behind him were numerous policemen. At the foot of the stairs well away from them was a cameraman, with director Semon next to him. Semon, not leaving room for ad-libbing, had an exact idea of what he wanted, and he turned to his star and said calmly:

> Now listen, Hughie. When Winnie [the cameraman] begins to grind, you let out a yell, start to run down the stairs, and fall down most of the way. Then you guys in back start to come down, trip over him, and the whole bunch of you go down the steps head over heels to the bottom. When you get there, Hughie runs out the door, with his mouth open, you guys get up, look around a second, see where he's gone, and follow him.

The steps were real wood. Everybody had to wait while Winnie tickled his camera, peeked in it a couple of times, yelled to the electrician to move a battery of arc lamps three-quarters of an inch west by southwest and then took his stand grandly beside some "tripod-footed mahogany gulper of drama." Semon synchronized with Winnie and shouted an "All right! Grind!" upon which Hughie started coming down the stairs. Duncan hardly found words for what followed. When Hughie, slipping obediently on the fourth step down, fell and began to roll, the charge of Agamemnon's chariot were naught compared to it. Moving down the staircase, Hughie sent one mighty foot through the canvas wall to the right of him and a mighty paw through the banister to the left of him. The swarm of policemen rolled above him and broke in "a foam of squirming humanity" down to the bottom of the steps. Arriving, they turned, gasped, looked after Hughie, who had risen and fled through the door leading into the fractional setting room and hobbled swiftly after him. The exception lay panting on the ground, feebly calling for a rescuer. Hughie had rolled over him.

It was too bad for his boys, but Semon discerned they would have to take that scene over again. While the carpenter fixed the banister and the property man patched up the wall, he thought the rest of them might as well go out to lunch. The gasping one arose

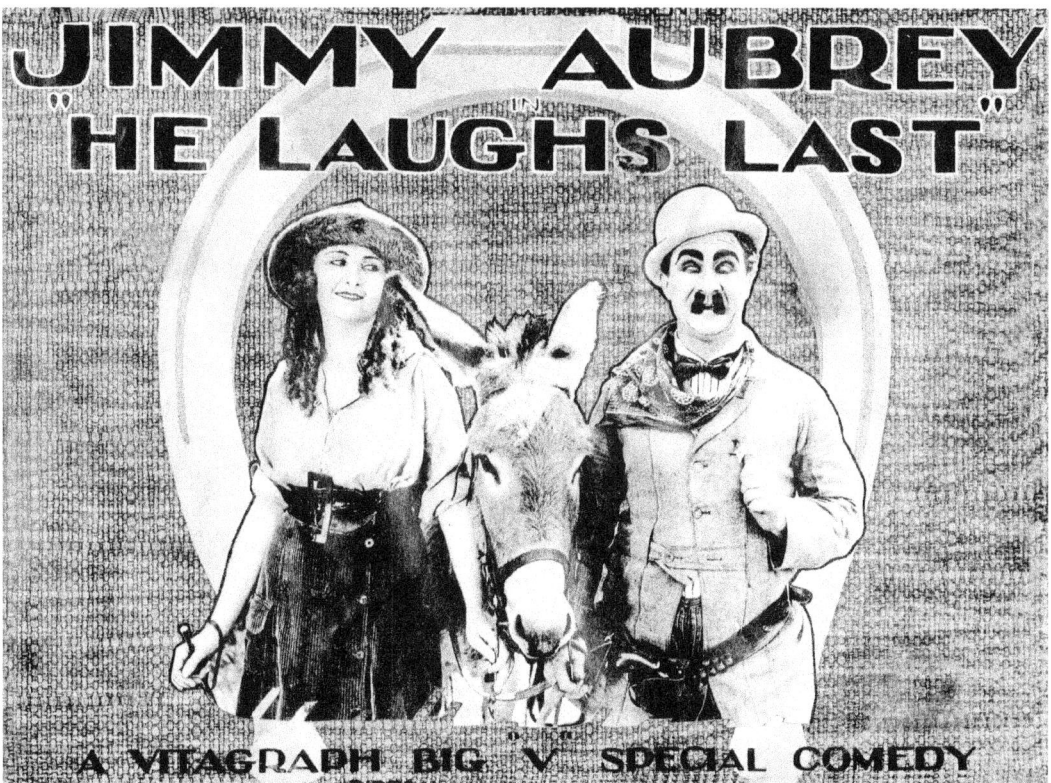

Dixie Lamont and Jimmy Aubrey in his post–Semon Vitagraph era. Lobby card for *He Laughs Last*, 1920 (author's collection).

and followed the rest out of the studio in the direction of one of the three restaurants in Flatbush. Semon reminded Duncan of Nero, after the Christians had been torn to pieces, saying, in a bored way, "Take out the bodies and make little bits of the meat out of them for the palace pets." Duncan said he hoped that some actor would strew flowers over Semon's grave someday, too.[22]

In November 1916, Vitagraph began releasing their new brand *Big V Comedies* as a result of a contest joined in by the members of the Vitagraph family. It was meant to replace the cumbersome name Hughie Mack Comedies, but was still starring their 400-pound comedian along with others of coordinate drawing power such as Jimmy Aubrey. Corporate design followed right on the new brand's heels in the form of a distinctive animated title piece and benignly illustrated subtitles. Films were promised to be complete far in advance of their release dates in order to avoid a loss in quality, typical of rushed work.[23] For the fall season, director Semon and about six members of the Sea Lions were sent to the West Coast to continue with their comedy productions. For Larry it was the first time in nineteen years to be out west. This time his projects received growing attention, as he began reappearing in cameos that were extremely successful with audiences. Larry would work out a piece of business that did not have the remotest thing to do with the story, apply bright white clown makeup, misfit shoes, flared blue overalls, a green coat with brass buttons and an all-hail cap. He would come dancing along in a park and try to catch a butterfly or admire a flower, just anything to attract attention. In the foreground the real business was unfolding, mostly some kind of struggle. As Larry was nearing to see what was going on, there was another shot of him. He would take the role of a bystander. Normally, the struggle resulted in throwing something; the purported target would bend over and Larry would get it right in the face—a pie, a bucket of water or a vase filled with a gooey substance. He would fall and look straight into the camera with a dazed expression. His character was not new, but the dub type that he used to employ in cartoons, a sort of Missouri show-me-kiddo that was but a caricature of himself. People started writing asking who that "fellow" was and demanded more as they found him the funniest man on the screen.

In mid-April 1917 Larry returned to Vitagraph's New York studio (joined by Earl Montgomery, Eddie Dunn, Joe Rock and Joe Basil) to make ten Big V comedies starring Jimmy Aubrey. The increasingly popular Hughie Mack had in the meantime been signed by Henry Lehrman's L-KO Kompany. Although filming on the West Coast was considered stressful because of its relatively impassable locations, Larry would have given anything to be allowed to return to Los Angeles. He was far from fulfilling his schedule because the local police were always in his way. They might have remembered him for his fake counterfeiting activities five years ago, and were still eyeing him. After his twelfth trip to the Brooklyn police station in order to explain just why he had been obstructing traffic on Fulton Street, the leading business thoroughfare of the suburb of Manhattan, Semon entered a state of desperation. He felt it impossible to make comedies in Brooklyn without fighting the entire police department or being willing to pay a fine or accept a jail sentence in order to complete the picture. He had expected to finish a comedy a week, but instead it took him eight weeks to complete three of them. Here we first get an idea of Semon's reputation of being behind schedule, which was not to be blamed on his perfectionism alone. He usually filmed anywhere from 5,000 to 15,000 feet of celluloid to get a single reel of 1000 feet (averaging 10 to 13 minutes) in its polished form.[24] Larry told *Motography*:

> Every time we shot off a firecracker we have been yanked to the police station to explain just why we did it. Jimmy Aubrey, my leading man, has been arrested three times because he happened to put foot on a private lawn. They just appear to be looking for us all the time. The trouble is that the people of the East, while enjoying looking at the motion pictures, know very little about the making. In the west, especially at Los Angeles, the people know all about the making of pictures. There is no hubbub when a company starts to work in the streets. A crowd may gather and the police may appear, but instead of hindering the direction, they help the director by taking care of the crowds.[25]

On April 6, 1917, the United States approved the resolution to enter the First World War. A few weeks later, Larry underwent physical examination and, like his father, was spared recruitment. This time it was not owed to a lame leg, but imperfect vision, forcing Larry to wear glasses off screen. Vitagraph saw it as their duty to keep the spirits of warstruck America high. They would reinforce the production of "happy" films, in order to let the American citizens forget their hardships for some time. The Vitagraph comedy company now quadrupled from one to four. One took up work in Brooklyn with Edward Earle and Agnes Ayres. The others were destined for Los Angeles. As their target, Vitagraph president Albert E. Smith had identified the millions of families who could hardly afford accommodation and food and whose sons were out on the killing fields. He considered it Vitagraph's duty to give these people every possible opportunity to laugh.[26] So in spite of world war and policemen, Semon kept plugging away and responded with propaganda films and spoofs of preferably German people handling weapons and military equipment. On the eve of his forty-fourth comedy for Vitagraph in early August 1917 the company announced a new series that would be produced in New York with Larry as its star. In the wake of Semon's growing popularity, Smith had approached him with the option to be featured, something he delightedly accepted, although in interviews he used to state that he never intended to be in the spotlight. Jimmy Aubrey slipped to second status, his temperamental and hard-to-handle character being another trigger for Larry to take over:

> My idea was to put slapstick into artistic backgrounds and unfold a connected story. I put these theories into practice with various comedians, but the work did not progress. They were types not suitable for every style of story. What I needed was a funny man who was not dependent upon eyebrows, moustache, funny gait, or makeup. So finally I went in and did the stunt myself.[27]

Larry *was* very dependent on makeup, although he started out with little or none. In fact, without painting his face and decent lighting, Semon looked old and tired. He needed makeup to underline his features because he was fair-haired with blue eyes and had no visible eyebrow contours. In studio photographs he would almost always apply makeup, even in those out of costume. When he did, he would come up with a face that made a tremendous impact and might rank as one of the most expressive and appealing in silent movies. Semon's particular assets were his well-proportioned bone structure and exceptionally glowing eyes that even show on poor prints.

In early December 1917, Semon renewed his contract with Vitagraph. In line with Smith's announcement, Larry, Joe Basil, Pietro Aramondo (later known as Pete Gordon) and Len Smith came back to Los Angeles. They were given a cordial welcome. As they had already passed the last winter at the Vitagraph Hollywood plant, it was decided to make their homecoming a roar, with William Duncan's cowboys forming the committee of arrangements. Much gun-shooting, rope-throwing and wild riding along with other festivities resulted.[28] On future occasions Semon would regularly be met at the station by members of his troupe all dressed in his soon-to-be characteristic style. They would force him to disrobe down to his underwear and don his comedy attire, after which he would be escorted to the studio.

Albert E. Smith's brother W. Steve Smith, Vitagraph's general manager, had advanced Semon's return in 1917 by engaging a troupe of acrobats and pretty girls so that the company could immediately go on producing on a lot enlarged at the expense of the Brooklyn studios. A huge part of the business would be shifted to Hollywood by 1920, although production in Flatbush continued until Vitagraph would fold. Concomitant with Semon's return, five Vitagraph film companies plunged into making new productions. One of these companies was the Blue Ribbon featuring Nell Shipman and Alfred Whitman; a second one was headed by director-star William Duncan and Carol Holloway; then there were the three Big V Comedy Companies: Semon's; Earl Montgomery and Joe Rock's; and one featuring Jack Dill and Caroline Rankin with their director, J.A. Howe. Semon would now settle on the West Coast. His connection to

New York had already been loosened as demonstrated by his 1916–1917 residence, the luxurious Hotel St. George on Brooklyn's Clark Street, once the largest hotel in New York City.

From the beginning, Larry was heavily investing in original gags to fill his pictures with breathtaking stunts. One of them included the flight of a bed through the roof of a house onto a set of telegraph wires. For this, a special grid had to be constructed.[29] Many of the stunts were heralded by the press, as were the sets—for instance an impressive reservoir surrounded by cliffs that had particularly been built for *Boodle and Bandits* (1918) on the Hollywood lot. It allowed horses and men to go over the cliffs and a bridge built from one side of the reservoir to the other.[30] In an earlier comedy, *The Battler* (1916), Semon made his action more authentic by staging the bout with as much atmosphere as people might have experienced in Madison Square Garden. He had a regulation ring constructed and used an audience of five hundred spectators.[31] *Bombs and Blunders* (1917) surprised patrons with a novel process of throwing custard pie. It was not done by hand, but with the use of the old bell-striking strength tester. With his huge mallet, Aubrey catapulted pies so high they hit adversary Eddie Dunn in the sky above, hovering in his aeroplane.[32] A special feature of *Turks and Troubles* (1917) was a cast with a not-to-be-surpassed array of pretty girls languishing and mermaiding on embroidered fabric, classified by Semon as "the sofa pillow brigade."[33]

A Villainous Villain (1916) caused a furor, since an automobile which Semon's stunt-

On location for Vitagraph's *A Villainous Villain* at Brighton Beach, New York, late August 1916, Hughie Mack, the robust comedian, Patsy De Forest, the vivacious comedienne, and Lawrence Semon, cartoonist and director, discuss how best to have an automobile loaded with comic policemen go off the end of the pier (author's collection).

men drove off the end of a Coney Island pier actually plunged into the water with all of them on board. Usually on dangerous scenes like these, dummies were used.[34] Montgomery and Rock were with good reason declared to be two of the most daring men in pictures. One scene made it into film history and was used for many advertisements, that of the two making an exceptionally long and difficult leap, a kind of roof hopping. According to Vitagraph, the stunt was performed without a safety net.

As funny as the Vitagraph Comedies appeared on the silver screen, the making of comedy films was no laughing matter. In 1916, Patsy De Forest was nearly blinded. She was working on multiple films at the same time and constantly exposed to the radium lights at the studio. Not before July 1917 did she fully recover.

In July 1916, John L. Flatow, a young and versatile stuntman, whom Larry had wooed away from the legitimate stage, suffered near-fatal injuries after jumping from a bridge and missing a vehicle. Flatow lost his grip on a rope and fell to the ground. He broke his nose and arms and crushed his feet and some ribs. Flatow was taken to Huntington Hospital where he had to undergo several operations. Seven months later, he began working again at the Brooklyn studios. Signing up with Vitagraph, the papers had ironically complimented Flatow on his ability to lie under railroad engines, fall from roofs, be shot and stabbed without having to resort to a hospital.[35]

Semon, quite handy with a rifle, had actor-stuntman Earl Montgomery put his arm in a sling. Both were working in a scene in which Montgomery was shaving before a small mirror with the mug nearby. Larry, holding two rifles, was to shatter both mirror and mug at the same time. He did it all right, yet the mug's fragments struck Montgomery in the arm, inflicting deep wounds. After first aid was administered by Miss Levering, Montgomery insisted he would continue work and brave Semon's rifles.[36]

Eighty feet off the ground, Larry (or one of his stuntmen) was being chased by villain Bill Hauber for *Solid Concrete* (1920). Both ran across a water pipe about fourteen inches in circumference. During the shooting of this scene, Hauber made a near miss, as the pipe was very old and the supports wobbly. Eyewitness Elizabeth Peltret remembered:

> Hauber chasing his chief, who was running at a fair amount of speed, increased his own speed suddenly, with the result that the pipe threw him flat. He caught himself instinctively with his hands and feet, tho we all realized that he came very close to going all the way over. The scene was N.G.'d and made over again, tho, as the cameraman remarked, it looked almost "natural," in other words, "done on purpose."[37]

When Hauber went over a cliff in a car near Griffith Park for *The Fly Cop* (1920), he failed to free himself from his position behind the wheel and was forced to remain in the machine during his 35-foot dive. Luckily Hauber cheated death and escaped without any fractures or internal injuries.[38] It comes close to a miracle that the number of accidents remained relatively small, measured against the challenges the cast and crew took during their daily routine. Hughie Mack on several occasions had a clay pipe shot from his teeth. This effect was achieved with a real rifle and a real bullet. Semon himself went through the same experience in *Bears and Bad Men* (1918) and once more counted on the expertise of his crew.

In order to get a good ending for *Jumps and Jealousy* (1916), 4,000 cigar box "bricks" were dropped from a height of twelve feet on Hughie Mack. He returned home with a reminder of the occasion in the form of nine bruises on his head.[39] Larry and other

members of the company had the same "pleasure" when breaking through a roof and a ceiling in *Passing the Buck* (1919). "Accidents happened very seldom" was something Larry used to stress, since they had most of their thrills "under absolute control" so that they were really no thrills at all.[40]

The making of *Bombs and Blunders* (1917) offered a very special kind of hazard, because it was "entirely outside of any human control" and so far the "most thrilling thing" that ever happened to Semon. The story was told to at least two journalists in at least two different versions. In any case, bombs were not restricted to the film's title. The company was down at Balboa, a seaside resort, carrying nitroglycerine and dynamite, box after box of high explosives. The question arose where to leave it. One of Larry's assistants insisted that he would not feel safe unless he had those explosives available for monitoring. Their car was not an alternative. So he took the boxes up to his room and stowed them under his bed. Larry had the next room.

That night, Larry woke up with the fuzzy impression that someone was having a heated dispute somewhere over a child. Then he realized that the assistant next door was talking in his sleep. Larry inferred that a sleep-talker could also be a sleepwalker, turned on the light and opened the door that connected his room with his. There his assistant was standing, a stick of dynamite in each hand. Larry expected any minute to arrive at Heaven's gates because he knew that the man had enough real stuff to put them both there, along with the building. There was no way of getting out either, except for the door through his assistant's room, since Larry's window was small and high above the floor. Larry was aware that any hectic behavior could result in waking up his assistant, who might drop the dynamite. Eventually some guardian angel on duty that night motivated Larry's assistant to put the dynamite down. In order to avoid a repeat of this situation, Larry invited himself to stay with him until the explosive had been used up for the film.[41] In the other known version, Semon was earwitness to a violent outbreak of profanity and counted the seconds towards a premature death, but this time his friend was sitting up in bed hugging a can of black powder. The dynamite remained untouched under his feet.[42] Given that Semon had coaxed the story a bit, the issue of the storage of explosives still lived with him.

The use of makeup—particularly that of greasepaint—meant another hazard as Joe Rock recalled when the troupe was out on the West Coast and miles away from makeup guru Victor Steurt:

> After working for four or five months with Semon, I developed a greasepaint infection. I would shave in the morning, and then apply Max Factor makeup which we used before Factor became famous. Max had a place down on Hill Street [Los Angeles]. Well, he put too much lead in the makeup, and we got lead poisoning, all of us, the whole company, right in the middle of a picture. We were out about a week. Anyway, with this infection I was trying to do various stunts, but missing badly those that should have been easy for me. Larry was giving me a hard time over it, thinking I'd been out the night before. He was a little bit jealous over the leading lady who didn't like him. She liked me, and he wasn't happy about that. He figured that we'd been out. We hadn't, but just the same I got credit for it. He was so mad that finally the assistant director [Joe Basil] said, "For God's sake, Larry, lay off him. Look at his face." I had a swollen left cheek and was burning with fever. I had to do a stunt that takes good health to do, one

Opposite: Playbill by cartoonist J. Norman Lynd for the 1920s re-release of Vitagraph's *Plans and Pajamas* (1917) showing Larry and the Vitagraph Beauties Brigade (courtesy Chris Seguin).

where I'm in an automobile, driving it, going fast up to a haystack. In the haystack were some solid bales of hay so that when the auto hit them, the impact would propel me over the haystack. There was something on the other side for me to fall on. Well, I wasn't timing it properly, and timing is everything in doing stunts. If they aren't timed right, you're going to get killed or hurt. Larry took a look at my face. "Why didn't somebody tell me?" he said. "Why the hell didn't you look?" Here I was, face out like that. I was laid up for fourteen weeks. That was the end of it.[43]

The friendship of Rock and Semon was henceforth ruined. Rock was yet still working for him when back in New York, but as soon as he could, he quit the Big V Riot Squad for good. Rock then teamed with Earl Montgomery and was promoted to star in films under the direction of C. Graham Baker.

· 5 ·

Growing Success

Larry's new contract meant new conquests. All-round actress Madge Kirby, *née* Whitehead, joined Semon for that season. In films she normally hid her dark hair under a blonde wig of frizzy curls and often played the fearless heroine. Born in London in April 1884, Madge came to America with her parents and a younger brother in 1886, settling in New York. About 1907 she married Morris Kirby and in 1908 they had a daughter, Audrey. Madge entered movies at least as early as 1912 with Ramo and Biograph of New York, playing bit parts for Griffith. Two years later she relocated to California, played opposite Rube Miller in Vogue comedies, and by 1920 she was a single working widowed mother. In 1922, Madge dropped out of movies and married Fresno district rancher Edward Frank Loescher. They separated thirteen years later, with unemployed Madge and her mother living on his support allowance. Madge was known for being hard-working and for her ability to bravely endure the wear and tear of filming. She preferred comedies to drama, as far as production was concerned, since they were not as nerve-racking but only affected the bones. Hence Madge had the guts to climb towers and to bear near-misses of automobiles bursting through café sets with just the same reaction that pulled her through chilly outdoor scenes in evening clothes.[1] Madge Kirby Loescher died on July 11, 1956, in Fresno, age 72.

Stunt specialist William Hauber (1891–1929) had switched from Mack Sennett and Foxfilm to join Semon's troupe. He was one of Semon's most valued men as he saved Larry time, money and umpteen injuries. An injury he had received while taking a fall for another studio made it necessary to reconstruct Hauber's backbone with silver wire.[2] When visitors came to the Vitagraph studios they could hardly tell who the real Larry Semon was, because Semon normally employed four stand-ins on the set, all clothed like him, all in his makeup and equipped with a *papier mâché* nose crafted after his.[3] One of them was usually Hauber. For four years, from about 1918 up to 1922, German-born Richard Talmadge was part of Semon's stunt crew. He and Hauber shared the stunts for some time, but then Talmadge went on to a career of his own. Hauber and Talmadge had learned to mimic Semon's movements and can hardly be spotted as doubles. (Hauber *was* a little larger than Semon, and of a more angular stature.)

Frank Alexander (1879–1937) was signed in 1918 to fill the gap that Hughie Mack had left and at 350 pounds joined the league of the heaviest comedians in film history.

Detective Larry Semon with Vera Steadman in *Traps and Tangles*, Vitagraph, 1919 (author's collection).

He could look back on a career at Keystone where he was a foil to Sydney Chaplin, Mack Swain, and others.

Another valuable addition to the Semon troupe was Hans F. Koenekamp. Koenekamp started with Sennett and did a stint at Fox Film before joining Vitagraph in 1917, from then on filming all the Semon comedies. Koenekamp recalled in an undated interview with Kevin Brownlow that Sennett was idle about then and some colleagues asked him if he would go over and talk with Larry Semon, who was having trouble. Maybe Hans knew somebody that would work with Larry. Koenekamp went over and decided he would work with Semon, entering a professional partnership that would last for eight years.[4] The "trouble" was presumably linked to the discord with Joe Rock that motivated more Semon co-workers to quit, one of them Patsy De Forest. Semon, who did not like to be mistered, but insisted that he be called Larry, was a controversial figure; he polarized people. Generally, though, he was very well-liked in the picture colony—on a personal and professional level. Theater owner Sam Bernstein thought him a great big kid and was sure if Semon ran for mayor he would have voted for him twice. Koenekamp described

Opposite: Janitor Larry, a few seconds shy of being chloroformed by an unidentified girl spy in *Pluck and Plotters*, Vitagraph, 1918 (author's collection).

Larry Semon, center, with the members of his successful "Athletic Club" (courtesy Marc Wanamaker, Bison Archives).

Semon as tough, affable and quite some guy and above all nice to work with. Semon's comportment depended on who he worked with.

Semon was highly regarded because he frequently organized and directed shows and benefits on behalf of disadvantaged actors and was able to assemble bills that could compete with the "big-time" circuits. One of the shows took place in the new Masonic Temple of Hollywood, staged by the town's Athletic Club (Semon was a charter member), and drew more than two thousand people. Included were stars of stage and screen T. Roy Barnes, Roy Atwell, Si Jenks, Victoria Allen and Lionel Belmore, while a flu-stricken Larry was conducting the orchestra.[5] The allied "Larry Semon Athletics" were a team of successful basketball players, one of them Karl Sidle.

Many former leading men who had been tickled pink to get extra work found it with Semon, as he was always "good for a couple of days"[6] when a hunger panic came on. The most famous instance was Stan Laurel, for whom Joe Rock lined up something with Semon when Laurel was out of work for a long period. This led to an intriguing though short-lived teaming of two comedy talents with a growing focus on Laurel. In the Semon comedies *Huns and Hyphens* and *Bears and Bad Men* (1918), Laurel undoubtedly acted on the level of a supporting player, although the latter film culminates in a

An early portrait of Larry Semon in profile in his favorite polka dotted tie by Albert Witzel, ca. 1919 (author's collection). The autograph is rubber-stamped.

fulminant chase involving a lot of rock and rope climbing by both Semon and Laurel. The sequences are notable for conceding both comedians balanced screen time and the enormous physical effort exerted. In many releases the final chase has been cut to a few feet, though. Recently, an Italian print resurfaced that seems complete and allows for re-assessing *Bears and Bad Men*. In *Frauds and Frenzies* (1918), Laurel had been put on equal terms with Semon so that this picture can be considered a Semon and Laurel team comedy. *Kinematograph Weekly* lauded the two artists: "Larry is doing time in conjunction with his friend [Stan Laurel], who is every bit as ingenious and athletic as himself, and very nearly as comic."[7]

Antonio Moreno saw some of the daily rushes for *Frauds and Frenzies* and declared that Laurel was funnier than Semon. This infuriated Semon. Allegedly he made sure that Laurel was first tied to a tree, then written out of the final chase sequence and immediately terminated. Likewise, Laurel and Hardy biographer John McCabe judged the Semon-Laurel relationship as one that was to fail owing to human shortcomings— Semon's:

> I think it should be remembered that between him and Semon there would be instinctive, indeed *automatic*, conflict. They were both born gagmen, but there was no mutuality of direction in their work at the time when they were together. Semon was interested in gags for *Semon*; Stan was interested in gags qua gags. He simply couldn't understand Semon's vanity in the matter. That is why Semon didn't last, and Stan went on to become the cornerstone of the most enduring comedy team in film history. To simplify it a bit, Semon was selfish, Stan wasn't.[8]

However, director and longtime Semon associate Norman Taurog acquitted Semon of jealousy and egotism. He credited Semon with being modest and most generous in giving screen time to other comedians, emphasizing that Semon was self-effacing. Funnymen such as Oliver Hardy, Frank Alexander and Bill Hauber never suffered from a lack of screen time in a Semon comedy. The same goes for Semon's female foils. In many films, Semon makes his first entrance only after considerable time is spent on the introduction that features players of his stock company. For example the first quarter of the one-reeler *Plagues and Puppy Love* (1917) passes without Semon; instead Florence Curtis is seen walking her dog and shaking off a bunch of stalkers. The impression that Semon was self-centered is undoubtedly also owed to surviving prints and footage in compilations which had been trimmed down to their star over the years.

Author Rob Stone sees the reason for Stan's departure from the Semon lot being the great influenza epidemic of 1918. On completion of *Frauds and Frenzies* the Vitagraph Studios, along with the bulk of the studios in Hollywood, had closed. In an effort to combat the spread of the flu, the Los Angeles County Health Department discouraged the gathering of crowds of people, while the film industry—in voluntary cooperation—temporarily shut down studios. Vitagraph would not resume work until November 4, 1918. Laurel, not being a contract player and needing to make a living, quit films and returned to vaudeville.[9] Other factors may be attributed to Mae Laurel, Stan's common-law wife, who has been described as a pest, as she constantly claimed exposure on the screen alongside her partner. Yet her face was not camera-friendly, she lacked the talent and could not take the simplest falls. Stan suffered because of his relationship with Mae, and had taken to drinking which made him unreliable.[10]

The layoff caused by the flu epidemic left Semon and the newly formed duo of Montgomery and Rock unharmed so that all of them managed to keep active. Both parties withdrew to make up new stories for their picture plays. Semon went to Riverside while Montgomery and Rock favored a cave in the mountains.

Much of *Frauds and Frenzies* is a rehash of the one-reeler *Stripes and Stumbles* Semon had produced earlier in 1918, which also featured two escaped convicts. But in that one, the players fall through the skylight of a film studio and don costumes, escaping the police. Semon often re-used ideas from earlier comedies and was technically rehearsing for greater spectacles. For instance, chunks of Semon's one-reeler *Spies and Spills* (1918) can be found in his two-reeler *Pluck and Plotters*, filmed a mere eight months later. Both pictures highlight a rocket-like vehicle by which scientist Madge Kirby dashes off through the sky, throwing bombs at villains. While trick photography in *Spies and Spills* still bears a makeshift air, *Pluck and Plotters* marks a quantum leap in camera technique and overall production. *The Star Boarder* (1919) was another pilot to be improved on: Larry, just set free from prison, desires to go back to jail as outside there is no Lucille. He happily changes clothes with his spitting image, escaped convict No. 13, in front of a tree. Both roles are played by Semon. That the two characters are swapping outfits can be told by a visible split-screen for which a dark tree trunk acted as prop. In *A Pair of Kings* (1922) Semon is a ruler who sidesteps revolution and a simple youth to step in for the king. The split screen is no more visible; the characters exchange their clothes by throwing them simultaneously at each other.

Right from the beginning, Semon was severely criticized for his repetitiveness. Albert E. Smith, who was running the company with a somewhat cold-hearted efficiency, feared his flagship might sink before it reached the pinnacle of success. In 1917, upon Blackton's temporary departure, he had re-entered the realm of production and rummaged through Semon's output. Just the same, the reworking of gags has to be viewed from different angles. The basic recipe of Semon comedies called for a reprise of particular ingredients. As Edwin Schallert once noted, it consisted of five canisters of giant powder, ten sticks of dynamite, one gallon can of gasoline, one script (if needed to flavor), forty odd gags, one pretty leading woman, one fat man, two monkeys (one human), one star comedian.[11]

In yet another run-in with Smith on the freshness of picture gags, Semon defended his philosophy by pointing out that he naturally drew on a bonded stock. He physically kept this stock as a scrapbook, packed to the brim with clippings of the cartoons he had drawn for the *New York Evening Sun*. He asked Smith if he could name half a dozen recent stunts that were new. Smith thought he could. Semon then showed him his scrapbook and proved to him that practically everything he mentioned was just a rehash of newspaper stuff that ranked from explosion ideas to mallets and pie-throwing. In Semon's words, some of the best of the recent humorous situations had been nothing but the revamping of old gags and the picturizing of jokes that had obtained a wide circulation. A famous gag employed in *The Grocery Clerk,* and to a lesser degree in his earlier short *Dull Care*, had been borrowed by Semon from a war comedy of a few years before. According to Semon, it did not draw a laugh because it was simply unnatural: A trail of gunpowder was laid to a house where some spies were hiding, the house was blown up, but the spies remained perfectly immaculate through the proceeding. When unwound as a gag, it was a yell—and besides it still clicks with contemporary audiences. Larry handed a farmer with a Ford a leaking can of gasoline. When the farmer had reached the machine, Larry dropped a match on the trail and the Ford, the farmer's whiskers, and the gasoline can all went up in a blaze of glory. Gunpowder was not the thing to use and people were not interested in spies either. But a Ford meant something and everybody had a slight fear of gasoline. So it was like a logical conclusion to Semon that the stunt of the leaking can, the farmer and the Ford should bring a big laugh, because people were aware that they might bump into a situation like this as well. (That this was technically not possible, though, has been shown on television shows and in lectures on physics.) The gasoline-match gag had already been used in *Dull Care* (1919) when Larry was trying to stop a gang of crooks from escaping in a car. He shot at its tank, the leak produced a fuse which was lit by Larry. Semon was sure that the very familiarity of this material really made it the more popular with the audience, especially if there was a new twist.

Yet Smith continued interfering with Larry's productions. Still driven by the idea that the rehash of gags was some kind of trademark, Semon made it a habit to let many of his 1918–1920 comedies end high and dizzy. The reprise was well done and came with surprising turns that never left the spectator dissatisfied. "High and dizzy" was a running gag that arched from film to film. Semon's comedies mirrored the results which he harvested as a prize comment gatherer. He used to drift into metropole houses and also to out-of-the-way theaters where old pictures of his were showing and, seat himself in a dark corner so that he could overhear what patrons said. Semon took notes, classified his results and had a regular staff of assistants who checked up on the laughs the gags brought. Much of the rapid development of his work was due to his scientific procedure.[12]

"[Larry] knew what he was doing all right," Hans F. Koenekamp used to say, much to the disapproval of their producer. Koenekamp was not only referring to Semon's gag mind but to his impeccable feel for motion. Koenekamp himself became noted for his ability to enhance comedy action with his growing repertoire of camera effects. The collaboration of the two led to a vast range of unique visual trademarks, such as Larry skidding to a halt during a chase, and then whisking around the corner. On the screen, this effect was always greeted by roars of laughter. To achieve it, Koenekamp would reduce his cranking speed to a slow turn just as Semon threw his feet out, braked, and then vanished around the corner.[13] Other beautiful effects were racing cars with rim in spiral design that went over telegraph wires with an ease as if they did in reality. Ancillary to Koenekamp's camera expertise, Semon had an excellent cutting crew. He often did the editing himself, which guaranteed a perfectly smooth transition from trick photography and miniature models to real life.

In an article of 1921, Semon was called the originator of the storyboard, then termed "illustrated scenario." To Semon the use of sketches for field continuity and story had been the norm since his earliest motion pictures days; surely this was owed to his cartooning past. Semon took it for granted and never talked about it, but passed the trend on to the whole film community. His storyboard was a stenographer's book of written directions for the action on one page, while the opposite contained a sketch illustrating the action or facial character studies, often of pretty girls. Semon would discuss his notes and drafts with his director and invited all members of his cast to consult the book whenever they thought it necessary.[14] Despite the storyboard and Semon's continuity, comedies were largely a matter of experiment. As soon as he had entered the screen himself, he allowed for more ad-libbing and studied every member of his company and they studied him. When Semon moved his foot or adjusted his hat, each one knew just what he was going to do. In an interview, he explained how he and his troupe proceeded with chase sequences:

> Do you remember the little fellow in *The Stage Hand* that grabbed me as I was going through the door? I turned and hit him, but never touched him. He anticipated my action, and the rest was easy. The only direction I gave for that scene was, "Boys, I'm going to run and you follow. If anyone of you can catch me, do so; but look out, for I am going to let go." The little fellow was the only one that caught me and he was ready to do his part.[15]

Semon often relied on the impact of industrial constructions such as gas holders or concrete factories and used their geometric shapes to aesthetic effect in chase sequences (*Humbugs and Husbands*, 1918; *Solid Concrete*, 1920). An outstanding film is *Hindoos and Hazards* (1918), one of Semon's last one-reelers. It shows how well he worked in the black and white medium, while its plot is as simple as effective in that it draws on the one theme of Larry protecting a valuable necklace from their lawful owners. Larry is trying to get rid of his persecutors and whenever he feels at ease, his opponents emerge from the remotest of hideaways as if they had been there long before his arrival. In one instance, Larry dashes like a bee-stung funambulist on telegraph wires across a street to which he has fled. As his antagonists creep up the poles from both sides, he leaps on a flat bed truck passing underneath, landing on a load of bricks, and finds himself again face to face with his adversaries. Resorting to an empty streetcar passing by, he takes a seat at the front of the car looking at his audience with an expression of deepest relief. In the twinkling of an eye, his enemies emerge from the other seats, prophetically expecting him. *Hindoos and Hazards* seems the only Semon film extant in this style. It creates tension from its situations, each growing towards the next, despite not striving too much for precipitation or speed, although the film is from beginning to end one big chase sequence. It's an unusual Semon film that capitalizes on surprises and still works with today's audiences thanks to its signature photography and Semon's acting, jointly making a trace of melancholy prevail. Koenekamp chose to shoot on roads that were far from the overcrowded Sunset Boulevard and positioned the camera at an angle that perspectively reduced the abandoned places lined with sketchy telegraph poles or concrete pipes. Only Larry and his stock company fill the picture; a random car driver bears a facial expression of profound anonymity and adds to the atmosphere of loneliness. Moments of fear alternate with moments of deceptive safety. *Hindoos and Hazards* proves that Semon took very well with a minimum of cast, scenery, budget and even story. And one little tidbit was visible in the print available for viewing, namely that in Semon's world, brick walls were ultimately held together by the wallpaper.

One of Larry's favorite pastimes was the golf links. He had studied the sport with Flintridge professional John Black.[16] In the nicely choreographed *Gall and Golf* (1917) and in the two-reeler *Golf* (1922), he gives proof of his accomplishment. One of his constant golfing companions in Los Angeles was Bobby Ross, high school golf sensation of Hollywood.[17] It was a standing joke between comedian Neal Burns and Semon to ask one another how their golf game was. One was expected to always answer that his game was rotten. "But one night, I guess I was a bit illumined with that which not only cheers, but also inebriates, and I told Neal the truth about what I thought of my game when he asked me. He kids me ever since."[18]

Rubber-stamped headshot of Larry Semon out of costume by Albert Witzel, Los Angeles, ca. 1919 (author's collection).

Before starting a day of shooting at Vitagraph, Semon would frequently take a few shots in the cold gray dawn.[19] Sometimes he went to play golf and let his crew wait all day. They knew that he needed to relax every so often, as he was the proverbial bundle of nerves. When Semon was ill with the flu (which happened often enough) and indeed stayed in bed (something quite unusual for him), he bought a pile of works of golf literature and studied it.[20] In private tournaments, Semon, known as the Demon Golfer, turned in a score of 37 for 18 holes. This was an achievement if judged from the fact that he was not a professional and that technique and equipment were cruder than today. During breaks, time was devoted to golf by the complete crew. The back end of the stage was open with fields out in the background. Koenekamp used to stand in the back end of the stage and shoot golf balls while the extras picked them up. In an interview with Kevin Brownlow he recalled:

> [Larry] would come down in the morning, didn't know what to do. "Koney," he'd say, "what are we going to do in this room?" We studied for a minute and if it didn't come out right we'd go and play—what you'd call—golf. So I started right off the bat with him on an open stage.

Couldn't smoke in those days, and he smoked quite a little. So I said, "What are you going to do in this scene?" He told me and I said, "All right, you go out and have your smoke and I'll have it ready for you." He kind of liked that, see. So that's the way we worked along, all through all his pictures.[21]

Spies and Spills left its mark on Semon's career as it was both a transition to technical perfection and a turning point for Larry's outfit. It was the first film featuring him in full costume, complete with chest-waisted baggy trousers, sizes too large, that accentuated the thinness of his body, white shirt, full makeup, a grin from ear to ear and a derby that imparted an extra thrill to his impact—his mouth so wide open that one is in awe of a budding lockjaw. Larry wore white socks as people always watched his feet when a chase was on. Yet there was still some experimenting when it came to details. For a short time, Semon sported a metal brace to one of his upper teeth for a dual effect: It faked a gash to give his impersonation of the boob the finishing touch—or rather to have his discolored front tooth aligned. It is best visible in a close-up in *Pluck and Plotters* (1918) while Larry is biting his enemy's leg, casually inducing a shark alert. This sequence is also remarkable for having been shot underwater. By 1919, Larry would have discarded the gash and conjure up a white front tooth in line with the others.

During the year 1917, Semon turned from little to no makeup to greasepaint, dark eye shadow, signature brows and eyes framed with dark pencil, either on the upper lid or with shapes completely outlined. The latter was a twist that opened his eyes significantly wider. It might have been necessary to contrast them owing to orthochromatic film that made blue eyes appear pale. Juxtaposing them with Stan Laurel's in *Frauds and Frenzies* show that Larry did not have to struggle with issues like these as his eyes photographed in a darker tone. Close-ups however reveal the whiteness of his lashes. In *Dull Care* (1919), his eyeshadow touched the arcs of his eyebrows; in *The Fly Cop* (1920) Semon applied Cleopatra-like accents to the outer corner of his eyes. His use of greasepaint increased from the beginning of the 1920s until he quit Vitagraph for good. In his early period, Semon left his lips uncolored, then towards the early 1920s he copied the makeup father Zera used to apply for his shows: his under lip rouged heavily, while his upper lip was left almost white to accentuate the leer. Semon always insisted that he did not grin nearly as foolishly in real life as in pictures and in fact used to look very studious in his off-screen glasses.

Views on Semon's natural looks vary. Author Anthony Slide points out that Larry, in makeup, was concealing his good looks.[22] Likewise, when the days of panchromatic film had arrived in the early twenties, director Norman Taurog wondered why Semon still hid his beautiful face behind a mask of chalk. Some sources believed Semon unattractive throughout, claiming he was exaggerating the absence of handsomeness by makeup. He was strange-looking and, in comedian Robert Foster's words, as if carved by a drunken puppeteer.[23] Author Gerald Mast described Semon's looks as if he "ran a kosher delicatessen on Mars."[24] Above all, Semon believed that people were put on Earth to make other people happy and if blessed with a funny face one should consider it an honor to use it in making others laugh.[25] Louella Parsons described Semon's looks along these lines:

> In a beauty contest Larry Semon would be in the also-ran class. But what is a mere matter of looks, when one makes one's fortune by doing stunts on the screen? Besides, in a brains contest

Larry Semon proudly showing off his outfit complete with derby and high waisted trousers in another rubber-stamped portrait by Albert Witzel, Los Angeles, ca. 1920 (author's collection).

he would come out near the top, and who is there who wouldn't rather have an abundant supply of gray matter than be listed as the Apollo of the cinema? Mr. Semon has never been asked to act as a tailor's model, advertise a brand of cold cream or permit his picture to be used as an example of manly beauty. Think what he has been spared.[26]

In about August 1919, Semon acquired co-director, Norman Taurog, who had been a child actor on the stage and appeared in films produced on the East Coast. After seeing himself on the screen, Taurog decided to become a property man—anything but an actor. He went west in 1915 and then experienced a swift rise: He received his training with Henry Lehrman at Fox Sunshine Comedies and got his first opportunity at directing when the rather indolent Lehrman chose to turn over chases to him. Twenty-year-old Taurog became responsible for complete films and attracted the attention of Semon, who was on the lookout for a new associate. Semon had asked Taurog about his salary

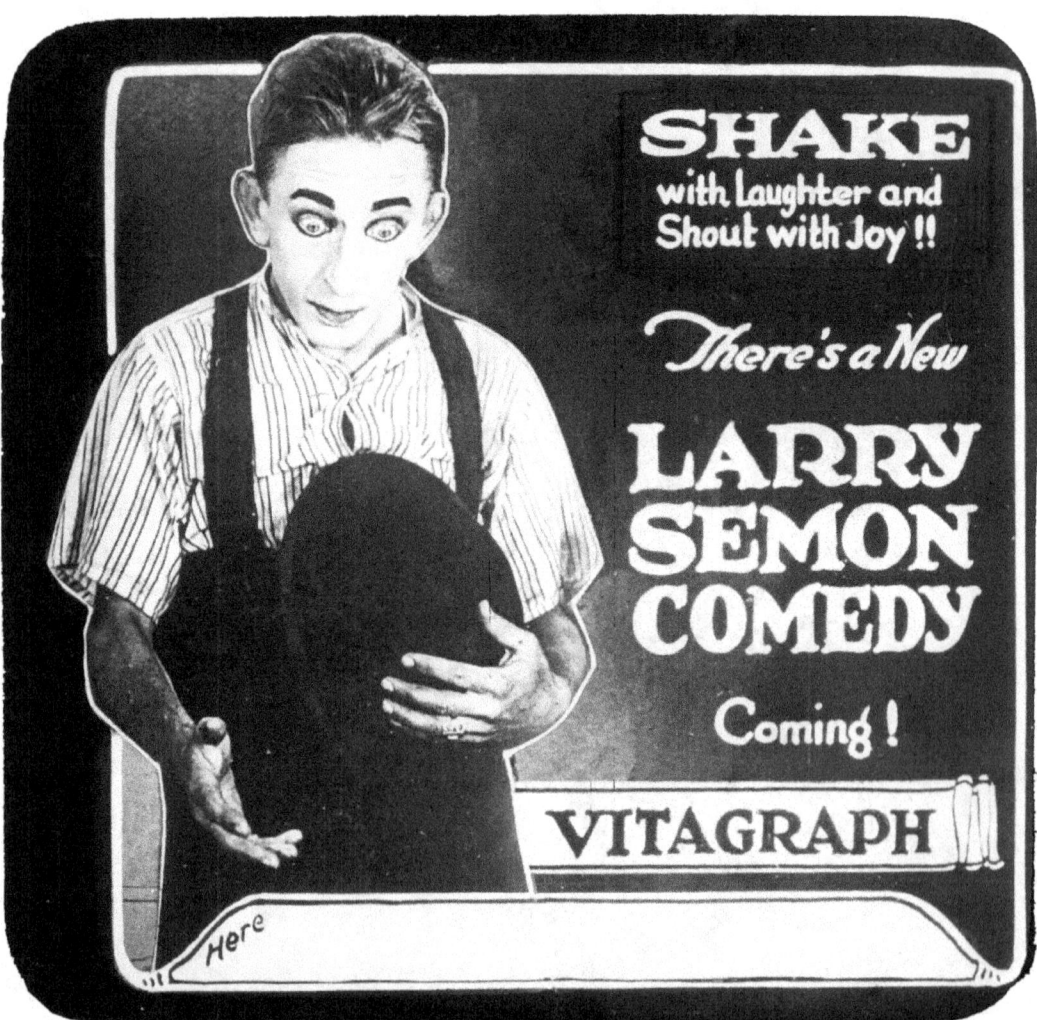

A glass-slide, used in the early days of cinema in order to advertise upcoming films, ca. 1919. Photograph taken from *Pluck and Plotters* (author's collection).

Farmer's Boy Larry has just had a motorcycle accident and reacts with his trademark dazed expression in *The Simple Life*, Vitagraph, 1919 (author's collection).

at Lehrman's and Taurog gave the amount with just the numbers "seven five," meaning seventy-five dollars, which Larry misinterpreted as $750. In the ensuing four-hour conference with "the Smiths," he was trying to get Taurog as much as this or even more—which he did. The story was amusingly recounted by Rob Stone[27] and Leonard Maltin,[28] respectively, who drew on different interviews with Taurog.

Taurog became Semon's assistant director-in-chief with full responsibility on the set as well as Semon's business manager.[29]

Another addition was comedian Oliver Norvell Hardy, who would often play villainous leads for Semon until 1926. Semon always knew a talent when he saw one and would give Hardy plenty of opportunities to prove his abilities, even as an assistant director. In 1919, Hardy played a cop as well as a janitor in *Dull Care* and *The Head Waiter*, and he is seen as an audience member in *The Stage Hand* (1920). In this film, Semon gave evidence of how deliberately chosen his actor-audiences were. Every player is a character study. At the beginning of the 1920s, Hardy was still with Jimmy Aubrey, but soon dismissed by him. Temporarily unemployed, Hardy found work on *A Lucky Dog* (1921), a pilot film for a proposed Stan Laurel series, who had grown bitter about vaudeville. After the filming of Semon's *The Hick* (1921), Hardy became a member of the Larry Semon stock company.

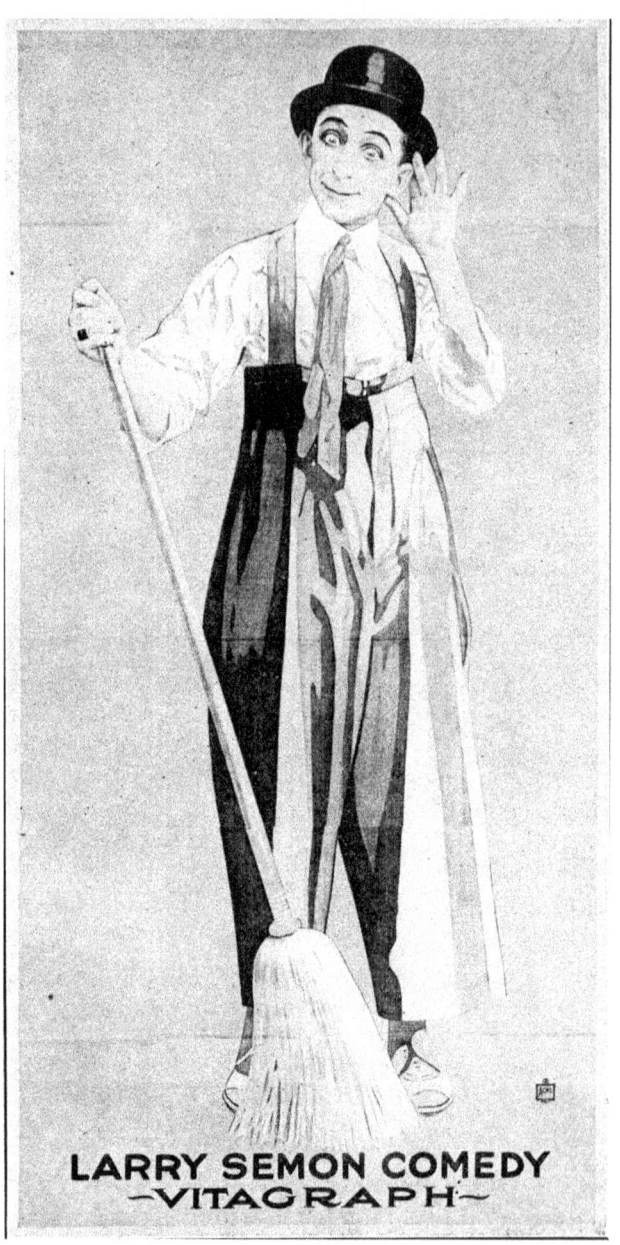

Three-sheet playbill of Larry Semon in his famous outfit, Vitagraph advertising material, 1919 (author's collection).

Semon more than once left the recruitment of players to mere chance and took the first who came and put them to work in a film. Frequently he chose people walking on the street or those who stopped by to watch. Guinn "Big Boy" Williams got his start at

Larry Semon's company. Later he was to become a busy, versatile player in westerns, drama, and comedy. Williams, with a well-developed body and destined to be an actor, arrived in Hollywood with $2.50 in his pocket and looked about for a film studio. He found Semon and his company working outdoors on a comedy. A large hole in the ground was needed for the picture and Williams, standing by, felt that the efforts of the workmen employed to dig the hole were half-hearted. He had not had any exercise for days, went over to one of Semon's workers and asked him to lend him his pick for just a minute. That worker was glad enough to turn it over to Guinn and he tore into the hole like nobody's business. Pretty soon everybody began to watch. Guinn guessed that they thought it was funny that anybody could be so enthusiastic about digging. Semon came over and offered him some work in comedies.[30]

Fifteen-year-old future journalist and founder of the Academy of Television Arts and Sciences Sydney Cassyd met Semon and worked for him for the first time in 1922. Semon had traveled to Rockaway Beach, New York, in order to film on location. The movie in question could have been *Golf*, although the scene Cassyd remembered does not appear in it (perhaps it was deleted). Cassyd's family used to go to Rockaway Beach every summer for a holiday. He told journalist Argentine Brunetti in 1980:

> As soon as I had learnt that Larry Semon was there, my companions and I gathered and went over to the place where he worked. We were excited because Larry was the one to make us laugh until we couldn't breathe any more. We were watching the production, when it suddenly came to a halt. Someone turned to us. I thought that we'd be chased away. We were all prepared to run when that someone pointed at me and said in a thunderous voice: "You come over here!" I was trembling. Until that moment I had not recognized Larry Semon and I didn't know that this was his normal behavior when he was not before the camera. Insecure and hesitant, I was coming closer. He said to me, "I need someone to fill a scene. Wanna earn half a dollar?" Half a dollar for one scene in a film with Larry Semon! That was a fabulous offer! Before I had a chance to recover from my surprise, Semon had taken me by the arm and pulled me towards a tree that was part of the scene. "You seem like a smart guy," he told me. "Do not laugh. When you see me fall into the well, make haste with the others." He turned and started with the scene. The well was fake, of course, but the water was real.[31]

Seeing him act, Cassyd had to bite his lip to keep from laughing: Semon moved in an absurd and ridiculous way and was very spontaneous. And he had this extraordinary agility. Cassyd's companions laughed out loud while he was making a great effort to not laugh as Semon had that stupid smile on his face. When Semon repeated the scene for the twentieth time, Cassyd's desire to laugh was gone. He had had enough, and was exhausted by running back and forth from the tree to the well. But Semon, as he started each new shot, was cooler and fresher than ever. After this introduction to Semon, Cassyd continued to work for him in the summer. His half-dollar finally turned into one dollar, back then a fortune. Cassyd was envied by his companions because he had been chosen to work in motion pictures with a star like Larry Semon. However, Cassyd always refused to say that he was working *with* Mr. Semon. It was working *for* Mr. Semon. He was domineering, if not the most demanding and despotic of all comedians. A terrible, pitiable and most unhappy man, condemned to make people laugh no matter what the expense, Cassyd remembered. The weirdest detail to him seemed the change that Semon's face went through when he had just stopped filming. His smile suddenly became tense. When he was working, he was serene, gentle, almost cute, but having finished the scene, his

Vitagraph playbill for Larry Semon films, ca. 1919 (author's collection).

expression became sullen, suspicious, almost aggressive. Semon never said "bravo" to anyone. He spoke only if an actor did not do what he wanted. Few words, but sharp; however not with Cassyd, who was just an extra. From the day Cassyd was "hired," for the span of the three summers he would work for Semon, Semon did not speak one word to him. He only conversed with an assistant director, and sometimes director Taurog, who Cassyd called a saint. In one instance Semon ordered his assistant director to tell "them" that they were not to move until he took a pie in the face. And while Cassyd and the other extras could perfectly hear what Semon had said, the assistant director rushed over to pass on Semon's order and did this with much verve so that nothing could go wrong. It comes as a bit of irony that Semon admired producer Joseph Schenck deeply for his way of getting close to people, learning what they knew and extracting truths from them as he talked to an extra man the same as he did to those with a huge paycheck.

Acrobat Richard Talmadge (1892–1981) would have loved a little more enthusiasm from Semon as far as his stunts were concerned. His most difficult achievements were those up in the air and he remembered performing on the wings of a plane in flight as he was tied up with chains. He also recalled a flight from the top of the mast of a ship for *A Pair of Kings*. It was a curved jump, so that he would not fall onto the ship. Talmadge doubled Semon and others—even his leading ladies. If Talmadge ran across Semon and Semon said nothing to him, it meant that everything had gone well; it was the best he could expect. Every stunt he had to do over again, because Semon was never satisfied. Semon worried over the effectiveness of every scene although he had his contract with Vitagraph and things were going well. If Talmadge did a 30-foot jump, Semon lamented that it would be most effective if it had been a 40- or even 55-foot jump. If Talmadge landed headlong on top of a haystack, Semon thought that everything would have been much more spectacular if the haystack was on fire. In compensation Talmadge was paid well and on time. With his five dollars per day, he received more money than everyone else on the set. Upon asking Semon, he soon was raised to seven dollars for each stunt. That the scenes were dangerous did not bother Semon. For him it was important that the whole thing worked. The rest did not matter. Despite his highly demanding job, and his too businesslike chief, Talmadge found his joint venture with Semon most inspiring. Should a scene appear too scary to him and he thought he could not do it, he modified it a bit. Nobody would notice. Talmadge worked for Semon for almost four years. During all that time, he had not seen him laugh once. When Semon invited his cast to see the footage shot the day before, everyone laughed like crazy in the projection room. But not Semon. So his cast, as they were watching, had to content themselves with their own laughter.

Norman Taurog remembered Semon in 1980 as "not a nice guy and quite different from comedians such as Jerry Lewis, who made people laugh even offstage." Semon, he believed, was too absorbed in his work for him. Keystone Kid Coy Watson's opinion of Semon: "[Larry] was very businesslike, but always funny to watch because his every move was original. As a boy I do remember my dad saying how much Larry, his pictures and his work were respected. When I did see him on or off the set, he was a very funny guy."[32]

Journalist Maude Cheatham had turned her observations exclusively to the needs of magazine readers. She described Semon directing *The Show* (1921) and how Larry managed—despite the interview—to answer questions, issue orders, offer suggestions

Agile and high-spirited Larry Semon conducting a brigade of songbirds. The birds were the result of post-production as they had been added to the photograph later. Photograph by Albert Witzel, Los Angeles.

and plan details for the scenes he was about to shoot. Cheatham and Semon were seated in the rear of an elaborate interior theatre set. More than a hundred chattering extras filled the seats and overflowed in the box in front of them. A dozen musicians were tuning their instruments in the orchestra pit, while shouting property men were busily arranging the stage. But through all this confusion, Semon remained undisturbed, his ideas clear and definite, his voice quiet and always low-pitched. His detachment from the surrounding noises, he explained, was due to his newspaper training. Semon's own view of himself and the people who worked with him was that he thought he had a great company, just chums working together. Harmony and happiness would be the precondition for good comedy. It was not all work with them, for they bowled, played golf every Saturday and had the best baseball team of Los Angeles motion picture people. Semon was sure that he could not be happy in any other life. He was too keen about acting; it was the producing end of the business that appealed to him. He said that someday he should put away the greasepaint and make big spectacles.[33]

During his early Hollywood era, Semon had a good time, if not the best of his life. Days were spent filming, nights dedicated to frolic. He kept his dinner clothes in his dressing room at the studio for fast access. When the developing room was overflowing with a thousand or more feet of film, then he was to be found—and always dress-suited—the central figure in the night life of Los Angeles. He was the Beau Brummel of the Vitagraph plant.[34] When not acting before the camera, Semon favored two sorts of fashion, one being the dapper young chap in smart evening clothes who occasionally dropped into the famous Coconut Grove with a party of friends to enjoy an hour or two of dancing. The other part was the sporty prep school boy in black and white checked cap, sunglasses and rough gray sweater with vivid purple stripes. When casual, Semon used to nurse a strange trouser habit: He preferred a model of striped trousers of a higher waist with a belt in a lower position, hips cut in a more protruding fashion. He seemed to have donned these trousers in nearly every snapshot taken between 1916 and 1928.

The Vitagraph Big V comedies meant money. By 1918, Semon was earning so much that he could easily indulge in his eccentricities. Semon loved cars and managed to buy three in succession. One was struck by a train, the second proved too small and the third still worked.[35] He purchased a fourth car a few months later, a "low-bung, high-speed auto that moved like a hurricane and ate gas by the gallon." But the genuine highlight was the amount of nickel that shone forth from every possible part of the auto. Even the wheels were nickel-plated.[36]

Semon, who read five Los Angeles papers and several dailies from New York, had settled in Hollywood and moved from the noble art deco Hotel Clark in downtown Los Angeles to a bungalow on Harold Way. Later he rented a modest, picturesque house at 2037 South Harvard Boulevard where he lived with three employees of Japanese descent, cook Frank Uyeda, butler James Takushi and chauffeur John Tanabe. With his ever-eager eye, Takushi was kept for tasks such as bringing Semon cigarettes with an instantly lighted match as soon as he held out his hand.[37] Takushi was one of the first disc jockeys ever under contract, for Semon worked better when listening to music, especially classical compositions and jazz reveries. As long as Semon was writing, his butler stayed in the same room for the sole purpose of playing record after record. Semon's pet cat, a maltese angora, always sat on Larry's desk as it gave him inspiration. One day, Takushi put a jazz record on the phonograph that contained rhythms to which the cat responded with shimmying movements. Semon was not too surprised as he knew that cats fell for the shimmy as a fish took to water. He decided that his cat was to star in *The Grocery Clerk*, in a gag that from today's perspective might have motivated animal rights activists to block the entrance at Semon's studio. In the movie, the cat walked into flypaper, got stuck and was rescued by Larry, who grabbed a giant pair of scissors and cut his feline friend from the mess. It walked off with just some remainders sticking to its feet that caused it to shimmy through the store. Back then, this gag created a furor in the social world. Many cat shimmying parties were expected to take place on the get-togethers of the happy few.[38] Unlike the cat, a chimpanzee in *Between the Acts* (1919) was not easy to handle. It had developed a bad case of "professional jealousy," as Larry's aptness at swinging on chandeliers and steam pipes and his ability to climb ropes was evi-

Larry Semon as Larry Cutshaw in heavy eyebrows in *Bears and Bad Men*, Vitagraph, 1918 (author's collection).

dently an intrusion on its heredity prerogative. In response the chimpanzee proceeded to show Larry some unusual tricks in fancy climbing over the sets. Semon stopped work and duplicated his every movement until the animal gave in and returned to its schedule.[39]

Apart from the cat craze, Semon started a new sport that hit fliers and photoplayers on the West Coast in no time. When he was playing golf, he drove a high ball from a hill. It went so far that his opponent thought he'd better get a plane and chase it. Semon soon after sent for a rented plane and hit upon the idea of actually chasing balls by plane. For this purpose he used gas-filled rubber (instead of gutta-percha) golf balls plus a sixteen-gauge double-barreled shotgun and fine birdshot. Out of twenty balloon-birds released, Semon shot down fifteen before reaching 3,500 ft. altitude. While chasing the "birds," the pilot performed all sorts of stunts, dips, turns and slides in order to bag the

Larry as an escaped convict in *The Star Boarder* (1919) is surrounded by a flock of pretty girls in this lobby card (author's collection).

game. Then called Balloon-Birds, its followers were shooting toy balloons from a speeding airplane. In 1922, it was one of the most exciting pastimes and bid fair to put clay pigeon shooting and other forms of similar sports out of the running for film stars and sportsmen alike. Semon was planning to stage a contest shoot, offering prizes for the marksman and pilot who bagged the majority of birds from the lowest altitude.[40]

Since the San Francisco radio station had inaugurated a service of storm warnings by the "wireless telephone" on which any person could "listen in," Semon was one of those citizens to install a receiving set at his residence, primarily to get weather reports. Every morning his secretary listened and handed the report to Semon. The small, moderately priced sets, then practical, were quite popular, since so many theaters and music stores were offering regular concerts over the airwaves. Semon used to entertain friends giving them a pipe organ solo from San Diego, a lecture from Santa Barbara, and market reports from Los Angeles. After dinner they danced at Semon's home to orchestra music from a local theater, amplified, which rendered the music as clear and loud as on the phonograph.[41]

While Semon's new interim contract of January 1919 passed rather unnoticed, the next deal he sealed with Vitagraph made the headlines. On November 20, 1919, he signed a contract with Albert E. Smith by which he was to receive $3.6 million during the coming three years for thirty-six comedies. One-third of the sum was to be paid each year for every batch of films. Semon's salary during that time was to range from $2000 to $3000 a week, according to the progress of the work. After the three years there was a chance that it could amount to a maximum of $750,000. To journalists and their readers alike, figures like these appeared astronomical. An average industrial worker of that period was earning less than $1000 a year.[42]

Twelve Semon pictures were to be made each year, one every month as it had been his habit since his first two-reeler *Huns and Hyphens* in September 1918. Only Charlie Chaplin's salary as a comedian was on the same level. Yet after deducting production costs, Semon's profit would not be as much as Chaplin's, who made fewer films per year, while Semon was scheduled to turn out one a month.[43]

Semon's value to motion pictures was enormous. Very few five-reel features played to a gross business of $150,000 outside of the pictures of the big stars; to pay $100,000 for a comedy, it had to bring in a third again as much. *The Call Boy's Chat*, a newspaper column, uttered criticism and hope alike now that Semon was financially on a level with Chaplin:

> [Chaplin] hasn't done anything worth mentioning since he signed [his] contract. The trouble with the screen comedian is that he only has a certain number of tricks and after he uses them he is through. Chaplin, in his first picture under the new contract, used up his stock-in-trade in the first reel of his first picture and the result was that it fell flat because after the first reel there was nothing to sustain the interest of an audience. It may be that Larry Semon will exercise more discretion and reserve some of his ideas for future films. If he does not, he will probably find himself in the same fix as Chaplin.[44]

Smith had made a trip to Los Angeles to close the multi-million dollar deal. Semon's signature to the contract was obtained significantly after midnight, ending a conference that lasted a little less than four days. Semon was not to receive all that money for his services alone; he had to pay out of it his production expenses. It seems a contradiction that some newspapers wrote that Vitagraph now provided Semon with carte blanche, in other words unlimited funds, to spend on his productions.[45] However, this meant that Semon could draw on further resources with regard to props and sets. The same day that Semon signed his next contract, *The Headwaiter* was booked as a featured offering at New York's Capitol Theater, then the world's largest place of entertainment.

Papers went overboard with malice from the *Telly*'s "I Knew Him When Club" that accorded Semon "lucky" and "unmitigated gall" as the two shabby reasons for his success. In typing the announcement, Vitagraph's typewriter's cipher key did obviously a shimmy. One former colleague averred that if anyone had told him and his colleagues at the *Evening Telegram* that Larry would climb to heights of affluence, everybody would have laughed at him and given him a couple of boots. He lacked originality, pep, versatility and objective and his output was closely bordering on an obituary.[46] President Smith spiked this derision by declaring that Semon had proved himself worthy of every cent he was paid. The "I Knew Him When Club" then pointed out that the Larry Semon they recalled was unable to "bulldoze editors out of shekels," but chose to fall silent hereafter. The retreat of the club was largely owed to a charitable New York newspaper that obviously purported to spare Semon his future problems with Vitagraph and other film ventures and sent him a flattering offer. Semon was asked to fix his own salary to return to his former work as a newspaper cartoonist. He turned it down as he preferred his job as a comedian.[47] After signing his big deal with Vitagraph, Semon took some days off with assistant director Mort S. Peebles to go duck hunting, his first vacation in two years.

Now Semon was a regular guest with the press, he inspired artists to compose the "Larry Semon Polka,"[48] he gave generous luncheons, and he made no secret of his happiness in being able to buy out drug stores and jewelry shops. At one event with the press, he introduced Uncle Jacob and Aunt Rosa Belle, two of the last three survivors of his family in the paternal line.

With Vitagraph eager to expand into the European market, the *Exhibitors Trade Review* conceded Mr. Semon talents in many directions. Yet he would be well advised to consider the foreign markets when he was thinking up his stories. Otherwise he would manufacture screamingly funny comedies for the United States, but miss the big outside field. As a negative example the paper picked *Well, I'll Be...* (1919). It partly dealt with poker, but few Britons played the game. Hence it was predestined to fail at their box office.[49] By the end of the teens, Semon Comedies had begun to capture Europe and other parts of the world. Even his one-reelers were welcomed and are still available in Italy. It does not seem that Semon did in fact slavishly match his films with the international market as far as U.S. American habits were concerned. Rather post-war retrospectives for cinemas and television stations took over this task and dubbed the films in their language, making them a huge success. Even without the dubbing, Semon's peppy way of acting and lust for life was a lingua franca.

Nicknamed "Zigoto," Larry was extremely popular in France and a special favorite with the poster and magazine artists who loved his French heritage still shining through in his facial features. They made the comedian's grotesque face and wide flapping trousers as familiar to all Parisians as Charlie's big shoes. At a fair in Milan, Italy, *Ridolini* films emerged as the most successful in an international cinematographers' contest and were awarded a gold medal. The committee had been viewing 100 pictures from the United States, England, France, Germany, Austria, Switzerland and Italy. Six movies per day were chosen and presented to the public.[50] The prevailing taste was further documented by M.E. au Bois, a fan from Brussels, Belgium, who revealed to *Mon Ciné* magazine that

> Zigoto is much superior to Fatty [Roscoe Arbuckle] and even to the too-mechanic Chaplin. M.E. au Bois does not see any obligation to admire everything Chaplin does. Zigoto is a first-class artist, too. His face is most expressive, very mobile and so fresh.[51]

American papers noted that Larry was a riot and a lot of people thought him better than Chaplin, Arbuckle and Lloyd. The *Los Angeles Express* wrote, "A Vitagraph Comedy with Larry Semon is a worthwhile addition to the main program. It's funny and appeals to people with intellect. And this Semon is an actor. He has original methods and an outstanding personality. Watch him grow!"[52]

In fact, Vitagraph tried to keep Semon in the dark that his face was known to millions in every corner of the globe, places where the names of Shakespeare and the Kaiser had seldom, if ever, been heard. He drew the crowds in Portland and in London and Bucharest, and some exhibitors thought the same held true for South Africa.[53]

· 6 ·

Womenfolk

In 1921 writer Malcolm Oettinger gained some deeper insight into the lives of top comedians and how they behaved off the screen. He knew that they worried over retakes and close-ups, over new gags and old situations, over the following day's schedule and the mistakes of the previous one. He also knew that their real-life personalities were distinct from the merriment they gave on screen. Completely unexpected was his encounter with Larry Semon *au naturel*, a pallbearer-like comedian who could hardly have been more lugubrious:

> He is indubitably one "of the gravest" looking mortals in Hollywood houses. His gangling height, his gaunt face, his hungry eyes all qualify him for a place in tableaux vivants picturing "Starving Afghanistan" or "The Forsaken" or "In the Wake of the Flood." His expression fairly gnaws at your heartstrings, strumming "Oh! Dry Those Tears." Semon walks as though the weight of the world rested upon his narrow shoulders, and if you encountered him on Broadway or Sunset Boulevard you would probably and pardonably look for the rest of the funeral cortege. But he works not in a morgue, but in a chuckle foundry.[1]

Oettinger had met Semon when the comedian was trapped in one of the deepest crises of his life. He was indeed "The Forsaken." Lucille Carlisle, in every respect his leading woman, had left him. But the story shall be told from the start.

As Semon was successfully developing as director and featured player, a young, attractive woman from Spokane, Washington, was working her way towards filmland, Lucille Zintheo. She was born Ida Lucille White in Galesburg, Illinois, on August 31, 1895, to a family of Irish and French descent. Already at an early age, Lucille's beauty shone through. She had inherited the good looks and the charm of her father Frank, who, in a desperate fight against his alcoholism, left the family when Lucille was just a baby. Early photos show a lively and bright girl of a warm personality with a captivating smile, an hourglass figure and lovely dark eyes and hair. For *The Agent* (1922), Lucille made such a realistic-looking Spanish senorita that one of the Mexican extra men hired for the piece came up to her and began to address her in rapid and fluent Spanish. Lucille had to send a hurry call for an interpreter.[2]

Opposite: **A playbill for *The Agent*, Vitagraph, 1922, with detectives Larry and Lucille, the latter here depicted as the generic flapper by cartoonist J. Norman Lynd (author's collection).**

As far as friends, Lucille was always popular with men. Sometime in the 1910s, she married and assumed her husband's name Zinther which she later turned into Zintheo. She was full of energy and somewhat liberated. According to a friend of both Lucille and her sister Melba, she left her first husband because he did not want her ice skating at night; this surely being not the whole story.

Lucille's other sister Helen (Edna Ellen) encouraged Lucille to enter a "Brains and Beauty" contest jointly conducted by *Photoplay Magazine* and manager-producer William A. Brady's World Film Corporation in 1916. It was the first contest announced by the magazine. Incidentally, Helen worked for *Photoplay* as a freelance writer and press agent. Lucille had already shown considerable acting talent, her current profession being a job in an office. In the end, Lucille mailed her photographs, one of her face and another in profile, along with a letter of 150 lines explaining why she wanted to be a motion picture actress. After a few months, eleven girls, from all parts of the country, received word that they had been chosen from 11,000 aspirants to be future film stars. Lucille was one of them. She had fully convinced the jury in an interview, stating that film folk had to lead clean, wholesome lives as she was aware that the camera was merciless and hedonism showed too plainly.[3] She also won accolades for her Barrymore-type profile that would later be the ruin of her career.

According to *Photoplay*, paradise was waiting for the contest's winners. After being given country-wide publicity with the use of every finalist's photograph printed in nearly every metropolitan paper, the girls were to pack their clothes, get set to have a "regular good time" and then take up work "as all film stars do." *Photoplay* continued that they would spend two weeks in and about New York City enjoying lectures, theater parties, studio lessons and other events under the tutelage of Maurice Tourneur, then director-in-chief of the World Film Corporation. Those who stood the ultimate test of fitness and talent were to be rewarded with a one-year contract and social diversions.[4]

Things turned out a bit different and Lucille and Larry were close to having a near miss. On their arrival in New York on September 14, 1916, the eleven winners expected to be mothered by William Brady's daughter, actress Alice Brady. However, they were all snubbed. Claire Lois Butler Lee, one of the shortlisted beauties, claimed that the campaign was a brilliant advertising scheme, but the film company "four-flushed" and even overlooked paying the costs for the trips. The bill was finally settled by *Photoplay*. The screen tests were supposed to be taken opposite Carlyle Blackwell and Irving Cummins, two men who would try them out in love scenes. But instead, the appointed actors stood at the door and matched pennies to see "which one should team up to make love to each girl as she appeared for her turn."[5] The girls protested, and gum-chewing, fluffy-haired Alice Brady was pressed into service to take over the hero's role in the love scenes, something that did not improve the situation. The director had to explain her every move.

The blow came when the girls were told to go home after four days at the Fort Lee, New Jersey, studios where the cameras had not even been loaded. All of them had failed the tests. Butler Lee, supported by the other girls, objected and opened headquarters for a lawsuit at *Photoplay*'s office in Chicago, preparing to sue the film company. She wanted $10,000 in damages.[6] *Photoplay* wisely came to the girls' rescue, paying for the remainder of the two weeks' visit. The magazine had a lot to lose.[7] In its November issue, *Photoplay* claimed that the current issue went to press too early to cover their experiences at Fort Lee.

Lucille Carlisle, Larry Semon and Al Thompson in *The Stage Hand*, Vitagraph, 1920 (author's collection). Lucille, knowing how every tint and shade of every color registered on the screen, chose a lavender ballet costume to photograph a soft white and lavender ostrich plumes for her hair to throw the particular light on her face that she needed.

On November 5, 1916, papers announced that 21-year-old Lucille Zintheo could secure a three-year contract with Lewis J. Selznick after she and the other contestants were tested by several New York film studios. *Photoplay* had remorsefully lined up something with the motion picture industry. Under the direction of Herbert Brenon, Lucille was chosen alongside Alatia Marton. For *Photoplay*, Lucille was the secret winner. Otherwise it cannot be explained why with every article that was published about the winning beauties, she graced each introductory page with an exclusive portrait. Lucille's first small role was at $75 a week in Brenon's *War Brides* (1916) with Alla Nazimova. Of more importance was her appearance in Brenon's follow-up production *The Queen Mother* (1917) with Florence Reed. Brenon pointed out that Lucille outlined a brief test scene in such a telling manner that he was convinced her intelligence would outweigh her lack of experience. Three more contestants were able to gain a foothold in motion pictures: Claire Lois Butler Lee, soon to be Lois Lee and showcased in Universal's *The Phantom Melody*, Helen Arnold signing with Daniel Frohman, and Mildred Lee, renamed Mildred Moore, to play leads with popular comedians Eddie Lyons and Lee Moran.

Brenon's working methods were the least acceptable for his actresses. He "failed" as Lucille once put it[8] and after a few months she was left with nothing. She went to Lexington, Massachusetts, where her oldest sister May Stevens was living and then to Detroit before her contralto voice won her an engagement with the Shuberts in New York. In the huge stage success *His Little Widows*, Lucille played Hyacinthe opposite Carter De Haven at the Astor Theater in May 1917. In the end, a sprained ankle prematurely ended Lucille's stage career. Still interested in film, she began to realize how little of acting and filming she really knew and took the advice of Cecil B. DeMille to heart that girls should work a few years in comedy as training for serious work.

After her accident, J. Stuart Blackton took Lucille under his wings at Lasky's for *Missing* (1918) and *The Firefly of France* (1918), another war story, where she played opposite Wallace Reid. In late May or early June 1918, the Semon picture *Boodle and Bandits* was filmed in Hollywood. Lucille makes a cameo appearance in the final scene, threatening Lightning Larry with a gun. The appearance marks her first traceable, though uncredited, appearance in a Semon comedy. Soon to follow was a larger role in *Bathing Beauties and Big Boobs* (1918), in which she plays one of the belles.

Lucille always listened and in doing so garnered a good grasp of colors and lighting. She knew how every tint and shade of color registered on the screen and refused to take chances in this respect. She began designing her own clothes for the screen, later setting trends for other Hollywood stars.

The leads in Semon pictures in 1918 were assigned to Madge Kirby. For a short

Larry Semon and Lucille Carlisle visibly in love, *Solid Concrete*, Vitagraph, 1920 (author's collection).

time, swimmer Vera Steadman took over and Lucille again appears only briefly in the 1919 comedy *Scamps and Scandals*. On the release of the following Semon picture *Well, I'll Be*, she was officially introduced to the public and changed her name to Lucille Carlisle as it "sounded better." This happened in the wake of Albert E. Smith's verdict that new arrivals at the studio had to change their names should there be doubts with regard to their pronunciation or "phonotactics."[9] "Carlisle" was reminiscent of a long white limousine, serenely gliding through boulevards. Smith thought the name "Charlie Chaplin" was a perfect example of a well-formed moniker, and it was easy to remember too. "Lawrence Semon" was changed to "Larry Semon" in order to avoid the accumulation of identical sounds. Semon's surname was left untouched, although the spelling did not necessarily suggest that the pronunciation was in the vicinity of "seaman" or any biological reproductive entities. In earlier vaudeville days and some film billings, advances had been made to establish "Seamon," but were soon dropped.

The Larry-Lucille union on screen also became a tight union off-screen, although Lucille claimed that she was going for keen-looking men like Thomas Meighan or Elliott Dexter and did not expect to be engaged nor married. Still in 1920, Lucille and Larry were hiding their relationship from the public, nevertheless joshing and fooling for the press. Semon was at his best and granted Lucille as much screen time as he did himself. The critics had already spotted his new leading lady and praised her looks and talent. She was the perfect counterpart to Semon, knew to take falls and gave performances that were as humorous as cordial and climaxed in a perfect impersonation of Semon in *The Simple Life* (1919). *The Los Angeles Times* exalted that Lucille was one of the most talented and loveliest girls ever to appear on the screen and wondered why no star-hunting manager was reaching out for her.[10] Larry and Lucille worked so well together that they developed into some kind of national institution, cherished by the film folk. Magazines celebrated their romance in regular updates. Their first personal appearance was at the Los Angeles Kinema Theater in conjunction with the screening of a Semon comedy. Lucille debuted in a steaming hot vamp dress and revealed Dame Fashion's latest mode. There was nothing she could do wrong. Larry introduced a sketch that in the eyes of journalist and critic Edwin Schallert needed "speeding up." Semon then delivered the novelty song "I'm Looking for the Man Who Invented Work"—in "too low a voice."[11]

Lucille was the first woman Larry became faithful to and it seemed that Lucille was enjoying Larry's company, too. In the final scene of *Solid Concrete* (1920), the butterflies are only too obvious with both of them. Lucille gave Larry a big silver ring with an onyx stone. After he wore it in a few pictures, people got to look for it, so he always wore it, as it seemed to bring him luck.

Until 1919, Larry was still married to Augusta, whom he had left back east with Virginia. His interest in wife and daughter had completely faded. Semon used to send them checks on a regular basis, a quite liberal allowance, without any accompanying messages. Communication from Augusta and Virginia's side was ignored. Larry did not even respond to the cute little drawings artistic Virginia had prepared especially for him. When he made a quick return to New York he did not advise his women and stayed at hotels. There must have been some secret joke about this on the set. When Semon had gone to the East Coast to settle some affairs with Albert E. Smith, his troupe in Los Angeles found their lives a bit gloomy. Finally his assistant director Joe Basil wired:

"Safe to return. Your wife and five children have left town." To which Larry made telegraphic retort: "They hanged your grandfather here last night. It was a pretty sight."[12]

Augusta and Virginia, bewildered at their treatment, wondered and worried. Along with Semon's silence their allowance was being gradually cut down. They decided to find out what made Semon behave like this—on site in Hollywood. Before getting on a train, they had wired him that they were coming. On their arrival, they found Hollywood nasty and cold. Nobody was there to welcome them. Nor did things change when they went to the Vitagraph lot at 1708 Talmadge Street. Access was denied because Larry had instructed the gatekeeper not to let them in. Phone calls did no good, as people would deny that Larry was around. He was not available at work or at home. Augusta booked a cheap hotel room and it dawned on her that she had been dumped. Nevertheless she wanted to see her husband to get things straight. After a few days, Augusta learned of a noted attorney who had an enormous influence on Semon and other film folk. This attorney, gruff and kind-hearted, knew about Semon's philandering and infatuation for Lucille and made him instantaneously materialize.

In his book *Sins of Hollywood*, the acme of tricky little stories long before the *National Enquirer* tabloids, former *Photoplay* editor Ed Roberts documented how the reunion of the Semon family unfolded: When six-year-old daughter Virginia recognized her father she joyfully bounced to his side and threw her arms around his neck. Semon immediately brushed her off, roughly loosening her tiny arms, and sneeringly turned to

Exterior of the Kinema Theater in Los Angeles, announcing a personal appearance by Larry Semon in 1920 (courtesy Robert G. Dickson).

distressed and tearful Augusta, whom he could not have treated more disdainfully. He was said to have uttered the words: "Still nagging, I see. Still hounding me! Well, what do you want?"[13] Augusta reportedly fell on her knees and begged her husband to come back to New York and to live with them. He turned away, whistling, and instructed his lawyer to let them get it over with. The maltreatment by his family-in-law and the concomitant offenses had led Semon to a quintessential showdown. The attorney explained to Semon, playing possum, that they were talking money in order to recompense the affection he was denying his wife and daughter. Therefore, it was up to him to pay his wife enough so that Virginia could be raised properly. Larry gave Augusta $100,000 with the pledge that she stay out of his life for good when they divorced in Philadelphia in 1919. He needed not have done so. The Rosenbaum family did everything they could to shut black sheep Larry out of the family. They would throw away or destroy everything that was remotely reminiscent of him and it explains why his photograph hasn't survived among the Rosenbaums. Larry would never see Augusta and Virginia again. If he did wish to see his daughter, he could not, because Augusta would not allow it. In the census of 1920, Augusta decided that her marital status was "widowed," certainly more out of bitterness than shame. Her experience with Larry proved rotten from beginning to end. It culminated in a train wreck in which Augusta and Virginia were involved back on their return to New York. One Samaritan approached them and asked whether they were okay. In fact they got off lightly.

Upon publication of Roberts' story in 1922, the Vitagraph marketing department immediately sent Larry out to play Daddy Santa Claus at a Los Angeles orphanage to mend the damage he had done to his image. Photo reporters snatched a candid in which a happy-looking Semon, still out of costume, balances a cuddly girl and a cute boy on his arms.[14]

Augusta and Virginia moved around a lot and soon Augusta would remarry. Husband number two was Henry Levy from Texas. Virginia spent a lot of time with relatives because stepfather Henry and stepsister Maxine did not like her. Levy went through Augusta's divorce money and when that money was gone, he too got rid of her. Augusta never got over the way her wealth had come and gone. Virginia found a better fate. People described her as a beautiful, humorous and charismatic woman, who loved people and made any party shine. Father Larry had evidently handed down quite a number of features, including his slender body, protuberant nose and lovely eyes. Although Virginia's eyes were hazel, they bore the same expressive quality. Virginia had also inherited her father's hands—well-shaped, narrow with straight fingers and pretty nails—and used them a lot for gestures. She was a night person, and for most of her life suffered from chronic insomnia. Augusta resented the fact that Virginia had a good marriage with Philadelphia dentist Reuben Matzkin because she felt superior to him and thought Virginia could have done better. Augusta and Virginia were not close, although Augusta lived with her when she was married. She found a lot of faults with her daughter, not exactly complimenting her with a frequent "You're just like your father!"[15]

Larry Semon comedies were designed to make people happy, especially children. They said that his face was so funny they just had to laugh. That her father was so nice to his film children, clowning with Aida Horton, cuddling and hugging others before the cameras in *The Hick* (1921) and *Trouble Brewing* (1924), yet rejecting his own daughter,

just added to the distress in Virginia's life. When she learned that her father had died, she simply shrugged her shoulders as if she could not care less. But Virginia did care. It is known that she contacted cartoonists and allied artists asking them what they thought of her father. Larry did care too. When he was hospitalized with pneumonia and just had two days left to live, Virginia received a telegraph in which she was asked to write her father as he would appreciate her message. Virginia died in 1961, at the age of forty-nine, from lung cancer that had traveled to her brain. Like her father, she was a heavy smoker, having taken up the habit when she was twelve. Virginia and Reuben had two daughters, Ruth Knapp and Lynne Whitcopf. Asked about Larry Semon, Lynne commented:

> I'm sure my grandfather was not the horrible person that Gussie made him seem. I learned about [him] when I was in early elementary school. It didn't mean anything to me that he was a big star because I had never heard of him. My mother never mentioned that he was a big star because she hardly ever talked about him. She just said what he did, but she didn't really know him because she was out of his life. My mother did not share much about her life. She really did not. She did not want us to have the life that she had. Her life was painful for her and she did not speak about it.[16]

In 1926, after Semon had married a woman just four years older than his daughter, a happy story was published about Semon's large fish bowl. With a closer look it might count as an allusion to his past marriage and desertion of Augusta and Virginia:

> Here is a fish story about a Hollywood father, Larry Semon vouches for it and it sounds like the stories often told about Hollywood Fathers. Larry has a large fish bowl in his back yard, which was filled with goldfish. Recently they began dying. Only two were left and strangely enough, they lived on and on. The others were forgotten and Larry failed to replenish the supply of fish in the bowl. The gardener rushed in one morning recently to say the papa fish had disappeared. Larry left his breakfast to grow cold while he helped in the search. No father was found, but a tiny baby fish was discovered in the bowl. Now what became of the father and why did he desert the child fish? So that's the story bothering Hollywood today.[17]

To the public, Semon's real marital status was never disclosed and he was believed a permanent bachelor. This would not dishearten him, as French *Mon Ciné* wrote and adjoined that he was too eccentric to make a woman happy.[18] Lucille had already determined that she intended to support Larry in three or four more pictures and then she would be ready for serious plots. In October 1920, papers announced that Lucille was going to leave for New York, particularly to conquer the stage, and destined for drama. Larry was said to be leaving Vitagraph as soon as he completed two more comedies, *The Suitor* and *The Sportsman*. This news was surprising as his contract still had another few years and he owed the company twenty-nine more comedies to complete the obligated thirty-six. Vitagraph, as *Photoplay* reported, would henceforth concentrate on other unnamed "Specials."[19]

There was an unusually long break between the releases of *The Suitor* and *The Sportsman*, although both were filmed in immediate succession in autumn 1920. *The Sportsman* would be held back until February 1921, whereas *The Suitor* arrived on the screen in November 1920. Several things were going on. For one, the frequent clashes Semon had with Vitagraph; the other, his private life tumbling down.

Opposite: **Just divorced: Wealthy Augusta Semon in fur, ca. 1920 (courtesy Lynne Whitcopf).**

Larry Semon's 16-year-old daughter Virginia in a portrait dated 1928 (courtesy Lynne Whitcopf).

Lucille remained off the screen for Semon's complete 1921 season, her absence creating a mild scandal in Hollywood. Some sources claim that instead of gaining more theatrical experience she had suffered a career-threatening nervous breakdown brought on by thirty months of continuous picture work without vacation. At the insistence of her family, she went east and entered a sanitarium.[20] Lucille's father Frank White was mentally unstable. Except for Lucille's eldest sibling May, all the other White sisters showed the same disposition. According to Lucille's nieces, there was in fact an interval of seclusion for Lucille, owing to nervous disorders; however, they could not recall when. Possibly it makes sense to combine these two aspects: That workaholic Larry was continually toiling on his films held true. Norman Taurog was in fact given full authority on set. Yet perfectionist Larry, blessed with an excellent story and gag mind, would sit for hours in conference with him and his gagmen in order to work out the plot and an abundant number of gags—something that meant everything to Larry. He would dedicate a whole day to shooting one scene and if displeased with it, start over the next day. This is what Norman Taurog recalled in an interview with Sam Gill at his home in Beverly Hills on August 17, 1966.[21] Robert Florey knew that Semon rarely went to bed before early in the morning. Instead he would rack his brain, chain-smoke his pipe and tie loose ends for the next day.[22] Semon's obsession with film might have taken prominence over his relationship with Lucille. He had a contract to fulfill, stipulating that he and she would still work even when they were ill.[23] He was said to have started production of *The Hick* (1921) some 36 hours after completion of *The Sportsman* and rather than be delayed he launched the others of his company on still another comedy.[24] If this is true, then Lucille was shortly part of this film, but had had enough and left, which made Semon interrupt his film work. Lucille, on the other hand, wanted a career for herself. Larry did not like that she was working so much as she did not need to. He would rather have her stay at home, but Lucille did not see it that way. Larry gave in to her as it was her "damn right." He did not like her decision, yet he was not protesting either.[25]

Ed Roberts described Lucille as a man-eating, gold digging parasite and did not

A highly sought-after Lucille Carlisle gives directions to yet another suitor (Richard Talmadge) while early birds Larry Semon and Dan Crimmins hide away in *Dull Care*, Vitagraph, 1919 (author's collection).

find their liaison a bilateral one. Her slave Larry was paying the bills for Lucille's extravagant lifestyle. Despite renting a house at Harvard Boulevard for himself, his life was revolving around Lucille's apartment in Los Angeles, for which he was also paying. The two were aware of the alerted moral authorities and as long as Larry was tied to Augusta, they did their best to conceal their affair to the public. Larry had given Lucille a handsome light blue limousine with chauffeur who picked her up at her residence and drove her to the studio. Larry left the place in a nondescript car and made sure that he and Lucille would never arrive at the studio together, as any hint of publicly displayed affection would have been too crude.

To Semon's regret, Lucille was playing head games with him, as Roberts maliciously observed. Larry wanted to marry her, but Lucille was rather drawn to the hotel life of New York where she teamed up with other men to indulge in an insatiable lust for life. Every day Larry would talk to her from Los Angeles and if he failed to reach her, he came home sick. When Lucille was not available for two days, Norman Taurog had to get a doctor for Larry.

Lucille returned to Hollywood from New York in the spring of 1921 so that newspapers presumed their marriage for mid–March at the Mission Inn in Riverside. Semon

Lucille Carlisle helps Larry Semon cross-dress in *Dew Drop Inn*, Vitagraph, 1919 (author's collection).

refused to confirm this. On her next stay in New York, Lucille wrote she was not coming back because things were going too well. Their engagement to wed was broken off. Larry cracked. Again Taurog put him under a doctor's care for a couple of weeks.

In this phase of love pains, Larry would come to the studio moody and miserable and unable to work. Along with Chaplin, Fairbanks, and Lloyd, he used to follow the habit of getting into a comedy mood before he could start filming. He would kid about for an hour as he had to feel funny to play it, just as actors had to feel drama in order to play that. Semon was haunted by the insight that everybody wanted to laugh, yet everybody seemed perversely saying, "I dare you to make me laugh!" He attributed this view to a lack of comedy in real life so that it was hard to make people believe it. When Semon began his daily work he was outwardly serious as a judge. Inwardly the glow of laughter was still there. As Lucille left him, all was gone. Larry himself would not speak of those days.[26]

One thing noticeable with the films, for example *The Hick*: Larry looks ill. This is particularly obvious in the last scenes when we get a close-up of his face. His youthful recklessness has vanished, a quality he would never regain. His situation was aggravated when a prop chandelier came down on his head harder than planned while filming the last scenes. His sickness and bruises kept him in a hospital bed for six weeks. According to the *Exhibitors Herald*, finishing the final scenes for *The Hick*, Larry wrenched his spine in a scene and, coupled with the injury, was threatened with pneumonia because of over-exposure in a water scene.²⁷ The latter was quite unlikely as there is no water scene in this picture. The closest possible short with a scene like that is *The Suitor*.

Semon's streak of bad luck seemed endless. The press told readers in mid–1921 that Semon had injured himself again. He was said to have jumped from a garage that was going over a cliff for the ironically titled *The Fall Guy*.²⁸ He gashed his leg and might have been killed, had timing worked against him. At present, he was in the hospital, designing an aeroplane for his "next comedy."²⁹ The second newspaper article was definitely a fraud. The next comedy that included an aeroplane was *The Bell Hop*, which had already been finished. Furthermore, from a mere economical perspective, Semon did not undertake jumps from roofs anymore. One of his last genuine daredevil stunts for Vitagraph can be seen in *Humbugs and Husbands* (1918), when Larry rushes upstairs and falls from a height of about ten feet, landing on his shoulder. But to take more risks like these, his bones were too expensive. He massively relied on the help of his stuntmen. This is not to say that he evaded every leap. In *Golf* (1922) for instance, Larry's rival Hardy replies to a hit from a carpet beater with another hit in the direction it came from. Larry falls over and lands flat on his face. Richard Talmadge remembered that the very agile Semon did little falls himself and never evaded the pies in the face, the feathers nor the pitch. He fell into wells and rivers, provided it was not too dangerous. Semon

An enraged Oliver Hardy is all set to prevent rent collector Larry from seizing his household goods while temporary leading lady Norma Nichols takes an appeasing attitude in *The Rent Collector*, Vitagraph, 1921 (author's collection).

wanted to do a lot more, but his insurance company would not let him. At the time of his alleged injury, Larry was in New York to confer with Albert E. Smith. Maybe he was also trying to find Lucille and win her back.

From here on, Semon demonstrated quite some bandwidth in leading ladies. He had trouble finding and holding onto an actress, his current romantic interest often coinciding with the lead role in his next film. After ex–Bathing Beauty Marion Aye, and Norma Nichols and Rose Code alongside Kathleen O'Connor, Semon was craving for a congenial Lucille and had screen-tested more than 200 beauties. He demanded that his new Venus be the comedy ABC—Apt, Beautiful and Cameraproof. She should not require trick light or lens to bring out her charms, but be a knockout even when filmed from unfavorable viewpoints. She would have to act while dramatic training would rule out comedy experience. To the right ABC girl, the salary was going to be limitless.[30] Finally, Semon stumbled across Eastern chorister and daredevil actress Ann Hastings, who had made a name for herself in serial productions and feature drama. Parisian-type Hastings was just about one year into a grand career and won praise in the papers for her petite beauty of rich warm coloring that increased her charm playing a lead in Pathé's serial *Hurricane Hutch*. People were reminded of comedienne Bebe Daniels. The few newspaper magazine clippings that survive suggest that Hastings was equipped with bee stung lips and lovely dark eyes. Semon had spotted Hastings in the Pathé serial and made a frantic series of long distance calls to which Hastings responded by dashing to Los Angeles. On the phone, they found a lot to talk about, since bright and eloquent Ann was experienced in slapstick farces. As a veteran she knew what it felt like to have one's face made the target of pie, cold cream and flour. Hastings had seen the business from both the hard and humble sides and could not imagine anything worse than the condition of an inexperienced girl trying to get into the movies during the early twenties. Semon and Hastings signed a joint contract on November 16, 1921, with the largest salary ever paid for a comedy co-star.

A studio portrait of Larry Semon by the time of his divorce and his affair with Lucille Carlisle, ca. 1919 (Media History Digital Library).

Contrary to some filmographies, Hastings never made an appearance in *The Sawmill*. Her scheduled introductory Semon film rather was what would later be entitled *The Show*, yet another superlative, as no comedy had devoured so much money before. Larry was planning to embark on an extended type of comedy that merged the old slapstick routines with the fanciest dress of drama and outshone regular musical comedies of the stage. Vitagraph's lot resembled a giant girl revue with the comedian as its little sultanic majesty. He built a theater in the studio and equipped it with seats, lights, boxes, hanging and stage fixtures. Larry had drawn upon New York's Winter Garden and other sources for one of the most spectacular assortment of young women dancers. About a hundred girls, some of them specialty performers, were trained for over a week by a revue expert before the camera began grinding. Simultaneously, Semon's press department was busy praising Ann's beauty while dressmakers had started augmenting her already huge wardrobe. Hastings was signed for three comedies during which she was to familiarize herself with Semon's "particular style of direction and story." Following that, a huge melodramatic feature was to be made with Hastings in the leading feminine role.[31] This nationwide announcement rang two buzzwords for Lucille: *high fashion* and *drama*. Being aware that she could do stark, cruel tragedy, Lucille always deplored that she had little chance to display emotion in comedy, as every close-up meant to show motion instead of emotion. She also used to design her own costumes, only to learn that her creations just showed in a flash.[32]

On November 19, 1921, Hastings told the press that her contract with Semon had not survived the past 24 hours. She eagerly added with a "glint in her eye"[33] that it was she who broke it. Hastings stressed that it was a personal matter—and one of business

Schoolkids Lucille and Larry in *School Days*, Vitagraph, 1920 (author's collection). Lucille looks authentic in a little girl's outfit.

between her and Semon. Manifestly fighting emotions, Hastings packed for her return to New York where she had just had a major success in a musical comedy. Semon pointed out it was nobody's concern and declined to engage in a personal controversy. In order to be on the safe side, he was reported to be ill, while his press agent thought it wise to keep his lips sealed. Larry had obviously fallen in love with Hastings and Hastings likewise was charmed by Larry. Lucille had heard of this bond and saw her chances diminish to ever be a leading lady again. Papers wrote that she coincidentally wired Larry after Hastings had left, but a different order of events is more plausible and fueled by an article by Grace Kingsley.[34] On her message that she was "in bounding good health again," Larry wired back the scanty three-word reply "Take next train."[35] He had lost personal interest in Hastings and withdrew from her.

Hastings claimed that she was planning for other matters back in New York City. But, her name hardly ever appeared in the papers again. One can only hope that her career had not been ruined by Semon. In the aftermath, his office would release press notes that the contract was annulled by the comedian himself because Hastings proved "temperamentally unsuited" for comedy[36] and that she did not photograph.[37] With Lucille coming home, *The Show* was subjected to a make-over. The girl revue never appeared in the film to the extent to which it had been rehearsed. Larry's scenes were discarded. Most of the footage later used for *The Show*, notably battles of cars and engines and doings on train tops, were finished under the direction of Norman Taurog. He had reserved tracks of the Pacific railway and executed his work so well that it became one of *the* most frequently cited scenes of silent movie comedies. The filming of the tank engine exploding must have been most hazardous also for the cameraman, as a huge object flew towards his lens, catapulted off by something unidentifiable the last second before impact with the crew. Some scenes with Lucille and Larry preceding the final train car chase and close-ups of Larry pursuing Oliver Hardy and his gang were later edited in.

When Lucille came back, Larry was appreciative. Again feelings were not considered bilateral. Roberts' account of Lucille's return proved the least flattering and most offensive, for the sake of higher sales figures. Otherwise it takes no stretch of the imagination to fancy Larry's hurt at being scored off by the woman whom he had been craving for in his darkest hours:

> That evening she recounted to a group of laughing and screaming studio pals the wonderful time she had in New York. She told of all the men she had met, and set the bunch roaring with glee again and again as she re-told her adventures. Yes, she is wanton—wanton and cruel and selfish. Think not that she "entertains" other men because she is so fond of their society—because she is a "man's woman." No, she is just a "gold digger." Larry's money is good—but it is not enough. And then he may be a great comedy star but he is not much for looks.[38]

Despite this, Larry had regained his good humor and droll conduct. He presented Lucille with a giant sapphire and was back on the red carpet of Hollywood's event halls. He found himself among the guests of Marcus Loew when the State Theater opened in Los Angeles in December 1921. Unimpeachably dressed, Larry was mistaken for a dignitary and called upon for a speech. He gravely moved down the aisle and ascended the stairway to the stage. Doing this, he illustrated his ability to fall down stairs in all kinds of fashions in no uncertain manner. The audience was overwhelmed with delight.[39] They had their Larry back.

An Italian postcard of "La Bella Dolly," aka Lucille Carlisle, with her nose in its original shape, ca. 1920 (author's collection).

In summer 1922, Lucille and Larry were all set to marry within a few days, yet any wedding news was soon denied and would not be brought up again. The quality of Lucille and Larry's relationship could easily be read from Lucille's finger and the presence or absence of a certain ring. In late 1922, Lucille shocked the motion picture capital with a complete nervous breakdown. Her absence from the media was redefined as an extended New York shopping tour. Paul Bern extended a helping hand. Lucille had last been featured in *No Wedding Bells*, filmed around November 1922, whose title seems to be too clear a message of the unfulfilled Semon-Carlisle affair.[40] Also, Lucille probably was fed up with Semon's way of direction. Syd Cassyd described her as very shy. When Semon was not satisfied with a scene and wanted to do it over again, she began to cry. Either in 1922 or 1923 Lucille reappeared on the set, but after that she was never seen again. Before her breakdown, Bern had helped Barbara La Marr find a sanitarium. While the two used to be romantically engaged, with Lucille there was no hint of romance—simply Bern's ever-present readiness to support anyone in distress and the willingness to secure the best of medical advice. After several months of seclusion, in April 1923, Lucille recovered and sought to resume her career.

Coinciding with her recuperation, Lucille had a piece of her nose reworked, the Barrymore-type shape not pleasing her. Her nose was slightly prominent, yet one of her distinguishing features. The medical intervention was sold to the public as inevitable because Lucille's septum bore a slight deflection since the day she fell from a rocking chair when an infant. Although some papers were happy for her and her new face as of late in classical alignment, something had turned out terribly wrong. Since January 1923, Lucille had been tied to her home, because her operation had induced an infection which was in turn caused by a weak immune system owing to her mental state.[41] Mrs. Sydney Chaplin had been in similar straits before Lucille and had her nose touched up by the same surgeon. Instead of tenderly removing a cartilage from the tip, the result was an olfactory member irreparably indented, which made her sue that surgeon for $100,000.

Soon after, Lucille was in the hospital again, where some other plastic surgeon took the necessary steps to fix the outcome of her operation.[42] Juxtaposing before and after images prove that Lucille should not have opted for a nose job; it marred the naturalness of her face and let it appear tragically artificial if viewed in profile. Lucille herself was shocked at her surgeon's work. The change of her facial expression caused her humiliation and great unhappiness. Allegedly, the result cost Lucille the lead as Esmeralda in *The Hunchback of Notre Dame* to Patsy Ruth Miller. However the film had been released before her operation so that the real reason rather lay in her natural nose, the director not casting her but driving her to have it changed. Later, Lucille appeared at Paramount in a dramatic role in Victor Fleming's *Adventure* which was based on Jack London's novel.[43] This seems to have been her last film, although she would keep a lifelong connection to the motion picture industry. Her association with Fleming explains why her niece, another Lucille, whom she had agreed to raise, was up for the role of Scarlett in *Gone with the Wind*.[44]

Time and again, Lucille's shattered nerves rebelled, so she had to return to the care of doctors whilst Helen Carlisle was grieving over the misfortunes of her sister. It was topped by Helen's ill-fated attempts to make a fortune as an actress and scenario writer for which she had given up a career in vaudeville and the magazine business. Helen, deciding that she would rather be dead than a failure, slashed her wrists and swallowed poison. She died on June 2, 1928, in the general hospital of Los Angeles. It was her second attempt to kill herself.[45] Helen had also submitted her photograph when *Photoplay* was casting the nation for its future film stars, but never even placed. In 1912, she had won a writing contest with the *Detroit Free Press*, which paved the way for her to write for various cinema magazines. People valued her ability to produce unconventionally refreshing texts and considered her one of the best motion picture magazine writers.

Lucille left the motion picture industry before 1930. She married Leland H. Millikin, a successful businessman who sold expensive cars, and remained married to him until her death. When sister Melba's husband passed away in 1932, Melba suffered a nervous breakdown. She asked that Lucille and their mother Della raise her daughter, the younger Lucille, who was then about thirteen years old. They agreed to do this and lived together in Spokane, Seattle, and Los Angeles. Although Melba eventually recovered and remarried several times, she never took the younger Lucille back to raise her. So Aunt Lucille was financially responsible for both Lucille and her own mother.

Lucille groomed her beautiful niece for a career, but was very disappointed when she learned that the younger Lucille wanted a family more. In connection with World War II, Lucille Carlisle made some radio appearances against U.S. involvement in the War. She belonged to a group called *Mothers of America* and acted as their voice.

Photos that survive show a still very beautiful Lucille. People who met her were truly impressed and recall her as a smart and worldly person, who loved baseball and had a great sense of humor. The bulk of memories about Lucille, however, center on her career, swallowing up most of her personality.

Lucille Carlisle died on October 19, 1958, in Los Angeles, probably due to liver disorder. She had been a drinker like her father, but had given it up. But the damage might have already been done.

· 7 ·

The Flawmill

When the members of Larry Semon's company reached into their mailboxes in late April 1922, each one read a letter with a notice sent by their producer: Their services were no longer required.[1] Except for Larry, everybody had been released. Behind the dismissal were his activities on the Vitagraph lot. Again Larry was way behind schedule and beyond any financial allotments. This time it took him twelve weeks and $150,000 to make his latest two-reeler *A Pair of Kings* (1922). Normally, production of two-reel comedies of any other studio rarely went beyond two weeks' time and often took less. But it looked as if Larry was making his own rules again and had tied up the company completely for himself. The delay would have forced him once again to step right out on a new production, yet Vitagraph stopped him, since their legal proceedings had not

Larry Semon and Lucille Carlisle conspiring in *A Pair of Kings*, Vitagraph, 1922.

brought on the result hoped for. Semon's behavior was certainly not a matter of chance, but had several reasons to it. In the old days a two-reel comedy could be made for $5,000 to $10,000, and no theater thought of paying more than $5 or $10 a day for a comedy. Most of them paid about $3. But competition became keen. Mack Sennett, Fox, Harold Lloyd, Semon and several other producers found that in order to keep up with Chaplin and Arbuckle, they had to put more time, money and expensive stunts into their comedies, with the result that costs ran high.[2] The other reason lay at a deeper level.

A Vitagraph-Semon war started in 1920. In June, Semon was again back east to confer with Albert E. Smith. Full of pride, he brought the negative of his latest work, *The Stage Hand*, which officially was the reason why he took the train east right after completion. Behind the scenes, other topics were being discussed from which both parties emerged discontented. Larry felt betrayed by Vitagraph, as in 1919 they had promised him carte blanche to draw on their resources. But they did not keep out of his business of picture-making and were constantly issuing instructions impeding his work. To no avail he had been telling them they were making a mistake unless they kept their hands to themselves. An ace up his sleeve, Semon wanted Smith to release him from his contract and to grant him a new deal at more than double the salary. Another company was offering him $5000 a week instead of the $2500 he was getting. Furthermore that company would ask him

Mustached Larry Semon tries to make his exit from Vitagraph in *The Suitor*, 1920, with Frank Alexander (second from left), Al Thompson in striped tie and others (author's collection).

The Sportsman: Armed sultan Frank Alexander, a deathly scared Larry Semon and his companion, Vitagraph lobby card, 1920 (author's collection).

to make six pictures instead of twelve. Smith did not come around. He insisted that Larry be kept under the conditions agreed on in November 1919. Vitagraph had invested hundreds of thousands of dollars popularizing Larry throughout the world. They would not let go.

A few days later, Larry was lining up his producing proposition in Los Angeles. He had rented studio space elsewhere and was negotiating distribution with United Artists and First National. This news was fodder enough for Smith's rage. Larry Semon had breached his contract with Vitagraph. In August 1920, Smith ran an advertisement in *Wid's Daily*, a warning directed towards the trade in order to block advances to steal motion picture stars, announcing litigation and prosecution of everyone who dared to try to entice their comedian away. Semon, he stated, would be going steady with the company until December 1, 1924, unless before that date he delivered thirty-six films.[3] According to the terms of the contract, filed with the suit, Semon was to make twelve two-reel comedies a year for three years. Five pictures had been released and number six, *The Suitor*, had just been completed. Vitagraph declared it was practically impossible for their star director and comedian to deliver more than a total of seven pictures during the first year.

Smith's advertisement was appreciated by the theater owners. They were also discussing the institution of drastic action on stars, directors and producers who were contract-jumping and contract-breaking. For quite some time they had been struggling owing to delayed delivery of motion picture products. Larry now brought the matter to a head.[4] Since a release from his contract with Vitagraph was not feasible, he decided to extract himself by all means. This meant milking Vitagraph's funds to an illicitly crazy extent until the company felt that their losses were too drastic to keep him. Back in New York, Larry had already threatened to do so.[5] Nevertheless, in answer to Vitagraph's statements he published a counter-advertisement in which he claimed that there was no foundation to believe that he desired to quit the company and accept a contract with another producing company. Larry concluded: "I believe I voice the sentiment of all reputable persons and organizations connected with the film industry when I say that they too will likewise resent any such blanket charges as these which, without naming anyone, cast the stigma of alleged secret dealing upon an entire industry."[6]

It is intriguing that of all things, *The Suitor* (1920) was the straw that broke the camel's back. On September 4, 1920, Vitagraph filed the largest suit in the history of Southern California, swamping the media with a thicket of figures. The company held Larry guilty of a $400,000 breach of contract. In exact numbers they wanted $407,338,22, although the amount varied according to the paper that published it. Vitagraph alleged that the defendant deliberately increased the costs of his productions through delays, carelessness and waste to an unreasonable sum to end his agreement with them. Semon was also charged for debris he had left behind when finishing *The Suitor*. He had used aircraft, a plane and a balloon from which to film the plane. In the last scene it crashed. Vitagraph had to take care that they were not financially ruined by other productions, most notably *Dead Men Tell No Tales* (1920) with an all-star cast directed by Tom Terriss. He had been given permission to blow up an old freighter bought by Vitagraph for $45,000. Had it gone wrong, the company would have had to ante up another fortune.

The Vitagraph-Semon case was unusual as the company did not ask to be released from their mutual contract, but insisted the star settle the damages and continue his employment. The legal point involved was to whether or not stars and directors could deliberately and willfully beef up the cost of their pictures to a prohibitive figure in the hope that the producers would cancel their contracts.

Larry countered by filing a cross complaint against Vitagraph for a million dollars, claiming they were undermining his reputation through defamatory ads in trade papers. He was supported by Attorney Phillip Cohen, who asserted that Vitagraph had held the comedian up to "hatred, contempt, ridicule and caused him to be shunned and avoided."[7] Smith's advertisement would make people infer that Larry was a willing party to a plot or conspiracy to steal him away from the company. In response to Vitagraph's accusations, he asked that the contract be legally terminated by the court.

As for wastefulness and extravagance, Semon stated that he was given an inefficient and incompetent supporting company. Among other things, he claimed that the technical department supplied him with a mannequin of a woman that was so hideous and cheap that he had to throw it away. As a consequence he was forced to delete the part of the script that called for the use of the dummy. In another instance, Semon had ordered an easily breakable statue of a man, which would immediately disassemble when hit by an automobile. Instead he was furnished with a statue, which partly wrecked the automobile upon impact. Vitagraph in turn countered with another complaint and charged Semon for $210,958,60 that had piled up owing to five more Semon comedies.

At the same time, Semon was experimenting with costly triple-exposures for *The Sportsman* (1920). Until then, double-exposure had been run of the mill, while an increase was still rated as special. Viewing extant prints, triple-exposures seem to be completely

Oliver Hardy beats Larry's ears in *The Bell Hop*, Vitagraph, 1921 (author's collection).

missing from the picture. Alternatively, the technical novelty might have been woven in so skillfully that it was not noticeable. To expect three Larrys acting simultaneously seems obvious, but was not put into practice. Instead the technique could have been used to spare Semon performing cheek to cheek with a real lion. Yet in that case double-exposure would have sufficed, but again those scenes look real, since the lion reacts to Semon's hectic behavior. The only candidate that remains for triple-exposure is a painting of a man who flees into the artwork's background when a real lion enters the room. Further, there is a villain who runs into the aforementioned lion. The villain first shrinks, then makes his exit around the next corner.

As measured by the immense production costs, errors in continuity make *The Sportsman* even more enjoyable. In the opening scene, Larry puts up a fight with a jackrabbit that is evidently operated by a puppeteer as the hare's ears flounder in awkward fashion. This was evidently intended. The hare resorts to an underground corridor with two apertures. Larry plugs his gun into one hole and pushes it deeper so that its barrel pops out on the other side while the hare escapes. When Larry fires the gun, the backlash is only visible with the part on his side. The rest of the barrel peeping out remains motionless.

On the list of fixed expenses was a furniture warehouse in Hollywood, kept busy supplying Larry with smaller items to smash up. A potter was continually at work furnishing reproductions of art treasures so that he would have plenty of bric-a-brac to demolish. At this stage, Larry's costumes were crafted by the same tailor who made his formalwear. His overalls, at $35 apiece, were made out of broadcloth so that they would not tear, with especially strong shoulder straps. Larry used up about two pairs in each picture, though, and nearly a dozen pairs a year. His derbies met a worse fate than any other part of his costume, since they were always getting hit.[8] To get a highest degree of authenticity and realism, Semon equipped his comedy with every detail possible making jobs and costs ensue. For *The Barnyard*, farmhand Semon had to employ a real farmhand to take charge of the actual chores to be done. In the big barn setting, Semon found use for nearly every variety of domestic animal, and they needed to be regularly fed and cared for when the actors had left. One morning, a knight of the road was spotted fast asleep in the big barn setting at Semon's studio, when the night watchman was making his early morning rounds. The tramp explained that he had come along that way in the moonlight, saw the big barn with a lot of nice comfortable hay inside and did not realize it was a prop barn. The watchman was so touched with pride at this tribute paid to Semon's realistic settings that he made the tramp a cup of coffee before his departure.[9]

A further case of high expenditure was *The Grocery Clerk*, the first title Semon delivered after signing his $3.6 million deal. For the film he destroyed the patrol wagon of Hicksville, which means that part of the chases were filmed in the state of New York so that he was forced to ship part of his company there. The patrol wagon had been crafted in the days when Abraham Lincoln was splitting fence rails. In an act of motorization it was updated by adding a motorcycle that was fastened to the shafts in order to replace the old-time horse. Hicksville with the desire to forge into prominence caught Semon's attention as he was always looking for something odd. Once he had singled out something that fit the pattern of the weird, he would give it the once-over. The police force and motor bus were loaned to Semon, yet no one thought to ask him what he intended to do with it. For days Semon was the idol of the citizens, drawing masses to the place.

During a wild ride the inevitable happened. The old patrol and the modern iron horse parted company. The up-to-date went on and the historic wagon found a place in oblivion. Semon generously reimbursed the Hicksville officials for their loss. Now they had a brand new motor patrol wagon.[10]

That Semon was paying a lot of attention to even minor matters can be exemplified by *Her Boy Friend* (1924). Film historian Denis Gifford reports that while writing a review for the picture, he spotted a small headline on a newspaper on the third run-through. It read, "All the News That Fits We Print."[11]

There were even instances of expense when Semon knew to stop. While he had ships sink or buildings explode and carpenters rebuild the settings until he was satisfied with the sinking and explosion, it was some piece of glass that actually mattered: In making *The Bell Hop* (1921), the smashing of an immense mirror was an event of the week at Vitagraph's Hollywood studio. Everyone in the neighborhood was on hand to see it. Larry, in front of the mirror, sees the hotel manager approaching. Constant abuse has taught him that the presence of the manager means trouble. Not to be outwitted, Larry takes a smash at the manager, crashing the mirror in pieces instead of punishing the boss. This was one scene in which it was generally understood that there was to be no retake. The high cost of mirrors made this necessary.[12]

Within the next few months, Semon was spending more of his life in court than anywhere else, clearly not in the studio. There was not much opportunity to enjoy the new home in the Hollywood foothills on 1938 North Vine Street opposite Mae Murray's, nor his newly attained position as honorary member of the Los Angeles Overseas Club.[13] Semon's overall situation was aggravated by his troubled time with Lucille. Norman Taurog found himself fully responsible for pictures and produced some Semon comedies largely without the star himself. That Larry was being headhunted by another company was fur-

"Larry Semon, as he really is," photographed at the entrance of his home at 1938 North Vine Street, ca. 1924 (author's collection).

ther steamed up by a newspaper note that forecast the starring of either Harry "Snub" Pollard or Larry Semon in the comedy two-reeler, *Androcles and the Lion*.[14] Larry was never involved with this film, though.

Another picture that cemented Larry's rocky relationship with Vitagraph was *The Sawmill* (1921). There was nothing about it that would justify the extraordinarily long production schedule or the large budget. Larry had spent over three months on a location that looked like a cross between an army commissary department and a lumberjack's camp. He had traveled to Hume Lake, an artificial lake in the Sequoia National Forest of Fresno County, California, about 500 miles north of Hollywood. More than a hundred people were busy building Semonville. It consisted of permanent log cabins and other structures for the company of over seventy-five cast and crew people, while the women members of the company had hotel accommodation. After the film's completion, those log cabins that had not been subjected to some of Semon's traditional blasts were torn down.

The finished product did not justify the expense. Some early film rushes brought to Los Angeles by Taurog were the least promising and when Larry sent word from Hume Lake in late September 1921 that he would require one set at Vitagraph's Hollywood studios, this gave Albert E. Smith a migraine. To him *The Sawmill* was by far Larry's weakest effort. From a financial standpoint Smith regarded the picture an atrocity.[15] Something that Smith maybe never became aware of, but what would have made him detonate on the spot is a very obvious editing error in some prints of the picture. One of Semon's stuntmen had leapt from a timber cottage (or rather a dummy had been tossed from the roof) and ruggedly landed on a raft. After the cut, Larry stood in and remained in a pushup-like position for a moment, waiting for his cue.

The traditional delay in the production of *The Sawmill* was caused by the enormous logistics, Larry's fight with Vitagraph and some other factors. Interviewed by Kevin Brownlow, Hans F. Koenekamp said:

> We had good deals—had the cooks out of the Alexandria Hotel. We all got settled in for the day and we were to start work the next day. Eating breakfast—*voom*—the government man steps in. We had a bad fire. We need everyone on the line. So we fought fire for three or four days. I packed a gun because of bears and things like that. Stayed all night on the fire line. Big fire, too; finally ended with 500 men fighting that damn fire. The fire would burn the top of the trees—you'd stop it down here and sparks would fly across and start another fire.[16]

The fire of August 1921 was one of the worst in recent memory in the Sequoia National Forest. All people in the vicinity were forced by law to help subdue the flames. Leading actresses Kathleen O'Connor and Rose Code forsook their hotel rooms and worked side by side with the men, while others took charge of impromptu field kitchens with food. In the end, more than 2,000 acres of forest containing nearly half a billion feet of lumber had burned. Larry finally started on his comedy after a considerable delay, as the smoke took weeks to clear. Instead of folding their tents and returning to the studio, Larry and his cast and crew vacationed in the permanent log cabins constructed to house everyone during the film's production—with Vitagraph paying. Despite its dramatic effect, the fire was not worked into the picture at all.

Taurog recalled that a pack train bringing supplies to the Semon unit had fallen over a 300-foot cliff with the result that the members of the company were on half-rations for nearly three days. New supplies were transported by burros who easily and unerringly climbed the dizzy trails of the Western mountain.[17] The cutdown in supplies was so bad on the troupe that Koenekamp developed the idea of making a new fuel from the discarded sawdust and wasted film. He mixed the two ingredients into a brick that burned very hot and long, yet there was not enough waste film to manufacture the new fuel in any quantity. Nevertheless Koenekamp could furnish "cinema logs" for the fireplaces of Semon and many members of the company, the cost being practically nothing but the labor.

When Semon and Taurog were stopping over in Fresno, a local theater man approached them with the news of Virginia Rappé's untimely death after attending a party with Roscoe Arbuckle. Taurog had been director and a personal friend of Virginia's, having supervised her in *The Luck of the Irish* among others. Taurog expressed his deepest regret to his former boss and Rappé's fiancé, Henry Lehrman, in a telegram and offered to help in any way.[18] Lehrman asked Taurog to take charge of her body and to arrange her funeral in his stead. Allegedly, Lehrman also encouraged him to take part in the prosecution of Arbuckle, whom he blamed for Virginia's death. Larry had been close friends with Rappé as well, some sources even believing that theirs had been a lifelong bond. Rappé, prior to her film work in Hollywood, had lived in New York until 1902 and then in Chicago. She came to California in 1916 and associated with film pioneer Fred Balshofer, who knew Larry and introduced the two. At Rappé's funeral, Larry and Taurog were two of the central figures, whilst the other members of Semon's company acted as pallbearers.

The High Cost of Filmmaking, Lesson 1, *A Pair of Kings* (1922): Larry Semon and Phil Dunham are wracking their brains to think of a quick end to their checkerboard game (author's collection).

The Sawmill made enough money to make Smith's jaw drop. Its climactic thrill that culminated in the blowing off of the log cabins was well-liked by patrons and exhibitors. They extolled *The Sawmill* as the best Semon comedy to date. Larry, they said, outdid himself. He had created something new.

In early April 1922, things brightened even more. Semon won the first round in the Vitagraph lawsuit. Federal District Judge Bledsoe held that certain sections of the complaint filed against Semon were too vague and dismissed the entire original complaint.[19] Vitagraph resented the judge's decision, but did not take up the suit against Semon again. Yet they were looking for something they could hold against their star comedian and warrant the dismissal of the members of his staff in the spring of 1922. This time it was *A Pair of Kings* (1922). One of Larry's extravaganzas was another Class A setting, the *West Montok*, a freighter laying in San Pedro, Los Angeles Harbor and a fancy castle erected on the Vitagraph lot. Then there was this checkerboard. Larry spent two days alone arranging it for a bit of footage in the picture's opening scene in which his men are cleared off. In the end, he had to call Lawrence M. Lewis, checker champion. Lewis placed the men so that the player made but four moves to jump nine men and three kings. It took him five minutes.

A Pair of Kings is doubtlessly a good picture. Spoofing *The Prisoner of Zenda* (1922), Semon displays first steps towards straight acting and does it well. The plot convincingly develops into a nightmare with antics performed like clockwork and state-of-the-art stunts. Playing the mean king, Semon borrows the nastiness of Erich von Stroheim and offers a convincing performance. He admired von Stroheim for his ability to put life on the screen without the thinnest veil of its sordidness and would be a fan of *Greed* (1924). According to Semon, the picture was brutal realism, but tendered an education in dramatic technique.

By late May 1922, peace had come to the rival parties: Vitagraph and Semon had buried the hatchet and signed a new agreement effective June 5, 1922. Larry would begin production on a new comedy in a flash: *Golf* (1922). As in his early Vitagraph days, he was his own producer, albeit this time imposed by Smith. The allowances Vitagraph conceded their biggest star were still quite generous. Semon was to produce ten comedies for which Vitagraph paid upon the delivery of the negative, together with an agreed $45,000 each for the first five and $50,000 each for the next five. The main tenor of a letter from Albert E. Smith to general manager W. Steve Smith reveals that the company was doing everything to keep Semon content. Vitagraph built him his own studio with two stages, one completely covered. The studio was said to have been the most modern and elaborate in the moving picture world, with Mayor George E. Cryer of Los Angeles, Lucille Carlisle and a distinguished array of visitors digging the first spade of dirt. Vitagraph conceded Larry the use of his studio for free. They would also develop his negative, strike a positive, and supply the editor to cut the picture. Vitagraph would provide Semon with currency while he was to bring everything else, including his own lights, sets and casts. Orally, Smith and Larry agreed that he could erect sets on the company's lot when need be, provided he got permission first. Larry was allowed use of Vitagraph's outdoor sets that already existed on the lot, though not for free while the company expected a weekly expense for the production of Larry Semon Comedies at about $6,500. Albert E. Smith ended his letter with the words:

I want to interpret this agreement in the most liberal way, and if there are any little things he wishes us to do, try and help him as much as possible. This should take from your shoulders all the worry and annoyance of handling Larry's company, and I hope our relations from now on will be amiable and amicable. Larry will probably take up with the Hollywood Bank the question of financing his productions, and if there is any way we can help him to do this, without committing ourselves for more than what the contract calls for, we'll do what we can to help him.[20]

Smith was determined to support Semon with the objective that at least the company would not struggle earning money. On his return from New York, Larry did not only boast a new contract but also headlined with the news that he was leaving Vitagraph, as the company would release him from his deal. The agreement was a verbal one under the condition that he complete some eight or ten pictures the contract still called for. Larry again did not have many opportunities to work on his pictures, as he was expected back on the East Coast within a month to handle the legal details of the arrangement. The information the press was provided reads fuzzy to the extent that Larry's deal had still some little time to run, "something like 18 months or two years."[21] Larry believed he could meet Vitagraph's requirement by the first of 1923 and was currently organizing a company in order to finance a future independent production. First National was going

A Pair of Kings: Larry trying to escape from Fred DeSilva, 1922. As Larry is not yet in full makeup, the shot is probably from a rehearsal (courtesy Bob Correia).

to make him a good offer since he would come to their ranks at the time Chaplin was finishing his contract. Chaplin went in for productions of a more serious nature.

Larry had been conferring with Albert E. Smith over the possibility of feature films. Negotiations were already on in order to secure several stories that would fit the extended format. Feature films were necessary as Vitagraph and other film companies could not get the theaters to pay as much for two reels as they paid for five. The result was that the comedy, if it was to be profitable, had to be the feature of the bill. Hence Mack Sennett was coming along with *Down on the Farm* (1920), Chaplin was planning a five-reeler and Fox released a five-reeler. The thing to be learned was whether the public wanted a five-reel comedy, or whether they preferred their laughs confined to two reels. If they liked long comedies, the producers would be able to get high rentals for them and would prosper. If not, the comedy producers would go back to two-reelers and would have to be content with being classed as second in importance and receive second money.[22]

In July 1922, Norman Taurog started his own company for one-reel comedies as he had reportedly severed connections with Larry and signed with Century. With Vitagraph's budget restrictions, Larry simply could not afford his favorite director any longer. Three years later, Taurog would make a brief return to Semon for the two-reel *The Cloudhopper*.

A few days after Taurog's own company had been announced, Larry narrowly escaped fatal injuries when his motor car was struck by a streetcar in Hollywood. He was hurling his heavy car, twisted its wheel sharply and skidded alongside the streetcar, damaging his own car badly, but preventing a head-on collision. The *New York Morning Telegraph* of July 23, 1922, averred that Semon cheated death thanks to his training in stunts and thrills. They attributed to him the remark that it was too bad that the camera was not set up on this scenery. It was Semon's idea of a thrill, all right.

Larry's professional and private life bore some similarities as they were both unsteady. After ending his love affair with Lucille Carlisle, he had a relationship with comedienne Doris Deane before Deane married Roscoe Arbuckle.[23] Semon also associated with leading lady Kathleen Myers. She appeared in Larry's last Vitagraphs and, like Lucille, brought sex appeal to his comedies. In *The Midnight Cabaret* (1923), in a pretty risqué costume and long-legged, she is the delight of every male visitor and blesses everyone from a garland swing. Kathleen was the daughter of S.C. Myers, a steel magnate of Newark, New Jersey.[24] Visibly slimmed down, she played opposite Larry in *Horseshoes* (1923) and went over to Al Christie as female lead to comic Jimmie Adams and took occasional fliers into more dramatic roles including Tom Mix's *Dick Turpin* (1923).

In winter 1922, Larry stated that upon the completion of his present contract with Vitagraph he would build a million dollar Hollywood studio and produce under his own banner with the help of eastern and Los Angeles capital. The relation between Semon and Vitagraph had become unsteady once again.[25] Needing rest, Larry resorted to a steam yacht of one of his well-to-do friends and sailed out of the harbor of Los Angeles for two weeks. This did not help much, as a few days later Larry had a severe case of the flu brought on by playing golf during a heavy rain.[26]

The return of the Vitagraph-Semon fight also had to do with Larry's exhausted imagination. Exhibitors had started complaining that after they ran a bunch of Semon films they lost their laugh appeal on account of a certain sameness in them all, but Larry still meant money. With films such as *The Bakery* (1921), *The Counter Jumper* (1922) and

Lobby card for *The Counter Jumper*, Vitagraph, 1922, showing Lucille Carlisle, Oliver Hardy and Larry Semon in photographic and cartoon images, with cartoon by J. Norman Lynd (author's collection).

The Gown Shop (1923), Larry was making another comedy along the lines of *The Grocery Clerk* (1919), the prototypical Semon comedy, often judged as his finest. The same could be said for *The Show* (1921) which was a rehash of *The Stage Hand* (1920), which in turn was a reworking of *Between the Acts* (1919). Author Rob Stone justly noted that the things Semon was doing were in fact funny, but not original. The plots were just too predictable. The large amount of footage showing different people getting soaked in whitewash, raw eggs, molasses and allied produce were tiring. It is a pity that the great gags of the pictures could not lift the films' overall impression, but as Larry would realize too late, a comedy was more than the presentation of a succession of gags. Despite conceptional repetitiveness, the films still exhibited a Semonesque quality of the ever–good-humored, swift-moving chap. With regard to gags, *The Barnyard* is noteworthy for a pair of shoes that seem to cavort by themselves but are found to have mice inside them. The trick photography along with the walking egg in *The Counter Jumper* was all excellently executed and Semon's signature can clearly be seen in the flawless handling of the puppets. The dancing shoes kept experts wondering whether Semon had operated them with wires, but in the end, they determined that he had chosen stop-motion for better results. *The Bakery* is memorable for a chase sequence that develops when rival bake shop inhabitants Oliver Hardy and Larry Semon jump onto a large revolving display case meant for the presentation of pies. The ensuing running gag with Larry, who occasionally seeks shelter within the display, and Oliver giving pursuit, is remarkable in that it was shot in one take. The footage unmistakably displays how able Larry and his company were and that much of the action was left to improvisation.

Larry held on to his philosophy of well-matched scenes. It was conceded in the industry that Semon's continuity came close to perfection. There was no overlapping of scenes and the linking of his close-up action with full shots was always seamless. One of the most thrilling examples of his continuity is the final chase of *The Bakery*. Mere pluck and the law of physics equip Larry and his enemy to brave a pursuit on a ladder. Both parties cling to either side, and capitalize on its balance point when fence posts and trucks get in their way. For *The Bakery*—a definite "self-rising uproar of fun"[27]— Semon had hired half a dozen authentic bakers and made the film culminate in a roar of black paint and vats of dough. Finally, the players had to be cut out of their clothes with knives and scissors.

Editing greatly contributed to a smooth and speedy development of action as with the puppet duckling in *The Barnyard* that gets tipsy drinking home-brew and seamlessly turns into a real-life one. Less impressive are films such as *Oh, What a Man* (1927) where the escape of biker Gertrude Astor and Larry on a tandem painfully switches to back projection and miniature models, simply because Larry did not have the funds any longer.

Notwithstanding the surging criticism, Sid Grauman believed in Semon comedies and booked them for his new Metropolitan Theater at a record price. Until the house opened, the films were featured at Grauman's Third and Broadway house. For the opening of *Golf* at Grauman's million dollar theater, Semon presided at a delightful dinner for paper folk. The only disappointment of the evening was the absence of Lucille, who was suffering from a heavy cold. Amidst the harassment from many sides, the *Duluth Herald* dedicated some cordial lines to the comedian:

> Larry Semon has spent the last couple of days and a bankroll in seeing New York, the town where he used to work as a newspaper artist. In spite of his phenomenal screen success, he still wears the same size skimmer.[28]

It is to Larry's credit that he did read reviews and unpredictably even rebooted his fiction factory much to everyone's advantage. *Horseshoes* (1923) is a charming film that elaborates on a constant urge for hide and seek. It is enriched by magic antics such as a flying top hat, a billiard strike that would upstage any upcoming world records and a thrilling chase sequence of a cleverness that is on a par with Larry's masterpieces of the late teens. For the billiard scene one can only hope that Semon at once hired an expert to work out the stop motion sequence in which one ball is enough to send all the others away. *Lightning Love* (1923) was so original that some contemporary film company nicked the idea of chasing their protagonist by a streak of lightning up and down a flight of stairs and through various sets and scenes. Larry himself spent some weary days animating the lightning by scratching the bolts onto the film. Finally, the plagiarist company was not allowed to release their movie. The mere filming of *No Wedding Bells* (1923) made Semon popular in Los Angeles' Chinatown. Lucille Carlisle, being close friends with Anna May Wong, was one of the few people from the outside allowed access and could line up admission for Semon's whole company so they could shoot many of the scenes on location. The work created so much interest among the celestials that Larry Semon's studio was besieged daily during the making of the comedy by Chinamen telling him just how to do his film work. He was invited to join both the Hip Sing and On Leong tongs, but Semon declined, as joining one or both would have forced him to take sides, and he did not care to mix up in any tong war as he had his own with Vitagraph.[29]

Early spring of 1923 had rumors flying that Larry was at last going to give the independent market a go. For Vitagraph he had to produce two more films, one of them reckoned a two-reeler, the other one a feature of five or six reels. Only feature-length comedies were to follow; successful stage plays and feature stories appearing in magazines or published books were considered. According to Larry, "If they don't like me, the story will sell the picture."[30] Stage plays by George M. Cohan were given priority for the moment. While in Chicago in late May 1923, Larry inked a contract with the TruArt Film Corporation. With their headquarters in New York, TruArt was affiliated with Tiffany Productions and supervised by M.H. Hoffman, general manager. The new contract called for the completion of six "superfeature" comedies in the next three years. Production would begin in autumn at the Fine Arts Studio where Mary Pickford and Douglas Fairbanks did some of their best work.[31] Distribution was intended to be on a franchise basis. The contract ranked as one of the largest individual agreements ever entered between an

Larry Semon, Oliver Hardy and Fred DeSilva have something to settle while an unidentified woman and Marta Sterling look on in *The Gown Shop*, Vitagraph, 1923 (courtesy Bob Correia).

actor and a producer. Hoffman and Larry then left for New York to cover stage rights and copyrights. TruArt had "committed" itself to the star for an extended period of time and stepped in for Vitagraph's erstwhile carte blanche so that a high-end output would result.[32]

Again, concrete dates varied a bit so that the production schedule finally read: *The Girl in the Limousine* to start in December 1923, followed by *The Wizard of Oz* in April 1924, *Let's Go* in September 1924 and *Yankee Doodle Dandy* in November 1924.

The signing of the contract was given much attention, even more than the one in 1919. Now a bunch of journalists was hovering at Larry's Biltmore suite trying to get word out of him about his latest conquest. Larry had brought his posse. He was lolling in an armchair, a couple of broken ribs and his damaged collarbone held in place by large strips of plaster, while his barber shaved him. During the filming of *Lightning Love*, he had suffered these injuries. As the newswriters became more intrusive, Semon chose to handle the situation with his face semi-serviced. He planned to engage as many stars and near-stars as needed for reasons of time and money because it was surely easier to direct a good actor or actress. The films were to be enriched with the traditional hokum, thrills and stunts, big sets, heart interest, and the best photography attainable. As for monetary plans, the TruArt concern would put money in two banks, plus a special drawing account for Larry in the next three years and a percentage of the profits that would bring his personal receipts to more than $3 million. His desire to make big spectacles was finally coming true. Yet he knew that this was the last contract he was going to sign and that he made up his mind that they would have to show him the dough.[33] One commentator reflecting upon Semon's statement came to the conclusion that he was going to pass up his art after those three years, as it was the least gratifying.[34]

While conferring with his new managers, productions were conveyed for the next season. Negotiations were also underway in Los Angeles with the Orpheum Circuit whereby Semon would play a brief vaudeville season before work on his own productions, his program to be filled with patter, dance, a stunt and a film.[35]

Life for Larry had not only brought a splendid professional perspective, but also a new heart interest. He fell in love with beautiful Coletta Ryan, a celebrated opera singer who had learned her art in Munich, Germany. She impressed one critic so much that he compared her ability to sing the high tones with the powerful talent of Geraldine Farrar and Maria Jeritza. Another critic termed her perhaps the most noted of all musical comedy prima donnas.[36] Larry and Coletta had been friends for some time according to members of the musical show company of Shubert's *Passing Show* to which Ryan belonged by contract. Papers began to speculate that Larry and Ryan were engaged or even married. Larry silenced the rumors with the rather harsh statement that he had never asked Coletta to marry him, and that he had never told her he loved her. However, he had sought to have the musical comedy actress become his leading lady before the camera, namely for *The Girl in the Limousine*, after Lucille Carlisle was unavailable. But Coletta was tied up with the Shuberts for six months more and could not appear in pictures during the life of her contract.[37]

When Semon came to Chicago about four weeks later, the press was breathing down his neck again. He had come over in order to take Coletta to lunch and was destined to return to California a bachelor. Coletta, a guest in the same hotel, evaded the journalists' queries and said that it was better to "ask Mr. Semon."[38] One newspaper even printed that she wished the engagement stories were true. This was the last time the press talked about the Semon-Ryan relationship. Months later, Larry vainly negotiated with vaudeville actress Mabel Bardine to support him in *The Girl in the Limousine*.[39] Doris Kenyon, who played the part on the stage, would not play it on the screen. She simply would not go to Hollywood to make pictures. Her interests were all there in New York where she was going to open in a stageplay in the fall of 1923.[40]

TruArt and Larry had slipped into New York party mode and showed this to the metropole. Larry was spoofed by friend Will Rogers at the Follies and a series of special parties and dinners was given in his honor.[41] Upon his reception, a parade of three cars chased itself around Times Square and supplied the citizens with some stunts. In the first car was Larry and some movie people, in the second and third a nondescript bunch holding home-made signs on poles with the inscription "Welcome Larry Semon with the Three Million Dollar Contract." A cameraman accompanied the outfit and documented the scene for some newsreels.[42] The *New York Times* joked:

> With a careless dash of a solid gold fountain pen, Larry Semon, the comedian, signed a $3,000,000 contract with the TruArt Film Corporation today. The ink used was also gold. Mr. Semon wore his new gold suit and the notary public who witnessed the deed had hair like spun gold. The golden sunlight filtered down upon the scene through the windows of the Grand Central terminal, where the ceremony took place. Mr. Semon and Mr. Hoffman of TruArt wanted the contract signed under settings in keeping with the dignity and immensity of the transaction.[43]

Larry knew he had found the way out from his association with Vitagraph. Yet he had reckoned without his host.

W. Steve Smith, by then vice-president of Vitagraph, was miffed and declared that he knew nothing of the contract. Semon, he asserted, still was committed to Vitagraph to produce two more comedies. Eight of the ten had been delivered. The remaining two would be produced within three months on a more elaborate scale than any heretofore screened. Smith was not surprised that Semon had signed with TruArt. However, he thought it was understood that Semon had agreed with Smith's brother Albert on the fact that he would not enter into a contract with any other production concern until the Vitagraph Company had been given an opportunity to bid for his services.[44] The liberal verbal agreement that Semon could leave Vitagraph after fulfilling his contract had fallen flat. W. Steve Smith even thought it self-evident that Semon would advise him why he left Los Angeles for Chicago. In a rushed attempt to appease his alma mater, Larry advertised in *Film Daily* the following lines:

> Owing to the widespread publicity which attended the recent signing of the contract between TruArt Film Corporation and myself for the production of feature-length comedies, and the various reports in the daily press of the country concerning this contract, I desire to announce, on behalf of TruArt Film Corporation, the Vitagraph Company of America and myself, that under my present existing contract with the Vitagraph Company, there remain two two-reel comedies to be produced of the standard that I have made heretofore for that company.
>
> If earnest effort and the sincere desire to give you worthwhile attractions count for aught, then I honestly believe that the two comedies still to be produced under my present contract will be superior to any I have ever made before.
>
> The full details regarding my future production plans will be announced by TruArt, immediately upon the completion of my Vitagraph contract.[45]

Trouble Brewing, another film title symptomatic for the Semon-Vitagraph relationship, was Larry Semon's final film for the company. Detective Larry displays his affection to popular Carmelita Geraghty in this Italian postcard, ca. 1923 (author's collection).

Semon soon delivered the rather rural *Horseshoes* (1923). Yet he was lagging behind with his last film for the Vitagraph contract that was to expire on September 1, 1923.[46] TruArt forces wanted to rush preparations with three motion picture comedy writers eagerly adapting *The Girl in the Limousine* to the screen, but found their advances blocked. Larry filmed his last Vitagraph in about September 1923. Prior, Albert E. Smith, laboring under the exhibitors' pressure, had issued instructions to head editor A.A. Jordan to determine whether it was possible to piece a new Semon comedy together from the discards of past efforts. Ten days later, on September 17, Larry showed up with a film he handed in for approval, *Moonshines*. Immediately, Albert telegraphed his brother Frank that he refused to accept *Moonshines* as it was a cheap production with a cheap cast. The list included names such as Oliver Hardy, Pete Gordon, James Donelly and Carmelita Geraghty. The latter, a former magazine writer, appeared in one of her first roles and was to be a WAMPAS baby only a few months after finishing the film.

President Smith persisted that *Moonshines* was not in the class of Semon's other pictures as if he had ever genuinely approved of his output, and that it had the charm of a low-budget Aubrey comedy. Semon for his part had successfully explored the usability of outtakes from past productions and included the blowing-up of old buildings used in other pictures. The film was returned to sender with the obligation that Semon do something to make it better. His electrical equipment would be held in order to protect Vitagraph on their money advanced. Semon was preoccupied with his new contract and had little time to deal with *Moonshines*' improvement. Finally Vitagraph paid for the picture because they had to fulfill their contract with theaters. The film was released in March 1924 and now bore the telling title *Trouble Brewing* (1924).

Trouble Brewing was believed to be a lost film, yet a third-generation, videotaped version from a clear Spanish print was available for assessment. The film is by no means bad. Prohibition detective sergeant Larry eagerly battles alcohol abuse. The very idea that Semon made a film about this is funny, as he used to supply his cast and crew with rum-stained Coca Cola and always meliorated private dinners with a fine drop. People kept whispering that Larry "opened champagne like water" and that "it tasted that way anyhow."[47] Certainly, Larry applied his old recipe of presenting gags in a row, but the running gags deserve to be considered. Contrary to Smith's furious telegraph in which he complained about numerous rehashes, he was either driven by a dislike of Larry or the latter did in fact spare the time to reshoot scenes. In one, blindfolded Larry fights a war with his opponent who wants to trap him in a barrel filled with water. With incredible certainty, Larry tiptoes on safe ground and avoids the hazard that is placed on his ever-changing path. Finally, Larry outwits his antagonist and makes *him* fall into the barrel. The bulk of the scene, which has Larry and his enemy impressively ballet around each other, was shot without interruption. Reminiscent of *The Sawmill* is a chase on blocks of ice that defies gravity. Another worthwhile moment is when Larry snatches bottles away whenever his "clients" try to take a sip. Afterwards he tries to catch a drinker who is hiding behind a sheet on a clothesline, but discovers that it is a child drinking from his milk-filled bottle.

How Larry satisfied Vitagraph's final demands could not be determined. At any rate he did not shoot a feature-length production for them, but was in the end set free, leaving the relationship sour. Of the thirty-six films agreed on in 1919, he had only made twenty-four.

When writing his autobiography in the 1950s, Albert E. Smith did not even mention Larry Semon. Though Semon generally had a good time at Vitagraph, he was yearning for a producer personality he found in Joseph Schenck. To Semon he was the biggest man in the film world: Schenck knew production and cared to work at pictures and not sit down in a New York office.

With Larry's departure, the label Vitagraph practically disappeared from the scene, as the company was sold to Warner Bros., Inc., in spring 1925. It made Warner Bros. one of the largest independent distributors in the country. The Vitagraph Studio in Brooklyn, a 20-acre studio in Hollywood, a laboratory there and a large library of motion pictures of historical value, real estate and all subsidiaries of the film company were included in the sale. The future products of Vitagraph were to be distributed worldwide, since the players and stories under contract formed part of the purchase.[48]

When not struggling with Vitagraph, Larry showed signs of being an environmental activist. He and his neighbors were trying to stop the laying of a sidewalk near their homes in Franklin Circle, as it meant the destruction of beautiful pepper trees. Their letter of protest was addressed to the City Council,[49] and rejected by them.

March 16, 1924, marked a turning point for the worse; Vitagraph began legally contesting Larry's signing with TruArt. TruArt was not interested in a court battle and, away from the headlines, dropped Larry's contract.

· 8 ·

Image Change

Stripped of a deal and now needing a new contract, the greatly in demand Larry Semon soon found it with Chadwick Picture Corporation, an independent company established in 1915. Producing activities were still executed in New York and in 1925 transferred to Hollywood. With company president I.E. Chadwick and supervisor Leon Lee, Semon signed a contract around May 10, 1924, that guaranteed him his long ambition to produce feature-length pictures, now labeled De Luxe Comedies, a series of five-reelers. Chadwick had secured the rights to *The Girl in the Limousine* and *The Wizard of Oz* and aligned with First National Pictures for distribution. *The Girl in the Limousine* went into production in mid–May 1924 with Claire Adams taking the female lead. It was completed a few weeks later.

Semon invariably talked freely about his view on films and how he updated himself on the requirements of a trade that was changing on a daily basis. Producing slapstick comedy had become difficult. The re-releases of Semon's Hughie Mack and Jimmy Aubrey comedies met with absolute silence from the patrons. Audiences no longer laughed at acrobats who fell down and piled on top of each other. The first tendencies against throwing pies and other soggy missiles at the heavy were around in the late teens. Fans inquired why comedians and comedy producers could not give them a connected story. D.W. Griffith, Maurice Tourneur, Thomas Ince and others had injected into dramatic productions comic situations that convulsed the audience through refined elements. Mr. and Mrs. Sidney Drew had proven that comedy need not be so roughhouse with horseplay or slapstick antics. Charlie Chaplin, Larry Semon, Harold Lloyd and others fell prey to the temptation to exploit some rough stuff of an earlier vintage. But their genius partially redeemed them. Otherwise comedy producers had chosen to abandon all sensible methods. The endless chase in a car or on motorcycle, with scenery racing past in a fuzzy mass, was not only regarded as a sign of their lack of new ideas, but a fairly good criterion as to the state of their minds. The possibilities in screen comedy had not yet been tapped, many fans believed. They were all waiting patiently for the day when they could watch one that would give them a maximum of laughter with a minimum of darned foolishness.[1]

By 1924, comedy-making had turned into an art, Lloyd and Chaplin leading the way. The man—not the act—was the attraction. Highly paid writers were kept busy day

Larry Semon as Tony Hamilton is lured into a car by a fake female, and an ensuing chase results in a life-threatening stunt scene, lauded by critics, in *The Girl in the Limousine*, Chadwick/First National, 1924 (author's collection).

and night thinking up gags with maybe one out of a hundred suggested usable and original. Semon insisted that he still did not intend to take a step up the ladder of "so-called art" in the field of comedy drama. For him it was slapstick first, last, and always[2] and so it was for the many exhibitors he had asked. Comedy had to make people laugh out loud, or it was not worth a tinker's dime.[3] Just a few months later, Semon realized that his comedy had to change and that he was in the process of being overtaken by his peers, should he not—literally—act and rethink his secret of success:

> All this means that the art of pantomime must be developed and improved. And this is what has happened with the screen comedians. The successful comedian of today must not simply grimace and gesticulate wildly. He must have restraint; he must get the utmost out of a humorous situation by some simple expression or gesture.[4]

If there was slapstick, then some logical reason should justify it. Knowledge of how to construct a story was essential for a comedian of his day, having turned from mechanic to dramatist. It seems a pity that Semon failed to recall his great Vitagraph two-reelers of 1918, 1919 and 1920. On the one hand they were filled with mirth, on the other hand they also had their quiet moments with gags developing from the situation. Semon's current ideas on comedy were not new. Back in 1920 he had told Edwin Schallert that

Larry Semon as Tony Hamilton and Claire Adams as Betty Fraser take care of a little monkey in *The Girl in the Limousine*, Chadwick/First National, 1924 (author's collection).

there had to be reason in the comedy. It was not possible to bang people over the head with battle axes and blow them up without a show of purpose. To add to his new recipe of good motion picture comedy, Semon postulated the presence of thrills that left an audience tense and excited. Their emotions wrought up, they were eager and willing to laugh at some funny scene, welcoming it as relief.

In order to punctuate *The Girl in the Limousine* with gasps, Semon was looking to break records. Supposedly he performed one of the most dangerous stunts, at the time one of the longest drops ever cranked for the sake of a movie thrill. To this end, he dove more than a hundred feet through space, equivalent to nine stories. Semon dropped backwards without looking and landed safely in the large net that had been installed to catch him.[5] It was topped by a thrill that might have taken the star's life. The stunt might have bankrupted Chadwick if Semon had been seriously injured or worse if the film, a few weeks into production, had never been completed. It was part of a race alongside an express train with two motorcycles and one heavy limousine. The limousine driver slammed on the brakes and the vehicle skidded, making two complete circles, and threatened to topple over. Semon claimed he was forced to skid the car twenty-seven times to film the scene correctly.[6] He hired the train for an entire week to shoot the action scenes. Some shots had to be redone up to eighty times.[7]

For *The Girl in the Limousine*, Semon prescribed himself everything but a life of luxury. He saw himself on a par with every athlete preparing for a championship. Apart from being his long-serving assistant director, former lightweight boxer and instructor during the war, Joe Basil was Semon's trainer and pushed him through a hard schedule full of wrestling, handball, boxing and jogging. All of that was done in between shooting and thought vital to prepare Semon for dangerous stunts. The film is unfortunately lost, so any attempt at determining the degree of credibility have been curbed. Although Semon was a top sportsman, it is difficult to conceive that he did the hazardous stunts himself. It is however intriguing that in *The Cloudhopper* (1925), Semon is up in the air fighting a crook on the wings of a plane. Apparently, it is all Semon himself, no back projection, no stand-in. Now that he was with another company and often eager to perform more stunts, it could have been possible that he allowed himself more freedom. At least the hard training had changed something about Semon's body. In harmony with the script, Larry was to appear in a woman's silk pajamas. No garment in the studio came close enough to "fitting" him. So the studio dressmaker was called to do a rush job.[8]

Apart from Joe Basil, *The Girl in the Limousine* reunited two more old friends, C. Graham Baker, who joined forces with First National and had been advanced to chief scenario writer, and comedian Charlie Murray, once with Zera's troupe.

Never did Semon advertise a film more than *The Girl in the Limousine*. Long interviews and press kits were released, which had not been the case with any other Semon production up to this time. *The Girl in the Limousine* was a welcomed film by some reviewers. Grace Kingsley, with whom Larry was a personal friend, wrote in the *Los Angeles Times*:

> Larry has done so well with his first translation of stage farce to picture form that we wish he would do a lot of them. He certainly has a flair for doing it—a difficult task at which most comedians fail dismally. He and Doug MacLean seem to be indeed the only comedians who have successfully translated stage farce into pictures.[9]

Earlier, in 1924, Semon had posed for artist photographer Lejaren à Hiller. He portrayed the tragic clown Pagliacci in a series of four selected prints. The photo layout was a campaign to back Semon's image change and to justify his joining the artist league in motion pictures.

A studio portrait of Larry Semon by Porter S. Cleveland, Hollywood, ca. 1924 (courtesy Scott Hayden).

The *Girl in the Limousine* brought no great stampede to the box office and it failed with those who went inside. With an elongated two-reeler that, according to most of the reviewers, was just a reworking of old gags, what did Semon expect? *Variety* termed it a disappointment and criticized Semon for too much slapstick. For most of the footage, Semon had even discarded his usual makeup and costume.

Owing to the failure of his first feature-length film, Larry was well advised to return to two-reel comedies. He did, and they were distributed through Chadwick-Educational and quite a success with both moviegoers and the critics. In *The Girl in the Limousine*, Semon's eye makeup still was reminiscent of his Vitagraph era, and he kept his derby hat, but he would alter his appearance in this later Educational phase.

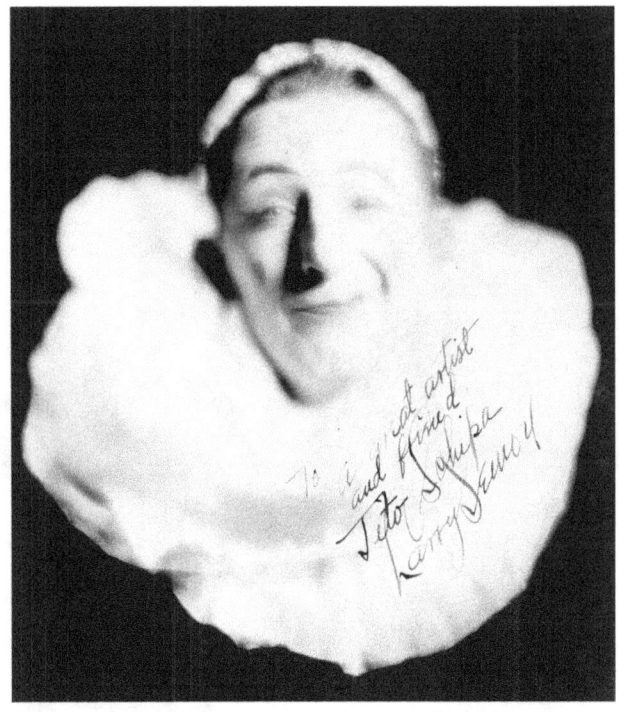

Semon's first steps towards being "an artist": posing for Lejaren à Hiller as Pagliacci in 1923 (author's collection). The photograph is inscribed to "tenore di grazia Tito Schipa."

Even earlier, on Christmas 1922, an admirer had presented Semon with a deviation from his familiar outfit. Semon regarded it fondly for a few moments, then hung it in the studio wardrobe and returned to his regular costume. He then commented: "It can't be done."[10] *Variety*'s criticism for *The Girl in the Limousine* was particularly unfavorable when terming Semon nothing more than a clown lacking "wistful poignancy."[11] This was the time for him to bid his clown character farewell.

Semon's first two-reeler for Educational, *Her Boy Friend*, was released on September 28, 1924, just two months after *The Girl in the Limousine*. Semon felt under pressure as exhibitors, critics and patrons were eyeing him, curious what he would come up with after the first failure in his career. The story took well and the film was received accordingly. The *Film Daily* rejoiced and wrote that the doings in the short reeler would thrill even the most hardened thrill-chasers. The cast was fine and the gags worth talking about.[12]

One thing critics did not talk about explicitly, yet did not take well at all, was Semon's new outfit and character, the result of Semon's hasty decision. It did not connect with patrons the way the boobish character had done. Now Larry was dapper in tie and well-ironed slim fit trousers. Max Factor was responsible for his new makeup[13] and remained his consultant up to his last movie. He let Semon's eyes appear smaller in applying dark color to the lower waterline. Expressiveness, and more importantly youthfulness, was waning. There was something gray, dull and edgy to Semon's appearance. Larry had chosen a hat that did not match his facial bone structure. That derby just seemed to com-

In Chadwick-Educational's *Her Boy Friend* (1924) Larry has to accept that his love interest Dorothy is already married to another man (Fred Spencer) (author's collection).

plement his features; the new hat did not. His new alter ego had even given up smoking. Yet there was another change: Surely not for the sake of vacillating tastes but for reasons of age, Semon's ample blond hair was getting thinner. Like his father Zera who had a pronounced semi-bald head in his thirties, Larry was also balding. From about *No Wedding Bells* on, Semon started to comb his hair back and used pomade on- and off-screen. At least in films he sometimes applied a hairpiece, but was not too particular about this, as scenes from *The Cloudhopper* show Larry with hairpiece on *and* off. Combined with his new makeup, it was giving him a more mature appearance.

That Semon, who possessed a good if not irrevocable taste for visual effects, decided to work so massively against his former character, the one he had developed and refined for more than seven years, is painful. In the course of time, Semon will have internalized many traits of his former on-screen persona. To eliminate it—and in doing so losing parts of himself—was one of the worst decisions he could ever have made. Semon was trapped in his own ambitions to please without allowing himself time to develop.

In succession, Semon released further featurettes which were good films, *Kid Speed* (1924), *The Dome Doctor* (1925) and *The Cloudhopper* (1925). In addition, he gave a behind-the-scenes stint in the six-reeler *Go Straight*, which has been lost. It documented Semon's work in the studio. While *The Cloudhopper* allowed for good stunting, the other three films were less spectacular and introduced the more frequent use of full-scale models. For *Her Boy Friend*, however, a jump off the top rigging of a sailing ship was reportedly done by his new leading lady Dorothy Dwan. Dwan later confessed that she had to be doubled before Tom Mix taught her to take stunts herself: "I could swim a little in a tank but was deathly afraid of the ocean, and dive I could not."[14]

Accompanying the release of his first Educational two-reeler, Semon signed a contract with the McClure Newspaper Syndicate of New York and Philadelphia. He obligated himself to turn out a daily comic strip based on his film persona from early October 1924 on. The comic strips were syndicated to newspapers throughout the U.S. and Canada.

For his Educational featurettes, Semon was looking for a new leading lady. This was his first order of business on his arrival back from New York, where he had attended First National's preview of *The Girl in the Limousine*. Without the usual advance rave, Semon was eager to find a photogenic female foil. On July 17, 1924, more than a dozen shortlisted candidates flocked to the F.B.O. Studios on 780 Gower Street where Semon had his office. He selected Dorothy Dwan, a petite young actress of big soulful blue eyes and red-gold hair. Even with his new lead, Semon said goodbye to his former type of

Larry and Dorothy in Chadwick-Educational's two-reeler *Kid Speed*, 1924 (author's collection).

woman, as before he tended to pick voluptuous, dark-haired, dark-eyed beauties. Prior to the screen test, Semon had already spotted Dorothy's photo in a magazine or casting catalog and invited her to take part in the screen test. Dorothy's mother, Nancy Smith, was used to campaigning for her daughter. When she knew that a certain director was preparing to start a movie she compiled photos of Dorothy showing her in the costumes of the period to be filmed and warranting that she photographed a brunette with bluewater eyes. With another tailormade set of photos she approached Semon and succeeded in inducing him to select her daughter.[15] Dorothy and Semon had met before while Dorothy was working on Vitagraph's *The Silent Vow* (1922), her first big picture, but they were just introduced. Nancy became one of the first actors' agents in Hollywood and would later rise to the heights of being president of the WASPS (Women's Association of Screen Publicists), whereas Dorothy evolved as the pet of fan magazines.

Dorothy's life began in Sedalia, Missouri, on April 26, 1906, as Dorothy Belle Ilgenfritz. Mother Nancy, once Dorothy W. Wallace, was a descendant of Scottish patriot Sir William Wallace. Dorothy's father, Melvin Ilgenfritz, was said to be a descendant of Thomas McKean, one of the signers of the Declaration of Independence. When Nancy was the youngest teacher in Independence, she eloped with Melvin, son of the Ilgenfritz Hardware Company. Theirs was an unfortunate marriage which resulted in a serious on-and-off relationship. For some time, Nancy and Dorothy remained in Sedalia with Dorothy turning heads at a young age and winning a local beauty contest. In between, Nancy resorted to California where Melvin followed her to attempt a reconciliation. A note was given by Melvin contending it was to relieve him for some time of all support of his wife and child. He never had the money. Finally, the couple obtained a divorce in about 1915.[16] Nancy remarried, this time to young Lieutenant Colonel George Hughes Smith in El Paso, Texas, who adopted Dorothy. When he retired, the family went to live in Philadelphia, where socialite Dorothy received her education at Miss Hill's, a fashionable girls' school. However, Smith returned to the army during the World War. Contrary to various sources, obviously fueled by Dorothy and Nancy themselves, he did not die a heroic aviator in the war in France, but returned home sick. In an attempt to help

Larry Semon's new discovery and future wife Dorothy Dwan, studio portrait ca. 1924 (author's collection).

him recuperate, the Smith family once lived in the Pocono Mountains of Pennsylvania. In 1922, Smith succumbed to pneumonia,[17] leaving Nancy so much money that she would never suffer any financial struggle.

Dorothy nursed several professional interests. One was to be a church organist if not a critically acclaimed musician. It made her practice every day on the pipe organ of the First Science Church in Philadelphia. The organ training got in her way when she had to take up jazz for a picture, but was unable to catch its swing. An even greater ambition was to conquer the legitimate stage. Nancy did not think the stage advisable when her daughter had just left school so they came west and tried pictures instead.[18] Nancy had an old friend who was affiliated with Universal Pictures. She could convince him to write a letter of reference to a Universal official. Armed with the letter, they piloted towards Los Angeles. Extra work in the movies was almost thrust upon Dorothy whereas another source suggests that with her first paycheck of $5 she was told she would never be a success because she did not film well.[19] But having tried pictures just for the novel experience, Dorothy lost interest in her career as a musician and was not eager to go back home either.

Since "Smith" as a surname may not have looked that appealing on a marquee, Dorothy decided in favor of a more musical moniker. Yet it was not to be too theatrical either. *Dorothy Vernon of Haddon Hall* was running at the time and someone suggested it, but it was ruled out as being too obvious. In the end, Dorothy assumed the name "Dwan" as she admired director Allan Dwan.

Playing extra bits at Universal did not seem to be leading anywhere, so mother and daughter focused on the other studios. One day, King Vidor held an impromptu beauty contest, with Dorothy chosen to be one of the young ingénues in *Wine of Youth* (1924). As it seems the fate of so many people who started in film, Dorothy's scenes were deleted except for one: She was carrying on a flirtation with a handsome young man, while her face was hidden behind a cushion. Only a pair of well-shaped legs was to be seen. Nevertheless Vidor helped Dorothy out of obscurity as he had the young beauties of his impromptu contest photographed and printed in a fan magazine. Semon, as mother Smith claimed, chanced upon this photo and considered Dorothy for a possible lead.[20] What this article kept quiet about was that Dorothy had already done some more notable work, such as in *Shadows of Paris* (1924) with Pola Negri and in Cecil B. DeMille's *Triumph* (1924). When she met Semon, she was involved with a James Cruze picture, at the time in production at Lasky's. Semon declared that he stood ready to give Dorothy every opportunity to develop her talent in comedy leads. He gave the contracting of his new beauty a romantic twist in that he claimed he had already met her at a masquerade party. Semon said that even with the masks on, he knew he loved the girl.[21] In fact, only three weeks after signing Dorothy for *Her Boy Friend*, in early August 1924, mother Smith, now Semon's press agent, announced the engagement of Semon and her daughter. Mrs. Smith, once bitten herself, first had to dispel her objections as she thought her daughter too young. Marriage was to follow the completion of Larry and Dorothy's first joint feature-length film, *The Wizard of Oz* (1925).

Larry and Dorothy were frequently seen dancing at the Coconut Grove, Dorothy looking splendid in white gowns. A little gossip was seeping through when the papers wrote that incidentally, more than one year before, Larry and Lucille Carlisle had been doing the same. Semon was earnestly considering casting Dorothy's lot with his for life. He tried three or four times to propose to her but did not have the nerve. Finally when he reached New York he asked for her hand via telephone and her answer was to take the train that next day to follow him into the metropole.[22] Dorothy however recalled that Larry proposed between forkfuls of dinner one night at the Coconut Grove: "I was so surprised I nearly choked on my salad, but I said yes. But I told him he would have to be pretty romantic the rest of his life to make up for it."[23]

In response, Dorothy had a little onyx ring made, just like the one Lucille had once given to Larry—his being only a few sizes larger. Coincidentally, it had been Larry's hands that first attracted Dorothy. She used to watch them instead of listening to him when he was directing her picture and believed that she could tell all about him by the way he used his hands. On the occasion, Semon's old mates remembered how unhappy he was in a former love affair right in the middle of his contract with Vitagraph and how faithful he had been. They were happy for him and thought he deserved a lot of bliss.

In the middle of August 1924, a supper party was given by Semon at the Coconut Grove in honor of Dorothy. The head of the menus read: "Eat, Drink, and Be Merry— It Won't Be Your Wedding." Along with some rare jewels, Semon handed his fiancée a large block of stock in his recently founded Larry Semon Productions as a betrothal gift, proving that even if head over heels he was a "sensible lover."[24] The paparazzi had already spotted that each course of the supper was sweetened by a kiss bestowed by Semon on his fiancée, a proceeding he fondly imagined was sub rosa.

Contemporary press articles never forgot to mention that 36-year-old mother Nancy Smith just looked a few years her daughter's senior and could easily pass as her sister. While Dorothy was always good for a remarkable scale of expressions, her mother constantly drew upon a serious face, often a tilted head. To fuel Nancy Smith's attractiveness, Vitagraph veteran Betty Blythe, also present at the Coconut Grove, but with a different party, was said to have been completely fooled by her appearance. Semon was already seated at the table before his guests were served, holding the hand of fiancée Dorothy on one side and that of his future mother-in-law on the other. Betty, passing by, laughingly called out to Semon that she did not see how he got away with holding two girls' hands at the same time. Then she was introduced and made a blushing apology. This anecdote gives a piquant touch considering that Betty Blythe embodied the epitome of liberalness, at least on celluloid. She was one of the first actresses to appear nude before the camera.

One day, Dorothy took her mother to Yellowstone National Park to film scenes of Tom Mix's thriller *The Canyon of Light* (1926). They were seated together in an automobile when a gang of Day Scout hikers arrived at the location. They had come to see broncho buster Mix in action. When they spied the two women, the captain of the gang gave them the once over. Then he turned to his sergeant, pointed to Dorothy Dwan and announced: "She's Miss Dwan. I saw her in *Spuds*. She's Tom's leadin' lady." "Naw," replied the sergeant. "You're all wrong, kid. Tom always picks the prettiest ones for leadin' ladies," and pointing to mother Nancy he clinched the argument, "That's Dorothy Dwan!"[25]

Dorothy must have felt what was to come when Semon, encouraged by the success of his Educational shorts, turned to a project he had been craving for so long, his slapstick screen version of *The Wizard of Oz*. Dorothy remembered, "[Larry and I.E. Chadwick] lost their shirts because they didn't know what in the hell they were doing!"[26] Yet spirits were still high. On January 22, 1925, Larry and Dorothy were married. The ceremony was squeezed in between Semon's early afternoon and evening appearances. Only the day before, he had obtained a marriage license and found a pastor who would unite them in short order. In the late afternoon, the Reverend Dr. Oliver Barnhill performed the ceremony at the Fordham Manor Reformed Church in the Bronx in the presence of a few friends. Although the ceremony was a simple one, Dorothy's sophisticated garment compensated for every absence of glamor. At the church, she was clad in a mustard-colored velvet frock trimmed with brown chenille, gold embroidery and a gold-laced hat. Later she wore a gown of white and silver and an accessory white shawl painted with bright colors. She was escorted by her mother, who had come with her by train from California for the wedding. Earle Hammons, president of Educational, acted as best man. Semon's stage performance on his wedding day was attended and maybe even roasted by 200 delegates from the Friars Club with many motion picture people and fans present. For his evening performance, Dorothy also appeared on the stage and was introduced by her husband. Their dressing room was packed with hothouse roses and the exits were crowded with folks waiting to see Hollywood's latest honeymooners. The newlyweds asked at which door the most people had assembled and that was the one they chose as an exit. Semon was eager to give everybody a close-up of his bride and Dorothy wanted to let as many people as possible see her husband. The couple spent their honeymoon in the city and remained there for ten days. In an interview on his wedding day, Semon still spoke of a $3 million contract and told journalists that on its expiration he would quit acting and produce and direct pictures starring his wife. Acting, he said, was really a woman's business, not a man's.[27]

During his wedding week, Semon was doubling the two Brooklyn houses, Bushwick and E.F. Albee. Semon's arrangement was considered daring by bookers. The E.F. Albee was expected to attract vaudeville patrons from all over Brooklyn, the balance of that season on its unusual magnificence. The Bushwick and Orpheum, both Keith-booked Brooklyn houses, would have to fight to retain their usual business for a time at least so the Semon playing of the new house and the Bushwick was not figured to aid the latter houses particularly.[28] The previous week, he had appeared at the Palace Theater. His appearances proved a huge success. Above all, the press raved about his well-modulated recitation of Robert W. Service's ballad "The Shooting of Dan McGrew" that was also circulating as a film version by the Sawyer-Lubin company for Metro. It tells of the dramatic hate between two men, an actual happening in the days of the Yukon gold rush. On January 9, 1925, Semon played at Keith's Riverside for one night only. The bookers of vaudeville convened to look Semon over and were startled at the warmth of his reception when he was announced. They knew the applause could not have been planted. There had been no advance billing and nothing said; Semon was going on cold. He told a few gags and made his Riverside stint look like a personal appearance. After the show he asked $2,500 for one week or $4,000 to double in two houses. Semon had been offered $3,500 by the Loew Circuit for one week at the State, New York, but declined. Of his Palace appearance a reporter wrote:

> Larry wound up the turn with a neat speech in which he thanked his audience for their "kindness to me." It's the first time "kindness to me" ever has been heard on a vaudeville stage, in a

speech or for any other reason. And pictures had to do that, too! Some of the speech-making gang believing it suffices to say "Thanks, folks, I would like to do some more but the show is too long," maybe should go to Hollywood for a while. While the Semon act isn't weighty, Semon stands that off himself. Through shifting his line of material it causes what ordinarily would sound impossible, make good for him. The Palace Monday night decidedly liked this comedian.[29]

A critical view of Semon's performance was not long in coming: Journalist Aloysius M. rephrased the general wish that so many film actors and actresses please stay away from the spoken stage and spare audiences their personal appearances because they were just shattering illusions. Semon could not sing any more than shabby-voiced Ed Wynn or constantly out-of-tune Ganna Walska. He was accused of being unable to balance out this shortcoming as he did not offer an aesthetic treat as a glimpse of Gloria Swanson.[30]

Now that Larry and Dorothy were married, papers were scattered with good little wifey articles about Dorothy and testimonials of perfect nuptial bliss of a couple that "proved quite the contrast to each other."[31] In one, the newlyweds were spending a hilarious time redecorating their home on Vine Street, in another they were trying out their new DeForest Radiophone receiving set. One leitmotif within the happy couple framework was parties, with excellent bridge player Semon always letting his guests win. While Dorothy insisted that upon their marriage only a simple platinum ring with their initials was crafted free from ornaments, Larry purchased a Studebaker Standard-Six Coupe. Only a year later, upon their first wedding anniversary, Dorothy let that virtue of modesty drop, went into conference with her husband and the result was another wedding ring set with thirty-two diamonds for wear on dress occasions. Dorothy's eccentricity was that she would not go to bed at night without a glass of water by her bed. She seldom drank it, but declared she could not go to sleep unless it was there. At an early stage of their marriage, an image was shaped that presented Dorothy as a rebel to the public. Together with Dorothy Sebastian she ushered a score of bathing beauties that insisted on wearing one-piece bathing suits. Along with the season's smartest vogue of white sailor pants, the bathing suits were banned by the Venice police with help from religious organizations. Only one exception seemed acceptable: That the beach belles wore the two pieces in combination, in other words a bathing suit under their balloon pants. Any counteraction was evaluated as immodest, indecent and immoral.

> I've got just as much right to be footloose and wear white pants on the beach to keep the sunburn off my legs as these old codgers have. The old codgers' idea of a good time would be holding a parade of buxom-waisted matrons wearing old-fashioned corsets and cotton stockings. Before you know it, a bunch of these self-elected censors will be saying what style of chemise we should wear. They'd very probably advocate canvas teddy bears.[32]

Dorothy did not get far with her protest. In June 1928 she had to stay away from film work. She was confined to her bed from too much sunburn in Catalina and was bandaged in linseed oil, unable to walk.[33]

Larry and Dorothy loved to have guests and entertain them. Once director Robert Leonard visited them. He was earnestly discussing art and pictures after dinner in their dimly lit living room and he sat right down on a dozen phonograph records that Dorothy had left on the sofa. The records all smashed. Semon determined that it really was not Leonard's fault, but poor Leonard was horribly embarrassed. He arose hastily, sat down again on the other end of the sofa and pop-smash went another dozen records that had been left on that end.[34]

In another story, Dorothy and Larry were visiting Semon's manager, director and actor Earl Montgomery, whose mail was generally addressed to Hollywood, but who had for the next five days all parcels and personal mail redirected to the Orange County Jail. His imprisonment was an unfortunate outcome of the newlyweds' infatuation. Dorothy tarried at Balboa taking pictures. Semon remained in Hollywood shooting the final scenes for *The Cloudhopper*. One night, Dorothy called and told him that she would have to stay overnight in Balboa and asked him to come down to the place. Larry, exhausted from a long day's work, asked Montgomery to drive him. After leaving Santa Ana, they chose the wrong road and headed for Laguna. Finding out their mistake, Montgomery and Semon had just turned around on the San Diego highway and were dashing towards Balboa when the police sirens blew and state motorcycle Officer Yoder singled them out. Semon tried to appease him with the words: "I'm Larry Semon, the comedian," as he jumped from his automobile. "You are," replied Yoder coolly. "Well, you make me laugh."[35] He wrote out a ticket alleging that Semon was travelling at more than 53 miles an hour and handed it to Montgomery.

"Chauffeur or no chauffeur, five days in the county jail," Justice Morrison decided.[36] For Montgomery the sentence was a sad affair and even indignant because newspapers identified Montgomery as Larry Semon's gentleman driver when reporting about his arrest. Montgomery was eager for the judge to know that he was not a chauffeur, but a vital member of the Larry Semon company. Since he found himself in the process of shooting a picture, he asked that he have a little time to serve this sentence and in a self-referential utterance told impatient Justice Morrison that the picture dealt with airplane races and train races. "When will the picture be finished?" he asked. "April 14, we think," Earl answered. "Then I expect you to check in at the Orange County Jail on April 15. Now, the next case."

Montgomery's advent at the prison was quite different from that of most jailbirds. He looked comparatively cheerful being accompanied by four people from Larry Semon's studio, whose arms were packed to the brim with radio sets, loudspeakers and sufficient wire for distribution in all the cells. On top, Montgomery sported a card from the sheriff of Los Angeles County testifying that he was proficient in the use of the broom and mop, in the case the jail needed spit and polishing within the next five days. Arriving early, Montgomery spent his pre-incarceration time at the jail monitoring the installation of the radio. The sheriff did not allow an aerial on the jailhouse roof, so he resorted to the First Presbyterian Church next door.

Semon had told miserable Officer Yoder who he was as he built on a former encounter with a chief of police while producing *A Pair of Kings*. That constable thought two speeding autos were carrying a masked bandit gang in a nerve-wracking chase. He took up pursuit, overtook the party and forced them to halt, only to find that the two cars contained the comedian and hard-boiled film sailors wearing bandanas across their faces. They were hurrying home from a location trip to San Pedro. Semon explained that the bandanas were used to protect their faces from the biting wind. It has been reported that the officer apologized with the words, "The city's yours—come again," to which Larry Semon replied, "Come up and watch us work, the studio's yours."[37]

Should he not be talking *to* his wife, Semon was talking *about* her. He was in seventh heaven and when he was, he turned into a practical joker without sparing anyone. Ruth Tildesley recounted:

> Larry fairly shone. None of the other husbands could compete with him. Dorothy bore it like a veteran. She sat back with that perfect wifely air of "he's very clever, but I know he's forgotten how to do it."
>
> When he borrowed my much-prized Estelle Taylor Christmas handkerchief, I feel sure she suffered with me as he gave it an odd twist, calmly set fire to it and let it burn for a second or so before dipping it in his fingerbowl. The forced smile on my lips was wearing off when he suddenly flipped the handkerchief in the air and returned it—not even one smudge on its fair surface, if you'll believe me!
>
> "You look just the way I feel sometimes," smiled Dorothy, shaking her soft, fair curls. "How would you like to have a magician in the family? Just as you're in the act of powdering your nose, perhaps, off goes your puff, gaily cavorting in mid-air. How he does it is just as much of a puzzle to me now as it was the day I married him."[38]

Though not sharing her husband's fascination for conjuring, Dorothy picked up his interest in cartooning and delivered doodles of her husband's likeness on the set.

Dorothy's persona was eyed by the public and assigned a lot of labels. Mae Edington, the English novelist, termed her the perfect type of American girlhood while others accorded her a spiritual beauty. Dorothy was constantly reminded of the fact that, along with Jobyna Ralston, she was the chubby type and that she had to obligingly furnish the prevailing outline of less content. Mother Nancy immediately let fanzine readers in on her daughter's diet that consisted of her heaviest meal about midnight and only a cup of coffee in the morning.[39] And of course she had another story handy: Dorothy, determined to clean the living room herself, whirled around to preserve her shape, head swathed in white bandana, sleeves rolled high. Promptly Semon's prop boy Don, who had called in to get Semon his goggles, mistook her for some new maid and fell in love with her.[40] Another boy, who had a crush on Dorothy, was Syd Cassyd: Semon signaled him one day to bring Dorothy a glass of water on the set. He recalled being mesmerized when he saw her.

Despite Semon's love for Dorothy, he was quoted as having said that there was nothing more attractive than a woman of forty, with her mind alert, experience and poise that a girl could not touch.[41] Semon alluded to Nancy Smith, whom he adored. Smith had always acted as Dorothy's manager and publicist. After Larry and Dorothy's marriage, she handled his production publicity as well taking over from Milton Howe. When Semon signed Dorothy, Nancy did publicity work free of charge for him, regarding this as valuable experience. Soon after, she was contracted as Semon's publicity manager, and clients began to arrive in increasing number; writer Gertrude Orr and actresses Margaret Livingston, Vera Reynolds, and Elinor Faire were among the first. She rented a little office and proved so successful that the place was to become a suite. When everyone else was weeping depression, Nancy Smith could tell of a 32 percent increase for 1930, and she employed a staff to aid in the work.[42] Smith had been belittled as one of those movie mothers who were hanging around on sets and living off their daughters, becoming pests for directors. She invested a lot of energy into dispelling this picture and defended what she endured for her daughter. Otherwise Dorothy would not have shone in the spotlight. Nancy worked like a Trojan for Dorothy, who repaid her, not in money, of which she had no need, but by giving her a job that kept her from settling down into the usual tedious routine of middle age.

Even when some mothers were not in direct reach of filmmakers, they had left their mark on their children. Semon noted that Hollywood kids were becoming more and more screen-wise since they had evidently received excellent coaching from their mothers, as he observed. When Semon was directing *Stop, Look and Listen* (1925), he used twenty-five children for some little old red schoolhouse scenes. Larry needed to get a close-up of himself with a group of children for the schoolhouse sequence; the children were supposed to rush around as he sat on the floor. The scene was rehearsed successfully, but when the cameras started grinding, Larry was completely hidden from view by two little tots who stood in front of him and took the close-up straight into the camera.[43]

Larry, Nancy and Dorothy were said to have had the strongest friendship and that the loyalty they shared with each other was one of the outstanding highlights of Hollywood home life. Semon confided to the Writer's Club in Hollywood that for years he had produced comedies about mothers-in-law, written gags on them and told jokes on them. When Dorothy and he were married, everyone kidded him about having a mother-in-law of his own. He solved the difficulty by making her his press agent so she could talk about him all she liked without hurting him. If she had not liked him, he would have gotten publicity anyway.[44]

With all the public bedlam, things turned serious when Semon's favorite project became the subject of attention: *The Wizard of Oz* with Semon as the Toymaker and the Scarecrow, Oliver Hardy as the Tin Woodman and Dorothy as Little Dorothy. Over $300,000 was poured into the production. Chadwick boasted that it had taken them six months to film and since its first announcement, streams of letters and inquiries had been flowing into their offices.[45] Plans were made to roadshow the movie with a New York legitimate theater for its Broadway presentation. Chadwick executives wanted to give it a Broadway showing at one of the big houses with a special presentation and assuring it an indefinite engagement. There were also contemplations of a stage version in New York in late winter of 1924. Semon played the Scarecrow after Fred Stone turned it down for reasons of age; he could no longer dance limberly enough to suggest a Scarecrow's bonelessness. The new stage production was to coincide with the film's world premiere scheduled for February 7, 1925, at the Forum Theater in Los Angeles.

Previously, on February 3, the National Film Corporation threatened to tie up the proposed countryside premiere of the production. William LaPlante, president of the National Film Corporation, told the management of the Forum Theater that in the case of any public exhibition on February 7 of the Oz picture, his concern would institute injunction proceedings and damage action against the theater. The problem was that National Film Corporation had produced *The Wizard of Oz* a decade ago with "Smiling Billy" Parsons as its star and claimed that they had never disposed of either the American or foreign rights. Chadwick Pictures then asked the court for an injunction in order to stop LaPlante from interfering with the premiere, and they succeeded. On February 7, 1925, *The Wizard of Oz* opened at the Forum Theater. The first five days at that theater brought more money into the box office than had been received in any other week in the history of the house. It was the first attraction to remain at the Forum for more than one week. At the completion of its third week, although the business seemed to warrant

Larry Semon in *The Wizard of Oz*, a somewhat spicy adventure, Chadwick Pictures Corporation, 1925 (author's collection).

a further extension of the engagement, it was necessary to withdraw the film due to the several other local bookings that had been arranged.[46]

Meanwhile, LaPlante with his action indicated that there was going to be a lot of court action. Chadwick was going to fight it through and finally did. They went ahead with their tremendous releasing campaign among state rights' buyers and "road showmen" including merchandising and lavish premieres in most major cities. However the film was not put into general release until the summer of 1925,[47] and there was never a theater production with Larry Semon. The hold-up meant terrible losses for Semon and Chadwick, aggravated by the fact that despite its promotion, box office receipts were lukewarm, not to mention tepid reviews. Dorothy also took part in advertising *The Wizard of Oz*. She was under contract with the Los Angeles County exhibit management and represented the city at the Missouri State Fair in her home town of Sedalia. The local theater had obtained the film for the first two days of Fair week and hired Dorothy for personal appearances, during which she signed thousands of autographs.[48]

That LaPlante was so ticked off by a pending copyright violation is surprising because Semon's *The Wizard of Oz* had little to do with the original story even though L. Frank Baum's son was one of its scenario writers. Its production caused Semon's satiation with the charm of fairy legends and he tended to henceforth reject other works of that genre with the exception of Brenon's *Peter Pan* (1924), which by the way clung closely to the original story. In *Oz*, Semon returned to his old slapstick routine with some drama thrown in. Disillusioned and disappointed fan letters were headlined "Mr. Semon, How Could You?"[49] and reproached him and his producers for desecrating Baum's legacy by butchering a well-loved plot. They were complaining about the gooey messes and atrocious and aged slang that had taken its place. Semon owed an apology to all those who had read the Oz books. Professional critics recommended the film for children's use only. At least for some critics Semon did a bit of Harold Lloyd pathos fairly well when giving Dorothy a lollipop and he played the old man character of the puppeteer to perfection. G. Howe Black was highlighted for his true comedy sense and Mary Carr, the screen's greatest mother, developed her small part to the max.⁵⁰ But this did not suffice. Grace Kingsley, attempting to save Semon from losing face in the business, wrote:

> Larry Semon is not going to confine his art to two-reelers anymore. Having made a howling success of *The Wizard of Oz*, he feels heartened-up to step permanently into the feature-length comedy. The comedian is receiving all sorts of substantial encouragement in his decision to quit the short-reel subject for good. Many offers are reaching him by various companies. One of these, it is understood, is from Paramount, now releasing the Harold Lloyd, Douglas MacLean and other comedies. He has several other important offers as well.⁵¹

In *Oz*, the vases, pots and statuettes which audiences see broken over the actors' heads were made of plaster and were quite brittle. It was an indoor sport at the comedy studios to "crown" somebody with a breakaway of this kind, after which that somebody usually appeared to go cross-eyed and then slowly drop to the floor. To do it when the other fellow was not expecting it—sneaking up behind him and crowning him—was the big object. One day Semon had a huge vase to crash over the villain's head. He was to throw it from a balcony when the villain tried to steal the girl. The boys in Semon's crew thought it would be a laugh to get him under the balcony and tip the vase over him. A small detail on the breakaway vase needed attention, so he substituted the heavy original for one scene. This was what Semon got on the head as a specimen of studio wit. He awoke in a hospital when he came to.⁵²

During the early part of the picture's production, Larry was annoyed that he had to slow down because Hardy with his excess weight could not keep pace with him. One can readily imagine Semon's surprise when the slow, heavy Hardy suddenly went by him like a shot out of a cannon, performing the most incredible leaps and gymnastic gyrations imaginable. This time the situation was reversed; Semon could not keep up with Hardy. Even when the director and cameraman had called "cut," Hardy was continuing with his mad race. Finally he slowed down and, once he had caught his breath, explained that an active bumblebee had injected itself inside of his tin wardrobe and had become very busy. Larry was shortly thereafter discovered trying to corral several bees in a bottle to be kept for future contingencies when he might want to speed up the supporting cast.⁵³

As early as March 1, 1925, papers announced Dorothy's farewell bid to comedies, as she was moving on to playing opposite George Walsh. For romantic reasons, one more two-reeler was planned with Semon, coming to life as *The Cloudhopper* (1925). Soon, Semon signed with British Exhibitors' Films for the distribution of his pictures in England. A possible delayed further honeymoon to London in summer 1925 was hoped for and a promise made by Semon to produce a film in Great Britain. He also considered travelling to Italy as its citizens had taken their Ridolini so much to their heart that he had a bigger following there than Chaplin.⁵⁴

The Perfect Clown (1925), the last starring picture for Chadwick, was completed July 17, 1925, but according to other sources filmed from mid–July to mid–August, overlapping with Semon's new contract. Semon did not take the director's role, but left it to Fred Newmeyer, a longtime associate of Harold Lloyd. In *The Perfect Clown* Larry is entrusted with a bag containing $10,000 which he is to deliver to a bank. After a series of mishaps and Larry's safe arrival, the bag is found to be empty, his employer having given him the wrong one. According to the *Chicago Daily Tribune*, "Mr. Semon is a hard worker, but he IS NOT FUNNY."⁵⁵

Larry on the occasion of his morning workout in Chadwick's *The Perfect Clown*, 1925 (author's collection).

Semon's next feature length film was *Stop, Look and Listen* (1926). After Chadwick's grave problems, Semon saw his own bankruptcy looming. Several production companies had rented out space or equipment to Larry Semon. He was unable to pay their bills so a joint action against Semon was advocated. Publicity representative Regine Crowe had already taken legal action. She alleged she was employed by Semon for eight weeks in the latter part of 1924 at a weekly $35. Her task was to boost Semon's entrance into vaudeville, but he did not reimburse her for her work and expenses. As a result, Semon had a judgment for $330 placed against him when he failed to defend the lawsuit in the Fifth District Municipal Court. Justice Davies also permitted an attachment to be filed against Semon when placing a bond for double the amount of the judgment with the court.[56]

Facing a financial breakdown, Semon turned out film after film. Another feature-length one, *My Best Girl* was crammed into the schedule in spring 1925 without advance advertising. Dorothy termed the vehicle a special present from Larry for her. He had long promised to feature her as a star, but over the months completely forgot about it and only Dorothy's gentle prodding made him act. The money was simply not there. Semon restricted his involvement to directing and to collaborating on the scenario with his wife, while Joseph Swickard accepted the male lead. The picture was about a chorus girl and it fell into oblivion before it ever received any public attention. It is doubtful whether it ever premiered at all, yet was listed underneath a promotional photo for Dorothy in the papers.

Rumors were flying that Semon would direct Mabel Normand in Chadwick's *Sunshine of Paradise Alley* and other announcements spread the word that he was busy assembling a cast for *The Count of Luxembourg*, his next full-length feature comedy for Chadwick. The production was intended to be even more elaborate than *The Wizard of Oz*, with many lavish sets and a cast of well-known players in support. But the Blizzard of Oz had blown away Chadwick's financial resources and Semon had to find a new contract. Nevertheless, Chadwick went on searching for a comedian to replace Semon.[57]

· 9 ·

The Perfect Frown

Semon was entering a phase in his career during which he would be handed around a lot. For a start, he was to direct himself in a series of eight feature comedies of at least five reels to be made during the next two years for Pathé. The cost of the pictures was $100,000, not much, considering that Semon's Vitagraph two-reelers used to devour at least the same sum. Semon would be getting a percentage on distribution besides a salary of around $2,500 a week.[1]

The new Semon contract was signed in late July 1925 between the Pathé Exchange and Larry Semon Productions, Semon's new producing company. It was organized in Hollywood entirely by Los Angeles capital, with quite a number of big shots in high positions. Its president, principal backer and sponsor was Captain Harry M. Rubey, who also presided over the Manufacturers and Wholesalers Credit Corporation of Los Angeles; John H. Adams, former president of the Mid-West Theater Operators, Inc., was Semon's business manager; local attorney Clyde Harms, general counsel. Larry Semon Productions—aka Larry Semon Studios—was also trying to develop talents and had Broadway dancer and comedian Kitty Kelly under contract; she excelled in Charleston contests.[2] Semon was thought to enrich Pathé's already ambitious program of "quality feature attractions," which included Harold Lloyd's *The Freshman* (1925). A Larry Semon series was believed to prove positive box-office productions. Later it was even intended that Semon take Lloyd's place when the latter left Pathé for Paramount.

The first comedy for the new corporation was a picturization of the Broadway musical comedy success *Stop, Look and Listen*. Pathé asked Semon to do something entirely different from anything he had yet attempted. Semon decided to appear in a straight acting role that would be a relief from playing the clown. The film did not make critics roar and completely failed at the box-office. It must have hurt Semon that the *Miami Herald* called *Stop, Look and Listen* a "typical Larry Semon vehicle."[3] In fact, the film's showdown is reminiscent of the debris that resulted in the final scene of *The Show*. An inexpensive train engine was employed for a chase and did not survive the production process.

Semon's films meant a financial downfall for Pathé and to himself. *Stop, Look and Listen* used to rank as a prize comedy story that evaded the grasp of motion picture producers for a number of years. The play was considered such good story material for a feature comedy that it had been sought as a vehicle for very big film comedy stars. Finally

9. The Perfect Frown 153

Bull Montana trying Dorothy Dwan's shoe in a publicity shot for *Stop, Look and Listen*, Larry Semon Productions/Pathé, 1926 (author's collection).

Semon got hold of it after several months of negotiation and paid a top sum for the screen rights.[4]

Stop, Look and Listen is a lost film. That no print of the film is known to be extant is especially deplorable as it seems to be a missing link in the evolution of the later Larry Semon.

After completion, Dorothy and Larry went to New York for the purpose of buying another Broadway success to adapt to the screen. Having scrutinized twenty-nine shows in thirty days, Semon was disappointed at his options. Most plays lacked the comedy elements that would allow for a screen transfer, but were replete with sex themes, and language that was not "clean humor":

> Apparently, the New York playgoer has become so blasé that it requires something of this nature to arouse him out of his mental lethargy. Unless a play has a few such mental shocks, it is seemingly destined to "flop."
>
> The condition is anything but healthy. The modern trend is retrogressive. My friends cannot accuse me of being a purist, but some of the productions left a positive bad taste. Perhaps I am old-fashioned, but I have not yet "progressed" to the point where I can enjoy the obscenity and profanity that dominate the New York stage today. If the box-office receipts are a criterion, it would seem that the producer is taking a risk if his play is not risque.[5]

The few shows appropriate for comedy films would shake Semon down for $40,000 to $100,000 for the title alone. He decided to keep his habit of writing his story around the title already famous and delivered *Spuds*, the film to break his bank. Eugene V. Brewster noted:

> I ran across my old friend Larry Semon the other day and he took me over to the F.B.O. studio, where he is doing a five-reel comedy called *Spuds*. Years ago I thought that Larry would by now be giving Lloyd, Chaplin and Keaton a hard run for first place, but he seemed to have gotten a bad break in the last few years and did not progress as he should. I am, however, still betting on him and hope yet to see him quite at the top among the first comedians of the screen. He showed me the first reel of *Spuds* and it is as good as anything I have seen by any of the comedians of the screen. If the other four reels are as good as the first, he has a sure winner, but—alas!—he says that they won't give him enough money to finish the picture properly. And that's the way things go. His backers must be blind![6]

Since his sponsors had turned away, Semon decided to fall back on his own capital and like a gambler he invested heavily in *Spuds*. The original story, written by John A. Moroso for *Everybody's Magazine*, had been purchased by Pathé. The basic plot bore a

Spuds (Larry Semon Productions/Pathé, 1927) was the film that brought on Larry Semon's bankruptcy. Hazel Howell as Bertha from Berlin, Larry Semon as Spuds and Dorothy Dwan as Madelon are shown in a hand-colored American lobby card (author's collection).

striking resemblance to Semon's one-reeler *Somewhere in Any Place* (1917) with Hughie Mack and Jimmy Aubrey in the leads. Semon played a potato-peeling boob private who gets mixed up in an enemy camp and through no brilliance of his own is the means of retrieving a stolen pay car just in time to prevent the execution of his superior. The film did not find many followers and the reviews did not meet Semon's expectations, to put it mildly. He was accused of having tried starring in a "travesty on war pictures,"[7] leaving nobody surprised that he wanted to become a director. The story, it was said, plodded along at a slow pace, while the whole production was an ill-assorted array of the comedian's talents and sat between two stools, leaving critics wondering whether it was comedy or drama.

Semon had given his last dime for the film. The only thing that helped lower production costs was a rainstorm that had conveniently hit Los Angeles. It supplied the necessary mud for the trenches on the F.B.O. lot and enhanced a scene with a huge tank wallowing most realistically across the front. A monkey was one the most expensive stars of the cast because he held up production several times. The monkey, clever and vivacious, earned $25 a day; at least his Italian master did. As many representatives of his species, the monkey was afraid of revolvers. One day he was terribly agitated for no known cause. Semon and the monkey's master could not get him to do anything whatsoever. At last the master presumed that there had to be a revolver somewhere and sure enough, on looking around, they found the weapon almost hidden among papers on a desk in a distant corner. The monkey had spied it and refused to work until it was removed. He was fastened to the end of a long, thin piece of black silken cord so that he could not get away. In a previous scene he had escaped and for hours spent a jolly time high in the rafters. Finally he left the building and lost himself several blocks away, much to the distress of his master. The crew combed the neighborhood for their little simian star. After an endless search it was Semon himself to rescue the monkey in the backyard of a bungalow.

A sequence in which Larry is hiding behind a couch near a steam-pipe, when the monkey comes in and turns on the steam, created another significant hold-up during filming. For two hours the monkey's master kept training his little fellow to sneak in and unscrew the handle of the radiator, but no steam was used during these rehearsals because it would frighten the animal. As the trainer limited himself to making the motions of turning the handle, the monkey would look at him and imitate the movement, constantly cheeping his willingness to do the best he could. When the monkey had been sufficiently rehearsed, the lights were turned on with the camera grinding while he turned the radiator handle. Clouds of something that looked like steam emerged. This scared the monkey off and again he disappeared from the set. Fortunately the scene was not spoiled. Semon and his cameraman wanted a retake, but for the life of them, they could not get the monkey to go near the radiator again, because hissing steam meant danger to him. The next day, Semon and his crew were trying it again and coaxed the animal into doing the stunt successfully.[8]

The shooting of *Spuds* revealed to Semon that Dorothy Dwan had an unusual gift for pantomime, making up for the often uttered criticism that she was hardly ever allowed to be more than eye candy: "I never realized how much of it she has, until we made *Spuds*. And then, in the scene where she hid in a barrel and signaled to me from behind the soldiers' backs, I suddenly became aware of the fact that she was doing some perfect miming. Instead of just a pretty ornament for my comedy, I found I had an actress in the company."[9] Semon was a great counterpart in this film, especially when he pantomimed to Dorothy that Kewpie Morgan would cut his throat if she exposed his hiding spot to him.

With *Spuds*, Semon could not be blamed for having made a bad picture, quite the contrary. The film was a premium production, a carefully filmed movie. Yet Semon's screen persona did not click with contemporary audiences. Whether the film was comedy or drama was not at issue. The comedy elements were a means to find comic relief in a hapless war situation despite some of them coming across as unmotivated. In one scene Larry makes his broom move without touching it. As the print available was a restoration after the film had been considered lost for decades, supporting and explicatory scenes might still be missing. Some gags of animated paintings were significantly enhanced replications of *The Sportsman*. Semon also took a peek into the past of his cartoon days, with an homage to Chaplin whose likeness he draws and animates for Madelon Dorothy. The genesis of the Charlie cartoon was filmed without displaying that Semon did it. The camera view is reduced to the sheet of paper, a pen and some artist's hands which are recognizable as Semon's with his short fingernails and his onyx ring. Yet the scene produced funny responses. When Semon was sitting in a neighborhood theater of Los Angeles noting the reaction of the audience to his five-reel comedy, a cynical fan questioned, "Wonder who he got to draw for him?"[10] Semon reportedly got hot under the collar. He had received more proof that his presence and favor among famous people was waning dramatically.

Norman Taurog watched Semon's downhill path from a distance.

> [Semon] wanted to do bigger, better and more important things. But do not try the impossible with your eyes closed. The success blinded him, reduced him worse than me. How can you think of doing Romeo and Juliet, Francesca da Rimini and just imagine…. Macbeth and gangster movies, in film, always with a floured face, filling the scripts with the same ridiculous cataclysms, with the same pies in the face and all those absurd falls? Of course, it was a fiasco after another. He wanted to be the first, the greatest comedian of all time. He thought: If I make the audience laugh for an hour and a half instead of just twenty minutes like the others, I am the king.[11]

Semon, on the other hand, was once quoted by Bob Monkhouse in his *Mad Movies* series as seeing himself as the second best comedian. Asking him who would then be the best, Semon answered that the others were still fighting on it.

In order to help recoup her husband's losses, Dorothy had to accept any possible film offers as a freelancer. She found them in westerns with one of Hollywood's foremost stars, Tom Mix. In late 1925, the film business was beginning to take its toll on her. Upon her return from New York with Larry, she suffered a nervous breakdown, the ultimate reason being that she had driven a car over a cliff and resorted to Soboba Hot Springs to recover.[12]

Pathé's contract called for a "special mission" on Semon's part. He was not only to direct and produce, but also develop comedy directors and later to sign some of the biggest New York comedians for the screen. To put it bluntly, studios did not believe any more in Semon as a box-office star and chose to shift him to a steady place behind the camera. Semon diluted any rumors about his star sinking and eagerly explained that the motion picture industry was desperately looking for good comedy directors and talented comedians. It would take a real comedian to direct another comedian on the screen, so who would fit more perfectly than Semon himself? For his new task of converting comedians from stage to screen, he was trying to get hold of greats such as Al Jolson, Eddie Cantor and Harry Green. Nothing came of the director-comedian project with the one exception of Robert Florey, whom Semon knew from his old Vitagraph days and would meet again as a colleague at Paramount. Semon taught him how to direct chase sequences.[13]

One player who sought Larry's advice was Lew Cody, who consulted Semon during a troubled period in his career. Semon suggested that Cody play villains with a sense of humor with the result that Cody's career took off again.

The comedian who made the greatest impact on Semon in his later career was Harry Langdon. Larry's admiration for this comedian becomes particularly clear in the opening scene of Larry's final work, *A Simple Sap* (1928), where his once-swift acting had been slowed down so much that one sees Langdon's influence. In 1925, Semon judged him a genius who was marking time, but who should have stayed with Sennett, as others were going too fast with him. Langdon still needed to learn about a lot of angles and gags which would require a couple of years' experience. But Semon knew that Langdon was destined to be a big success.[14]

It is quite impressive how many Semon projects evaporated. In June 1926, vaudevillian and prolific male impersonator Kathleen Clifford told columnist Louella Parsons that she had just agreed to play a part in *The Gob* with Semon, bringing to the screen her famous male characterization which got so much attention in the United States and in Europe. After finishing the film, Clifford and Semon would appear in a one-act stage play running in Los Angeles for three weeks then go directly to Europe for an indefinite engagement. Greatly welcomed was the idea that Clifford would do an imitation of Semon and Semon would do one of her—a sort of dual imitation stunt. Other projects that never saw the light of day and stalled during negotiations were at least two feature films for Cecil B. DeMille which Semon was to direct. He was also briefly considered as director for Mildred Davis Lloyd. On top, rumors persisted that Semon and Harold Lloyd had been negotiating that Larry would direct Lloyd's next comedy and possibly others. Since his beginning with Hal Roach, Harold wanted Semon to direct him. In May 1926, Semon took quite a detached attitude to the whole matter:

> I have talked only in a general way to Mr. Lloyd about directing him in pictures. We never reached the stage where we even talked terms or where Mr. Lloyd made any proposition to me. There is no one in the business whom I would rather direct than Harold Lloyd, for I have always been the greatest admirer of his work and of his personality, but I would like it understood that at no time has Mr. Lloyd made me a proposal that I might either accept or reject.[15]

Semon indeed took his hat off to Lloyd. To him, who judged himself a "serious bird"[16] personally and who went to the cinema not only to be entertained but also with the desire to study the technique of his fellow workers, Lloyd was a real tonic. His *Hot Water* (1924) made Semon forget technique, direction, situation and everything connected with production, but rather he laughed his head off. A few weeks later, Semon affirmed that negotiations had continued. However, he decided against a project with Lloyd. One problem was the high salary that Semon commanded, because Lloyd needed months to

A brief stint at the Mack Sennett Studio: Still from *A Dozen Socks*, 1926, with Alice Day in checked trousers and Danny O'Shea surrounded by unidentified beauties (courtesy Robert Kiss).

produce a film. For another thing, Semon was convinced that a rival comedian could hardly better himself by being directed by his competitor.

An enterprise that did see the light of day was Semon's engagement under Mack Sennett to direct Alice Day and Eddie Quillan in a new series of Pathécomedies, their first short to begin at once in the summer of 1926. Semon directed the two-reelers *Pass the Dumplings* (1927) and *The Plumber's Daughter* (1927) and worked out the script for *A Dozen Socks* (1927).[17] The latter was available for viewing and suggests that Semon bowed to the style of his new client, yet employment ended after completing the three films. At the same time, he received an offer to go on the Keith vaudeville circuit on a year contract which he turned down because then it would have overlapped with the filming of *Spuds*[18] and obviously with another commitment with the Orpheum circuit. His tour is hard to date yet it probably took place in the fall of 1926. In any case, Semon went on a tour from coast to coast which included Portland, a show town he greatly enjoyed. Nothing can be traced newspaper-wise, yet it is known that he told writer Elizabeth Lonergan much about it and that she documented the interview in her "English publications," as she called them.[19] Of the tour, one anecdote has survived: On the way east, Semon and his megaphone wielder Joe Basil had chosen the same train as Ben Turpin, who provided entertainment. Even more so when they stopped off at a wayside station at some place in Kansas to have coffee. In order to tease and startle the waitress, Turpin all of a sudden thrust his face through the window, but the girl was experienced in handling funsters and emptied a glass of water in his face. Poor Turpin drew back, complaining that he had millions laugh—to have cold water poured on him in Kansas. "No!" Semon sympathized, "she didn't even warm it first!" They nearly missed their train and had to speed. Turpin bid the waitress farewell and had to have the last word: "Next time you see my eyes on the screen I hope they haunt you."[20]

Of undetermined outcome was Semon's involvement with the Standard Pictures Corporation, founded in July 1926 and distinct from its namesake associated with William Fox. The company was a non-theatrical venture destined to specialize in high-end pageants and other educational movies to meet the demands of churches, women's clubs and schools. The president was Dr. C. Sidney Maddox, Semon came on as director-general, and George E. Bradley, once involved with First National, was their vice president. The company's own censor board assembled honoraries from colleges, universities and superior courts, who were to review all stories, approve casts and assign directors. Semon stated that they had selected their first production and hoped to start shooting within the second week of August 1926. Players such as Earl Williams and teenage Mary MacAllister had been lined up to appear in their pictures (*Salvage* was the first), believing that box-office names spelt success. The non-theatrical field was thought to have unlimited possibilities and that its surface had not been scratched. Despite their primary object to release through educational institutions, the company felt their productions were of such a standard that the theatrical field would be glad to talk business with them.[21] The first production started with a delay of a few weeks and was released on October 1, 1926. Neither *Salvage* nor other scheduled titles could be traced as having come into touch with patrons. Within a short period of time, the Standard Pictures Corporation—the way it was planned—disappeared from the scene. In 1938 another company of the same name was registered that incidentally bought the old Vitagraph studios from Warners Bros. Another Standard Pictures Corporation existed as an Indian film company well into the 1940s.

Dorothy stayed home waiting for calls. She soon developed a growth on her eye necessitating an operation and possibly jeopardizing any nice role that came along. She had been invited to play the lead in a film for Rayart, *Perils of the Coast Guard* (1926) with Cullen Landis and Jimmy Aubrey. Whether or not she accepted depended upon the eye, which was given first priority for the next four weeks, which Dorothy was to spend in a dark room.[22] Things turned out so well that she could appear in the film. Following her ocular problem, she injured herself during the filming of *The Great K and A Train Robbery* (1926) with the Tom Mix Company in Colorado, re-staging a historic train robbery. During production, misfortune was plentiful. Mix, intending to swing from the top of a speeding train to a rope high in the air, fell to the ground and hurt his feet so seriously that he needed to recuperate in Colorado Springs. Dorothy slipped down a high bank to the railroad track, spraining her ankle so badly that production was delayed awaiting her recovery.[23]

Dorothy never really made it big in motion pictures but, in order to support the Semon household, she contented herself with being a leading lady instead of striving for drama or thrilling characterizations. In 1926 she had at least nine leading roles, many of which were with Mix. Dorothy's peers said that she showed no temperament and displayed loads of skill and ambition which would guarantee her constant employment as a freelancer. She was toiling hard, a striking feature that she shared with her husband. With the assistance of Mix, Dorothy became an expert horsewoman and excellent swimmer. In *The Great K and A Train Robbery* she was required to do horseback riding in a chase for miles, and for *Perils of the Coast Guard* she needed to swim a long distance in the Pacific Ocean during late winter. When still filming with Semon, Dorothy studied to develop into a professional dancer preparing for the role of a dancing teacher in *Stop, Look and Listen*. Her performance won her lots of praise, not just because of her terpsichorean skills. Right on the evidence of her background in organ and piano playing, Dorothy had taken up studies at the Olga Steeb School in Los Angeles with the awareness that music made one impressionable to emotions. Dorothy also learned to golf because another scenario demanded it and she drove her own car and many others. For *Spuds* the press harvested Dorothy's seven-year education in French which predestined her for the role of Madelon. The close-ups called for correct pronunciation, else one familiar with French could tell it was not French being spoken.[24] However, Dorothy's overall influence on *Spuds* was not that significant. Otherwise she would have prevented Semon from using the title card "Je ne c'est pas," the faulty transcription for the homonym "Je ne sais pas" ("I don't know").

In conclusion, Dorothy surprisingly found that she had had neither hard knocks nor great struggles and laughingly said she would have been a better actress if she were to fight her way to the top. She appended the fateful words that she expected to get hers sometime and that it would be good for her.

Image-shaping continued. Papers said Dorothy had an indifference towards the future and the priceless gift of a happy disposition. In fact, it was up to Dorothy to play the adult. Semon was either on top of the world or down in the depths and needed her calm and unspoiled outlook on life to keep him from floating off on a cloud or drowning under the sea.[25] Dorothy had gotten to know a Larry Semon who had greatly changed within a couple of years. Early photographs of young director Semon show him all aglow; later pictures show his eyes had grown tired and sad.

Semon strained Dorothy's nerves by dropping cigarette stubs into dinner dishes after eating. She assigned it to thoughtlessness. He did not realize how rank the odor was from cigarettes in coffee cups. Dorothy went into their kitchen time and again to find the cook frowning or sulking over this state of affairs. In fact, Dorothy and Larry lost gems of cooks over just this habit.[26]

Spirits were kept high for the press when Secretary of Labor Davis visited the Hollywood studios, reuniting with his "old friend" Larry Semon. He said that if he were not in his responsible position, he would probably be associated with Semon and finance his pictures.[27] In the evenings, Larry and Sydney Chaplin surprised parties and topped them with sleight of hand tricks while Dorothy was trying out multi-colored mascara at the studio and sponsored net stockings of a coarse mesh in place of chiffon or silk. She introduced another new fad to Hollywood when she fastened a bus conductor's coin box to her knee, filled it with money and locked the box so that it was safe from sticky fingers.[28] For further publicity, Larry and Dorothy were stating that they were well off. They entered in the Hollywood game of collecting; Dorothy a sewing box made before the Civil war, Larry a Confederate seal smuggled out of Vicksburg during the siege. Then the couple added a brand new Packard Hupmobile Eight roadster to the Semon fleet of cars. Of course the two never failed to pose with their latest conquests for the photographers.

Another streak of bad luck hit Larry. Going to the circus that day was a very expensive proposition for both Jack Ford and Larry Semon. It might not have cost so much had they driven their own cars but, as they carpooled with Mrs. Ford and Mrs. Semon, they decided to park their cars in front of the Semon home and drive with a friend. When they returned from the circus, the rear tires had been stripped from both cars.[29] Soon after, as a kind of sinister pre–Christmas surprise, on December 23, 1926, Semon had an entire automobile stolen. Twenty-one-year-old Clifford Vanciel of Van Nuys chose Larry's Hupmobile in order to escape from an earlier misdeed. A few days later, Vanciel drove to Van Nuys and appropriated someone else's license plates and placed them on Semon's only to burglarize the San Fernando police station. Now equipped with a gun, holster and a police officer's badge, he sallied forth in search of adventure and induced two young women to ride with him. Driving through Lankershim, he was spotted by a police officer who had been searching for him and a chase begun. At a road crossing the officer forced Vanciel to stop. While being questioned the crook suddenly shifted gears, backed clear of the police car and sped off. The officer took up the chase at breakneck speed and again corralled Vanciel at the place where he had summoned him before and placed him under arrest. During the chase, Vanciel threw the gun, holster and badge out of the car. He pleaded guilty to grand larceny.[30]

Spuds was released in February 1927, some two months after Semon had secured another new contract, this time with one of the biggest, Paramount Pictures. He was booked in the triple capacity of writer, director and comedian and his first job to conceive the script for the Wallace Beery film *Taking the Air*.[31] Later this job was given over, presumably to cartoonist Paul Terry. Semon's change to Paramount was a shift in producing companies, as the Larry Semon Productions were unable to finance any further projects. West Coast executive B.P. Schulberg dolled up Semon's arrival as "a move of the greatest importance," particularly in times in which comedy was so sought-after by the public that the "value of a man of [Semon's] versatile genius is immeasurable."[32] Next to writing and directing a piece of light comedy, Larry was encouraged to don the greasepaint once more to play a few scenes as well. He might even star in a feature at a later date. The announcement refers to two pictures in which Semon had to be subordinate: Eddie Cantor's *Special Delivery* (1927) and Josef von Sternberg's *Underworld* (1927).

Special Delivery was called one of those studio mistakes. Without Cantor, who wanted to make his own story ideas come to life in a picture, it would have been a complete failure. Cantor played postman Eddie, whose strict father impresses on him that he must not return home until he had earned a fortune. Eddie's chances at success were slim, those of writer and comedian Eddie Cantor were even waning: A sum exceeding $200,000 had already been invested by Paramount when the film flopped at a preview in a Los Angeles theater. It was brought back to the studio and Semon had to replace a director by the name of Will H. Goodrich, the pseudonym for Roscoe Arbuckle.[33]

When asked for his contribution to the film's success, Semon was most hesitant and apologetic, as he had no intention to stab the struggling Arbuckle in the back. Arbuckle was trying to make a comeback as a director. He had been accused of actress Virginia Rappé's death in 1921, resulting in his fall from grace with the public. Although he was finally acquitted, his career was down the drain and he died of a heart attack in 1933.

The role Semon played during the scandal could not have been an easy one. When Arbuckle found himself in deep trouble, Semon demonstrated his support for his colleague publicly, putting his own reputation at risk and daring to be ground between two parties. Following a comic performance by Arbuckle at the Marigold, a pleased crowd had formed around him, yet creating the absurd situation of leaving him standing alone, weary from the capers and falls with which he had tried to entertain his audience. First Willie Howard strode out eagerly and shook Arbuckle's hand. Then Semon plunged through the barrier and embraced him, and many others followed.[34]

In 1927, Arbuckle signed a new vaudeville and film contract that would make him two million dollars, first directing Marion Davies in *The Red Mill*. After finishing, another director was sent for, and he gave the Arbuckle film a complete makeover. Next, Arbuckle was appointed director for Eddie Cantor on *Special Delivery*. After the preview, Paramount saw the film's only chance was to turn it over to Larry Semon for doctoring.[35]

Today, *Special Delivery* is remembered as a film directed by Roscoe Arbuckle, while Semon goes uncredited. Several contemporary newspapers confirm that it was chiefly directed by Semon. A still from the set shows Semon in his typical director's outfit, complete with baker's boy cap and gray cardigan. He stands next to fully equipped mailman Cantor, who has postpaid "Baby"—actress Tiny Doll—in his pocket. The author owns a two-sided autographed page, on one side Semon's signature; on the other Cantor's, who inscribed, "This makes me three minutes late."

Semon, in his own words, bound by his contract, was forced to take the film under his wing. They gave him eight days to fix it up. Larry had no other choice. Before long, half a million dollars would be tied up in the production and not a chance of recovering even half that amount.

The first sitting had brought it all to light. Except for one reel, *Special Delivery* had to be reshot. Semon took Cantor out in the street scene and had him deliver mail. Without any opportunity for retakes, Semon and Cantor worked their way from street corner to street corner on the set, building in the best possible laughs and gags. Every scene had to be accepted "as is." There was one sequence that never made it to the screen due to the fact that Cantor and his canine foil were cut from the same cloth. Said Semon:

> That was after the dog ran in and grabbed the "weenies." Cantor is a nervous fellow, you know. Highly excitable and almost afraid of his own shadow. I had a dog that had worked with me for years. The dog was nervous and excitable, too.
> If you treated the dog quietly and gently, all was well, but yell at him and he would get so nervous he would try to take your leg off. We started the scene, and I told the trainer to let the dog run on the set.
> We got that much and we shot the part where he grabbed the weenies. Then Cantor lost his head and decided he wouldn't give the weenies to the dog, and the pair of them tussled a couple of minutes when Cantor attempted to kick the dog to make him let go.
> Then the dog lost his head, too, and sank his teeth in Cantor's leg. It was an hour before we could restore Cantor. He ran all around the set, moaning. "He bit me! He bit me! He bit me!" The damage was not serious, but thank heaven, we did not have to shoot the scene again.[36]

Semon was a big fan of Cantor's. For a long time, he had wished to direct him and develop him as a screen comedian, but when Semon was with Pathé, things turned out different. Now that his wish came partly true, he would have fancied better conditions than a time limit of eight days for a six-reeler.

Special Delivery was not liked by the critics of the day as it remained in the shadow of Cantor's previous effort *Kid Boots* with co-star Clara Bow. With every intellectual demand put aside and minus *Kid Boots*, it is an entertaining film whose charm has grown during the past decades. Cantor's simpleton face could even go without a story. The plot develops in a running gag fashion and culminates in a Semonesque chase. Since Semon found new ways of combining chase elements, the pursuit offers another highlight. One memorable scene takes place in a Dutch snack bar. Waitress Jobyna Ralston hole-punches Eddie's coupon card more than once to attest her affection for him. Goofy Eddie drops his card, only to find that the spiked sole of another customer has left enough holes to secure Eddie free meals for the rest of his life.

When Semon was picked for *Underworld* (1927), his return to the screen was greatly heralded by the press. Semon was to play a featured comedy role, that of Slippy Lewis,

Playbill for *Underworld* (1927) featuring George Bancroft alias Bull Weed and Larry Semon appearing in a supporting role as "Slippy" Lewis (author's collection).

a gentleman crook who dresses appropriately for every crime. Accordingly, he was said to have kept track of his new picture by the number of suits he had donned since it started. He was to wear seven of them, all of extreme cut, loud pattern and distinctive appearance.[37] Josef von Sternberg had taken over the directorial role from Arthur Rossen, who had developed the script in collaboration with Ben Hecht and was soon fired by Paramount. *Underworld* was von Sternberg's last chance to prove himself in Hollywood, and the film was expected to be a complete failure. In the end, the film became one of the biggest box-office hits of 1927, enthused the critics and influenced a genre of modern gangster films that flourished in the decades to come.

Though often assigned the title of the "first gangster film," *Underworld* stood in line with Griffith's *Musketeers of Pig Alley* of 1912. In that *Underworld* was set in Chicago, the metropole which during Prohibition had hundreds of gangland killings, it was in touch with the headlines of the day. Still it was one of the first American-made films of an expressionist atmosphere, long ago created in print by scenario writer and newspaper reporter Ben Hecht.[38] The film gets audiences involved in the constant struggle between the underworld and police and among the gangsters themselves. Clive Brook as Rolls-Royce, Ricardo Cortez as crook-in-chief Bull Weed and Evelyn Brent as Weed's moll Feathers were cast for the other leads. In a last-minute decision, the Cortez part was given to George Bancroft.[39] The bulk of the footage was shot in the studio, but the scenes showing the heart of the metropolis were taken in downtown Los Angeles during rush hour. The hurrying crowds were too focused on getting home to realize they were being caught by a battery of cameras. During shooting, a practical joke was played on George Bancroft. Locked in the steel cell of a jail set he was told by director von Sternberg to fall asleep for a scene. It was late in the evening and Bancroft had toiled all day. He closed his eyes and paid no attention to what was going on around him. Fifteen minutes later he looked up. The stage was dark and quiet. No one was around. Brook, Brent, Kohler, Semon, von Sternberg, cameramen and electricians had all tiptoed away.[40]

At first, Semon protested against his role, for he did not judge himself familiar with the humor of gangsters. Yet he had to earn a paycheck and met with the laconic reply by von Sternberg to "find out." Old newspaperman that he was, Larry finally went at the job as a reporter would have, put gags into the crime melodrama and got a real kick out of his job.[41] Heavy-browed Bancroft as Bull Weed now had a humorous companion in Slippy Lewis, whose laughter he would turn into bitterness.[42]

The final version of *Underworld* must have nearly broken Semon's heart. His role, in minimal makeup, had been pared down to a minimum in length and it seems utter mockery that he was "pleased to note that it registered at just the moments he had hoped it would."[43] As a result, reviewers judged him in comparison to the protagonists in a pejorative tone:

> Evelyn Brent is very attractive and she gives a capable performance as "Feathers." Sometimes Mr. von Sternberg shows that he is too fond of posing her looking away from the persons with whom she is supposed to be conversing, but that is his fault. Larry Semon springs into this story as a comic character, but his efforts are a monkey wrench in the machinery.[44]

If someone was watching *Underworld* and was completely unfamiliar with Semon—had never seen his picture or any of his films—he might have been intrigued by his first appearance, since he has such a great entrance with a fragrance dispenser and hanky. But as the film goes on, it makes people wonder what Slippy's purpose was and why he was given so little to do. Slippy has some nice moments during the gangsters' annual ball, but they have no reason to be there. It is obvious that they were cut short. In one scene, Slippy threatens a cloakroom attendant with a water pistol. In another he is behind a rail spitting pellets at Bull Weed who is next seen towering directly behind the surprised Larry. A smoke-inhaling routine following Slippy's resort to the bar was better in *Her Boy Friend* (1924) when detective Larry was playing opposite Alma Bennett. Slippy is also visible in the courtroom scenes and on the exterior steps of the courthouse.

Semon's appearance in the film, albeit elegant and well-played, sometimes hounded, is perhaps its only failing as it seems out of place. Allegedly, von Sternberg idolized Semon, but in the end he did not know what to do with him. Other sources believe that von Sternberg, being described as a vain and unpleasant man who had to draw on someone else's script, regarded Semon as a "low" comic interfering with the tone of his drama.

Consulting the original script for *Underworld*, of which more than one version is extant, it becomes clear that Semon had quite a considerable part in the film, yet it would be too much to call Slippy Lewis integral to the plot. To list but a few changes: Slippy is constantly following Rolls-Royce, here still called Weasel, at the gangsters' party, and imitating his every move as if to reinforce his own importance by linking with him. A marquee-like electric sign announces Bull Weed's failed jailbreak, while Slippy entertains the watchman of the sign with some amusing sleight-of-hand tricks. Probably this sequence, notably the message on the sign, proved to be clumsy and labored and thus impeded the momentum. The details of the failed jailbreak do not matter to the basic plot—suffice to say it went wrong. The final version of *Underworld* known today ended in Bull Weed's arrest. Originally, its end was extended: At a railroad station, Slippy bids Feathers and Rolls-Royce goodbye as they are traveling to a new life. The final lines read: "Slippy waves. Waves again. His face is a study. He takes a huge silk handkerchief from his pocket and sniffles as we … fade out." This sequence probably did not survive the editing process as it was too much kitsch and hampered the final dramatic impact of Bull Weed giving in, realizing that Feathers deserted him.

Had Semon been granted more screen time, the film might have helped establish him as a character actor, since a great number of reviewers thought he gave the picture "genuine relief" of well-balanced acting, not exaggerating his work nor giving it too much free rein.[45]

Considering Semon's premature demise, it is macabre to note that he kept more or less in character off the screen when he startled Hollywood by driving to work in a hearse. He drove right into the Paramount Studios as the car was ordered by von Sternberg. Another morbid occasion was Dorothy Dwan's cat party she gave for her girlfriends in their living room. Larry needed to stay upstairs until all the girls' partners arrived. It was a habit that the head of the home presented the female guests with flowers. Semon sent each one a bouquet of lilies of the valley which made the place look like a wake as Dorothy jokingly remarked.[46]

Financial problems made Larry sell his house on Vine Street. He moved with

Dorothy to a ranch a few miles outside Hollywood. Before long, his former residence, which he had once purchased for $35,000 without even so much as a collapsible staircase, would make room for a motorway. Semon lived like a lord, as long as he could. But not only did he lose his home in California, his apartment in New York was also gone and so was his house by the sea. Apart from his still existing collection of automobiles, Larry's pet diversion was now growing vegetables. One of his fads was a brand of Japanese radishes that were so long that they seemed more like enormous carrots. Surviving photos prove that Larry was indeed sinfully successful as a gardener.

The Semons did not see much of each other, their professional paths independent of each other. On Larry's birthday in 1926, Dorothy, on location with the Tom Mix troupe at the Royal Gorge, made sure to wire some of her girlfriends. She asked them to go over to Larry in order to help him forget his loneliness. Alice Day served the birthday cake and surprised a party of men friends who had convened and already called in for the same reason.[47] When one was not at work in a studio, on location, or appearing on the stage, one was often in a hospital bed. In November 1927, Dorothy was just starting a Fox picture when throat trouble stopped her and she had to have her tonsils removed. A few months earlier, Semon had surgery performed on his nose, sparking curious fan mail whether it did any good or whether he had preserved the shape of his olfactory bulb. In remembrance of her ancestors that had sailed on the *Mayflower* to the United States, Dorothy was preoccupied organizing a "*Mayflower* of the Movies Club" in the hope of making it an active factor in the social life of Hollywood. Eligibility for membership was based on genealogical principles as they had become *en vogue* among various patriotic and pioneer societies.[48] Dorothy was so overwhelmed with work that she could not handle the signing of her promotional photos, but left it to a secretary who continually twisted the letters of her surname to "Dawn."[49] The first time in weeks that Dorothy and Larry spent together was on the occasion of the Dempsey-Tunney boxing fight in Chicago. It did not cost Dorothy a cent to get there, while the rest of the leading women in Hollywood were still counting their coins. Dorothy interrupted her picture *Silver Valley* with Tom Mix, jumped from Chicago to Sedalia and Warrensburg, Missouri, to visit her two grandparents, finished her film with Mix and dashed off to Canada for another movie.[50] On June 29, 1927, 24-year-old Ethel Hall (Draper), doubling for Dorothy in her scariest scenes, was battered to death on the rocks of the rapid Merced River during production of Tom Mix's *Tumbling River* (1927). Hall was scheduled to be abandoned by the villain of the picture in a canoe and to be rescued just in time by Mix as she neared the river rapids. Before Mix stepped into action, the canoe was set adrift. It overturned so that Ethel Hall was swept into the rapids and dashed against a boulder which led to her fractured skull. An actual rescue followed, but on her way to the hospital she died. The Fox organization was under so much pressure that Hall's death halted production just for a few hours.[51] They announced that it cost them near $200,000 to settle the loss.

When Dorothy returned to Hollywood late in September 1927, Larry was getting ready to promote his new Educational two-reelers on a roadshow being booked by Loew's

Opposite: **Larry Semon and Marie Astaire in the Educational comedy *Dummies*, 1927 (author's collection).**

State. Dorothy fancied joining future shows; however, tandem performances would never be realized. Larry was still under contract to Paramount but had been lent to Educational for a series of eight two-reel comedies that were to be produced within twelve months.[52] Chadwick would again act as producer, although Semon also invested money in the productions. The first three shorts had already been completed: *Dummies*, *The Stunt Man* and *Oh, What a Man!* The latter was a takeoff on *Underworld* with Gertrude Astor playing the role of a female Bancroft while Semon appeared as a detective. Semon was confident, thinking he had a lot of good gags in this picture. Semon and Astor make an effective juxtaposition: Determined that Detective Larry shall not be complicated in her affairs and because he has been so nice to her for knocking out all his own men, Astor tucks him under her arm—a feat she *could* do, as she was much larger than Semon. She then bundles him out to his motorcycle and sidecar. *Oh, What a Man!* unveiled to a lukewarm reception. Like his other Educationals, exhibitors shoved the film off to the children's corner.

Educational was going strong on the comedy end, planning to release more than 100 short features. Their roster of jesters included comedienne Dorothy Devore, who was to appear in all of the eight Educationals with Semon. A vaudeville veteran, she ranked as the last female funster in two-reelers after several seasons in feature-length pictures. At fifteen she had produced and toured in her own revue, used to be the lead in a musical comedy and hit Hollywood when she was seventeen soldiering on to the short subject and going places in filmland. In the end, Devore did not appear in any of Semon's new Educationals. In her stead, Dorothea Raynor, Marie Astaire, Gertrude Astor and Bee Amann played opposite Semon. Strangely, Babs Leonard was hired as Semon's foil a few days after his new contract with Educational was made public. Yet ten minutes after signing, Leonard received serious injuries in an automobile accident so that her physicians determined it would be a month and a half before she could appear before the camera. As a result, she never played with Semon having suffered severe shock, a broken collarbone and her face cut by flying glass when a truck impacted her car. After recovery Leonard was afraid of riding in the ordinary type of automobile again. Instead she helped make sales figures rise for Stutz Verticals of the eight series. Those cars had a low center of gravity that prevented overturning, steel running-board side bumpers, safety glass and powerful hydrostatic four-wheel brakes.[53]

Keeping pace with the general Hollywood trend, Larry Semon was making plans to build his own studio in an area on Ventura Boulevard that was being developed. He figured that he could cut down production overhead to a greater extent. He was paying $1500 a month for lot space at F.B.O., where his Educational shorts were made. For his new studio, he had purchased two acres of land. It was an absurd thought since at the time he was not even able to pay an insurance policy.

Larry was given six weeks for his vaudeville tour; after that he was to return to make three more comedies, of which only one was realized, albeit much later, in December–January 1928. After the scheduled film productions, he went on an eight-week tour. Larry's weekly salary in vaudeville amounted to about $2300 and he was a prominent guest at several hotel luncheons where he paid for his warm meals by private entertainments. He started out in Detroit in mid–October of 1927, traveled to Cleveland, then worked up to Buffalo and Pittsburgh and ended his tour in Canton, Ohio, in late November, giving at least three performances a day. In Buffalo, Semon's show was broadcast at the Loew's *Buffalo Evening News* radio from station WMAK and despite his attacks of "microphonitis," i.e., mike fright, he managed to put over a good act.[54]

Contrary to his waning favor with exhibitors and patrons, Semon's vaudeville performances were received with greatest kudos. He showed that he could not be fully appreciated by a review of his film activities and that he was worth seeing on stage. Many people preferred his vaudeville acts to his film persona because Larry performed without raising eyebrows and grinning foolishly. He had a regular vaudeville company and entertained his audience for thirty minutes singing, hoofing and clowning. As in juvenile days, he did several encore numbers. Larry Semon left vaudeville in early December 1927 in order to return to his comedy picturemaking on the coast and put the finishing touches to his next story for Chadwick-Educational while en route from New York.

Together with Dorothy Dwan, Semon re-entered the stage, in a charity act at the Christmas Benefit in Los Angeles. It was quite rightly billed as the biggest show of the year. The 300 stars to appear were ushered by top act Ziegfeld star Lina Basquette. Other highlights included Laurel and Hardy, Joan Crawford, Marie Dressler, Clyde Cook, Renée Adorée, Viola Dana and Our Gang. More names were added to the bill up to the last minute. Entry was at reasonable prices, while about 6000 shrine seats were available. Next Semon continued appearing on stage in Los Angeles during the Christmas holidays and was billed for Loew's for the New Year's Celebration of 1928.[55] His Christmas afternoon performance was so warmly welcomed that the audience clung to their seats and refused to leave Semon and his partner Rube Wolff even after they had seen the entire entertainment.

The holidays were filled with more activity: Semon was eager to set up another record with Jack Holt and Adolphe Menjou. They called themselves "three hard-boiled eggs,"[56] going to spend the day playing golf, only relocating in the latter part of the afternoon to the Christmas dinner and tree at their homes. Semon's golf game would be played with the new set of hand-made clubs Dorothy had ordered for him. His Christmas surprise for Dorothy, literally a surprise with his bankruptcy creeping up from behind, was a chic sedan he kept in a neighbor's garage. When she was not about, he sneaked to the car and polished it to perfection.

Semon's newest two-reelers were creating no big impact on the box-office. He reacted to it in his vaudeville shows with the joke about the old lady who always went to see his pictures because she never had to stand in line. On the bad side, the story prevailed that Educational was seeking to cancel its agreement with him. Earle W. Hammons, president of Educational, denied this and confirmed that Larry was still under contract and reconfirmed that he had been granted a leave of absence to play eight weeks of vaudeville and picture theaters. He declared that the comedian would return and complete his series of six subjects. Strikingly, the number of two-reel films that Semon was to deliver had been reduced from eight to six. Hammons ironically continued that Semon was ahead of his schedule, having three or four finished.

About the turn of the year (1927 into 1928) Semon completed his last known film, the two-reeler *A Simple Sap* that had been filmed on the Hal Roach lot. In the female lead was German-born Philippine "Bee" Amann (1905–1990), who worked under a long-term contract for Chadwick. Soon after her birth, her family migrated to the United

Earle W. Hammons, president of Educational Releasing Corporation, visiting Larry Semon, dressed loud, at the FBO Studios, ca. 1927 (author's collection).

Notorious Nora alias Gertrude Astor has found a new love in inept fly cop Larry Semon in the Educational comedy *Oh, What a Man!*, 1927 (author's collection).

States. Amann returned to Germany in 1928 and became a star. During her career she also worked for Alfred Hitchcock.

"I'd rather be hit by plaster than by a custard pie," Larry once remarked when things were still going well for him in cinemaland. He always insisted that he did not like to be identified with pie-throwing and he kept custard away from his comedies.[57] Yet in the final scene of *A Simple Sap*, Semon would close—with a custard pie in his face.

• 10 •

From Broke to Breakdown

Hollywood's chief conversation on February 5, 1928, was Larry Semon. One day earlier, he had appeared before Judge I. Mulville, who cited Semon into municipal court at Los Angeles because he could not pay a judgment of a few hundred dollars in connection with an insurance premium. Semon frankly admitted he was penniless, his exact words being "I'm broke and $80,000 in debt."[1]

Semon did not state his current salary, but according to *The Daily Constitution* of Chillicothe, Missouri, it was understood to have been $1,250 a week. Semon was still under contract to Educational, his agreement with Paramount having expired. He declared that he had no money or other assets with which to pay his debts, having lost all his money in motion picture ventures, particularly the picture *Spuds* which he chose to finance almost entirely himself and which had failed miserably. The fact that he drove to the courthouse in an expensive sedan made his statements seem implausible, yet he testified that the car belonged to his wife. It was the one he had presented her with on Christmas 1927. Larry was terribly disappointed by his former associates because there were a lot of bills that he was not responsible for. Efforts were being made to obtain judgments against him personally instead of Larry Semon Productions Inc., which handled his film producing activities.

A few days later Semon was sued for additional back taxes for 1923, but was really struck hard on March 13, 1928: He showed up in Federal Court and asserted in a voluntary bankruptcy petition that he owed $454,639.87.[2] The sum included secured and unsecured claims and accommodation papers. With regard to assets, Semon on this day came up with $300 to pay his debts with, though he hoped to keep half. His only possessions were household goods and wearing apparel. To be on the safe side, Dorothy had purchased Semon's household goods from her own separate earnings, rendering them exempt from seizure. Semon's most conspicuous creditors were the Cinema Finance Corporation, holding the motion picture *Spuds* for loans or advances, Larry Semon Productions—not to mention attorneys, doctors and cafés.[3] The cafés and other places featured prominently because Larry Semon had continued partying despite his awareness that he was rapidly sliding toward complete financial ruin.

Part of Semon's problem: back income taxes, as he had faced financial problems at an earlier stage in his stellar career. It started when Semon's money was tied up from

The star also rises: Doll-faced Dorothy Dwan as Molly Graham playing opposite Tim McCoy as Lt. Crane in MGM's *Riders of the Dark*, 1928 (author's collection). It was one of the last westerns she appeared in before attempting to leave that genre.

1920 through 1922 in his lawsuit with Vitagraph. His complete financial breakdown could even have resulted as soon as 1922, had Judge Bledsoe not dismissed Vitagraph's complaint. Otherwise Semon would have been made to pay his employer more than $500,000. At that time his friends rejected the idea that he had any such sum. Soon after, the government came after Semon for $10,000 when he was only able to raise a bit more than half of it. This made authorities attach his home for the remaining amount due, and resulted in Semon selling his Hollywood house in 1927.[4]

When the creditors were descending, so were the journalists. Reviewing the real-life pratfall of the sorrow-faced comedian who now put something "really genuine in his doleful expression,"[5] they came to the conclusion that the figures of Semon's past million dollar contracts had been nothing but inflated publicity stunts. In this vein, his talents were questioned down to its very beginnings when penning and inking for the papers. The cartooning abilities that years ago had been his key to motion pictures were exposed to be not much. Now that he had lost it all, this dean of custard pie throwers let his wife Dorothy Dwan do all the acting for the family. Mountebank Semon deserved his decline.

Just how much Semon had fallen out of favor with cinema patrons and exhibitors was mirrored by a little story about film comic Tyler Brooke, who approached a new gateman at the Fox lot and asked for admission. While stepping through the big iron gate, "the gateman reached for Brooke's coat collar and halted the actor. 'No visitors allowed on this lot, mister!' 'But,' said Brooke, 'I am working here in a picture.' The gateman closed the gate in Brooke's face: 'Stay out of here! I know who you are. *You're Larry Semon!*'"[6]

Another paper rather benevolently observed that even those who made it to the class of the higher paid had no warrant for permanent wealth. Within the past six months, Theodore von Eltz, Helen Lee Worting and Virginia Brown Faire had also filed for bankruptcy. Yet insolvency was of course far from the poorhouse. Charles Ray was one of those to lose almost everything he had when attempting to finance his own movies. Nevertheless, his name was sure fire at the box-office.[7] So was Semon's name with the vaudeville patrons—or at least they hoped so. Definitely not all of his appearances did well. As Semon did not have a clear field, he was merely relying on the strength of his name and calling. When he set out with an inadequate sketch during the week of January 2, 1928, at the Metropolitan in New York, his tour only lasted two weeks instead of eight.[8] With the goal to reimburse his creditors, Larry tried again with new material and went on another vaudeville tour while Dorothy closed and sold their ranch and moved in with her mother. By February 26, 1928, Larry had already resumed his life on the stage. His route was up and down the Eastern seaboard including Philadelphia. Although his star was sinking, in March 1928 the *Emporia Gazette* of Kansas thought it worth mentioning that Semon and Adolphe Menjou were passing through the town and that their Santa Fe train No. 20 would arrive in the early evening. This news would make people go to the station and greet them.[9]

During the last third of April 1928, papers announced that Semon had been booked for a vaudeville tour of the English music halls and planned to open in Birmingham in May.[10] Another note said that Virginia Lee Corbin, popular movie ingénue, and Larry were soon to appear at the local Keith-Albee Orpheum houses in New York.[11] Corbin would appear in a skit with songs and dancing, while Semon would deliver a monologue, both acting under the tutelage of Charles Morrison, but not jointly.[12] Semon's name is however absent from the bills. Instead, the Publix Theaters Corporation arranged for him to make six personal appearances between New York and the coast. Of these, at least three stints could be traced, namely for Waterloo and Davenport, Iowa, and later Chicago. As before, "the very dapper" Larry wowed the people and was accorded to be "seemingly anxious to please his audience."[13] At the same time, Dorothy Dwan was leaving horse opera western films to further her career. For a start, she had been signed for the leading role in *The Virgin Queen* (1928), an early Technicolor film. On a parallel activity elsewhere, Bert Clinton, the Larry Semon of the stage, was reputed to render the closest impersonation of the screen comedian ever seen and met with considerable success.

When the real Larry Semon played Waterloo, the *Evening Courier* ran an interview that could rank as Larry's last known and, possibly, an exclusive to that paper only. Semon disguised his current vaudeville tour as a welcome rest from the tremendous hardships of rough-and-tumble comedy acting. His words come as a sad analysis of his own failures. Audiences, he claimed, were too smart, demanding plenty of action, new thrills and gags every minute of the time. Having abandoned his own excursion to the realms of Harry

Langdon–like comedies, Semon concluded that fast-moving comedies, if indeed they ever waned in popularity, were growing steadily in favor.

His final statement seems incredible and scary. From an external viewpoint one gets the impression that he had listened and would from now on be wise enough to refrain from larger projects. At the end of his present tour he planned to return to Hollywood, direct for a time and then appear in a new series of pictures. Yet he insisted "No more two-reelers. You can't even get started in two reels."[14]

Semon did not specify which company he now signed with. However, a month prior, papers announced that he would go on salary with Educational. The company was incidentally boosting its profits by re-releasing Semon comedies with footage from old Vitagraph negatives—without stating this in the contracts, though.[15] Other big film producers were wooing Larry in the wake of his *Underworld* appearance in order to secure him for more dramas.[16]

After Waterloo and Davenport, Semon's vaudeville tour nearly disappeared from the scene as far as reviews are concerned. In early May, Semon played Chicago's Forest Park Theater, a week later the Senate. In between he appeared at the Regal at a midnight show connected with a memorial fund for the late Florence Mills. Joining Larry were celebrities such as Bill Robinson, Tom Mix, and Jazz "Lips" Richardson. Semon was back in California by the second half of May, as he acted as best man when Nancy Smith married retired oil tycoon Charles Sollars in Pasadena. Smith and Sollars had been schoolmates in Warrensburg, Missouri, and met again when they both chose to make Los Angeles their home. Sollars resided at the Biltmore and Nancy soon joined him.[17] In mid–June, Semon returned to Hollywood and entered into a golf tournament with Harold Lloyd and A.H. Palmer.

On July 27, 1928, the Motion Picture Capital Corporation sued Larry Semon Productions in an assigned claim for twenty promissory notes valued at approximately $100,000. The first note dated back to 1925 and contained twenty counts.[18] Although the matter was addressed to Larry Semon Productions and not Semon himself, this news helped trigger Larry's collapse.

August 7, 1928, marked the day Semon was brought to the desert ranch of Dr. Harris S. Garcelon in San Bernardino, near Victorville. About two months later he was dead.

· 11 ·

Slow Motion

Semon's final days were framed with short newspaper articles and those press releases to some extent supplied by Nancy Smith Sollars. In view of the fact that Semon's grave nor his death certificate, at that time, could never be found, researcher Steve Rydzewski and the author suggested in 1999 and 2000, respectively, that there were some inconsistencies to Semon's death and that he may have even faked his tragic departure.[1] Since the official reporting did not overlap with some things Dorothy Dwan later said and two telegrams that were given to the author by Semon's family do not fit in as well, all available information shall be reviewed in detail.

According to film historian Richard M. Roberts, who interviewed Dorothy Dwan shortly before her death, Semon fell ill while playing vaudeville in Chicago. An exact date could not be confirmed. The *Schenectady Gazette* noted that soprano Lillian Daley was the last one to appear with Semon on stage and that she continued with the act until Semon broke down. Daley and Semon did play opposite one another in 1927, but in 1928 their tours had headed in different directions.[2]

At least it seems that Semon returned to California, since he and Dorothy appeared at the traditional Friday night party at the Montmartre after her performance in *Lombardi Ltd*.[3] On August 3, 1928, Dorothy had opened in a very minor role in the successful play written and staged for the first time in 1917 and revived at the Hollywood Playhouse. She was one of the young film actors preparing themselves for talking movies by going in for actual stage experience. It also marked her first encounter with cue lines.[4] As the play premiered on a Friday, it is probable that Dorothy and Larry were at the Montmartre on that August 3, 1928. That the press noted the couple's attendance not later than August 26, 1928, can be explained by the fact that the Montmartres were too private to be greatly mentioned, yet not to be ignored either. Writer Grace Kingsley combined her review with the real event of Carl Laemmle's party in his palace on the top of a knoll in Benedict Canyon.

August 7, 1928: According to Semon's death certificate, from now on he was under the care of Dr. Harris S. Garcelon to whose private sanitarium he had been taken. The sanitarium was out in the desert, eight miles from Victorville, in the county of San Bernadino. It was one of the most prominent places when it came to the treatment of tuberculosis. Many screen actors had undergone rest cures at the Garcelon ranch and some sources called Dr. Garcelon a nerve specialist.[5] The Garcelon ranch had gained regional fame as it encouraged health and pleasure combined. Only two years earlier, a group of Los Angeles capitalists of the exclusive Mojave Lake Club had bought the ranch of 300 acres on the Mojave River. More than a million dollars were invested and a corps of engineers put to work to make this oasis in the desert into something still more beautiful. Their task was to plan and build a large clubhouse, a chain of golf links, numerous cottages and a comprehensive scheme of landscaping. Another feature was a camp with all the accoutrements of early day placer mining so that those who desired exercise could swing the pick and shovel and in doing so add to the amusement of the other guests who would see the ancient equipment in operation. Despite selling his premises, Dr. Garcelon retained an active interest of his ranch property.[6] Dorothy Dwan recalled, "I was wired that Larry had been taken ill and was going to Victorville and you know what that meant. Larry was being handled by these two guys, I don't know who they were. But they wouldn't allow me to see Larry. They told me I had to stay away from him until he was better. They wouldn't let me see him at all."[7]

It remains a mystery where Dorothy was and what she had been up to when Semon found his way to the sanitarium. He was presumably removed to Victorville at night, while Dorothy was appearing on stage with *Lombardi Ltd*. Some articles noted that "when [Semon's] condition became serious, Dorothy cancelled her engagement in *Lombardi Ltd.* to rush to his bedside."[8] *Lombardi Ltd.* would resume its former success and played ten weeks in Hollywood.[9]

Given that Dorothy was not allowed to see her husband, Jimmy Aubrey's reminiscences of his last encounter with Semon, which he revived in an interview with film historians Sam Gill and Jordan Young in 1976, seem the more surprising. Known for his salty language and his lack of hospitality with interviewers, Aubrey let only Joe Rock emerge unscathed in his memory; everyone else he ever worked with was a no-good son of a bitch, including Laurel and Hardy. So he set out to complain about his former Vitagraph director Semon and appended a remarkable utterance: "He wanted no one but himself, and tried to get me out. And do you know who he came to at the end, when he was dying out there in the desert? Me, the last person he calls—me—and so I run over there just before he died."

August 22, 1928: The nationwide press noted on many front pages that Semon suffered a nervous and physical breakdown about August 15 after his return from a national vaudeville tour. His family had said that physicians believed it would be at least three months and perhaps a year before he recovered. Dorothy Dwan had "closed the ranch and gone to live with her mother." On August 21 he was taken to a private sanitarium to recover from his ailment.[10]

Nancy Smith issued the note that Semon was unable to assimilate food on account of his nervous condition and was so weak that he slept most of the time. His mind was perfectly clear and doctors who had examined him attributed his illness solely to a collapse of his nervous system.[11] *The Riverside Daily Press* informed their readers that Semon might never be able to return to the screen or the footlights; according to the Victorville sanitarium, Semon had not responded to therapy for a nervous breakdown. The date Semon began his treatment at Dr. Garcelon's had been increased to "six weeks ago."[12]

September 23, 1928: Unlike other sources, the *San Francisco Chronicle* reports that

Dorothy Dwan was still in *Lombardi Ltd*. She enjoyed a party that actress Lois Wilson gave and which started with supper early in the evening so that several guests playing in legitimate shows could come, eat and visit and get to work on time for the evening show.[13]

September 27, 1928: Because of the many inquiries from friends regarding Semon's condition and the many rumors being circulated concerning his illness, Dorothy thought it wise to issue a statement from Dr. Garcelon through the *Los Angeles Times*:

> Mr. Semon has been under my care at my home near Victorville for two months, suffering from a nervous breakdown and complicated stomach trouble brought on from overwork and nervous strain while on tour in the East last spring. It will require many months of complete rest before he can even consider returning to his work. He is in a very serious condition.[14]

Dorothy would visit her husband on a weekly basis. She even turned down a contract with the Henry Duffy Players in Portland because of Semon's illness.

September 28, 1928: *The Waco News Tribune* observed that while Semon was waging a fight for his life at the Garcelon Ranch, Dorothy was watching anxiously at his bedside and countless friends were waiting for news of his condition.[15] The same day, *The Buffalo*

A telegraph signed "Dorothy Dwan Semon" to Larry's daughter Virginia, October 6, 1928 (courtesy Lynne Whitcopf).

Courier Express reported that Semon had been unable to shake off bronchitis and suffered a complete nervous and physical breakdown. This news summoned Dorothy and Nancy from Hollywood.[16] Around this time a press release was sent out to the news agencies. It was accompanied by a photograph of Larry and Dorothy "on the ranch out at the Mojave Desert" with Semon "recovering from his nervous breakdown." Semon reads the daily paper and Dorothy looks on. In the background there is a giant floor lamp and the reader is led to believe the photo was taken on August 10, 1928. This actual photograph, along with accompanying snipe, sold at auction in November 2012.[17] Your author lost out on the photo and is therefore not in a position to identify or verify its true date or origin. That same photo was used in the *Brooklyn Standard Union* one day after Semon's death, but the quality is so poor it could not be reproduced in this book.[18] However, there is some clue that the shot dates back to as early as 1925. To begin with, Dorothy's hairdo is still bobbed. From 1927 on, she kept up with the general trend that swept cinemaland and grew her hair long.[19] Already in May 1927, two good news items emerged from the Semon household—or rather mother Nancy's typewriter: Dorothy's hair had significantly grown and she had found a solution to put her tresses under control.[20] In *Square Crooks*, a Fox film with Dorothy Appleby, Dwan sports hair down to her shoulders, as can be told from a still. The film was copyrighted on February 22, 1928. The same state of hair length can be noticed in a photo during the making of *A Simple Sap*. Semon receives his film makeup from Max Factor, while Dorothy is witnessing his transformation.[21] Pictures of Dorothy after Semon's death show that she did not cut her hair. Furthermore, Semon still appears comparably cheerful in the said photograph. Owing to his oft-undernourished childhood days, he had always been of gangly appearance. He stood 5'7" and in his better days weighed 133 pounds.[22] When financial disasters began to pile up, he significantly slimmed down and appeared emaciated. His face had also grown old, showing deep wrinkles.

September 30, 1928: The *Trenton Evening Times* says that reports of Semon's grave illness are exaggerated.[23]

October 5, 1928: In her interview with Roberts, Dorothy Dwan said that she heard back from Semon's two mysterious helpers who asked her to come to the ranch. San Bernardino and Los Angeles lie at a distance of about 60 miles and from today's perspective can be reached by car in 90 minutes. Back then the journey was longer.

> It was very strange. I finally got a call from them and they said, "Come on down here, he wants to see you now," so we drove down to Victorville and it's the strangest thing you've ever seen. First, they bring me into this dark room and Larry's laying in the bed on the far side of it. Just one dim lamp. I can hardly make him out and they won't let me get near him. We talked for a few minutes, and he tells me he's getting better. Then the doctor tells us we have to leave. My mother and I go back to Los Angeles and two days later I get another call saying he's dead.[24]

On October 6, 1928, a telegraph was sent by Dorothy Dwan Semon from Victorville to Larry's daughter Virginia Semon, then residing at 2622 Rosedale South, Houston, Texas. It was received via Western Union, Houston, 6:05 a.m. Pacific Standard Time (Victorville) would have been 3:05 a.m. The text of this telegraph contradicts what Larry had told Dorothy, i.e., that he was getting better:

YOUR FATHER CRITICALLY ILL AND NO HOPE OF RECOVERY—STOP—THERE IS NOTHING YOU COULD DO—STOP—I KNOW HE APPRECIATED YOUR MESSAGE AND

REALIZED ITS CONTENTS.
DOROTHY DWAN SEMON

It could have been that Dorothy and Nancy were summoned in the middle of the night to see Larry and they sent the message after their visit. This would explain why this message was dispatched so early in the morning. However, since Semon had told Dorothy he was recovering, there would have been no reason for prematurely upsetting Virginia.

The same day, at 12:15 a.m. Pacific Coast time, Nancy Smith reportedly told the press that Semon was very low and that little hope was held for his recovery. It was doubtful if Semon, weakened by his nervous collapse, was strong enough to fight off the pneumonia. She specified that Dorothy and she would remain with him until there was some change.[25] Nancy's statements crossed with a report that came from the desert town. It stated someone purporting to be Dr. Garcelon had telephoned that Semon had succumbed to his malady. The report was judged credible in view of a message dispatched "this morning" to Los Angeles newspapers by Nancy, in which she said the comedian had contracted pneumonia and was not expected to live. The *Modesto Bee and News*

A second telegraph signed "Dorothy Dwan Semon" to Virginia Semon, October 8, 1928 (courtesy Lynne Whitcopf).

Herald added to the confusion: According to them, Semon never toured in the summer of 1928, but had been confined to his ranch for a considerable time before being put over to the isolated desert resort of Dr. Garcelon.[26] Allegedly there was no direct communication with the Mojave "hospital" because it had no telephone and was situated in the desert beyond Victorville across the San Bernardino mountains, as the Associated Press pointed out. Nancy Smith had left "her hotel," whose location was not specified, for the Mojave retreat to be with Semon.[27] Despite the lack of telephones, the *Emporia Gazette* knew that "a telephone message from the ranch" where Semon had lain seriously ill for several days declared that Semon had not died up to 11 o'clock but that he was in a "very low" condition.[28]

October 7, 1928: Again setting aside the fact that Semon's own ranch had been sold before Semon went on tour in spring 1928, the *San Bernardino County Sun* wrote that at midnight, in other words the turn of the day, it was announced that frail little Larry Semon "might not live through the night" and that he was stricken with a "mysterious ailment."[29] There was just one little hint in the news that Semon was "getting better," in accordance with what he told Dorothy when she came to Victorville to see him:

> Rallying only slightly yesterday, Semon was last night again (October 7) in a "very critical condition and possibly would not live through the night," physicians attending him at the Garcelon Ranch near Victorville said. Semon, who is ill with pneumonia, had not been expected to live through Saturday night but rallied slightly yesterday morning. He relapsed again last night, however, and was on the verge of death. The comedian went to the Victorville ranch two months ago to recuperate from a nervous breakdown.[30]

Two days after Dorothy had just seen her husband, she received another call telling her that Semon had died.[31] This must have been on October 7, 1928, a few hours before Semon's official date of death on October 8, 1928. Precisely, it was a Monday morning, at 3 a.m.[32]

As printed in the *Los Angeles Times* the same night, Nancy Smith had said via telephone that they did not believe Semon could live through the night. She and Dorothy were at Semon's bedside.[33] In a telegram Smith advised the *Times* that Larry had developed pneumonia and there was little hope of recovery.[34]

October 8, 1928: At 12:32 a.m. another telegraph to Virginia Semon was received at the Western Union Office, Houston. The telegraph's origin was again Victorville, dispatched on October 7 at approximately 9:30 p.m.

YOUR FATHER HAS PNEUMONIA. IMPOSSIBLE TO LIVE THROUGH THE NIGHT = DOROTHY DWAN SEMON

If Dorothy's memory was right, she would still have been in Los Angeles at that time and could not have sent the telegraph herself. At this point of time (October 7, 1928) she might already have received the message that Semon was dead.

According to his death certificate, Semon succumbed to lobar pneumonia, which had fought for five days. Contributory was pulmonary tuberculosis from which Semon had been suffering for two years, possibly having contracted the disease in Chicago. He did not undergo an operation, nor was there an autopsy.

October 8, 1928: The first newspapers report that Semon had met his maker. His body was taken to San Bernardino where simple funeral services would be held. Victorville is about an hour away from San Bernardino, especially back in 1928 when the major route was over some steep mountains, so he might have gone by train. In keeping with the wish of the survivors for a quiet and private ceremony the time and place of the funeral service would not be made public. The simple funeral rites were indeed another element that disturbed Dorothy as she told Roberts. Larry's helpers called her and advised her he had special instructions as to how he wanted his funeral and she was to follow them to the letter.

Semon had instituted a closed casket before his cremation and that only six hand-picked people were to attend: Dorothy, her mother, husband Charles Sollars, Christian Science reader Mrs. B.W. Cruickshank, her assistant, and the undertaker. Semon's body was to be cremated immediately after the service and it was announced that his ashes would be sent to Philadelphia. Semon was said to be cremated at Mountain View Cemetery and Mortuary. But *The Los Angeles Times* wrote that after the services, Semon's body, not the urn, would be shipped to Philadelphia for burial beside his mother and father, which was not possible because Zera and Irene rest at different graveyards. Irene (Rea) Semon is buried at Philadelphia's Fernwood Cemetery, Zera at the city's Beth El Emeth Cemetery along with his father and brother Judah. Semon's death certificate disambiguates the question about the state of his body for shipment: He was cremated on October 9, 1928, when still in San Bernardino. The *Times* continued that Semon's sister,

The Italian playbill for *Ridolini e la collana della suocera* (1952), a compilation movie narrated by Tino Scotti (author's collection). It contains scenes from the Vitagraph comedies *School Days, His Home Sweet Home, The Star Boarder, The Hick*. The still is from *Frauds and Frenzies*, 1918.

Mrs. H.C. Cunningham, resided in Philadelphia, which held true. Her alleged visit to Semon several weeks earlier is rather doubtful. She had already made arrangement for the burial.[35] Dorothy collapsed under the strain on the day of Semon's death. According to Nancy Smith, Semon died in his sleep, although he became conscious several times and recognized Dorothy.[36]

October 9, 1928: Funeral services were held in a small mausoleum chapel hidden away at Mountain View Cemetery and Mortuary in San Bernardino that afternoon. The press called it a "solemn, pathetic closing chapter of the life of the star, who had brought happiness and cheer to millions."[37] Services were indeed held privately.[38] Semon's body lay in a gray and silver casket covered with two sheafs of flowers and a spray of roses placed there by his widow. Dorothy, Nancy and Sollars drove directly to the cemetery from Hollywood where Dorothy had been under the care of a physician since Semon's death. The party entered the chapel, awaited by Christian Science reader Mrs. B.W. Cruickshank. Behind closed doors, the simple ceremony of death was enacted. The question is how, with all the privacy, the press knew these details. Nancy Smith must again have been the source of the information. Outside, a few people attracted by the cemetery in the belief that Hollywood stars would be present, wandered near the mausoleum. They drew closer as grief-stricken Dorothy and her attendants left the chapel following the services which were completed in less than thirty minutes. Dorothy, clad in all black with large hat of the same color that partially hid her face from the curious, entered her car and was quickly driven away. Waiting patiently near the chapel was a sad figure whom few people recognized *sans* makeup: Snub Pollard, said to have been a pal of Semon's in his early picture days. Pollard was drawn to the cemetery in hopes of one last glimpse of his old friend. But as was announced, the funeral was private and no one else admitted.

At the close of the service, the body was cremated and the ashes would be forwarded to Philadelphia where members of Semon's family stood ready to supervise their interment in the family plot. The J.R. Rich Company of Victorville was in charge.[39]

Theaters began screening the last pictures Semon had completed before his serious illness. Several thousand letters of condolence reached Semon's relatives. They came from fans and admirers from all parts of the country and around the world.[40]

October 10, 1928: Dorothy left in the afternoon by car for the Santa Maria Inn, where she intended to stay a few days recuperating from her nervous condition. She was going to spend part of her time at the Huasna Ranch in San Luis Obispo County.

· 12 ·

Fade Out

With the articles on Larry Semon's dying juxtaposed, the question remains whether he departed on October 8, 1928, or whether he took a different way out. One thing is sure: This question will never be answered to anyone's satisfaction.

In favor of his untimely death are the signs of grave illness that Semon in fact did show. That he had contracted tuberculosis had been known to the film world, or at least some of them.[1] He displayed the clinical picture of weight loss, weariness and weakness. Robert Florey saw Semon for the last time when Larry was filming *Underworld*. Florey said he had changed. He did not talk much and it appeared that he did not recognize his old friends.[2] When Larry played the Earle Theater in Philadelphia in March 1928, people at the house who knew him from his old days sensed that he was not the same. His youthful vigor and cleverness had disappeared.[3]

If someone was to break down, it was Semon. With his unhealthy lifestyle, regular sleep deprivation, constant tobacco use, continuous work on his film and stage projects without a serious break since 1912 and his worries about their outcome, endless trials in court, contracts cancelled and the threat of a difficult future—did he have any other choice? Most prominently, Semon was dropped by his former employers, although he delivered good work. Paramount gave him projects and took them away from him, cut them to a ridiculous amount and made him deliver an enjoyable film within an unlikely period of a few days. His erstwhile work of which 75 percent meant a fine and memorable output did not count the least. Nobody believed in Semon any longer. The bitterest pill was his former associates of the Larry Semon Productions, who were passing the buck and did not care about their own responsibilities.

What made matters worse was the disappointment with his peers. Despite the rough style with which he might have handled people on the set, Semon was known as a generous person. In his better days, he used to invite his former colleagues who were not as successful as he to his home in Hollywood and did everything to help them—something he was concealing to the public.[4] But these colleagues were not close to him. When he was in need, he did not get much in return. Semon would understandably have ended up in a tremendous depression. Asked in 1980 whether Semon had friends, Norman Taurog stated that there was nobody he knew of. Semon had lived for his work and would have given his life for his job—which in the end he did.[5]

Alan Sylvester quite similarly reviewed Semon's life as having been given to him by Hollywood and to have also been taken from him by Hollywood. He knew that Semon had been worrying tremendously over his finances. Being forced into bankruptcy broke his heart. Sylvester believed that Semon's continual brooding over his troubles brought on his nervous breakdown. Then Sylvester came up with something unexpected, naming benefactors who helped Semon to get rest and attention: "Tom Mix and a few loyal friends."[6] So Mix could have been one of the helpers Dorothy neglected to identify or at least recall. There was in fact a link from Mix to Dr. Harris Garcelon. Garcelon once built a guest ranch where early cowboy movies were filmed, including the Tom Mix and William S. Hart westerns.[7]

Just the same, Semon had chosen the emergency exit, either through death or social suicide. For Dorothy Dwan the nightmare would continue. About a month after her husband's death she suffered injuries during the filming of a western near Bakersfield. She was trotting sidesaddle for the first time when her foot caught in the stirrup and she slipped to the ground. The horse dragged her a considerable distance before actor Ken Maynard could save her. It was impossible for her to continue working for some time.[8]

The harassment did not stop. Day after day some new cases were emerging in which back income taxes caused grief and hardship to screen actors. In 1929, Internal Revenue Collector Galen H. Welch filed in Federal Court an income tax lien against Larry Semon for $14,419.97. It was indicated that the lien would be amended against the estate of the late motion picture star. In other words, Dorothy was responsible.[9] She had earned an estimated $4,000 since her husband's death. The government at once descended upon her and instructed her to pay Semon's back taxes, taking every cent she had. Dorothy had been paying her husband's hospital bills, funeral costs and for two suits he never lived to wear. Burdens like these left her in a state of nervous collapse. Mother Nancy financed Dorothy's trip away from Los Angeles so she could rest.[10]

After Larry died, Dorothy lost interest in her own film career and, despite her preparatory training with *Lombardi Ltd.*, did not like the thought of talking pictures. One year after her last movie with Ken Maynard, he called her and begged her to do a talking film with him. So Dorothy made *The Fighting Legion* (1930), a story of the old rip-roaring west, in which Maynard single-handedly cleans up a typical bad town. She hated the experience and quit films for good, working as a press writer with her mother.

Semon never made talkies and departed just when sound was becoming standard. Taurog always regretted this as he said Semon had a beautiful strong voice. It was, however, not suitable to his comical character.

Nineteen thirty was the year in which Dorothy's life took a major upswing. She extended her career into the world of the oil business. Like her mother before her with her marriage to oil magnate Charles Sollars, Dorothy and Paul H. Boggs of Beverly Hills wed in Los Angeles on May 26, 1930. Boggs was the son of the Union Oil Company's vice-president and one of their employees.

There was another reason for Dorothy to withdraw from pictures. Unlike the working mothers, she insisted she would devote all her time to their son, Paul Boggs III. The marriage however did not turn out a happy one. In 1935 dispatches from Hollywood announced that Dorothy was seeking a divorce, charging Boggs with desertion. The couple had been living separately for three years.[11] Again Dorothy's life was accompanied by nervous breakdowns which for some time held up the execution of a major abdominal operation.

Traces of Dorothy Dwan soon became scarce, if it was not for the memories of broadcaster and newsman Scott Hayden. He met Dorothy in the summer of 1957 when he was thirteen years old. Dorothy drove from California back to see her family in Missouri. She was a niece of good friends of Scott's parents. Her aunt, knowing of Scott's fascination with silent movie comedians, mentioned his interest and told Dorothy she had to stop by and see him. Dorothy drove up in a late model Thunderbird convertible with her boxer dog that had made the trip with her. Scott remembered that she was very pleasant and interesting to talk with. She was a large woman (not fat, but just big-boned). He was about 5'7" then, and when standing, they were eye to eye. Dorothy was wearing a summer house dress, no stockings and red pumps. She had applied hardly any makeup except for lipstick. Her hair was curly and mostly gray with dark highlights, short and slightly wind-blown, but not messy. She was very outgoing, seemed happy and smiled a great deal. When not smiling, she had a sparkle in her eyes. Her voice was kind of deep—maybe from the cigarettes, of which she smoked quite a number, as almost everyone did then.

> Meeting her ... was a pretty heady experience. I was excited, thrilled and even a little scared, I think. But she was so nice and easy to know that those apprehensions went away. Still, to be a silent movie buff and to have a silent movie star in your home, well, that was really something. At that time, I had only met a few stars, and certainly none came to see me.[12]

Scott did not see her again but after he grew up and moved to California he had her phone number and address and was always going to get in touch. But, as things happened, he never did. He seemed to remember that Dorothy sold real estate.

Dorothy Dwan died Dorothy Buckels in Ventura, California, on March 17, 1981, age 74, from lung cancer. She was cremated at Grand View Cemetery in Glendale. Her ashes were scattered at sea, probably off Santa Monica.

By the time of Semon's death, many members of his earliest stock company had developed nicely. Joe Rock became a minor star and afterwards a respectable and prominent film producer. Bill Dunn was the owner of a prosperous casting agency in Hollywood. His brother Eddie had a long career in movies with W.C. Fields, Laurel and Hardy, Harry Langdon and many others. Frank Brule was selling insurance in Brooklyn.[13] Hughie Mack, however, died on October 13, 1927, at his home in Santa Monica of heart failure. When he drew his final breath he weighed 356 pounds.[14] Another early stock company member was Jack W. Hoins, although he was never mentioned in the publicity. Jack served a while as one of the "Semon cops" (or rather the Big V Riot Squad) and later became a journalist for the *Brooklyn Standard Union*. On his old chief's death he wrote:

> Many Brooklynites will note with sorrow the passing of an old boss of ours who, although only a youngster years ago, was a veteran laugh producer. Larry Semon, comes word from Hollywood, has heard the final "cut" order from the Great Director. Like many small men he radiated energy and humor. It was strange that Larry Semon should take his last great fade-out almost a year to the day that Hughie passed away in his Hollywood home. We can't help but feel a personal loss, as will many Brooklynites, who spent some of their years in the old Vitagraph studio. The doctors may have high sounding names for what brought about Larry's death. Knowing his tireless efforts to make the world laugh, and knowing how hard Larry

A collage of Larry Semon's artwork for the *New York Evening Telegram*, 1910–1911, and the *New York Evening Sun*, 1915 (courtesy Fulton History, composed by Claudia Sassen).

strove to put his best into everything he did, we can only feel certain that he just burned himself out ... at thirty-seven (sic!) years of age ... another victim of that worn and maltreated phrase ... *laugh, clown, laugh.*[15]

Semon's stuntman William Hauber followed on July 17, 1929. He died along with motion picture cameraman Alvin Knechtel when their airplane crashed after a spectacular 2000-foot fall two miles west of the Metropolitan Airport. During flight, Knechtel had fainted, which caused him to slump forward on the control stick. This made the plane "wing-over" and dive tail first toward the ground. Hauber, seated in the rear cockpit, was powerless to prevent the tragedy. Owing to the whirling, looping motion of the aircraft on its downward drop, Hauber could not climb out and jump. Hauber and Knechtel had finished their day's work on *The Aviator* and were looking for a suitable location to film a forced landing. The fatal accident was believed due to Knechtel, whose life had been an eventful one. He had been ill with a psychiatric disorder for the last five days but insisted they continue filming over the protest of motion picture officials.[16] Hauber, like the proverbial black cat with its nine lives, had often braved death and so often saved the life of Semon. It was strangely coincident that the fatal flight should be fraught with the element of the spectacular, far beyond anything his work in motion pictures had dared him to attempt.

Norman Taurog died on April 9, 1981, at the age of 82 in Palm Desert. He had a long career in the movies. In 1930 he won an Academy Award and later filmed with Elvis Presley. After retiring he taught at the University of California School of Cinema.[17]

Hans Koenekamp survived them all. He became a special effects expert with Warner Bros. and photographed productions such as *Moby Dick* (1930). Koenekamp received the Award of the American Society of Cinematographers in recognition of his contributions to motion pictures. He retired in the early 1960s and died, age 100, at his home in Northridge, California, in 1992.[18]

As everything is transitory, many of Larry Semon's films, the originals on 35mm nitrate, are now gone. Nevertheless, the bulk of his oeuvre survived. This is partly owed to Raymond Rohauer, who in the 1960s bought from Warners a huge collection of Semon's 35mm Vitagraph films. About a year before he died, Rohauer made arrangements with the Library of Congress to donate most of these films. Other benefactors such as Joe Rinaudo of California have paid for the restoration of several titles whose current status is not known at the time of this writing. After World War II, the Italian and Spanish peoples' enthusiasm was responsible for keeping Larry Semon's memory alive. In the seventies and eighties, German television showed Larry Semon films on a weekly basis; his face is still known to people of this country to the present day. And as absurd as it may sound, all the film dupers in this world contributed to the rescue of Semon's best work, to which the author counts everything he did between 1918 and 1921.

Larry once said that admonition summed up his philosophy of life. He evolved it through encountering some most disheartening obstacles and he believed overcoming them by grimly refusing to be beaten, regardless of the consequences.[19] Like his grandfather and father before him, he had lost everything. He was anxious to make good, but it was not in the cards. Ironically, a few days after Semon's death, Sidney Goldin, the first to give him a chance in motion pictures, filed for bankruptcy. Like Larry, he had no assets; with better luck, maybe a nicer future.[20]

Famous people's last words always make a good citation. Semon's last words went unknown. Hans Koenekamp recalled when their unit was done for the day, Semon used to exclaim what might have made Larry's perfect epitaph: "Oh hell, let's go home."[21]

Appendix:
"Magic, Past and Present, Exposed"

Listing of Semon's column "Magic, Past and Present, Exposed." Published in the Sunday supplement of *The North American*, Philadelphia, and usually accompanied by his cut-out paper toys.

07/11/09 No column article; Punch and Judy: A Whole Show for the Children.
07/18/09 "Black Art" #1; Cut-out by M.A. Hayes.
07/25/09 "The Talking Head" #2; The Funniest of Fancy Dancers.
08/01/09 "Trunk Trick" #3; The Wrestlers.
08/08/09 "Decapitation Illusion" #4; Cut-out by M.A. Hayes.
08/15/09 "Basket Trick" #5; Hunters, Tiger & Gorilla: A Cut-up Picture Puzzle for the Young Folks.

"Kaptin Kiddo's Hobby Horse"

08/22/09 "Levitation" #6; The Hippodrome Jr., The Ringmaster & the Elephant.
08/29/09 "Tricks Relating to Spiritualism" #7; Donkey, Monkey & Clown.
09/05/09 "Growing Roses on the Stage" #8; Horse & Rider for the Jr. Hippodrome.
09/12/09 "Spiritualistic Manifestations" #9; The Dancing Chinaman, an Amusing Cut-out.
09/19/09 "Japanese Tricks" #10; The Jolly Professor: A Practical Jumping Jack.
09/26/09 "What Can Be Done With Playing Cards" #11; The Monkey on a Stick: A Working Toy
10/03/09 "Spiritual Cabinets" #12; The Jolly Tar.
10/10/09 "'She' (Cremation Illusion)" #13; Willie Westinghouse's Airship.
10/17/09 "Changing Liquids" #14; Sambo & His Mule.
10/24/09 "The Dice Box" #15; Lively Jester.
10/31/09 "Magical Cooking" #16; Marionette Brigand.
11/07/09 "The Box and the Platform" #17; Dancing in the Barn.
11/14/09 "Making Coffee On the Stage" #18; No cut-out toys.
11/21/09 "The Hat of Plenty" #19; The Artist's Dilemma.
11/28/09 "The Inexhaustible Coconut Shell" #20; The Seesaw.
12/05/09 "The Double Box Mystery" #21; Sambo & the Giraffe.
12/12/09 "More About Cards" #22; Christmas Hold-Up Kaptin Kiddo.
12/19/09 No column article; Santa Claus Cut-Out for Christmas.
12/26/09 "Flight of the Favorite" #23; Uncle Sam's New Year Greeting.
01/02/10 "A Spiritual Cabinet Built Upon the Stage" #24; The Lion Tamer.
01/09/10 "Where Is She?" #25; The Jolly Blacksmiths.
01/16/10 "The Vanishing Assistant" #26; Simple Simon And The Pieman.
01/23/10 "A Wonderful Levitation Illusion" #27; Eskimo Family: Cut-Out That Smacks Of The Frozen North.
01/30/10 "The Paper Bag and Box Mystery" #28; A Jolly Jingling Johnson Jigger Cut-Out.
02/06/10 "Several Small Tricks" #29; Wriggling Willie.
02/13/10 "A Mysterious Prisoner" #30; A Cut-Out Valentine.
02/20/10 "A New Cremation Illusion" #31; A Cut-Out Family of Arabs.
02/27/10 "The Triple Box Mystery" #32; The Wizard's Album.
03/06/10 "A Chapter on Handcuffs" #33; A Japanese Family: A Pretty and Interesting Cut-Out.
03/13/10 "The Milkcan Mystery" #34; Kaptin Kiddo's Hobby Horse.
03/20/10 "Escape from the Packing Box" #35; Dubbalong, Scow And Johnson in a Backyard Serenade.
03/27/10 No column article; Charming Ethelinda.

Filmography

BY PATRICK SKACEL AND CLAUDIA SASSEN

This filmography lists all movies for which an appearance or involvement of Lawrence "Larry" Semon could be documented. We provided as much information as possible, including survival status, copyright and release dates, cast lists, plots and reviews. In some cases we were able to add details about the original length of a picture: in feet for U.S. releases, in meters for German releases. It was our goal to draw on authentic reviews other than press releases and blurbs from trade papers, whenever possible. Titles are listed chronologically by their initial release dates.

We decided to incorporate information on contemporary German prints as they might be helpful as a reference point for restoration. Whenever the film is not known to be extant, we stretched the plot information so that it became distinctive for identification.

Regarding the length of pictures, it is impossible to provide an exact running time, since the cranking speed and projection speed were not standardized, varying from 16 frames per second or less up to 25 fps and faster. Both cameras and projectors were operated manually, resulting in different speeds screened from projectionist to projectionist.

Unless stated otherwise, our sources were the Vitagraph release synopses and the Catalog of Copyright Entries, Motion Pictures 1912–1939 by the Library of Congress, 1951. We also did data mining via watching as many films as possible.

The length of the uncut German releases does not mean that they feature additional scenes. Rather, the Germans loved indulging in intertitles, often adding lines where the original print would go without. Normally between 10 and 15 intertitles were used per reel.

Starting in the 1910s, several cameras were installed or different takes were employed to create a domestic negative and another one for the foreign market. At this writing, we were not able to determine any differences in takes or camera angles for Semon films.

The survival status normally refers to 35mm prints. With the inexorable deterioration of unidentified film material that waits for discovery in remote vaults, cineasts nowadays have to fall back on prints that were at times duped for the 8mm market of home projectionists. Whenever we knew of the existence of any remote print of a Semon film, we give its status as "extant." When we state that the film exists as a 16mm, 9.5mm or 8mm print, we normally refer to inaccessible private collections from which the film was normally transferred to video. To help those who would like to enjoy Larry Semon films in nearly complete amateur prints, we have added a list of home movies that still circulate at online auction sites.

Larry Semon's filmography may never be completely or correctly documented as his earliest attempts at film studios prior to Vitagraph have poorly been accounted for. In a 1925 newspaper article, Semon declared that up to the present day he had been responsible for the direction of 300 films,[1] a number that appears exaggerated. Giving it a second thought, Semon's first movie attempts probably had the status of "one-shot" consumables, even shorter than one reel. Considering that he still found himself in a learning-by-doing period with most of his attempts making it into the trash can rather than a distributor's office, in the end, a total of 300 films does not seem too far-fetched. Semon's Vitagraph films and later movies taken together amount to about 133 pictures which were diligently produced. So it is quite plausible that he made about the same number of films in the years 1914 to 1916. Among these films was his assistant work for Frank Daniels at Vitagraph before he took over as main director, assembling his own casts and crews. Semon delivered his earliest films for the Universal Studios from circa 1914 on; no one title can be named. Neither is the case for his stay at the Mittenthal Film Company in Yonkers, New York, where he started at about the same time. Semon was serving for Mittenthal as director, scenario writer and maybe even comedian, as can be inferred from an interview that Sam Gill and Jordan Young conducted in 1976 with James Aubrey.

Only one film before Semon's advent at Vitagraph can be verified: *The Fiddler* (1915) for Novelty, Mutual. On IMDb, Semon is listed as director for the Thanhouser-Mutual Company two-reel comedy *The Baby and the Boss* (1915). Only the second reel is extant. No document can be tracked down that confirms his contribution to the picture. *The Baby and the Boss*, or at least the footage available for viewing, does not tender comical traits and is rather a documentary of local doings in New York. As Semon seems to have indulged in comedy from his very beginning in motion pictures, the lack of comedy elements comes over as strange. Yet there are some hints that would not necessarily rule out Semon's contribution. The film was released in late November 1915, *The Fiddler* in mid–December 1915, both through Mutual. Also, the picture was produced on location in New York, showcasing the city's mayor, other officials and the local police force. Semon's career as cartoonist and journalist may have helped in getting access to these people.

In 1915, Semon became active for Palace Players, New York, as director and scenarist, although no titles coinciding with Semon have been verified. Palace Players began production in mid–1915. For the 1915–16 season, comedies directed by Edward Warren were filmed with C.M. Ackerman and Suzanne Westford in the leads. It is possible that Semon contributed to the scenarios. Only a handful of film titles for this period could be tracked down: *Oh You Maggie*,

The Double and the Devil, *Mrs. Dustin-Stax's Transformations*, *Jealous Jane's Janitor* and *Tramp and the Rubberking*.[2] No further information on these pictures is available.

Abbreviations

BFI: British Film Institute, London, UK
CCB: Cineteca del Comune di Bologna, Italy
CF: Cineteca del Friuli, Italy
CFU: Československý Filmovy Ústav–Filmovy Archiv, Prague, Czech Republic
CM: Camillo Moscati Collection, Milano, Italy
CNC: Archives françaises du film du CNC, Bois d'Arci, France
DFM: Det Danske Filmmuseum, Copenhagen, Denmark
DIF: Deutsches Institut für Filmkunde, Filmarchiv Wiesbaden, Germany
EYE: EYE Film Instituut Nederland, Amsterdam, Netherlands
FC: Filmoteca Catalana, Barcelona, Spain
FD: Filmmuseum Düsseldorf, Düsseldorf, Germany
GEH: George Eastman House, Rochester, New York, USA
JH: Estate of John Hampton, Los Angeles, USA
LoC: Library of Congress, Washington, D.C., USA
MoMA: Museum of Modern Art, New York, New York, USA
NFA: National Film Archive, London, England
PS: Sammlung Patrick Skacel, Frankfurt am Main, Germany
PTC: Piero Tortolina Collection, Italy
RFC: Ripley's Film Collection, Rome, Italy
UCLA: University of California, Los Angeles, California

One-Reel Comedies

1915

The Fiddler, **alternate title:** *The Violinist*; **survival status:** unknown; **release date:** December 20, 1915; **director:** Lawrence Semon (?); **writer:** Lawrence Semon (?); **produced by:** Novelty-Mutual; **cast:** Lawrence Semon; **plot:** Ravenously hungry Hans gets kicked out of a German band. He chances upon an eventful evening at the house of a Sausage King, devours the refreshments and becomes the darling of the occasion when he is mistaken for the famous violinist Strensky, who has failed to show up. Hans' life is put at risk when the real Strensky finally arrives, but the Sausage King buys Strensky off with a generous check. Hans and Lina, daughter of the Sausage King, plight their troth, and mamma rejoices. According to Larry Semon, this was the first film he appeared in (Ciné-magazine, April 11, 1922); **review:** Rather a slapstick sort of an offering in which much sausage eating and other eccentric happenings occur. Some audiences might find the comedy amusing, but it lacks refinement (*Moving Picture World*, December 20, 1915).

Other Mutual comedies which Semon might have contributed to and scheduled for the November–December season were: *Charlie's Twin Sister* (Novelty); **release date:** November 29, 1915; *Betty Burton, M. D.* (Novelty); **release date:** December 1, 1915; *A Janitor's Joyful Job* (Novelty); **release date:** December 6, 1915; *A Musical Mix-Up* (Novelty); **cast:** Edwin Pickett; **release date:** December 8, 1915; *A Girl, a Guard and a Garret* (Beauty); **cast:** Carol Holloway, John Sheehan, William Carroll; **release date:** December 13, 1915.

1916

Tubby Turns the Tables; **survival status:** unknown; **©:** February 9, 1916; **release date:** March 3, 1916; **copyright:** LP7611; **director:** Lawrence Semon; **writers:** Lawrence Semon and C. Graham Baker; **produced by:** Vitagraph; **cast:** Hughie Mack (Tubby), Adele de

Garde (Stenographer), Bert Binns (First Crook), George Binns (Second Crook), Billy Whitney (Banker); *plot:* Cleaning man Tubby is sent to work for a wealthy banker, who wants to donate his fortune to charity. Two disguised crooks sally out to steal the money. Tubby's powerful vacuum cleaner pulls off the crooks' disguises; *review:* Hughie Mack and a vacuum cleaner create most of the fun in this one-reel comedy. The idea is novel and has been cleverly produced by Lawrence Semon... (*Moving Picture World*, March 18, 1916, 1853).

Terry's Tea Party; **survival status:** unknown; ©: April 6, 1916; *release date:* April 28, 1916; *copyright:* LP8059; *director:* Lawrence Semon; *writer:* George McManus; *produced by:* Vitagraph; *cast:* John T. Kelly (Father), Kate Price (Mother), Jewell Hunt (Daughter), Doc Donohue (Count), Lawrence Semon (Valet), James McCabe (Dinty), Hughie Mack (Son); *plot:* Father wants to go out with his buddies who are waiting in a nearby restaurant. While Mother is preventing Father's escape, "The Count," the owner of the restaurant, is beaten unconscious by a beer keg thrown by Mother. When he wakes up, Father hires a gang of roughnecks for the count's hasty departure. To please Mother, Father volunteers to search for the roughnecks and stands as a hero after finding them at the restaurant; *review:* With John T. Kelly to head the cast, this one-reel comedy is a strong reminder of the Harrigan & Hart style of Irish humor. George McManus ... has been liberal with the laughs, and [the cast] support[s] Mr. Kelly with evident relish for the task (*Moving Picture World*, May 13, 1916, 1181).

Out Again, In Again; **survival status:** unknown; ©: April 18, 1916, March 3, 1920; *release dates:* May 12, 1916, March 22, 1920; *copyright:* LP8138, LP14818; *director:* Lawrence Semon; *writer:* George McManus; *produced by:* Vitagraph; *cast:* John T. Kelly (Father), Kate Price (Mother), Jewell Hunt (Daughter), Hughie Mack (Tubby), Donald McBride (Burglar); *plot:* Once again, Father desperately wants to go to the restaurant next door. In order to foil his escape, Mother makes him take off his clothes and go to bed. Tubby tries to elope with their daughter, but chooses the wrong window and enters Father's bedroom instead. Father disposes of intruder Tubby with a gentle tap on his head, takes his clothes and heads off for some drinks; *review:* The situations are laugh-provoking and full justice is done to them by the company (*Moving Picture World*, May 27, 1916, 1536).

More Money Than Manners; **survival status:** unknown; ©: May 8, 1916; *release date:* May 19, 1916; *copyright:* LP8246; *director:* Lawrence Semon; *writers:* C. Graham Baker and Lawrence Semon; *produced by:* Vitagraph; *cast:* John T. Kelly (P. Oodles), Kate Price (Mrs. Oodles), Jewell Hunt (Lucille Oodles), Templar Saxe (The Duke de Luxe), Genevieve Russell (Duchess de Luxe), Hughie Mack (Hector McMush); *plot:* The Oodles family wants to enter society, so they invite the Duke and Duchess de Luxe for dinner. The bad table manners of the Oodles insult the Duke and he demands satisfaction.

The Battler; **survival status:** print known to be extant, but further information is not available; ©: May 10, 1916; *release date:* May 26, 1916; *copyright:* LP8302; *director:* Lawrence Semon; *writers:* C. Graham Baker and Lawrence Semon; *produced by:* Vitagraph, Lawrence Semon; *cast:* Hughie Mack (The Battler), Edward Dunn (The Champ), Billy Baxter (The Villain), Claire McCormick (The Girl), Danny Hayes (The Trainer), Doc Donohue (The Crook); *plot:* Hughie, the battler, is offering $50,000 if he fails to knock out any ten men in ten minutes. Ed Dunn, the champ, decides to be one of the ten, but instead of his fists he intends to use gas bombs constructed by crook Billy Baxter; **additional information:** No print was available for viewing, yet in all probability Semon used "Billy Baxter" as a pseudonym. For *A Jealous Guy* it could be confirmed through title cards that Semon and Billy Baxter were identical; *review:* When they wrote *The Battler*, C. Graham Baker and Lawrence Semon gave us something different. Hughie Mack ... introduces a new form in the manly art of self defense. When he is pitted against a champion, he uses the "gas bomb wallop" with wonderful effect. The things that follow at the fight club are too funny to be related (*Moving Picture World*, May 27, 1916, 1521).

Losing Weight; *survival status:* unknown; ©: June 20, 1916, April 3, 1920; *release dates:* June 30, 1916, April 12, 1920; *copyright:* LP8575, LP14946; *director:* Lawrence Semon; *writers:* Lawrence Semon and C. Graham Baker; *produced by:* Lawrence Semon; *cast:* Hughie Mack (Hughie), Jewell Hunt (Jewell), John Flatow (Mr. Smith); *plot:* Overweight Hughie tries to lose weight via special training, but all his efforts fail and he gains another 150 pounds. Frustrated he returns to his former eating habits: beefsteaks, potatoes and beer. Oddly enough, he starts losing weight on his newly invented special diet.

The Man from Egypt; *survival status:* extant (35mm [EYE], fragment: 16mm [LoC]); ©: June 30, 1916, April 30, 1920; *release dates:* July 14, 1916, May 10, 1920; *copyright:* LP8652, LP15060; *director:* Lawrence Semon; *writers:* Lawrence Semon and C. Graham Baker; *produced by:* Lawrence Semon; *cast:* Hughie Mack (Heroic Hughie), Jewell Hunt (Jewell Moneybags in release-synopsis, Jewell Mazuma in credits), John Flatow (Man from Egypt), Harry Hammil (High Priest), Kate Price, William Shea; *plot:* Hotel bellboy Hughie scares off a guest and assumes his identity. In the guest's room he finds a large ruby and an invitation from a millionaire and his daughter. While they are meeting, a sheik makes attempts on Hughie's life and tries to steal the ruby.

A Jealous Guy; *survival status:* extant (35mm [EYE]); ©: July 15, 1916; *release date:* July 28, 1916; *copyright:* LP8707; *director:* Lawrence Semon; *writers:* C. Graham Baker and Lawrence Semon; *produced by:* Lawrence Semon; *cast:* Hughie Mack (Hughie Hunk, a Detective), Jewell Hunt (Mrs. Winsome, His Sister), Billy Baxter alias Lawrence Semon (Wildo Winsome, Her Wedding Gift), Edward Dunn (Butler), Vica Raymana (Maid); *plot:* A man, deeply in love with his wife and extremely jealous, presents a valuable necklace to her. Their crooked servants plan to steal it. The wife's brother Hughie, a detective, gets on the butler's trail, but the husband thinks that he is his wife's secret lover. It takes some time before things are sorted out—just in time to catch the servants; *review:* Lawrence Semon, in directing the picture, made capital of every comical situation. Interiors are entirely acceptable.... The photography throughout is excellent (*Moving Picture World*, July 29, 1916, 799).

Romance and Rough House; *survival status:* unknown; ©: August 2, 1916, May 6, 1920; *release dates:* August 11, 1916, May 17, 1920; *copyright:* LP8871, LP15093; *director:* Lawrence Semon; *writers:* C. Graham Baker and Lawrence Semon; *produced by:* Lawrence Semon; *cast:* Hughie Mack (Hefty Hughie), Patsy de Forest (Romantic Rena), William Shea (Her Father), Edward Dunn (Lieutenant of the Black Hoodwinkers), Pierre Colosse (Big Chief of the "Hoods"); *plot:* While trying to protect his sweetheart Lucretia, Hughie inflicts a wound in the shape of a cross on his own cheek. A gang of nihilists think that he is their new chief, whom they just have never seen before; *review:* The photography and lightings are worthy of comment, as they are particularly fine. The hand of Lawrence Semon is seen in the direction, which is certainly all that could be desired. Hughie is exceptionally droll and his support is also very good ("Two Vitagraph Comedies on General," *Motography*, Vol. XVI, No. 7, August 12, 1916, 366).

There and Back; *survival status:* extant (35mm [MoMA]); ©: August 3, 1916; *release date:* August 11, 1916; *copyright:* LP8881; *director:* Lawrence Semon; *writers:* Lawrence Semon and C. Graham Baker; *produced by:* Lawrence Semon; *cast:* Hughie Mack (Hughie Homer), Patsy De Forest (Mrs. Homer), Frank Kingsley (Hen Pecke), Alice Mann (Mrs. Hen Pecke), Edward Dunn (John Dubo), Ethel Corcoran (Mrs. John Dubo), Josephine Earle (The She Detective), Harry Hammil (Hank Hardrug); *plot:* Hughie and two of his friends sneak away from their wives to visit a cabaret where they start flirting with two girls. The wives grow suspicious and hire a female detective to track their husbands. She soon finds them in the cabaret. Right at the moment when the angry wives appear at the cabaret, Hughie manages to sneak out and return home. On his wife's return, Hughie demands to know where she has been; *additional information:* Dr. Sigmund Stark, physician for the New York studios of the Vitagraph Company, returned from Camp Whitman for a few minutes on

Friday and arrived at the studio just as director Larry Semon's troop of funmakers in fantastic costumes were leaving the yard with a battered brass band. Seeing him, they turned and marched around the yard at his back, tooting their tattered trumpets and banging their ragged drums. Used to such doings, the doctor did not realize that he was the object of their affection for several minutes. When he did, Uncle Sam's bold medical adviser flung honor to the wings and fled, to the joy of the rest of the studio (*Motography*, August 19, 1916, 441).

A Villainous Villain; **survival status:** unknown; ©: August 24, 1916; *release date:* September 8, 1916; *copyright:* LP9022; *director:* Lawrence Semon; *writers:* Lawrence Semon and C. Graham Baker; *produced by:* Lawrence Semon; *cast:* Hughie Mack, Patsy De Forest, William Shea, Harry Hammil, Ed Dunn, Joe Simberg, Frank Brule, Daniel Hays; *plot:* A master crook kidnaps Hughie's girlfriend. She is tied to one end of a rope, while the other end is tied to a car. The car and the girl fall into the water and a wild chase by boat follows. Now Hughie gets entangled in the rope, but he is able to grab his girlfriend and rescue her.

Love and Loot (original title) *An Amateur at Heart* (alternate title); **survival status:** unknown; ©: September 9, 1916; *release date:* September 15, 1916; *copyright:* LP9082; *director:* Lawrence Semon; *writers:* C. Graham Baker and Lawrence Semon; *produced by:* Lawrence Semon; *cast:* Hughie Mack (The Hero), Patsy De Forest (The Heroine), William Shea (Her Father), Edward Dunn (The Crook), Frank Brule (The Burglar); *plot:* Thrown out by his girlfriend Patsy, Hughie goes in for a career as a burglar. Years later he accidentally chooses Patsy's house to break into.

Sand, Scamps and Strategy; **survival status:** unknown; ©: September 16, 1916; *release date:* September 22, 1916; *copyright:* LP9133; *director:* Lawrence Semon; *writers:* C. Graham Baker and Lawrence Semon; *produced by:* Lawrence Semon; *cast:* Hughie Mack (Percy Pickles), Patsy De Forest (Little Nell), Edward Dunn (Crafty Casper), William Shea (Father); *plot:* Percy pays the mortgage for his sweetheart's father. The creditors seek revenge and capture the girl. Percy needs to save the girl from a fiery furnace and from the edge of a cliff; *review: Sand, Scamps and Strategy* sets a pace for fast and furious fun that even the agile Hughie and his comedy pals will find it hard to live up to (*Moving Picture World*, September 23, 1916, 1978).

She Who Last Laughs; **survival status:** unknown; ©: September 23, 1916; *release date:* September 29, 1916; *copyright:* LP9177; *director:* Lawrence Semon; *writers:* C. Graham Baker and Lawrence Semon; *produced by:* Lawrence Semon; *cast:* Hughie Mack (Spencer Spunk), William Shea (I.M. Wealthy), Patsy De Forest (Vera Wealthy), Cathryn Palmar (Ruth Sleuth); *plot:* Vera Wealthy, heiress to the Wealthy estate and Spencer Spunk's girlfriend, fakes her own abduction after a quarrel with her father and goes for a walk in the park. Father thinks Spencer is behind the kidnapping, and Spencer, to clear his name, goes on a rescue mission.

Walls and Wallops; **survival status:** unknown; ©: October 30, 1916; *release date:* November 13, 1916; *copyright:* LP9428; *director:* Lawrence Semon; *writers:* C. Graham Baker and Lawrence Semon; *produced by:* Vitagraph; *cast:* Hughie Mack (Police Sergeant), William Shea (The Chief), Patsy De Forest (His Daughter), Ed Dunn (The Villain); *plot:* The police chief's daughter, kidnapped by gangsters, finds herself in the villain's dance hall den. The sergeant and some other policemen take up pursuit; *review:* There is whirlwind action from start to finish in this comedy.... The Director, Lawrence Semon, who is part author, has kept the fun going at a fast and furious rate.... The photography has succeeded rather well in keeping up with the rapid action (*New York Dramatic Mirror*, November 4, 1916, 34).

Jumps and Jealousy; **survival status:** unknown; ©: November 8, 1916; May 21, 1920; *release dates:* November 20, 1916; May 31, 1920; *copyright:* LP9477, LP15157; *director:* Lawrence Semon; *writers:* Lawrence Semon and C. Graham Baker; *produced by:* Vitagraph; *cast:* Hughie Mack (The Masher), Patsy De Forest (The Mashee), James Aubrey (Her Husband); *plot:* Hughie, always flirting with the girls in the park, is chased by a cop and a friend of one of the girls. Later that day he gets involved in a bedroom war with Jim and Patsy; *review:* Average Comedy. Four years old but gets by (*Exhibitors Herald* [on a re-release], March 15, 1924, 90).

His Conscious Conscience; *survival status:* unknown; ©: October 28, 1916; *release date:* November 27, 1916; *copyright:* LP9421; *director:* Lawrence Semon; *writers:* Lawrence Semon and C. Graham Baker; *produced by:* Vitagraph; *cast:* Hughie Mack (Hughie McTurbs), Patsy De Forest (Patsy Darling), Harry Hammil (Old Man Darling), Ed Dunn (Thief); *plot:* Hughie is in love with Patsy, but he still needs her father's approval and he is sure that the old man will say no. When the days' proceeds of the local cinema are stolen, Hughie encounters the thief at home, face to face with Patsy's father, who is waving a gun. Hughie accidentally recovers the money and learns that the father always wanted him as his son-in-law.

Hash and Havoc; *survival status:* extant (35mm [FC]); ©: November 11, 1916, March 29, 1920; *release dates:* December 4, 1916, April 19, 1920; *copyright:* LP9506, LP14981; *director:* Lawrence Semon; *writers:* Lawrence Semon and C. Graham Baker; *produced by:* Vitagraph; *cast:* Hughie Mack (The Chef), Patsy De Forest (The Cashier), James Aubrey (The Boss), Ed Dunn and Frank Brule (The Waiters); *plot:* At a restaurant, the chef, the boss and the waiter are all in love with the cashier, which results in the wrecking of the kitchen and the dining room.

Rah! Rah! Rah!; *survival status:* unknown; ©: November 14, 1916, May 18, 1920; *release dates:* December 11, 1916, May 24, 1920; *copyright:* LP9517, LP15136; *director:* Lawrence Semon; *writers:* Lawrence Semon and C. Graham Baker; *produced by:* Vitagraph; *cast:* Hughie Mack (Our Brave Hero), Patsy De Forest (Our College Widow), James Aubrey (Our Jealous Rival); *plot:* Jim hires some actors to scare Hughie in a haunted house, as Jim wants to prove to Patsy that Hughie is not the bravest man in the world. Patsy's hero is disgraced when all actors strip off their disguises. A gang of counterfeiters takes all valuables from everyone present, and Hughie gets his chance to show that he is a brave man indeed; *review:* The humor is of the slapstick variety. While there is no story worthy of consideration in the comedy, there is considerable active effort to encourage laughs which are quite successful (*New York Dramatic Mirror*, November 18, 1916, 34).

Help! Help! Help!; *survival status:* unknown; ©: November 6, 1916, February 28, 1920; *release dates:* December 18, 1916, March 15, 1920; *copyright:* LP9466, LP14807; *director:* Lawrence Semon; *writers:* Lawrence Semon and C. Graham Baker; *produced by:* Vitagraph; *cast:* Hughie Mack (Lifesaver), Patsy De Forest (The Girl), William Shea (Mr. Henpeck), Nellie Anderson (Mrs. Henpeck), Ed Dunn (Mr. Hubby), Adele De Garde (Mrs. Hubby); *plot:* Hughie is a lifeguard, who cannot swim but loves to flirt with the ladies. When a child gets pulled out far into the water, he comes to the rescue; *review:* There is some ingenuity in the action and in the way the laughs are worked up (*New York Dramatic Mirror*, November 4, 1916, 34).

Shanks and Chivalry; *survival status:* unknown; ©: December 12, 1916, April 21, 1920; *release dates:* December 25, 1916, May 3, 1920; *copyright:* LP9729, LP15040; *director:* Lawrence Semon; *writers:* Lawrence Semon and C. Graham Baker; *produced by:* Vitagraph; *cast:* Hughie Mack (Ye Lover), Patsy De Forest (Ye Princess), William Shea (Ye King), Jim Aubrey (Ye Prime Minister), Ed Dunn (Ye Lieutenant), Vida Ramon (Ye Ladye-in Waiting); *plot:* If it was up to the king, princess Patsy would marry the prime minister. But she is in love with Hughie. The prime minister kidnaps the princess. Hughie, after an exciting escape from being buried alive, routs the prime minister and rescues the princess; *review:* An amusing burlesque on the medieval drama (*New York Herald*, December 4, 1916, 7).

1917

Speed and Spunk; *survival status:* unknown; ©: December 13, 1916, March 19, 1920; *release dates:* January 1, 1917, March 29, 1920; *copyright:* LP9731, LP14910; *director:* Lawrence Semon; *writers:* Lawrence Semon and C. Graham Baker; *produced by:* Vitagraph; *cast:* Hughie Mack (The Bachelor), James Aubrey (The Husband), Patsy De Forest (The Wife); *plot:* Hughie is a real nuisance, flirting with every girl around, especially with Patsy, much to the annoyance of Patsy and her sweetheart Jack. Hughie finally tries to kidnap Patsy. Jack follows Hughie's car by airplane and throws a bomb down on it.

Bears and Bullets/Bullies and Bullets; *survival status:* extant (35mm [BFI, DFM]); as *Bears and Bullets* © November 29, 1916, re-released as *Bullies and Bullets* ©: December 13, 1916, March 23, 1920; *release dates:* January 8, 1917, April 5, 1920; *copyright:* LP9732, LP14916; *director:* Lawrence Semon; *writers:* Lawrence Semon and C. Graham Baker; *produced by:* Vitagraph; *cast:* Hughie Mack (Him), Patsy De Forest (Her), James Aubrey (A Person); *plot:* Hughie and Patsy are in love. Jim tries to separate them by telling Patsy that Hughie is unfaithful and telling Hughie that Patsy is not true to him.

Jolts and Jewelry; *survival status:* unknown; ©: January 9, 1917, December 10, 1919; *release dates:* January 15, 1917, December 29, 1919; *copyright:* LP9937, LP14529; *director:* Lawrence Semon; *writers:* Lawrence Semon and C. Graham Baker; *produced by:* Vitagraph; *cast:* Hughie Mack (Bunco Charley), James Aubrey (Slippery Ike), Alice Mann (Miss Glitters); *plot:* A new invention, an electric warming blanket, is demonstrated before an invited audience. Two crooks shake everyone down for their valuables

Big Bluffs and Bowling Balls; *survival status:* unknown; ©: January 12, 1917, December 10, 1919; *release dates:* January 22, 1917, December 22, 1919; *copyright:* LP9976, LP14528; *director:* Lawrence Semon; *writers:* Lawrence Semon and C. Graham Baker; *produced by:* Vitagraph; *cast:* James Aubrey (One Bluff), Hughie Mack (Another Bluff), John Costello (Father), Alice Mann (His Offspring); *plot:* Alice's father is a bowling fan and wants a son-in-law who is hooked as well, so he decides to bestow his daughter to the winner of a bowling contest. Hughie and Jim, rivals for the hand of Alice and absolutely unable to bowl, get ready to learn the game; *review:* Amused the crowds (*The Brooklyn Daily Eagle*, February 6, 1917, 14).

Somewhere in Any Place; *survival status:* unknown; ©: January 20, 1917, November 25, 1919; *release dates:* January 29, 1917, December 15, 1919; *copyright:* LP10050, LP14476; *director:* Lawrence Semon; *writers:* Lawrence Semon and C. Graham Baker; *produced by:* Vitagraph, Lawrence Semon; *cast:* Hughie Mack (Capt. S. Service), Alice Mann (His Stenographer), James Aubrey (Mr. "X," a Spy); *plot:* When a spy steals a valuable map, Capt. Service, who was responsible for the safety of that map, is condemned to death. His only chance is to return the map by six o'clock.

Rips and Rushes; *survival status:* unknown; ©: January 29, 1917, January 7, 1920; *release dates:* February 5, 1917, January 26, 1920; *copyright:* LP10088, LP14622; *director:* Lawrence Semon; *writers:* Lawrence Semon and C. Graham Baker; *produced by:* Vitagraph; *cast:* James Aubrey (His Lordship), Hughie Mack (Vernon Rastle), Alice Mann (Girlie), John Costello (Her Old Man), Joe Simberg, Earl Montgomery, Pietro Aramondo, Murray Simberg, Edward Dunn; *plot:* Dancing teacher Hughie and Jim are both in love with the same girl. While Jim is spying on Hughie and the girl, he ruins his trousers, and Hughie rips his own pants. Hughie and Jim flee holding screens to conceal their hairy legs from onlookers.

He Never Touched Me; *survival status:* unknown; ©: January 27, 1917, February 6, 1920; *release dates:* February 12, 1917, February 16, 1920; *copyright:* LP10074, LP14721; *director:* Lawrence Semon; *writers:* Lawrence Semon and C. Graham Baker; *produced by:* Vitagraph; *cast:* James Aubrey (A Crafty Lawyer), Hughie Mack (A Weak-Kneed Husband), Alice Mann (His Wife), Hattie Delaro (Her Strong-Jawed Mother); *plot:* Jim plans to marry Hughie's rich mother-in-law. In order to increase his chances, he invites himself to breakfast at Hughie's house. The meal evolves into a fight between the two men. Hughie defeats Jim and throws him out.

Cops and Cussedness; *survival status:* unknown; ©: February 5, 1917, January 26, 1920; *release dates:* February 19, 1917, February 2, 1920; *copyright:* LP10118, LP14677; *director:* Lawrence Semon; *writers:* Lawrence Semon and C. Graham Baker; *produced by:* Vitagraph; *cast:* Hughie Mack (The Pride of the Force), James Aubrey (Oliver Otbun), Patsy De Forest (Cook), Edward Dunn (First Cop), Jack O'Hara (Second Cop); *plot:* Cook Patsy loves crook Jim. Cop Hughie recognizes

Jim from a photo and tells Patsy all about him. Hughie hides in Patsy's house and awaits Jim. Joined by another cop, they finally capture him.

Masks and Mishaps; **survival status:** extant (35mm [LoC]); ©: February 19, 1917, February 21, 1920; *release dates:* February 26, 1917, March 8, 1920; **copyright:** LP10224, LP14763; *director:* Lawrence Semon; *writers:* Lawrence Semon and C. Graham Baker; *produced by:* Vitagraph; *cast:* James Aubrey (A Much Married Man), Vivian Marshall (His Jealous Wife), Ed Dunn (A Bill Poster), Billie Leslie (His Dame), Virginia De Lillies (The Countess); *plot:* To escape from his dominating wife for a night, Jim goes to a masked ball with another lady. Dressed as Pierrot and Pierrette, they find out that another couple has also chosen that set of costumes.

Guff and Gunplay; **alternate title:** *Guffs and Gunplay* (in release synopsis); **survival status:** extant (35mm [BFI]); ©: February 28, 1917, January 7, 1920; *release dates:* March 5, 1917, January 19, 1920; *copyright:* LP10270, LP14621; *director:* Lawrence Semon; *writers:* Lawrence Semon and C. Graham Baker; *produced by:* Vitagraph; *cast:* James Aubrey (Black Ike), Ed Dunn (Sheriff Dawson), Josephine West (The Gal); *plot:* Sheriff Dawson is the town's hero until a gunman named Black Ike captures him and forces him to hold up a stagecoach. Ike escapes and the sheriff is deeply humiliated, but a girl goes after Ike. Ike instigates a shoot-out in the dance hall. The girl knocks Ike out by shooting a lamp hanging above his head.

Pests and Promises; **survival status:** extant (35mm [LoC]); ©: March 13, 1917, February 11, 1920; *release dates:* March 12, 1917, February 19, 1920; *copyright:* LP10376, LP14744; *director:* Lawrence Semon; *writers:* Lawrence Semon and C. Graham Baker; *produced by:* Vitagraph; *cast:* James Aubrey (The Mayor), Edward Dunn (The Boss), Dorothy Armstrong (The Girl); *plot:* Jim and the father of his sweetheart both run. Jim wins the election, but he does not keep the promises he made to the town's bosses, so they plan to create a scandal by having him caught with a vamp.

Footlights and Fakers; **survival status:** unknown; ©: March 16, 1917, November 21, 1919; *release dates:* March 19, 1917, December 8, 1919; *copyright:* LP10397, LP14463; *director:* Lawrence Semon; *writers:* Lawrence Semon and C. Graham Baker; *produced by:* Vitagraph; *cast:* James Aubrey (Props, on reissue sheet: Jim), Edward Dunn (Grips, on reissue sheet: Ed), Dorothy Armstrong (Leading Lady; on the reissue sheet this role is credited to Alice Mann), Joe Simberg (Her Husband); *plot:* Jim and Ed are property men working in a theater. They start flirting with the leading lady, much to the annoyance of her husband. Then the two ruin the show by turning on a water hose full force, leaving the cast and the audience soaked; *review:* It is mighty clever. Get it (*Exhibitors Herald* [on a re-release], May 26, 1923, 82).

Turks and Troubles; **survival status:** extant (35mm [BFI]); ©: March 21, 1917, November 12, 1919; *release dates:* March 26, 1917, December 1, 1919; *copyright:* LP10414, LP14429; *director:* Lawrence Semon; *writers:* Lawrence Semon and C. Graham Baker; *produced by:* Vitagraph; *cast:* James Aubrey (A Soldier of Fortune, on reissue sheet: Jim), Edward Dunn (Haffed, the Terrible Turk), Dorothy Armstrong (The American Girl; on the reissue sheet this role is credited to Alice Mann), Joe Rock and Earl Montgomery (The Other Two); *plot:* An American girl and her father have been imprisoned by Haffed, the Turk, but she manages to call Jim, a soldier of fortune, for help. After an unsuccessful first rescue attempt, he disguises himself as a female dancer and turns Haffed's head.

Dubs and Dry Goods; **survival status:** unknown; ©: April 2, 1917, January 28, 1920; *release dates:* April 2, 1917, February 9, 1920; *copyright:* LP10500, LP14687; *director:* Lawrence Semon; *writers:* Lawrence Semon and C. Graham Baker; *produced by:* Vitagraph; *cast:* James Aubrey (The Boss), Ed Dunn (The Shipping Clerk), Joe Simberg (The Shoplifter), The "Big V" Riot Squad; *plot:* A shoplifter roams around in Jim's department store. Ed, the shipping clerk, offers help and disguises himself as a woman.

Flatheads and Flivvers; **survival status:** extant (35mm [FC]); ©: April 7, 1917, December 20, 1919; *release dates:* April 9, 1917, January 5, 1920; *copyright:* LP10528, LP14548; *director:* Lawrence Semon; *writers:* Lawrence Semon and C. Graham Baker; *produced by:*

Vitagraph; *cast:* James Aubrey (Ima Crook), Ed Dunn (A. Boob), Harry Deroy (Bing Bangs), Nina Trask (Bessie Bangs); *plot:* Two rivals, a secret service agent and a representative of the king of Bulgonia, each try to convince a professor to hand him the professor's new invention, a very powerful explosive.

Bombs and Blunders; *survival status:* unknown; ©: April 13, 1917, February 16, 1920; *release dates:* April 16, 1917, March 1, 1920; *copyright:* LP10575, LP14757; *director:* Lawrence Semon; *writers:* Lawrence Semon and C. Graham Baker; *produced by:* Vitagraph; *cast:* James Aubrey (Timothy Oogle), Nina Trask (Helen Truelove), Ed Dunn (Jack, Her Sweetheart), The "Big V" Riot Squad; *plot:* Jim tries to flirt with Ed's sweetheart Helen. Helen rejects his advances. Her sweetheart Jack comes to her rescue by plane.

Hazards and Homeruns; *survival status:* unknown; ©: April 21, 1917, December 26, 1919; *release dates:* April 23, 1917, January 12, 1920; *copyright:* LP10612, LP14571; *director:* Lawrence Semon; *writers:* Lawrence Semon and C. Graham Baker; *produced by:* Vitagraph; *cast:* James Aubrey (Gideon Glassarm), Ed Dunn (Nat Twirler, Rival Captain), Dan Duffy (Ima Bugg, a Baseball Fan), Dorothy Armstrong (Sadie Bugg, His Daughter), Frank Alexander (Heeza Tonn, a Catcher); *plot:* Jim and Ed compete for the hand of Sadie. They are also rivals on the baseball diamond. Ed's gang kidnaps Sadie and Jim starts the pursuit, leaving his team without a pitcher. However, he rescues Sadie *and* wins the game.

Boasts and Boldness; *survival status:* extant (35mm [EYE], fragment: 16mm [CM]); ©: July 6, 1917; *release date:* August 6, 1917; *copyright:* LP11072; *director:* Lawrence Semon; *writers:* Lawrence Semon and C. Graham Baker; *produced by:* Greater Vitagraph; *cast:* James Aubrey (Jim), Lawrence Semon (Villain); *plot:* Jim and his wife spend their honeymoon on a train with a large shipment of gold. A bandit holds up the train. Jim's wife orders him to capture the villain; *additional information:* Vitagraph on their first New Big V Comedy: "On August 6, Greater Vitagraph will release the first of its new series of rollicking Big V Comedies. These comedies, which are of the slapstick variety, but refreshingly devoid of the pie-hurling element, are produced under the direction of Lawrence Semon, who plays the leading male role and also collaborates with Graham Baker in writing the scripts. In the cast supporting Mr. Semon are some of the most intrepid performers before the camera, chief among whom are Joe Simberg, Earl Montgomery, Joe Basil and Ed. Dunn. All of them are trained acrobats, recruited from circus and vaudeville stage to provide laughs and thrills for the Big V Comedies. The new series of comedies will be characterized by some of the most remarkable trick photography ever seen on the screen. The new stunts in cinematography which are being concocted by Cameraman Len Smith and Director Semon are calculated to create a furor in film circles when the first of the new Big V Comedies is released" (*Motography*, August 11, 1917, 296); *review:* There is a snap and a dash about the business of this one-part athletic farce that makes it very laughable. It is well produced and acted (*Moving Picture World*, August 18, 1917, 1086).

Worries and Wobbles; *survival status:* extant (35mm [EYE]); ©: July 9, 1917, May 27, 1920; *release dates:* August 13, 1917, June 7, 1920; *copyright:* LP11062, LP15179; *director:* Lawrence Semon; *writers:* Lawrence Semon and C. Graham Baker; *produced by:* Vitagraph; *cast:* James Aubrey (Wandering Boy), Joe Simberg, Earl Montgomery, Pietro Aramondo, Ed Dunn; *plot:* Jim's wife catches him drunk and orders him to go to bed. Jim outwits a burglar and switches clothes with him; he then makes his way out on the ladder the burglar used to break in. Soon Jim's wife enters the bedroom to ask for forgiveness; *review:* This has no particular plot and develops only a fair amount of humor, though well handled for this type of humor (*Moving Picture World*, September 1, 1917, 1389).

Shells and Shivers; *survival status:* unknown; ©: July 9, 1917, March 27, 1920; *release dates:* August 20, 1917, April 26, 1920; *copyright:* LP11063, LP14982; *director:* Lawrence Semon; *writers:* Lawrence Semon and C. Graham Baker; *produced by:* Vitagraph; *cast:* James Aubrey (Major Life Miserable), Ed Dunn (General D. Bility), Lillian Mann (The Girl Spy); *plot:* A furious battle between a major (Jim Aubrey) and a general

(Ed Dunn) develops. A Red Cross nurse volunteers to lure the major into the general's hands, but her cover is blown. Just when she is about to be put to death, the fights start again, because the lunch break is over; *review:* A war-time burlesque of rather an entertaining sort. The manner in which shells dart back and forth through the air and pursue frantic victims is really very amusing. Rather a clever idea with Lawrence Semon directing (*Moving Picture World*, August 4, 1917, 813).

Chumps and Chances; ***survival status:*** unknown; ©*:* July 14, 1917; ***release dates:*** August 27, 1917, October 14, 1918; ***copyright:*** LP11091; ***director:*** Lawrence Semon; ***writers:*** Lawrence Semon and C. Graham Baker; ***produced by:*** Greater Vitagraph; ***cast:*** Lawrence Semon (Comedian/Harold), Jewell Hunt (Girl), Jules Cowles (Father), Nellie Anderson (Old Maid), Joe Simberg and Earl Montgomery (Cops); ***plot:*** Larry asks his sweetheart's father for her hand. The father refuses and the daughter is put into the custody of her old maiden aunt. Larry tries to enter the aunt's house and free his girl, but several attempts at rescue fail. He finally climbs to her window using telegraph wires; ***review:*** This is as funny a picture as one could wish to see. It is full of laughs. This comedy is incredibly funny (*Moving Picture World*, August 4, 1917, 813).

Gall and Golf; ***length:*** 236 meters (Dansk version); ***survival status:*** extant (35mm [DFM, LoC], 16mm [CM]); ©*:* August 30, 1917; ***release dates:*** September 3, 1917, October 14, 1918; ***copyright:*** LP11324; ***director:*** Lawrence Semon; ***writers:*** Lawrence Semon and C. Graham Baker; ***produced by:*** Vitagraph; ***cast:*** Lawrence Semon (O.U. Dubb), Florence Curtis (Girl Crook), Earl Montgomery, Templer Saxe, Donald MacBride and Joe Simberg (Other Dubbs); ***plot:*** O.U. Dubb, a member of the country club, realizes that he cannot play golf without using bad language. He is being avoided, but things brighten up when he meets a pretty girl on the golf course; ***review:*** The comedy is mostly devoted to footage, showing Mr. Semon in attempts at clowning. The number does not go over very well, its only laughs being in the scenes showing the golf balls flying around. A few pretty girls help a little. A mediocre release (*Moving Picture World*, September 15, 1917, 1707).

Slips and Slackers; ***survival status:*** extant (16mm [CM]); ©*:* September 7, 1917; ***release date:*** September 10, 1917; ***copyright:*** LP11354; ***director:*** Lawrence Semon; ***writers:*** Lawrence Semon and C. Graham Baker; ***produced by:*** Vitagraph; Lawrence Semon (The Slacker), Nellie Anderson (The Bride), Harry Hammil (The General), The "Big V" Riot Squad: Joe Basil, Earl Montgomery, Joe Simberg, Charles O'Brien, Doc Donohue, Murray Simberg, Pietro Aramondo; ***plot:*** Larry is not sure whether he should join the army. He enters a recruiting office but, when he learns what kinds of examinations and tests all applicants have to go through, he gets cold feet; ***review:*** [Larry] is a slacker who is scared by the methods of testing recruits. These scenes are very funny. He compels the scrubwoman to marry him. Then he finds out that she is worse than the war. The best part is where he sits on a target that has been freshly painted. When he gets up the recruits mistake him for the target and begin practice (*Moving Picture Word*, September 15, 1917, 1707).

Risks and Roughnecks; ***survival status:*** extant (16mm); ©*:* September 12, 1917; ***release date:*** September 17, 1917; ***copyright:*** LP11402; ***director:*** Lawrence Semon; ***writer:*** C. Graham Baker; ***produced by:*** Vitagraph; ***cast:*** Larry Semon (The Boy), Florence Curtis (The Girl), The "Big V" Riot Squad: Earl Montgomery, Joe Simberg, Joe Basil, Pietro Aramondo; ***plot:*** A fan of all kinds of detective stories, Larry does not hesitate to rescue his girl from kidnappers just as all his fictional heroes would do; ***review:*** Some amazing acrobatic stunts. Everything and everybody moves so fast that the plot is soon left behind, but the supply of broad humor keeps pace with the action (*Moving Picture World*, September 29, 1917, 2010).

Plans and Pajamas; ***survival status:*** extant (35mm [LoC]); ©*:* September 20, 1917; ***release date:*** September 24, 1917; ***copyright:*** LP11436; ***director:*** Lawrence Semon; ***writer:*** C. Graham Baker; ***produced by:*** Vitagraph; ***cast:*** Florence Curtis (The Girl), Lawrence Semon (The Idler); ***plot:*** An escaped lunatic, the spitting image of a German spy, talks Larry into stealing some top secret papers.

Larry does not know that those papers are in fact only the plans for a new girls' dormitory; *review:* Up to the average of this brand of pictures (*Moving Picture World*, September 29, 1917, 2010).

Plagues and Puppy Love; *survival status:* extant (16mm [PS]); ©: September 25, 1917; *release date:* October 1, 1917; *copyright:* LP11461; *director:* Lawrence Semon; *writer:* C. Graham Baker; *produced by:* Vitagraph; *cast:* Florence Curtis (Florence), Larry Semon (Larry), The "Big V" Riot Squad: Earl Montgomery, Joe Simberg, Joe Basil, Pietro Aramondo; *plot:* While walking her dog in the park, Florence is flirted with over and again, even by a cop who she calls for help. Her boyfriend Larry, foreman of a derrick, intervenes and puts the others to rout; *review:* Plagues and Puppy Love is the odd title of a comedy that should cause smiles, ripples of laughter and then the loud hearty kind the next three days (*Utica Sunday Tribune*, October 21, 1917, 13).

Sports and Splashes; *survival status:* extant (35mm [LoC]); ©: October 5, 1917; *release date:* October 6 or 8, 1917; *copyright:* LP11499; *director:* Lawrence Semon; *writer:* C. Graham Baker; *produced by:* Vitagraph; *cast:* Lawrence Semon (The Luckless One), Florence Curtis (The Dancer), The "Big V" Riot Squad: Earl Montgomery, Joe Simberg, Joe Basil, Pietro Aramondo, Harry Cooper, "Big V" Beauty Squad; *plot:* Walking down the road, Larry finds a horseshoe and hopes that his bad luck will change for the better. He soon passes the horseshoe on to another man who was just thrown out of a cabaret because he could not pay his bill. This very moment, Larry is hit by a car and tossed into the cabaret, right into the seat of the non-paying guest.

Tough Luck and Tin Lizzies; *survival status:* extant (16mm); ©: October 17, 1917; *release date:* October 22, 1917; *copyright:* LP11575; *director:* Lawrence Semon; *writer:* Lawrence Semon; *produced by:* Vitagraph; *cast:* Larry Semon (Larry), Florence Curtis (Florence), Pietro Aramondo (Pete); *plot:* Once again a horseshoe does not bring Larry much luck, because he is hit by a car just when he picks it up and hit by another one when he rids himself of the horseshoe. He lands in the stranded Ford of Pete and Florence and accidently starts the car. It runs over Pete, who had placed himself underneath the vehicle to get it out of the rut; *review:* [This film] will be good for its purpose—to make you laugh (*Livonia Gazette*, April 12, 1918, 8).

Roughtoughs and Rooftops; *alternate title:* Rooftops and Ruffians (working title); *survival status:* extant (35mm [CNC, LoC], 16mm [FD]); ©: November 1, 1917; *release date:* November 5, 1917; *copyright:* LP11646; *director:* Lawrence Semon; *writers:* Lawrence Semon and C. Graham Baker; *produced by:* Vitagraph; *cast:* Larry Semon (The Janitor), Earl Montgomery (Monty), Joe Rock (Joe), Florence Curtis (The Girl), The "Big V" Riot Squad: Joe Simberg, Joe Basil, Pietro Aramondo, Ed Dunn; *plot:* In an office building, a gang of conspirators is all set to break a safe and snatch a banker's money. Janitor Larry and a girl try to foil their plan.

Spooks and Spasms; *survival status:* extant (35mm [CNC]); ©: November 28, 1917; *release date:* December 3, 1917; *copyright:* LP11764; *director:* Lawrence Semon; *writer:* Lawrence Semon; *produced by:* Vitagraph; *cast:* Larry Semon (Larry), Florence Curtis (The Girl), The "Big V" Riot Squad: Pietro Aramondo, Joe Basil, Al Rush, Tom O'Brien, James Brennon; *plot:* Poor Larry lives in constant dispute with his mother-in-law, who has an affair with a dancing master. During a melee with the dancing master, Larry is shot, at least by all appearances.

Noisy Naggers and Nosey Neighbors; *survival status:* unknown; ©: December 10, 1917; *release date:* December 17, 1917; *copyright:* LP11816; *director:* Lawrence Semon; *writer:* Lawrence Semon; *produced by:* Vitagraph; *cast:* Lawrence Semon (Larry), Florence Curtis, Madge Darrell, Pietro Aramondo, Leo Hayes; *plot:* When Larry falls in love with his neighbor Florence, his wife brings him to his senses by smashing a pitcher on his head. Things get even more out of hand when a ball of wool rolls from Florence's room into the apartment of Pete the poet, another secret admirer of hers.

1918

Guns and Greasers; *survival status:* extant (35mm [LoC]); ©: January 22, 1918; *release date:* January 28, 1918; *copyright:* LP11984; *director:* Lawrence Semon; *writer:* Lawrence Semon; *produced by:* Greater Vitagraph; *cast:* Lawrence Semon (Simp); *plot:* A western town is attacked by a Mexican gang just as Larry is about to count his gambling profits. Together with the lady dancer who helped him win the game, he tries to capture the gang; *additional information:* This was Larry's first comedy since his return to the West Coast from the Brooklyn studios.

Babes and Bombs; *alternate title:* Babes and Boobs (in copyright file); *length:* 825 feet; *survival status:* extant (35mm [BFI], 8mm); ©: February 2, 1918; *release date:* February 11, 1918; *copyright:* LP12021; *director:* Lawrence Semon; *writer:* Lawrence Semon; *produced by:* Greater Vitagraph; *cast:* Larry Semon (A Boob); Madge Kirby (His Wife), Frank Alexander (A Policeman); *plot:* Larry has curled up in his baby's cradle while the little child has to sit on the floor. His wife compels him to go shopping with her and the baby. Larry starts flirting with a pretty lady instead of minding the baby and causes a hopeless mix-up of babies and prams.

Rooms and Rumors; *survival status:* extant (35mm [LoC]); ©: February 15, 1918; *release date:* February 25, 1918; *copyright:* LP12064; *director:* Lawrence Semon; *writer:* Lawrence Semon; *produced by:* Greater Vitagraph; *cast:* Larry Semon (I.M. Insensible); *plot:* Drunk sap Larry accidentally enters the apartment of a married couple.

Meddlers and Moonshiners; *survival status:* extant (35mm [LoC, PTC]); ©: February 28, 1918; *release date:* March 11, 1918; *copyright:* LP12116; *director:* Lawrence Semon; *writer:* Larry Semon; *produced by:* Vitagraph; *cast:* Larry Semon (Simple Oswald); *plot:* Larry applies for a job as a revenue officer, ready to catch bootleggers.

Stripes and Stumbles; *survival status:* extant (35mm [LoC]); ©: March 5, 1918; *release date:* March 26, 1918; *copyright:* LP12144; *director:* Lawrence Semon; *writer:* Lawrence Semon; *produced by:* Greater Vitagraph; *cast:* Lawrence Semon (Larry), Madge Kirby (The Girl), Frank Alexander, Joe Basil, Owen Evans, Mortimer Peebles; *plot:* Larry, in love with the daughter of a prison warden, serenades her while a bunch of prisoners are trying to break out. Larry, on a ladder climbing up to his sweetheart's window, has his ladder and clothes stolen by the convicts and finds himself in the middle of a brawl.

Rummies and Razors; *survival status:* extant (35mm [LoC]); ©: March 23, 1918; *release date:* April 8, 1918; *copyright:* LP12212; *director:* Lawrence Semon; *writer:* Lawrence Semon; *produced by:* Greater Vitagraph; *cast:* Larry Semon (Larry); *plot:* Larry has a strange dream in which he sits on a park bench next to a quarrelling couple. Strangely, the wife begs her husband to continue to treat her roughly. Some time later, Larry runs into another fighting couple and, with the previous situation in mind, he hands the husband a club.

Whistles and Windows; *survival status:* extant (16mm [CM]); ©: April 5, 1918; *release date:* April 22, 1918; *copyright:* LP12281; *director:* Lawrence Semon; *writer:* Lawrence Semon; *produced by:* Greater Vitagraph; *cast:* Larry Semon (Oswald), Madge Kirby (Madge); *plot:* Madge is flirting with a neighbor. Larry is dragged into the events while trying to help the poor fellow, who is hanging on a girder after a hard punch from Madge's jealous husband; *additional information:* Apart from playing Oswald, Larry Semon also portrays a second character, a Russian duchess.

Spies and Spills; *survival status:* extant (16mm [CM]); ©: April 30, 1918; *release date:* May 13, 1918; *copyright:* LP12352; *director:* Lawrence Semon; *writer:* Lawrence Semon; *produced by:* Greater Vitagraph; *cast:* Larry Semon (Larry), Madge Kirby (Madge), Frank Alexander (Her Father); *plot:* Some spies have been instructed to get hold of a large cannon. Larry's dog fires the cannon and shoots the chief spy's plane down.

Romans and Rascals; *length:* 817 feet; *survival status:* extant (35mm [DFM], 16mm); ©: May 11, 1918; *release date:* May 27, 1918; *copyright:* LP12403; *director:* Lawrence Semon; *writer:* Lawrence Semon; *produced by:* Greater Vitagraph; *cast:* Lawrence Semon (Caesar and a Minstrel), Madge Kirby (Cleopatra), Pietro Aramondo, Owen Evans, Frank Alexander, Paul Rondas; *plot:* Some villains plan the downfall of Caesar (Larry), but the emperor trades places with a young minstrel who looks exactly like him. The minstrel defeats the villains and falls for Cleopatra.

Skids and Scalawags; *survival status:* extant (16mm [CM]); ©: May 27, 1918; *release date:* June 10, 1918; *copyright:* LP12462; *director:* Lawrence Semon; *writer:* Lawrence Semon; *produced by:* Greater Vitagraph; *cast:* Lawrence Semon (Rollo), Madge Kirby (Madge), Pietro Aramondo, Owen Evans, Frank Alexander, Paul Rondas; *plot:* Rollo and Madge try to elope from her father's house, but they are caught and Rollo is thrown out. After a long struggle, he manages to pick up Madge and escapes with her in his racing car.

Boodle and Bandits; *survival status:* extant (16mm [CM]); ©: June 11, 1918; *release date:* June 24, 1918; *copyright:* LP12532; *director:* Lawrence Semon; *writer:* Lawrence Semon; *produced by:* Vitagraph; *cast:* Lawrence Semon (Lightning Larry), Pietro Aramondo, Frank Alexander, Owen Evans, William Hauber, Madge Kirby, Lucille (Zintheo) Carlisle; *plot:* Lightning Larry, a two-gun desperado, and his gang are terrorizing a small western town. Their specialty is emptying the pockets of the saloon guests. Larry is finally captured by the lady sheriff.

Hindoos and Hazards; *survival status:* extant (35mm [RFC]); ©: June 29, 1918; *release date:* July 8, 1918; *copyright:* LP12619; *director:* Lawrence Semon; *writer:* Lawrence Semon; *produced by:* Vitagraph; *cast:* Larry Semon (Larry), Madge Kirby (Girl in Park), Frank Alexander (Necklace Thief), James Donnelly (Hindoo Chief), William Hauber (A Hindoo); *plot:* A tourist snatches an invaluable necklace from an Indian idol, which results in a bunch of priests pursuing him. He stumbles across Larry and thrusts the necklace into his hand. Larry does not want to part with the necklace, so a fast and thrilling chase begins.

Bathing Beauties and Big Boobs; *alternate titles: Big Boobs and Bathing Beauties, Wild Women* and *Wild Waves* (on release synopsis); *length:* 812 feet; *survival status:* extant (16mm [MoMA], 8mm); ©: July 15, 1918; *release date:* July 22, 1918; *copyright:* LP12663; *director:* Lawrence Semon; *writer:* Lawrence Semon; *produced by:* Greater Vitagraph; *cast:* Larry Semon (Lawrence), Madge Kirby (The Girl), Frank Alexander (Fatty), Lucille Carlisle (A Girl), James Donelly (Father); *plot:* During a sunny day at the beach, Lawrence and Fatty try to impress the father of a beautiful girl by faking a robbery. Real robbers are not far away.

Dunces and Dangers; *length:* 782 feet; *survival status:* extant (35mm [LoC], 16mm [CF], 8mm); ©: July 29, 1918; *release date:* August 5, 1918; *copyright:* LP12697; *director:* Lawrence Semon; *writer:* Lawrence Semon; *produced by:* Greater Vitagraph; *cast:* Lawrence Semon (Larry), Madge Kirby (His Wife), William Hauber, Owen Evans, Pietro Aramondo, Frank Alexander; *plot:* Creditors seize the belongings of Larry and his wife until nothing is left. When another three men knock on their door, Larry and his wife escape through a window, ending up high and dizzy.

Mutts and Motors; *survival status:* unknown; ©: August 24, 1918; *release date:* September 2, 1918; *copyright:* LP12777; *director:* Lawrence Semon; *writer:* Lawrence Semon; *produced by:* Greater Vitagraph; *cast:* Larry Semon (Larry); *plot:* A young woman tries to stop a car to bring her home. Larry offers help.

Two-Reel Comedies

Huns and Hyphens; *length:* 556 meters (uncut German release); *survival status:* extant (16mm, 8mm); ©: September 10, 1918; *release date:* September 23, 1918; *copyright:* LP12860; *director:* Lawrence Semon; *writer:* Lawrence Semon; *produced by:* Greater Vitagraph; *cast:* Larry Semon (Larry), Madge Kirby (Vera Bright), Stan Laurel (A Plotter), Mae Laurel (A Woman), William McCall (Customer), Frank Alexander (Cafe Owner), William Hauber (Waiter), Pete Gordon [Pete Aramondo] (Waiter), John Rand (Guest); *plot:* Vera Bright, Larry's girlfriend, has invented a gas mask approved by the government. At the secret hideout of a gang of German plotters, the girl's plans are stolen. Eventually, Larry rescues his girl and recovers the plans; *additional information:* Stan Laurel's first of three appearances with Larry Semon; *review:* This comedian, author and director has surrounded himself with a splendid company of players, and in his initial two-reel offering has striven for effects which he could not attain in one-reel length (*Moving Picture World*, September 21, 1918, 1726).

Bears and Bad Men; **survival status:** extant (16mm [CM], 8mm); **©:** September 28, 1918; *release date:* October 7, 1918; *copyright:* LP12933; *director:* Lawrence Semon; *writer:* Lawrence Semon; *produced by:* Lawrence Semon, Greater Vitagraph; *cast:* Lawrence Semon (Larry Cutshaw), Madge Kirby (The Slawsons' Daughter), Stan Laurel (Pete), William McCall (Stranded Actor), Blanche Payson (Stranded Actress), Mae Laurel (Scared Woman), Bessie and Brownie (Two Bears); *plot:* Larry, in the midst of a family feud, is deeply in love with their rival's daughter. He does not only have to watch out for the Slawson family, but also for two wild bears; *reviews:* More laughs than can be counted (*Utica Herald-Dispatch*, January 25, 1919, 3); The entire cast supply the picture with plenty of rough-and-tumble humor (*Moving Picture World*, November 9, 1918, 692).

Frauds and Frenzies; **survival status:** extant (35mm [CCB], 16mm [MoMA], 8mm); **©:** October 14, 1918; *release date:* November 18, 1918; *copyright:* LP11815; *director:* Lawrence Semon; *writer:* Lawrence Semon; *produced by:* Vitagraph, Lawrence Semon; *cast:* Larry Semon (Larry), Stan Laurel (Simp), Madge Kirby (Dolly Dare), William McCall (Warden), William Hauber (Prison Guard); *plot:* Larry and Stan are escaped convicts fighting for the love of Madge Kirby, unaware that she is the daughter of the chief guard; *reviews:* Lawrence Semon supplies enough energy and nerve in this two-part rough-and-tumble farce to win the admiration of any spectator. He risks his neck continually, and repeats his familiar brand old burlesque with all his old deftness (*Moving Picture World*, November 16, 1918, 760); It contains plenty of laughs worked up in a more or less legitimate way and is on a par with other comedies produced by Semon (*Exhibitor's Trade Review*, November 16, 1918).

Humbugs and Husbands; **alternate title:** *Husbands and Humbugs*, **survival status:** extant (16mm, 8mm); **©:** November 20, 1918; *release date:* December 2, 1918; *copyright:* LP13058; *director:* Lawrence Semon; *writer:* Lawrence Semon; *produced by:* Greater Vitagraph; *cast:* Lawrence Semon (Larry), Madge Kirby, Blanche Payson, William Hauber; *plot:* Larry tries to steal a police uniform from a cop, because all the girls have a crush on policemen and he wants to benefit from it. His plan backfires and he has to run.

Pluck and Plotters; **survival status:** extant (16mm [CM], 8mm); **©:** December 12, 1918; *release date:* December 23, 1918; *copyright:* LP 13162; *director:* Lawrence Semon; *writer:* Lawrence Semon; *produced by:* Greater Vitagraph; *cast:* Lawrence Semon (Janitor), Madge Kirby (Professor's Daughter), Frank Alexander (Chief of Gang), William McCall (Gangster), Jim Donnelly (Professor), William Hauber and Earl Montgomery (Gangsters); *plot:* An inventor asks janitor Larry to guard his newest stroke of genius—a flying torpedo and its small scale model—to be used against German spies. With the help of a woman spy, some crooks steal the model. Thanks to Larry, the model is returned to its inventor.

1919

Traps and Tangles; **length:** 590 meters (uncut German release); **survival status:** extant (35mm [LoC], 16mm, 8mm); **©:** January 10, 1919; *release date:* January 20, 1919; *copyright:* LP13273; *director:* Lawrence Semon; *writer:* Lawrence Semon; *produced by:* Greater Vitagraph; *cast:* Larry Semon (Detective Sparks), Madge Kirby (Sparks' Wife), Frank Alexander (Shop Assistant), Vera Steadman (His Girlfriend), Pete Gordon, William Hauber (A Gangster), Jim Donnelly (Old Cop); *plot:* Detective Sparks gets duped as he pays the reward for catching a crook to the crook himself. Later he and his wife get involved in the case of a beautiful lady's missing photo.

Scamps and Scandals; **length:** 530 meters (uncut German release); **survival status:** extant (35mm, 9.5mm [PS], 8mm); **©:** February 1, 1919; *release date:* February 17, 1919; *copyright:* LP13367; *director:* Lawrence Semon; *writer:* Lawrence Semon; *produced by:* Greater Vitagraph; *cast:* Larry Semon (Larry), Vera Steadman (His Sweetheart), Frank Alexander (Her Suitor), Lucille (Zintheo) Carlisle (A Wedding Guest), William Hauber (Policeman); *plot:* The father of Larry's girlfriend is also Larry's boss, and he is not too happy with their relationship and Larry's escapades. He arranges her marriage to another suitor, but Larry and his sweetheart manage to escape.

Well, I'll Be...; *survival status:* extant (35mm [LoC], 16mm [CM], 8mm); ©: March 15, 1919; *release date:* April 7, 1919; *copyright:* LP13499; *director:* Lawrence Semon; *writer:* Lawrence Semon; *produced by:* Vitagraph; *cast:* Larry Semon (The Sheriff), Lucille (Zintheo) Carlisle (Susie/Vaudeville Sue), William Hauber (Crook), Frank Alexander; *plot:* Sheriff Larry is not respected by his folks. A gang steals $50,000; Larry gets the money back and rescues Lucille, who has been forced to work in the town's saloon. Lucille throws him off his horse and rides off with the money; *reviews:* The comedy is an excellent one (*Moving Picture World*, April 5, 1919, 128); It is a corker, and [Semon] will cheer you—and thrill you—with his brilliant comedy stunts (*Morning Star*, Wilmington, N.C., November 20, 1920, 9).

Passing the Buck; *length:* 548 meters (uncut German release); *survival status:* extant (16mm [CM], 8mm); ©: April 17, 1919; *release date:* May 5, 1919; *copyright:* LP13614; *director:* Larry Semon; *writer:* Larry Semon; *produced by:* Vitagraph; *cast:* Larry Semon (The House Detective), Frank Alexander (The Fat Crook), Lucille Carlisle (His Wife), Jim Donnelly (Hotel Proprietor), Louise Du Pre (The Manicurist), William Hauber (A Hindoo), Pete Arrow (Another Hindoo); *plot:* Distinguished house detective Larry has been assigned the task of protecting a set of antique Hinduist crown jewels that have arrived in an everyday bag. Crooked Hindoos show an interest in the jewels and exchange the bag for a similar-looking one with a bomb; *review:* Much of the comedy in this two-reel knock-about picture is new and goes over with a good deal of liveliness.... It is a very good specimen of this kind of farce picture (*Moving Picture World*, May 17, 1919, 1078).

The Star Boarder; *length:* 599 meters (uncut German release); *survival status:* extant (35mm [MoMA], fragment: 16mm [CM], 9.5mm, 8mm); ©: May 15, 1919; *release date:* June 2, 1919; *copyright:* LP 13724; *director:* Larry Semon; *writer:* Larry Semon; *produced by*: Vitagraph; *cast:* Larry Semon (Star Boarder and Little Joe, the Escaped Convict), Lucille Carlisle (The Warden's Daughter), Frank Alexander (The Warden), The Beauties Squad, among them Norma Shearer; *plot:* Prisoner Larry enjoys his time doing time. Accordingly, he tries to go back to prison after his premature release. He changes roles with an escapee, unaware that the guy has been sentenced to death.

His Home Sweet Home; *length:* 529 meters (uncut German release); *survival status:* extant (16mm [CM], 8mm); ©: May 24, 1919; *release date:* July 7, 1919; *copyright:* LP13764; *director:* Larry Semon; *writer:* Larry Semon; *produced by:* Vitagraph; *cast:* Larry Semon (The Husband), Lucille Carlisle (The Wife), Rose Gore (Mamma-in-law), Snookums (The Trouble Maker, a Chimpanzee), Frank Hayes (Some Family Member), Frank Alexander, Eddie Dunn, Joe Simberg (Crooks), William Hauber (Policeman), Bobby Ray (Guest); *plot:* Larry's mother-in-law rules the house with a strict hand. At a dinner party, trained chimpanzee Snookums snatches her pearls, but Larry bravely recovers them; *reviews:* There is a real plot to *His Home Sweet Home*.... Its casting, from a caricature standpoint, is declared to be perfect (*Moving Picture World*, June 28, 1919, 2000). The chase for the pearls enlists the grotesque activities of an ape of uncanny intelligence, a wonderfully trained bulldog and a cageful of monkeys in addition to the boisterous portrayal of bizarre characters contributed to the whirlwind speed of the subject by the star and supporting principals (*The Washington Post*, July 7, 1919, 5).

The Simple Life; *length:* 519 meters (uncut German release); *survival status:* extant (35mm [CCB, LoC], 16mm [CM], 9.5mm [PS]); ©: July 10, 1919; *release date:* August 4, 1919; *copyright:* LP13943; *director:* Lawrence Semon; *writer:* Lawrence Semon; *produced by:* Vitagraph; *cast:* Lawrence Semon (Farmer's Boy), Lucille Carlisle (Captain Tillie), Frank Alexander (Farmer), The Beauties Squad (Farmerettes), Frank Hayes (Police Officer); *plot:* Farmhand Larry loves the farmer's daughter Lucille, leader of the Farmerettes, but her father has chosen another man for her. The father sends for the magistrate who, after a thrilling car chase, ends up sitting on the hood of Larry's car. He weds Lucille and Larry right before their car crashes down a cliff. *review:* Larry Semon scores one of the great comedy hits of his career as a camera buffoon and gymnast. The action at all times exceeds the speed limits… . If all of the things happen on the farms of the country that happened on the particular one that Mr. Semon chose as the scene of his bucolic riot, the old high cost of living may be expected to remain aloft (*The Washington Post,* August 18, 1919, 5).

Between the Acts; *length:* 504 meters (uncut German release); *survival status:* extant (35mm [EYE], 16mm [CM], 9.5mm [PS], 8mm); ©*:* August 11, 1919; *release date:* September 8, 1919; *copyright:* LP14064; *director:* Larry Semon; *writer:* Larry Semon; *produced by:* Vitagraph; *cast:* Larry Semon (Larry, Handy Man/Drunkard), Lucille Carlisle (Manager's Wife, the Vamp), Frank Alexander (The Manager); *plot:* A traveling revue troupe is in town. Larry, the handy man, tries to protect Lucille from her husband, the strongman and manager of the show, and therefore causes complete chaos; *review:* Semon is a dandy. This comedy is one of his best. The cat and mouse alone keep folks howling (*Exhibitors Herald,* June 19, 1920, 82).

Dull Care; *alternate title: A Heap of Trouble* (working title); *length:* 561 meters (uncut German release); *survival status:* extant (16mm [FD], 8mm); ©*:* September 19, 1919; *release date:* October 6, 1919; *copyright:* LP14214; *director:* Larry Semon; *writer:* Larry Semon; *produced by:* Vitagraph; *cast:* Larry Semon (Larry, the Detective), William Hauber (The Crooks' Chief), Frank Alexander (Chief of Police), Lucille Carlisle (His Wife), Oliver Hardy (Janitor), Al Thompson, Jim Donnelly, Richard Talmadge; *plot:* At an apartment house, the town's mayor, the chief of police and their wives are robbed by a band of crooks. They took advantage of the mess caused by detective Larry and the jealous chief of police; *reviews:* If you know Larry, you'll know that this is a dandy picture (*Utica Herald-Dispatch,* May 12, 1920, 4); I can't see why they rave over Semon. My patrons do not and I can't see where he compares with Lloyd (*Exhibitors Herald,* October 30, 1920, 98).

Dew Drop Inn; *alternate title: One Wild Day* (working title); *length:* 645 meters (uncut German release); *survival status:* extant (35mm, 16mm [CM], 8mm); ©*:* October 7, 1919; *release date:* November 3, 1919; *copyright:* LP14276; *director:* Lawrence Semon; *writer:* Lawrence Semon; *produced by:* Vitagraph; *cast:* Lawrence Semon (Larry, the Detective), Lucille Carlisle (The Girl), Frank Alexander (Moonshine Mooney), The Beauties Squad (Female Follies Film Company), Frank Hayes (Directress), William Hauber (Moonshiner); *plot:* Detective Larry is on the trail of Moonshine Mooney and his gang. Together with the members of the Female Follies Film Company, who are filming on location not far from the moonshiner's hideout, Larry tries to capture the bad guys; *additional information:* Filmed on location at Lake Huntington. The German Board of Censors decided to delete several intertitles supplied by the translators for copyright holder Otto Schmidt. Forced into rhymes, they were so embarrassing that the Board feared a negative impact on the audience. Act 2, Title 11: "Köstlich mundet heut' die Suppe! Nachher kommst Du ran, kleine Puppe!" ("The soup is delicious. Later, I'll make love to you, you nice little package!"); *review:* Did not come up to expectation. Nothing to it. No better than his former comedies (*Exhibitors Herald,* June 19, 1920, 82).

The Head Waiter; *length:* 634 meters (uncut German release), 787 meters (original print according to Dutch HAPfilm catalogue); *survival status:* extant (35mm [LOC]); ©*:* November 7, 1919; *release date:* December 1, 1919; *copyright:* LP14412; *director:* Larry Semon; *writer:* Larry Semon; *produced by:* Vitagraph; *cast:* Larry Semon (Larry), Oliver Hardy (Cop), Lucille Carlisle (Cashier), Frank Alexander (Ex-Head Waiter), Max Asher (Gentleman of Leisure), The Beauties Squad; *plot:* During a strike, penniless and struggling Larry is hired for a temporary job as a waiter in a cafe. The strikers wreck the place and take Larry prisoner. Suddenly the picture fades into Larry's office where he discusses the script of the film with the writer. It seems that Larry does not like the script, but winks into the camera while the writer is being carried out after a collapse; *reviews:* Larry Semon has created an entirely new type of character. His creative genius as a cartoonist has again stood him in good stead as an author and comedian (*El Paso Herald*, November 8–9, 1919, 7); Though I usually like Larry Semon, I think this is the poorest comedy he has made. The stunts have all been used before, and it seems cheap all the way through. He can make good slapstick comedies though when he wants to (*Exhibitors Herald*, September 11, 1920, 98); Larry Semon, although he denies it in the last few feet of the film, surely found a comedy with enough "rough stuff" to satisfy him in this. It is replete with free-for-alls, slambang mix-ups and knock-down-and-drag-out battle royals. There are also bevies of pretty girls. Girls who would make any musical comedy famous, and whose "forms divine" would pack the bald-headed row in the most uncomfortable theatre in the most sophisticated town in the world. And there is one girl—Oh, Boy! There is one feature about this film, however, which is fortunately becoming more common in the comedies produced today. That is, the humor is not dependent entirely upon slapstick buffoonery. The slapstick is all right, at the right time, and to a certain point. But a skillfully injected touch of genuine character-portrayal, even if it is character caricatured, and an indication of pathos even if the pathos is really pathos, makes every comedy better and funnier. Mr. Semon has achieved this in *The Head Waiter* and therefore he has added something towards the proper gayety of democracies (*Asheville Citizen*, NC, January 11, 1920, 13); This is one of the old ones. Semon always satisfies, although in these older pictures he resorted more to bathing girls and less to trick and animal stunts which have made his later pictures so popular (*Exhibitors Herald* (on a re-release), April 21, 1923, 80).

1920

The Grocery Clerk; **length:** 580 meters (uncut German release); **survival status:** extant (35mm [LoC, CCB], 16mm, 8mm); ©: January 29, 1920; **release date:** February 23, 1920; **copyright:** LP14722; **director:** Larry Semon; **writer:** Larry Semon; **produced by:** Vitagraph; **cast:** Larry Semon (Chief Clerk), Lucille Carlisle (Postmistress), Monte Banks (Town Gusher), Frank Hayes (Female Customer), Frank Alexander (Big Ben), Pete Gordon, Jack Duffy; **plot:** Larry is chief clerk of the largest store in town. He works alongside his sweetheart, postmistress Lucille. When some valuable bonds are stolen from the safe in her office, Larry does everything in his power to get them back; **review:** Larry Semon has put more laughs, injected more originality, and got farther off the well-beaten paths than any ten comedians combined (*Bemidjy Daily Pioneer*, August 31, 1920, 2).

The Fly Cop; **length:** 626 meters (uncut German release); **survival status:** extant (35mm [CCB, LoC], 16mm [CM], 8mm); ©: March 19, 1920; **release date:** March 29, 1920; **copyright:** LP 14909; **director:** Lawrence Semon, Mort S. Peebles, Norman Taurog; **writers:** Lawrence Semon, Mort S. Peebles, Norman Taurog; **produced by:** Vitagraph; **cast:** Larry Semon (The Fly Cop), Lucille Carlisle (A Cabaret Queen), Frank Alexander (Cabaret Owner), William Hauber (Crook); **plot:** The story takes place in a Chinese underground cabaret, which also hosts an opium den. Detective Larry stumbles in and gives singer Lucille her necklace which was stolen by the villainous owner of the cafe. A wild chase through the cabaret and the den begins; **reviews:** Some excellent comedy business, equaled by a thrilling sequence on the roof tops, are elements which make this two-reeler ... one that will register as far out of the average line with all audiences (*Film Daily*, April 18, 1920, 27); Larry Semon proves a prime favorite in his new two-reel comedy ... which compels a laugh a minute from even the most austere (*Utica Herald-Dispatch*, May 12, 1920, 4); In scoring the picture in our Review Room, the pianist laughed so heartily that he could not play. We have eighty men in our orchestra. The stringed instruments and percussions will probably manage all right, but what about the men who are playing on the brasses and woodwinds? (*Exhibitors Herald*, March 24, 1920); Larry Semon comedies have the great advantage of having real, well connected stories, not just a hodgepodge of laughter-producing incidents dragged in by the heels without a semblance of continuity, and it follows that their titles must therefore be descriptive of the story. *The Fly Cop* is no exception (*Pioneer*, Bemidji, Minnesota, May 13, 1920, 5).

School Days; **length:** 640 meters (uncut German release); **survival status:** extant (35mm [CCB, DIF], 16mm [CM, LoC], 9.5mm [PS], 8mm); **©:** April 27, 1920; **release date:** May 3, 1920; **copyright:** LP15057; **director:** Larry Semon, Mort S. Peebles, Norman Taurog; **writers:** Larry Semon, Mort S. Peebles, Norman Taurog; **produced by:** Vitagraph; **cast:** Larry Semon (The Hired Man), Lucille Carlisle (The Daughter), Frank Alexander (Another Hired Man), Frank Hayes (The School Teacher), Jack Duffy (Principal), William Hauber (Bad Boy), Hugh Fay (Fiancé); **plot:** Little Lucille, Little Larry and their classmates love to play practical jokes on the teacher, the principal and parents' councils. Nodding off during the lesson, Larry dreams about a joint future with Lucille; **review:** The funny side of childhood is seldom appreciated by those who are passing through that period of their lives until distance has lent enchantment to the view.... But Larry Semon brings it all back to us in this wild farce, and it will indeed be a dullard who can restrain laughter while the clever comedian frisks about in little short trousers, inky fingers and a perfect genius for doing the wrong thing at the critical moment (*Bioscope*, July 8, 1920).

Solid Concrete; **length:** 528 meters (uncut German release); **survival status:** extant (35mm [FC], 9.5mm [PS], 8mm); **©:** May 27, 1920; **release date:** June 7, 1920; **copyright:** LP 15178; **director:** Larry Semon; **writer:** Larry Semon; **produced by:** Vitagraph; **cast:** Larry Semon (The Boob), Lucille Carlisle (The Boss' Daughter), William Hauber, Frank Alexander; **plot:** Larry works at a large concrete factory. He is in love with the boss' daughter Lucille, and so is the foreman. Larry teams up with some agents who try to coax Lucille's father into selling the factory; **additional information:** A camera was mounted onto a gondola filming Larry sitting in front, while the gondola rolls trough the factory; **reviews:** "[*Solid Concrete*] is primarily packed with roars and laughter, but quite inadvertently it is also an educational picture of no mean value. To insure a true to color production Mr. Semon ... looked for proper locations to form a background for this comedy. The story was written around happenings in a large stone quarry. A large quarry was pressed into service with the result that every phase of the industry was photographed with startling fidelity. No expense was spared to see that the yard was in full action while the scenes of the comedy were being enacted. Cranes and cars carrying crushed stone were in operation and the blacksmith' shops shot sparks merrily (*The Morning Star*, Wilmington, N.C., October 9, 1920, 14); Instead of depending upon novel tricks and bits of business, this latest Larry Semon two-reeler holds up only because of a number of thrills, photographed in remarkable fashion.... It's exciting and while not nearly as funny as the better productions turned out by the irrepressible Larry, has a number of whirlwind sections to overcome the deficiency (*Film Daily*, June 27, 1920, 28); This is one of Larry's best, but somehow it failed to pull. I think it was the silly title which meant nothing to so many people (*Exhibitors Herald*, October 2, 1920, 98); Larry slipped just a bit in this, as too much background detracts from his clever work (*Exhibitors Herald*, August 28, 1920, 84).

The Stage Hand; **length:** 644 meters (uncut German release); **survival status:** extant (16mm, 9.5mm, 8mm); **©:** July 16, 1920; **release date:** September 1920; **copyright:** LP15361; **director:** Larry Semon, Norman Taurog; **writers:** Larry Semon, Norman Taurog; **produced by:** Vitagraph; **cast:** Larry Semon (The Stage Hand), Lucille Carlisle (The Leading Lady), Thelma Percy (The Animal Trainer), Frank Alexander (Stage Manager), Al Thompson (Show Manager), William Hauber ("Props"), Jack Duffy (The Hero), Frank Hayes (Prima Donna), Oliver Hardy (Audience Member), The Beauties Squad; **plot:** Lazy stage hand Larry is found asleep in a rolled rug. He'd better have stayed there, because he only generates chaos—both on stage and backstage; **review:** Larry Semon long ago dispelled any doubts that might have existed as to his ability as a comedian and comedy director. *The Stage Hand* ... will certainly strengthen his position in the ranks of star slapstick comedians to even a greater extent.... A man gifted such as this comedian can easily figure out a variety of good stunts with this rich location as a background, and Semon certainly has made good on this end of his work. The gags and situations follow one another rapidly and many of them display an originality that adds considerably to their value. There are two scenes in which the action gets quite slobbery, one where the Negro receives splashes of white paint full in the face and the other where the comedy chorus girl falls into a barrel of murky goo. For the rest, however, the picture maintains a pace that is ever laughable and refreshing (*Film Daily*, August 22, 1920, 27).

The Suitor; *length:* 666 meters (uncut German release); *survival status:* extant (35mm, 16mm [CM], 9.5mm [PS], 8mm); ©: September 18, 1920; *release date:* October or November 1920; *copyright:* LP 15561; *director:* Larry Semon, Norman Taurog; *writers:* Larry Semon, Norman Taurog; *produced by:* Vitagraph; *cast:* Larry Semon (The Suitor), Lucille Carlisle (An Heiress), Al Thompson (A Lizard), Frank Alexander (The Major Domo), William Hauber (Cook), William McCall (Father); *plot:* Millionaire Manybucks does not want Larry to marry his daughter Lucille. He also has no time for The Lizard, another suitor. The Lizard and his henchmen kidnap his daughter. Larry pursues the kidnappers by motorbike and plane and rescues Lucille; *additional information:* The Suitor was greatly overlength when watched by the West Coast studio staff, just before it was shipped east. However, it was believed that any eliminating of the scenes would have to be made at the expense of the film's laugh value. A way out was found by shortening every scene in the entire film (*Motion Picture News*, October 2, 1920, 2635); *review:* For boys and girls of all ages.... Larry Semon isn't standing still, that's certain. He has improved his methods of funmaking immeasurably in the past months, and this two-reeler is packed with bright bits of business, clever clowning, and all-round good sense in sets and story.... A few more like this and Semon will be in the front rank of silent comedians (*Photoplay Magazine*, December 1920, 123).

The Sportsman; *alternate titles:* The Hunter, The Huntsman (working titles); *length:* 538 meters (uncut German release); *survival status:* extant (35mm [LoC], 16mm [CM], 8mm); ©: November 28, 1920; *release date:* February 6, 1921; *copyright:* LP15854; *director:* Larry Semon, Norman Taurog; *writers:* Larry Semon, Norman Taurog; *produced by:* Vitagraph; *cast:* Larry Semon (The Huntsman), Al Thompson (The Antique Collector), Lucille Carlisle (His Daughter), Frank Alexander (The Sultan), William Hauber (Chief Bodyguard), Hank Brooks (The Valet), "Bumps" Adams; *plot:* An antique collector and his daughter are held captive by a sultan. Together with huntsman Larry, who was also captured, they must escape the sultan and his henchmen *and* a horde of lions; *additional information:* Filmed on location at Catalina Island.

1921

The Hick; *length:* 617 meters (uncut German release); *survival status:* extant (16mm [CM], 9.5mm [PS], 8mm); ©: March 7, 1921; *release date:* March 10, 1921; *copyright:* LP16253; *director:* Larry Semon, Norman Taurog; *writers:* Larry Semon, Norman Taurog; *produced by:* Vitagraph; *cast:* Larry Semon (Larry), Marion Aye (The Farmer's Daughter), Frank Alexander and Frank Hayes (Guests at Cafe), Jack Duffy (The Farmer); *plot:* Larry is deeply in love with the farmer's daughter, but a dubious artist coaxes her into eloping with him. Larry takes up pursuit and finds her dancing in a shady cafe; *reviews:* We find Larry Semon draws better houses than any other comedian. All of his comedies are better than the average. Lucille Carlisle was missed a lot (*Exhibitors Herald*, May 28, 1921, 80); This Larry Semon comedy is not up to the standard set by its predecessors. A lot of money has been spent where more ingenuity would have brought happier results. The titles are inane and the "gags" have been used many times before by Semon and other comedians. The story is usual comedy collection of situations with a boob lover, city fellow and country girl. The best thing about it is the thrills resulting from Semon's acrobatic falls and the fact that it will entertain the slapstick fan (*Exhibitors Herald*, May 16, 1921, 73).

The Rent Collector; *length:* 635 meters (uncut German release); *survival status:* extant (35mm [CCB], 16mm [CM], 8mm); ©: April 8, 1921; *release date:* April 11, 1921;

copyright: LP16377; *director:* Larry Semon, Norman Taurog; *writers:* Larry Semon, Norman Taurog; *produced by:* Vitagraph; *cast:* Larry Semon (The Rent Collector), Norma Nichols (Leader of the Society Girl Settlement Workers), Oliver Hardy (Big Boss), Eva Thatcher (The Landlady), Pete Gordon (Barber), Frank Alexander (A Thug), William Hauber, Leo Willis; *plot:* Larry has secured a new job as a rent collector in a tough neighborhood. Soon he and a social workers' lady are kidnapped. Their getaway covers the whole district; *additional information:* After a chase with a policeman, Larry's face is clean although he had hit a telegraph pole with his bike and was catapulted away. In the next scene he is seen reading a paper sitting in front of a shack, his face dirty, only to have a perfectly clean face again when he enters the shack; *reviews:* A genuine laugh-getter. From start to finish the comedian keeps things going, and besides a lot of the old hokum that still gets laughs he has put in some new stunts that sent the Strand audience into roars of laughter.... The usual roughhouse and throwing contests are used and while it gets a bit "messy" for a while, the comedy is good. Perhaps the biggest joke is Larry playing Sir Walter Raleigh. He puts his coat over a puddle which happens to be a man-hole. The lady steps down—very much down—in fact she submerges (*Film Daily*, May 29, 1921, 20).

The Bakery; *alternate title:* The Bake Shop (working title); *length:* 604 meters (uncut German release); *survival status:* extant (35mm [LoC], 16mm [CM], 8mm); ©: April 28, 1921; *release date:* April 29, 1921; *copyright:* LP16435; *director:* Larry Semon, Norman Taurog; *writers:* Larry Semon, Norman Taurog; *produced by:* Vitagraph; *cast:* Larry Semon (Bakery Clerk), Oliver Hardy (Foreman), Norma Nichols (Owner's Daughter), Frank Alexander (Owner), William Hauber, Grover Ligon, Pete Gordon (Workers), Eva Thatcher (Customer), Al Thompson, Jack Duffy; *plot:* Larry works in a bakery and wreaks havoc—as usual. A member of foreman Hardy's gang swipes the daily receipts and scoots off. Larry catches the thief and returns the loot to the owner and his daughter; *review:* The action is brisk from start to finish and the entire production filled with laughs. Larry Semon does some good work and gets over some very good comedy effects (*Film Daily*, June 5, 1921, 19).

The Fall Guy; *length:* 1940 feet; 616 meters (uncut German release); *survival status:* extant (16mm [CM, PS], 9.5mm); ©: June 6, 1921; *release date:* July 16, 1921; *copyright:* LP16635; *director:* Larry Semon, Norman Taurog; *writers:* Larry Semon, Norman Taurog; *produced by:* Vitagraph; *cast:* Larry Semon (The Fall Guy), Norma Nichols (Prima Donna), Oliver Hardy (City Slicker); *plot:* In a dance hall, Larry rescues the prima donna of the chorus from the advances of a city slicker. When the city slicker steals her jewels, a wild chase ensues; *review:* A roar of laughter, new tricks, clever photography and excelling even Larry Semon's previous efforts (*Reading News-Times*, April 10, 1922, 7).

The Bell Hop; *alternate title:* The Bell Boy (working title); *length:* 660 meters (uncut German release); *survival status:* extant (35mm [LoC], 16mm [CM], 8mm); ©: August 29, 1921; *release date:* September 18, 1921; *copyright:* LP16905; *director:* Larry Semon, Norman Taurog; *writers:* Larry Semon, Norman Taurog; *produced by:* Vitagraph; *cast:* Larry Semon (The Bell Hop), Norma Nichols (Maid/Secret Agent), Oliver Hardy (Hotel Manager), Frank Alexander (Government Official), William Hauber, Al Thompson, Pete Gordon; *plot:* A government official puts some top secret papers in the safe of the hotel where Larry works. A gang of thieves manages to pinch the papers. A secret agent disguised as a maid and Larry join forces to get the papers back; *reviews:* Larry Semon gets away to a running start in this very funny comedy (*Exhibitor's Trade Review*, January 7, 1922, 402); Helped to pull crowds in (*Exhibitor's Trade Review*, October 22, 1921, 1440); Old-fashioned slapstick that tickles the kids (*Exhibitors Herald*, February 16, 1924, 78).

1922

The Saw Mill; *alternate title:* The Lumber Jack (working title); *length:* 1918 feet; 605 meters (uncut German release); *survival status:* extant (35mm, 16mm [GEH], 8mm); ©: December 12, 1921; *release date:* January 1, 1922; *copyright:* LP17350; *director:* Larry Semon, Norman Taurog; *writers:* Larry

Semon, Norman Taurog; ***produced by:*** Vitagraph; ***cast:*** Larry Semon (The Dumb Bell), Oliver Hardy (The Foreman), Frank Alexander (The Owner), Kathleen O'Connor (The Boss' Daughter), Ann Hastings (The Owner's Daughter), Al Thompson (Boss), Rose Code, William Hauber, Peter Ormonds, Pal the Dog; ***plot:*** The owner of a sawmill and his daughter conduct an inspection visit. Larry, on the run from the foreman, tries to win the heart of the daughter and gain the blessing of her father. Larry succeeds as he rescues his darling from mutinous workers; ***review:*** From the drop of the hat Larry Semon does nothing much but carve nice little slapsticks and great big slapsticks out of all the wood that is brought within the range of the camera. And when it comes to doing that same little thing Larry still is batting in the 400 class—and climbing steadily. He may have done better things in his own field of comedy than *The Saw Mill*, but if he did this writer regrets he missed the performance (*Exhibitor's Trade Review*, March 11, 1922, 1038).

The Show; ***alternate title:*** *Props* (working title); ***survival status:*** extant (35mm [LoC], 16mm [CM], 8mm); ***©:*** February 11, 1922; ***release date:*** March 19, 1922; ***copyright:*** LP17545; ***director:*** Larry Semon, Norman Taurog; ***writers:*** Larry Semon, Norman Taurog; ***produced by:*** Vitagraph; ***cast:*** Larry Semon (Property Man/Gentle Onlooker), Oliver Hardy (Stage Manager/Audience Member) Frank Alexander (Ballet Dancer/Wife of Man in Balcony), Lucille Carlisle (Leading Lady), Betty Young (Dancer), Alice Davenport (Audience Member), Al Thompson (Man Who Smuggles Family In), Pete Gordon (His Son), Frank J. Coleman (Humiliated Man in Audience/Woman With Bird Hat/Cop), Jack Miller (Villain), Grover Ligon (Bald Cop), William Hauber (Two Different Audience Members), Coy Watson, Jr., 40 chorus girls; ***plot:*** Lucille is the star of tonight's revue, while Larry has to content himself with the job as propman. He manages to ruin the event, much to the delight of villain Hardy, who takes advantage of that chaos and runs off with Lucille's necklace; ***additional information:*** For several years Lucille Carlisle had been designing all the gowns she wore on and off camera. Her costumes were copied by society leaders and other actors. For *The Show* she designed a gown of iridescent and black sequins (*Twin Falls News*, April 19, 1922, 2); ***review:*** [A] lively two-reel comedy. It is not so much from the acting of Semon, although he has some good legitimate humorous expressions, as the fast action that makes this passable farce. The story is not wonderfully clever, many of the stunts having been employed by other comedians before, but *The Show* is adequate for the purpose (*Exhibitors Herald*, March 11, 1922, 61).

A Pair of Kings; ***alternate title:*** *The Substitute* (working title); ***length:*** 2030 feet; 628 meters (uncut German release); ***survival status:*** extant (35mm, 16mm [CM], 8mm); ***©:*** May 12, 1922; ***release date:*** May 15, 1922; ***copyright:*** LP17870; ***director:*** Larry Semon, Norman Taurog; ***writers:*** Larry Semon, Norman Taurog; ***produced by:*** Vitagraph; ***cast:*** Larry Semon (Stranger/King August I), Lucille (Princess Lucille), Oliver Hardy (General Alarm), Fred DeSilva; ***plot:*** King August I has taken away the throne and kingdom from Princess Lucille. Upon his despotism, the king faces death threats. He decides to change roles with unsuspecting doppelganger Larry, and flees. Larry bravely stands up against all villains, rescues the princess and reinstates her to the throne; ***additional information:*** A small party of tourists were visiting Larry Semon's studio where he was making a new film. One happened to ask the meaning of the name Los Angeles and Larry, who was somewhat of an amateur linguist, volunteered the information that Los Angeles was only part of the order. In his eyes the complete name of this beautiful city was "El Pueblo de Nuestra Senora la Reina de Los Angeles" and it meant "The City of Our Lady, Queen of Los Angeles." He waited, but they had no more questions to ask (*Exhibitor's Trade Review*, April 15, 1922, 1399); ***reviews:*** With *A Pair of Kings* Larry Semon turns parodist.... [The film] depends largely on speedy slapstick for its impulse. The humor that has been so marked in the immediately preceding releases of the comedian is noticeable for its absence.... The picture is lavishly staged throughout (*Exhibitor's Trade Review*, June 24, 1922, 213); Can't say much for this one. It's one of the poorest Larry ever made. Nothing new in it.

If Semon don't do better it will be good-bye Semon (*Exhibitors Herald*, October 21, 1922, 88).

Golf; *length:* 1843 feet; 575 meters (uncut German release); *survival status:* extant (35mm,16mm, 8mm); ©*:* August 5, 1922; *release date:* August 8, 1922, or September 3, 1922; *copyright:* LP18121; *director:* Larry Semon, Tom Buckingham; *writers:* Larry Semon, Tom Buckingham; *produced by:* Vitagraph, Larry Semon; *cast:* Larry Semon (The Son), Lucille Carlisle (His Sister/The Blonde Flapper), Al Thompson (The Father), Oliver Hardy (The Neighbor), Vernon Dent (The Suitor), The Golfers: William Hauber, Fred Lancaster, Pete Gordon, Joe Basil, Vincent Dermott, Fred Gambold, Eva Thatcher; *plot:* Larry brings his golf-playing abilities to perfection by practicing at home. He destroys subtenant Hardy's dinner. Hardy has his eye on Larry's sister Lucille; *review:* [*Golf*] is funny enough to offset any melancholy effects.... In *Golf* the reviewer enjoyed himself more than he has in a long time.... *Golf* is a bit faster than Larry's usual slapstick and is sometimes as foxy as a lynx.... Larry Semon indulges in the customary succession of athletic stunts with a reckless abandon that fairly makes one's hair rise on end (*Exhibitor's Trade Review*, December 2, 1922, 36).

The Counter Jumper; *alternate title: The Store Keeper* (working title); *length:* 1865 feet; 617 meters (uncut German release); *survival status:* extant (35mm [MoMA], 16mm, 8mm); ©*:* December 1, 1922; *release date:* December 6, 1922; *copyright:* LP18470; *director:* Larry Semon; *writer:* Larry Semon; *produced by:* Vitagraph, Larry Semon; *cast:* Larry Semon (The Counter Jumper), Lucille Carlisle (Glorietta Hope), Oliver Hardy (Gaston), Spencer Bell (A Clerk), Al Thompson, William Hauber, Joe Basil, Eva Thatcher, Jack Duffy, William McCall, Reginald Lyons, James Donnelly, Fred DeSilva, a walking egg; *plot:* A trading post out west is owned by Lucille, Larry as jack-of-all-trades and Oliver Hardy as the villain. Hardy steals Lucille's valuable necklace; *additional information:* Before completing *The Counter Jumper*, the Larry Semon studio announced that he was going to go do a slapstick comedy with a general store of a trading settlement as a background.

He decided to do so since he was impressed several years ago with the possibilities of a comedy in a general store. Critic James W. Dean wrote on the occasion: "[Semon] should have been impressed long before that. Some of the earliest films were cracker-barrel comedies. His aim is to exaggerate life happenings and magnify them to such an extent that they are funny without becoming overdrawn. Rather paradoxical. The reason Semon has not become one of the great comedians of the screen is because he has not presented situations that might find a counterpart in the experiences of those who see his films" (*Niagara Falls Gazette*, October 21, 1922, 8); *reviews:* This latest Semon comedy has some brand new stunts, and despite the fact that a lot of the footage is slapstick and rough, there are laughs a plenty (*Film Daily*, December 3, 1922, 19); [A] number of things take place in these two reels that ought to make fun for the crowd.... The picture will go strongly in the city, but it is not risking much to wager it will do even more than that in rural sections (*Exhibitor's Trade Review*, December 9, 1922, 81); Larry is losing his punch. Have not used any of his comedies for about a year and this one has only one laugh and that where the egg sprouts legs and runs around. Larry, though, has stuck us eight beans per for five of these comedies. Is this the best or the worst? (*Exhibitors Herald*, October 6, 1923, 85).

The Agent; *alternate titles: The Gringo, The Sleuth* (working titles); *survival status:* extant (35mm [CFU, CCB], 9.5mm [PS], 8mm); ©*:* September 25, 1922; *release date:* September 27, 1922, or November 19, 1922; *copyright:* LP18238; *director:* Larry Semon, Tom Buckingham; *writers:* Larry Semon, Tom Buckingham; *produced by:* Vitagraph, Larry Semon; *cast:* Larry Semon (Federal Agent), Lucille Carlisle (Federal Agent, Undercover), Oliver Hardy (Don Fusiloil), William Hauber, Joe Basil, Al Thompson, Kittie Rinehart, Robert McKenzie, Harry DeRoy, Ed Wertz, Donald Maines; *plot:* Lucille and Larry as federal agents encounter moonshiners near the Mexican boarder. Soon they both have to retreat and fight to escape; *additional information*: Owing to overuse of this title, Larry was advised to not choose *The Sleuth* as release title. (See correspondence with Ligon Johnson, attorney at law, September 26, 1922); *reviews:* Larry Semon is in a rip-roaring comedy which makes up for the almost total lack of laughs in the feature film [*The Masquerader*].... Larry Semon limbers up the audience in a few moments (*Exhibitor's Trade Review*, December 2, 1922, 38); This is a good two-reel comedy and will please most any audience (*Exhibitors Herald*, February 16, 1924, 78).

1923

No Wedding Bells; *length:* 1976 feet; 628 meters (uncut German release); *survival status:* extant (9.5mm [PS], 8mm); ©: January 25, 1923; *release date:* January 30, 1923; *copyright:* LP18635; *director:* Larry Semon; *writer:* Larry Semon; *produced by:* Vitagraph, Larry Semon; *cast:* Larry Semon (Larry), Lucille Carlisle (The Girl), Oliver Hardy (The Father), Glen Cavender (Irate Husband), Kathleen Myers (His Wife); *plot:* In a secret hideout beneath the city, a Chinese villain mixes a potion that puts people into a hypnotic state. He kidnaps Lucille and tries the potion on her. Larry comes to her rescue; *reviews:* Up to Semon standard (*Exhibitors Herald*, March 15, 1924, 90); There is an abundance of action, but there is lacking the full quantity of Semon mirth in the situations (*Exhibitor's Trade Review*, February 10, 1923, 557); The action is lively and spirited along with splendid subtitles. The cast is adequate, the direction and photography above the average, and while more or less of slapstick variety, Semon steps on the safe side whenever a situation approaches vulgarity, resulting in comical screen entertainment or merit (*Motion Picture News*, February 10, 1923, 748).

The Barnyard; *length:* 1884 feet; 573 meters (uncut German release); *survival status:* extant (35mm [LoC], 16mm [CM], 8mm); ©: March 17, 1923; *release date:* March 26, 1923; *copyright:* LP18801; *director:* Larry Semon; *writer:* Larry Semon; *produced by:* Vitagraph, Larry Semon; *cast:* Larry Semon (Farm Hand), Oliver Hardy (Larry's Co-Worker), Frank Hayes (The Farmer's Wife), Kathleen Myers (The Farmer's Daughter), William Hauber, Al Thompson, Joe Basil; *plot:* Crooked oil operators try to force a farmer to sell his farm, because they assume there's oil on that property and on other properties in the neighborhood. Larry quietly scrounges the signed contract and dashes away by car, later by plane; *reviews:* It was our special pleasure on last Sunday afternoon also to witness again that awful screen comic, Larry Semon, in something having to do with a barnyard. There may be a worse actor in the world than Larry but such a condition is little less than impossible for us personally to understand (*Oakland Evening Tribune*, May 24, 1923, C.); At no time is there nothing doing, and amid the riot there is some fun (*Exhibitor's Trade Review*, April 28, 1923, 1090).

The Midnight Cabaret; *alternate title:* Cabaret (working title); *survival status:* extant (35mm [LoC]); ©: May 2, 1923; *release date:* late May 1923; *copyright:* LP18933; *director:* Larry Semon; *writer:* Larry Semon; *produced by:* Vitagraph, Larry Semon; *cast:* Larry Semon (Waiter), Kathleen Myers (Cabaret Performer), Oliver Hardy (Impetuous Suitor), William Hauber, Al Thompson, Fred DeSilva, Beauties Squad; *plot:* Celebrated cabaret performer Kathleen is tired of constantly being chatted up by the male audience. Larry, a waiter, tries to protect her from those lechers and therefore clashes with Hardy; *reviews:* In this, Larry depends not so much upon gags as upon farce to get laughs.... It is lavishly produced, the cabaret scene being unusually large, and there are dozens of pretty girls, headed by Kathleen Myers (*Exhibitor's Trade Review*, May 5, 1923, 1132); This is not up to Semon's standard, but nevertheless contains some good laughs. Mostly old stuff put across in a way that pleased (*Exhibitors Herald*, September 15, 1923, 90).

The Gown Shop; *length:* 465 meters (uncut German release); *survival status:* extant (35mm, 16mm [CM], 9.5mm [PS]); ©: August 14, 1923; *release date:* August 14, 1923; *copyright:* LP19307; *director:* Larry Semon; *writer:* Larry Semon; *produced by:* Vitagraph, Larry Semon; *cast:* Larry Semon (Salesman), Kathleen Myers (Head Saleslady), Oliver Hardy (The Store Manager), Pete Gordon (Presser), Fred DeSilva (Tailor), James Donnelly (Husband), Harry de Roy, Dorothea Wolbert, Otto Lederer (Audience Members), Frank Hayes (Wife In Audience), Spencer

Bell (Janitor); *plot:* Larry and Kathleen work in a fashion house, both madly in love. Store manager Hardy has nothing good to say about Larry and acts accordingly; *reviews:* Not up to the standard of former Semons, though satisfactory (*Exhibitors Herald*, December 29, 1923, 177); The comedy ... is the same rough-and-tumble and slapstick type with which Semon has been identified (*Moving Picture World*, November 17, 1923, 334).

Lightning Love; *length:* 596 meters (uncut German release); *survival status:* extant (8mm); ©*:* October 16, 1923; *release date:* October 23, 1923; *copyright:* LP19520; *director:* Larry Semon, Jimmy Davis; *writers:* Larry Semon, Jimmy Davis; *produced by:* Vitagraph, Larry Semon; *cast:* Larry Semon (A Suitor), Oliver Hardy (The Other Suitor), Kathleen Myers (Rhea), Spencer Bell (Butler), William Hauber, Pete Gordon, Al Thompson, Elma the Monkey; *plot:* Oliver and Larry are rivals for the hand of Kathleen. Their fight is interrupted by a heavy thunderstorm during which the house gets swept to the edge of a cliff; *review:* The manner in which Larry and the other principals are being continually struck by lightning and the way the lightning follows Larry all over the place is cleverly done and will bewilder the average patrons (*Moving Picture World*, November 17, 1923, 334).

Horseshoes; *length:* 566 meters (uncut German release); *survival status:* extant (35mm, 16mm, 9.5mm, 8mm); ©*:* December 10, 1923; *release date:* December 10, 1923; *copyright:* LP19684; *director:* Larry Semon, Jimmy Davis; *writers:* Larry Semon, Jimmy Davis; *produced by:* Vitagraph, Larry Semon; *cast:* Larry Semon (Larry), Kathleen Myers (The Grocer's Daughter), Oliver Hardy (Dynamite Duffy), James Donnelly, Jack Duffy, Spencer Bell; *plot:* Boxing champion Dynamite Duffy is defeated by Larry in a training match thanks to horseshoes in Larry's boxing gloves. Not very pleased about the outcome of the match, Hardy chases Larry through town; *review:* Exceedingly amusing—Larry Semon is one of the biggest "nuts" in the comedy game and there are few who can resist laughing uproariously when viewing his antics on the screen. His technique improves with each picture and in this latest two-reeler he certainly makes the most of each comedy gag (*Exhibitor's Trade Review*, December 22, 1923, 29).

1924

Trouble Brewing; **alternate title:** *Moonshines* (working title); *length:* 610 meters (uncut German release); *survival status:* extant (8mm); ©*:* March 10, 1924; *release date:* March 12, 1924; *copyright:* LP19984; *director:* James Davis, Larry Semon; *writers:* James Davis, Larry Semon; *produced by:* Vitagraph, Larry Semon; *cast:* Larry Semon (Dry Agent), Carmelita Geraghty (The Girl), Oliver Hardy (Bootlegger), William Hauber, Al Thompson, Pete Gordon; *plot:* Prohibition agent Larry closely watches the doings in and about a hotel. Reportedly, bootleggers do not only satisfy the in-house demand for booze, but also that of the neighborhood.

The Girl in the Limousine; *length:* 5630 feet; 1630 meters (uncut German release); *survival status:* unknown; ©*:* July 25, 1924; *release date:* July 25, 1924; *copyright:* LP20420; *director:* Larry Semon, Noel Mason Smith, adapted from A. H. Woods; *writers:* Avery Hopwood, Wilson Collison; *scenario by:* C. Graham Baker; *produced by:* Chadwick Pictures Corporation; *distributed by:* First National; *cast:* Larry Semon (Tony Hamilton), Claire Adams (Betty Fraser, the Girl), Charlie Murray (Ripps, the Butler), Lucille Ward (Aunt Cicily), Larry Steers (Dr. Jimmy), Oliver Hardy (Freddie Neville); *plot:* Tony and Freddie have been rivals for the love of a girl since childhood. While the girl returns Freddie's affection, sadly neglected Tony is kidnapped by a gang of muggers who use a man in woman's clothing as a shill. Tony is knocked unconscious, put into a pair of women's pajamas and rolled under the bed of his unapproachable sweetheart. Complications result from his efforts to dodge the husband and various guests. When the crooks steal the girl's jewels, Tony overtakes them and becomes a hero; *reviews:* For those who like prolonged knockabout farce (*Pictures and Picturegoer*, February 1925, 71); A picture which ought to prove a first class drawing card for big and little theatres, an amusing hot weather attraction without a dull moment in it (*Exhibitor's Trade Review*, July 12, 1924, 25); Larry Semon's first feature-length comedy is a disappointment. As farce it misses almost completely and as slapstick it is far too long.... Semon probably will never be a genuine farceur. He is a particularly bad choice, and, since the direction and the rest of the cast are couched in similar broad pie-throwing terms, the stage hit of Avery Hopwood and Wilson Collison loses almost all the farcical luster it possessed when produced as a play five years ago.... There can be no complaint on the score of action, as the film is brimful with it, although it does drag interminably toward the finish. The fight scenes are jammed with motion, and in the end a chase with autos, trains and motorcycles is well pictured. Semon is hard to take seriously in the quieter passages of the films. He is never more than a clown, lacking wistful poignancy when things go wrong.... What Semon needs for a long picture is pure roughhouse stuff with a barrel of new ideas (*Variety*, October 8, 1924, 30).

Her Boy Friend; **length:** 1011 feet (?)—only an edited version (based on Kodascope-print) is widely available; **survival status:** extant (35mm, 16mm [GEH], 9.5mm, 8mm); **©:** September 23, 1924; **release date:** September 28, 1924; **copyright:** LP20595; **director:** Larry Semon, Noel Mason Smith; **writer:** Larry Semon; **produced by:** Chadwick; **distributed by:** Educational; **cast:** Larry Semon (Larry, the Chief's Son), Dorothy Dwan (Iva Method, the Girl Detective), Frank Alexander (Slim Chance), Oliver Hardy (Killer Kid), Fred Spence (Headquarters' Hank), Alma Bennett (The Vamp), Spencer Bell (Dock Worker), William Hauber; **plot:** Detective Dorothy has been kidnapped by bootleggers. Larry, the police chief's son, is assigned to a rescue mission. An attempt to escape from a seedy club fails and Dorothy and Larry are brought aboard a sailing ship.

Kid Speed; **length:** 567 meters (uncut German release); **survival status:** extant (16mm [CF], 8mm); **©:** November 24, 1924; **release date:** November 16, 1924; **copyright:** LP20799; **photographed by:** Hans F. Koenekamp; **director:** Larry Semon, Noel Mason Smith; **writers:** Larry Semon, Noel Mason Smith; **produced by:** Chadwick; **titles by:** Leon Lee; **distributed by:** Educational; **cast:** Larry Semon (The Speed Kid), Dorothy Dwan (Lou DuPoise), Oliver Hardy (Dangerous Dan/Dan McGraw), Frank Alexander (Avery DuPoise), James J. Jeffries (The Blacksmith), Spencer Bell (The Speed Kid's Co-Driver), Grover Ligon, William Hauber; **plot:** Oliver Hardy and Larry fight over Dorothy's affections. Her father prefers Oliver, while Dorothy prefers Larry, so a car race will decide; **review:** It's a first-rate short reel. Some of the stunts, high jumps etc. will thrill even the hardened thrill-chasers... [Semon is] very amusing as the detective's son.... The gags are very good, the photography is excellent, and the thrills worth talking about (*Film Daily*, September 28, 1924, 11).

1925

The Dome Doctor; **survival status:** extant (16mm [PS]); **©:** Gauntlett & Co., April 27, 1925; **release date:** April 19, 1925; **copyright:** LP21408; **photographed by:** Hans F. Koenekamp; **edited by:** Sam Zimbalist; **director:** Larry Semon; **writer:** Larry Semon; **produced by:** Chadwick; **titles by:** Charlie Saxton; **distributed by:** Educational; **cast:** Larry Semon (Peter Pep), Fred DeSilva (Pierre Pep), Frank Alexander (Fuller Hulkinbulk), Dorothy Dwan (Dorothy), Earl Montgomery, Grover Ligon; **plot:** A tale of two competing businessmen—a hairdresser and the bald owner of a delicatessen—plus their two loving children, Dorothy and Larry. Larry offers Dorothy's father a chance to grow new hair through a miraculous machine. This is when all the trouble starts; **review:** Larry Semon is a good comedian when he has an appropriate vehicle, but *The Dome Doctor* is indeed a feeble gesture. There is in this film the wildest and most inane aggregation of ancient slapstick gags that have been assembled in a long while. The subtitles are strained and pointless, although it is evident that the title writer made a desperate effort to force a laugh without any manifest success. The film is entirely lacking in anything even faintly suggestive of a story; it is just a string of gags for the most part timeworn and mirthless. We would not bet too heavily on this one, although the name of Larry Semon may help to put it over (*Exhibitor's Trade Review*, April 25, 1925, 44).

Go Straight, **alternate title:** *When a Woman Turns Forty;* **length:** 6107 feet; **survival status:** unknown; **release date:** April 27, 1925; **director:** Frank O'Connor; **writers:** Agnes Leahy (screenplay), Ewart Adamson (story); **produced by:** B. P. Schulberg; **cast:** Owen Moore (John Rhodes), Mary Carr (Mrs. Rhodes), George Fawcett (Madison), Ethel Wales (Mamie), Gladys Hullette (Gilda Hart), Lillian Leighton (Gilda's Aunt), Robert Edeson (The Hawk), DeWitt Jennings (The Hunter), Francis McDonald (The Dove); as themselves: Anita Stewart, Larry Semon, Donald Keith, Le Roy, Talma and Bosco (illusionists); **plot:** Gilda Hart quits her life of crime and goes to Hollywood with her aunt. She finds work in a bank, falls in love with its president John Rhodes and is soon promoted to secretary to the head of the bank. Gilda's old gang finds her and attempts to talk her into knocking over John's bank, but she refuses and personally takes all the money in the vaults to his house. Breaking into the empty bank, the gang is arrested. Gilda confesses her former life of crime to John, and he quickly forgives her; **additional information:** Anita Stewart, Larry Semon, Donald Keith and other film notables appear in special studio sequences; **review:** *Go Straight* is one of those robust old melodramas which, if one cares to look at it from a satiric angle, furnish some amusement, as it has moments of unconscious humor and a mixture of good and bad acting. One sequence is devoted to scenes in a Hollywood studio, which are not uninteresting, although occasionally the thunder of the ruddy story switches to the falsetto of slapstick (*New York Times*, October 6, 1925, 30).

The Wizard of Oz; **length:** 6300 feet; 1892 meters (uncut German release); **survival status:** extant (35mm [NFA], 16mm, 8mm); **©:** June 27, 1925; **release date:** June 30, 1925; **copyright:** LP21623; **director:** Larry Semon; **editor:** Sam Zimbalist; **adapted by:** L. Frank Baum, Jr., Leon Lee, Larry Semon; **photographed by:** Hans F. Koenekamp, Frank Good, Leonard Smith; **art director:** Robert Stevens; **assistant director:** William King; **titles by:** Leon Lee; **produced by:** Larry Semon, Chadwick; **cast:** Larry Semon (Toymaker/Larry/Scarecrow), Dorothy Dwan (Dorothy), Bryant Washburn (Prince Kynd), Virginia Pearson (Countess Vishus), Oliver Hardy (The Tin Woodman), Charlie Murray (The Wizard), Josef Swickard (The Prime Minister), Mary Carr (Dorothy's Mother), G. Howe Black (Rastus), William Hauber, William Dinns, Frank Alexander (Dorothy's Guardian), Otto Lederer (Sly Diplomat), Frederick KoVert; **plot:** The Land of Oz, once ruled by Prince Kynd, has fallen into the hands of Prime Minister Kruel. Farmhand Larry has a crush on Dorothy, who is actually Princess Dorothea of Oz. Together with Price Kynd she is supposed to rule the Land of Oz; **review:** Mr. Semon, How Could You? Listen folks, if you want to see something that will make you sick, see *The Wizard of Oz* played by our eminent comedian, Larry Semon. Ye gods! I have been reading and re-reading the Oz books ever since I was a little girl and have been eagerly awaiting the advent of "the wizard" in pictures. Of course, when I heard that Larry Semon was to play it, I had my misgivings. But I surely wasn't prepared for what I got—a regular Semon comedy under the disguise of *The Wizard of Oz.* There were the usual gooey messes, flights and chases over housetops, the shimmying, frightened Negro, in fact, every old comedy gag that has ever been used. And then, on top of that, the fat man who crawled into a pile of tin to escape his pursuers—and emerged the Tin Woodman! Atrocious and aged slang was used in every possible place. Was L. Frank Baum's story so poorly written that no vestige of the plot could remain? Why should it be set to the tune of slang, rotten eggs and mud? Dear producers and all responsible for the pictures: When you are transferring a well-known and well-loved story to the screen, is it necessary needlessly to butcher the plot? Can't you learn to transfer it faithfully or not at all? Of course, I don't really mind a happy ending and such things being tacked on when they improve the story, but why, oh why, do you suppose the stories are as popular as they are? It is not because they are poorly written or the plots are faulty, Larry Semon, you owe an apology to the people who have read the Oz books, and do humble beg the pardon of Frank Baum's memory for the wrong you have done this story (Althea C. Russell, Chicago, Illinois, "Letters from Readers," *Photoplay,* December 1925, 12); The photoplay version of L. Frank Baum's famous fantastic spectacle ... is all that the author could have imagined or desired. The production has been lavishly produced, the air of fantasy has been retained, the trick camera effects are marvelous and the whimsical humor of the author has been retained and developed by Mr. Semon and his able acting ensemble.... Larry Semon [plays] the "Scarecrow" and it cannot be described, he must be seen to be appreciated.... Dorothy Dwan, Oliver Hardy and a very funny colored comedian, named G. Howe Black, all do their share in keeping the fun both fast and furious (*Nassau Daily Review*, December 26, 1928, 5).

The Cloudhopper; **survival status:** extant (35mm [MoMA], 16mm [PS]); **©:** Gauntlett & Co. June 22, 1925; **release date:** June 7, 1925; **copyright:** LP21575; **director:** Larry Semon, Norman Taurog, Steve Roberts; **writers:** Larry Semon, Norman Taurog, Steve Roberts; **titles by:** Charlie Saxton; **photographed by:** Hans F. Koenekamp, Len Smith; **edited by:** Sam Zimbalist; **produced by:** Chadwick; **distributed by:** Educational; **cast:** Larry Semon (Borden Rhoom/Getz A. Bunn), Dorothy Dwan (Dorothy Jack), Mickey McBan (Little Will Jack, Dorothy's Brother), Frank Alexander (Holden Jack, Dorothy's Father), Earl Montgomery ("Red" Shirt), Otto Lederer ("Alaskan Count"); **plot:** Larry is one of the guests at a charity bazaar arranged by the family of his girl Dorothy. Her father stores in his safe some papers which contain a top secret formula. Some crooks get away with those papers and Larry and Dorothy take up the chase; **review:** There is action galore in this comedy but nothing which will cause any laughter. The story lacks continuity because too much action is crammed into two reels. The final fade-out shows Borden lying upon the ground—the rest of the story being left for the audience to imagine. The scene in which Semon changes from one plane to another will prove thrilling. Your best bet in exploiting this picture is the well-known star (*Exhibitor's Trade Review*, June 6, 1925, 51).

My Best Girl; **alternate title:** *Youth Is Youth*; **length:** five reels; **survival status:** unknown; **release date:** June 1925(?); **director:** Larry Semon; **writers:** Dorothy Dwan, Larry Semon; **scenario by:** Dorothy Dwan, Larry Semon; **cast:** Dorothy Dwan, Joseph Swickard, George Austin; **plot:** A young girl hopes for fame by entering a chorus; **additional information:** The film was produced without any prior announcement. Although some sources mention this film (e.g., *LA Times*), no synopsis or official review could be located. However, Grace Kingsley wrote some lines after she had had a short preview: "I saw a bit of it in the projection room, and it looks like a knock-out. Miss Dwan has made remarkable strides in her work of late, and while one may have to discount a trifle what a fond bridegroom says, still this hard-boiled reviewer found fresh charm, incalculable technical improvement, and striking beauty in Miss Dwan and her work screen" (*Los Angeles Times*, May 24, 1925, 19).

The Perfect Clown; **length:** 5700 feet; **survival status:** extant (16mm, 8mm); **©:** November 16, 1925; **release date:** December 15, 1925; **copyright:** LP22003; **director:** Fred Newmeyer; **writers:** Thomas J. Crizer, Larry Semon; **produced by:** Chadwick; **photographed by:** Hans F. Koenekamp; **cast:** Larry Semon (Bert Larry), Kate Price (Mrs. Sally Mulligan), Oliver Hardy (John Mulligan), Dorothy Dwan (The Girl), Joan Meredith (Her Chum), Otis Harlan (The Boss), G. Howe Black (The Porter); **plot:** Larry is instructed to deposit $10,000 in cash at the bank, but it is late and the bank is already closed. He therefore is forced to keep the money overnight and protect it at all costs; **reviews:** This is called a comedy; why no one knows. Larry Semon works hard, but in vain.... [M]ultitudinous adventures which may amuse children but will not draw much laughter from the average adult. Mr. Semon is a hard worker, but HE IS NOT FUNNY.... [Dorothy Dwan] and the others in support of the star do their best to make a silk purse out of the sow's ear which is *The Perfect Clown* (*Chicago Daily Tribune*, January 9, 1926, 11); A very bad comedy with Larry Semon. Might have been funny in two reels (*Photoplay Magazine*, March 1926, 14).

1926

Stop, Look and Listen; **length:** 5305 feet; **survival status:** unknown; **©:** February 1, 1926; **release date:** January or February 1, 1926; **copyright:** LU22348; **director:** Larry Semon, assisted by Earl Montgomery and

Oliver Hardy, adapted from the musical comedy by Harry B. Smith, Larry Semon and Tom J. Crizer; *photographed by:* Hans F. Koenekamp, Jimmy Brown; *produced by:* Larry Semon; **distributed by:** Pathé; **cast:** Larry Semon (Luther Meek), Dorothy Dwan (Dorothy), Mary Carr (Mother), William Gillespie (Bill), Lionel Belmore (The Sheriff), B.F. Blinn (The Mayor), Bull Montana (The Strong Man), Oliver Hardy (The Show Manager), Curtis McHenry (The Porter), Josef Swickard (Old Actor), Frederic Kovert; *plot:* Luther Meek's girlfriend Dorothy strives for a stage career. On the initiative of Bill, Luther's stepbrother, she is hired to star in the local opera house. While the show is on, Bill and the manager do not only whip the show's receipts, but also the cash from the bank's vault. Cocky Bill accuses Luther, but eventually Luther can prove his innocence and capture the thieves; *reviews:* The earlier reels move along smoothly and are filled with typical Larry Semon gags that are good for a number of chuckles and will keep the average audience in good humor. Amusing burlesque has been introduced into the performance in which the girl stars her stage career, with everything going wrong.... [T]he action moves at a fast pace with straight punch melodrama ... sandwiched in with farce comedy (*Moving Picture Word*, January 23, 1926, 340); Larry Semon has one at last that is funny.... Mr. Semon works hard and to great effect. A competent cast supports him ably. Considerable money has been spent intelligently on sets etc., and the subtitles are snappy and to the point. Watching, your furtive smile develops into an ear-to-ear grin, and eventually medicinal laughter shakes you (*Chicago Daily Tribune*, March 3, 1926, 27).

1927

Pass the Dumplings; **alternate titles:** *Boarding House Story*, *Alice Day Boarding House Slavey Story* (working titles); **survival status:** unknown; ©: January 14, 1927; **release date:** January 16, 1927; **copyright:** LU23534; **director:** Larry Semon; **writers:** Randall Faye, Harry McCoy, Jefferson Moffitt, Gil Pratt, Phil Whitman, Clarence Hennecke, Hasso Price (script); **produced by:** Mack Sennett, Inc.; **distributed by:** Pathé; **cast:** Alice Day (Alice Hale), Louise Carver (The Landlady), Danny O'Shea (Officer Danny Donovan), Marjorie Zier (Mazie), Eddie Quillan (Eddie Jones), Thelma Hill, Alice Belcher, Barney Hellum, Andy Clyde; **plot:** Alice works as a servant in a boarding house. She is engaged to Eddie, a pugilist. Danny, a handsome police officer who has rented the best room in the house, makes advances to Alice. At the same time, she finds out that Eddie is untrue to her. Alice realizes that Danny will be the best husband for her. **Review:** There are some good gags in the motorcycle sequences and in the boarding house scenes, including Eddie's attempt to eat a sponge thinking it was a dumpling, which accounts for the title of the comedy. Slapstick fans should like this one (*Moving Picture World*, January 22, 1927, 282).

The Plumber's Daughter, **alternate titles:** *Alice Day Story*, *Semon Story* (working titles); **survival status:** unknown; ©: September 17, 1926; **release date:** February 12, 1927; **copyright:** LU23129; **director:** Larry Semon; **writers:** Phil Whitman, Harry McCoy, Grover Jones, Robert Eddy, Randall Faye, Earle Rodney, Clarence Hennecke; **produced by:** Mack Sennett, Inc.; **distributed by:** Pathé; **cast:** Alice Day (Alice Fawcett), Don Maines (Ed Fawcett), Eddie Quillan (Buddy Jones), Danny O'Shea (Danny Duncan), Alma Bennett (Alma Washburn), Evelyn Sherman (Mrs. Washburn), Billy Gilbert, Irving Bacon, Leo Sulky, George Gray, Dave Morris; **plot:** Eddie, a plumber's assistant, is in love with Alice, the boss' daughter. He invites her on a boat ride, but the boat capsizes and Alice is rescued by Danny, a wealthy young man. Alice's father fires Eddie and from now on Alice works as his assistant. An assignment leads them into Danny's house, but he does not recognize Alice and mistreats her. He realizes that he made a mistake and proposes to Alice, who finally accepts; **review:** There is a series of amusing situations, including one in which Alice disguises as a ragged boy to help her father, and is responsible for the house becoming flooded with water and is kicked and booted about by her hero before he discovers her identity (*Moving Picture World*, February 19, 1927, 577).

A Dozen Socks; **alternate titles:** *Love's Little Socks*, *A Socking Affair* (working titles); **sur-**

vival status: extant (16mm [PS]); ©: January 14, 1927; *release date:* March 13, 1927; *copyright:* LU23536; *director:* Earl Rodney; *script by:* Larry Semon; *writers:* Carl Harbaugh, Phil Whitman, Hasso Price, Jefferson Moffit, George Jesske, Harry McCoy, Earle Rodney; *produced by:* Mack Sennett, Inc.; *distributed by:* Pathé; *cast:* Alice Day (Molly Maloney), Danny O'Shea (Spike O'Brien), Majorie Zeir (Maybelle), Barney Hellum (Felix Dugan), Jack Dempsey, George Cray, Bobby Dunn; *plot:* During a training session, prizefighter Danny approaches Alice, Barney's girlfriend. Later, while in the audience of one of Eddie's boxing matches, Alice wheedles Barney into fighting Danny; *review:* It is a good number of the series and should prove amusing to the Alice Day fans and the public in general.... There are a number of good gags in this two-reeler (*Moving Picture World*, April 9, 1927, 574).

Spuds; *length:* 4930 feet; *survival status:* extant (35mm [UCLA, JH], fragment: 16mm [MoMA], fragment: 8mm); ©: February 4, 1927; *release date:* April 10, 1927; *copyright:* LU23535 ; *director:* Larry Semon; *writer:* Larry Semon; *photographed by:* Hans F. Koenekamp, James Brown Jr.; *produced by:* Larry Semon and unidentified backer[3]; *distributed by:* Pathé; *cast:* Larry Semon (Spuds), Alan "Kewpie" Morgan (Sergeant), Robert J. Graves (General), Hazel Howell (Bertha, from Berlin), Hugh Fay (Spy), Dorothy Dwan (Madelon, the Waitress), Edward Hearn (Captain Arthur); *plot:* In World War I France, a payroll car containing $250.000 is stolen while the responsibility of Larry's captain. Larry discovers the whereabouts of the car behind enemy lines by accident. To bring the car home, Larry drives it through the battlefield. He arrives just in time to prevent his captain from being shot; *reviews:* Stretching one reel of humor to five reels (*Motion Picture News*, April 15, 1927, 1376); Larry Semon thinks he is a good enough comedian to do without a story or situations. And of course you know otherwise. Larry has been doing this for years and it is really about time that he got wise to himself. Perhaps that is why he has turned his talents (?) towards directing for Paramount. This was apparently intended to be a hilarious travesty on the war but one is never quite sure whether it was meant to be comedy or pathos (*Photoplay Magazine*, June 1927, 137).

The Stunt Man; *alternate title:* The Strong Man; *length:* 507 meters (uncut German release); *survival status:* extant (16mm, 8mm); ©: October 27, 1927; *release date:* October 23, 1927; *copyright:* LP24579; *director:* Larry Semon; *writer:* Larry Semon; *produced by:* Chadwick; *distributed by:* Educational; *cast:* Larry Semon (Luther Meek), Jack Lipson (Seesal Sawmill, His Rival), Dorothy L. Raynor (Pearl), Charles Meakin (Her Father), Al St. John, Lillian Leighton, Peggy Taylor, Jerry Jarrette, William Dennis, Paul Dennis, Pasley Noon; *plot:* Dorothy is in love with a movie director and Larry is his antagonist. In order to win her heart, Larry applies for a job as stuntman on a movie set; *reviews:* This comedy is made up largely of exceptionally rough and tumble slapstick and will probably please fans who like this form of entertainment. There are a few ingenious situations but most of the gags are of a familiar type (*Moving Picture World*, September 24, 1927, 248); This one gives Larry a chance to stage all the old gags that most of the gag men out in Hollywood have forgotten. Larry wrote and directed this himself, which may be what's wrong with it. As a black-faced comedian, he is in the average run of that type, but he should let someone specializing in that work write his gags for him. It is cluttered with miniature sets that are amateurish. Larry will have to do better than this if he wants to get the real money (*Film Daily*, October 2, 1927, 7).

Underworld; *length:* 7453 feet; *survival status:* extant (35mm [GEH, MoMA]); ©: October 29, 1927; *release date:* August 20, 1927; *copyright:* LP24601; *director:* Josef von Sternberg; *story:* Ben Hecht; *adapted by:* Charles Furthman; *screenplay by:* Robert N. Lee; *produced by:* Paramount, Hector Turnbull; *cast:* George Bancroft (Bull Weed), Clive Brook (Rolls Royce), Evelyn Brent (Feathers), Larry Semon (Slippy Lewis), Fred Kohler (Buck Mulligan), Helen Lynch (His Girl), Jerry Mandy (Paloma), Karl Morse; *plot:* Lawyer and heavy drinker Rolls Royce is accepted as a member of Bull Weed's gang. He soon advances in the gang's hierarchy and also falls in love with his boss' girlfriend, but out of the respect for their leader they never establish a relationship; *additional information:* Semon's praise for Bancroft ... was of highest caliber. He thought Bancroft was one of the great actors of the day, a keenly intelligent fellow who knew pictures and picture values with the best of them (*Plain Dealer*, Cleveland, Ohio, October 28, 1927, 21); *review:* The totally different picture is here at last! ... [*Underworld*] is about the most amazing screen play I have seen in years. It is a powerful absorbing story of crime and violence literally taken from the life of a great city.... You will find much to admire in the performances given by the feature's players, George Bancroft, Evelyn Brent, Clive Brook and Larry Semon (*Reading Times*, Pennsylvania, November 21, 1927, 17).

Oh! What a Man; *length:* 470 meters (uncut German release); *survival status:* extant (35mm [EYE]); ©: November 28, 1927; *release date:* December 4, 1927; *copyright:* LP24728; *director:* Larry Semon; *writer:* Larry Semon; *photographed by:* Hans F. Koenekamp; *produced by:* Chadwick; *distributed by:* Educational; *cast:* Larry Semon (The Detective), Gertrude Astor (The Bandit), Jack Richardson (Her Pal), Silas Wilcox (Older Man), Willie Dennis, Paul Dennis; *plot:* Like every private eye in town, Larry is eager to arrest Notorious Nora, the leader of a gang of thieves. Nora's people turn against her and flee with a bag of previously stolen jewels. Larry involuntarily comes to Nora's aid and wins her heart by mistake; *reviews:* Larry Semon turns out a very pleasing number that carries a good batch of laughs (*Film Daily*, November 27, 1927, 13); Semon is done. This is far from good (*Exhibitors Herald and Moving Picture World*, March 24, 1928, 53); Do not consider this comedy suitable for children (*Exhibitors Herald and Moving Picture World*, April 14, 1928, 51).

1928

Dummies; *length:* 468 meters (uncut German release); *survival status:* extant (35mm [MoMA], 16mm); ©: January 2, 1928; *release date:* January 11, 1928; *copyright:* LP24841; *director:* Larry Semon; *writer:* Larry Semon; *photographed by:* Hans F. Koenekamp; *produced by:* Chadwick; *distributed by:* Educational; *cast:* Larry Semon (The Entertainer), Jim Donnelly (The Professor), Marie Astaire (His Daughter); *plot:* Larry forms part of a travelling medicine show run by a nice elderly man who calls himself "The Professor" and his daughter. Larry entertains the crowd with his dummy and a trained monkey while the professor sells his medicine to the audience. One day the professor's daily proceeds are pilfered; *review:* [Larry] has crammed a lot of gags in that have been done many times before (*Film Daily*, December 25, 1927, 8).

A Simple Sap; *length:* 608 meters (uncut German release); *survival status:* extant (35mm [CFU], 16mm, 8mm); ©: February 12, 1928; *release date:* February 12, 1928; *copyright:* LP25041; *director:* Larry Semon, Hampton Del Ruth; *writers:* Larry Semon, Hampton Del Ruth; *photographed by:* Teddy Tetzlaff; *produced by:* Chadwick; *distributed by:* Educational; *cast:* Larry Semon (It), Bee Amann (She), Walter Hiers (He), James Aubrey (Uncle Ezra), Billy Gilbert (Grandpa), Edwards Davis (The Nut); *plot:* The owner of a general store has embezzled funds from his niece's estate. He will have to go to jail if he cannot sell his store before noon, but all sales pitches fail; *review:* Children are about the only audience that will enjoy this slambang comedy. Perhaps there are a goodly number of elder folks in their second childhood who will also enjoy it. From our viewpoint it is generous to call it fair (*Motion Picture News*, February 25, 1928, 644).

Special Delivery; *alternate title:* Love Letters (working title); *length:* 5524 feet; *survival status:* extant (35mm [GEH]); ©: March 26, 1927; *release date:* May 6, 1927; *copyright:* LP23886; *director:* William Goodrich/Will H. Goodrich [Roscoe Arbuckle], Larry Semon; *photographed by:* Harry Hallenberger; *titles by:* George Marion, Jr.; *edited by:* Louis D. Lighton; *writers:* Johnny Goodrich, Eddie Cantor, Larry Semon; *produced by:* Paramount; *distributed by:* Jesse L. Lasky, Adolph Zukor, B.P. Schulberg; *cast:* Eddie Cantor (Eddie Beagle), Jobyna Ralston (Madge Warren), William Powell (Harold Jones), Mabel Julienne Scott (Mrs. Jones), Jack Dougherty (Flannigan, a Cop), Donald Keith (Harrigan, the Fireman), Louis Stern (John Beagle), Victor Potel (Nip, a Detective), Paul Kelly

(Tuck, Another Detective), Mary Carr (The Mother), Tiny Doll (The Baby); *plot:* Postman Eddie is not to come home until he has made $10,000. He therefore sets out to deliver letters with the hidden idea of capturing Blackie Morgan, a notorious crook, for whom a $10,000 reward is offered; *reviews:* Though the star has not the material that served him in *Kid Boots*, he has many opportunities for humor, of which he makes the most. He is well supported by Jobyna Ralston, William Powell and others. The settings are quite satisfactory, and the photography is good. Eddie Cantor as a U.S. postman shows his ability as eccentric dancer and comedian. Clever knockabout comedy (*The Bioscope (UK)*, August 25, 1927); The inimitable Eddie Cantor manages somehow to be funny in the midst of the oldest lot of comedy devices I have ever seen all gathered together in one picture.... Very tepid (*The Educational Screen*, June 1927, 279).

More Appearances

Screen Snapshots:

The one-reel series *Screen Snapshots* supplied intimate views of favorite film stars and met with great success at the box office.

Screen Snapshots, Series 1, No. 20; *release date:* February 22, 1921; *produced by:* C.B.C. Film Sales Corp.; *topics:* Larry Semon, Billy West, Tom Mix, Lilian Gish, Doraldina.

Screen Snapshots, Series 2, No. 22-F; *release date:* March 25, 1922; *produced by:* Jack Cohn, Lewis Lewyn; *distributed by:* Federated Film Exchanges of America, Inc.; *topics:* Semon and stars such as Wallace Beery, Harold Lloyd and Charlie Chaplin attending automobile races (*Exhibitor's Trade Review*, March 25, 1922).

Screen Snapshots, Series 3, No. 6; *produced by:* Jack Cohn, Lewis Lewyn; *distributed by:* Pathé; *topics:* Larry Semon, William Farnum, Blanche Sweet and husband Marshall Neilan, Ruth Roland and Edgar Rice Burroughs; *review:* The number is well up to the standard of the series and will please picture fans (*Film Daily*, August 6, 1922, 78); Larry Semon joining hands and dancing with a dozen girls arrayed in typical Semon garb (*Exhibitor's Trade Review*, August 12, 1922, 757).

Screen Snapshots, Series 3, No. 17; *release date:* January 14, 1923; *produced by:* Jack Cohn and Lewis Lewyn; *distributed by:* Pathé; *topics:* Larry Semon is seen in gala attire in an Actors Fund Benefit affair along with another nineteen top-notch stars; *review:* The scene itself is spirited and unusual, with each of the famous characters clearly and sometimes amusingly portrayed (*Exhibitor's Trade Review*, January 13, 1923, 357).

Screen Snapshots, Series 4, No. 15; *release date:* March 15, 1924; *produced by:* C.B.C. Film Sales Corporation; *topics:* Larry Semon, Monte Blue, Colleen Moore, Viola Dana, Walter Hiers, Conway Tearle, Barbara LaMarr, Norman I. Kelly, Blanche Sweet, Conrad Nagel (*Motion Picture News*, April 5, 1924, 1549).

Animated Hair Cartoons:

Animated Marcus Hair Cartoons, No. 3; by Edwin Marcus, cartoonist for the *New York Times*; *distributed by:* Red Seal Picture Corporation; *length:* one reel; *topics:* Larry Semon, Lady Astor, David Belasco, Clara Kimball Young and Billie Burke (*Exhibitor's Trade Review*, December 12, 1925, 37); *review:* By manipulating the hirsute adornments of some character, [Marcus] turns it into another by the mere removal of a beard to a hairdress of something similar. They are interesting short subjects particularly useful when a long feature picture is the order of the day (*Exhibitor's Trade Review*, January 24, 1915, 35).

Radio:

West Coast broadcasting, Station KNX (aka *Voice of Hollywood*): Laugh Month program: short addresses by Larry Semon, Dorothy Dwan and Walter Weasling of Pathé's Los Angeles office, December 26, 1925 (*Exhibitor's Trade Review*, January 16, 1926, 10).

Loew's Buffalo Evening News radio from station WMAK, stage appearance by Larry Semon, Ohio, November 3, 1927 (*Buffalo Courier-Express*, November 3, 1927).

Unconfirmed Appearances

For these listings on IMDb, Semon's contribution could not be verified by the sources available.

The Baby and the Boss; ©: ?; *survival status:* second reel extant (35mm [GEH]) *release date:* November 23, 1915 (?); *copyright:* ?; *director:* Larry Semon (?); *writer:* (?); *produced by:* Thanhouser Films Company; *distributed by:* Mutual Film Corporation; *cast:* Helen Badgley, Mayor Mitchel, city officials, New York police force; *additional information:* Filmed on location in New York; *plot:* A little girl wants to get her favorite policeman promoted.

Captain Jinks' Widow; ©: January 12, 1917; *release date:* February 12, 1928 (?); *copyright:* LP9936; *director:* Van Dyke Brooke; *writer:* C. Graham Baker; *produced by:* Vitagraph (*Motion Pictures*, 1912–1939, Library of Congress, 1951).

No copyright data could be found for these titles: *Captain Jinks' Nephew's Wife* and *Captain Jinks' Dilemma*, both 1917.

Screen Snapshots, Series 1, No. 20, February 22, 1921. Larry Semon, Wesley Barry, D.W. Griffith, Ruth Roland, Tom Mix and others (IMDb, retrieved June 1, 2014).

Possibly Semon also appeared in one a Screen Snapshots c. June–July 1923, being chased around Times Square on the occasion of the $3,000,000 contract he had signed with TruArt.

Unrealized Projects

Screen adaptation of George Cohan's *Money to Burn*.[4]

King Dodo (*Film Daily*, August 2, 1923, 4) Rights had already been secured for this film.

Money to Burn (Truart—*Indianapolis Star*, June 9, 1923, 7) To follow the release of *The Girl in the Limousine*, which originally had been scheduled for January 1924.

Let's Go (Truart—scheduled for September 1924) (*Exhibitor's Trade Review*, September 22, 1923, 757) The film was finally released by TruArt, starring Richard Talmadge.

Yankee Doodle Dandy (Truart—scheduled for November 1924) (*Exhibitor's Trade Review*, September 22, 1923, 757)

Taking the Air starring Wallace Beery; Semon was slated to be the scenario writer (*Motion Picture News*, January 28, 1927, 300).

The Count of Luxembourg[5]

Semon purchased the screen rights to *The Count of Luxembourg* around May 1925.[6] The film was meant to be a full-scale Semon vehicle, with him in the leading role and as director and producer. Filming was scheduled for Los Angeles for mid-1925, but it was delayed due to an illness of the then chosen director Arthur Gregor. After his recovery in late 1925, the film was made without Larry's participation.

©: December 14, 1925; *release date:* February 1, 1926; *copyright:* LP22116; *director:* Arthur Gregor; *writers:* Arthur Gregor, Jack Natteford, based on the operetta by Franz Lehár; *supervised by:* Hampton Del Ruth; *produced by:* Chadwick; *cast:* George Walsh (René Duval), Helen Lee Worthing (Angele Didier), Michael Dark (Duke Ruzinoff), Charles Requa (Secretary), James Morrison (Anatole), Joan Meredith (Yvonne), Lola Todd (Juliette)

The Gob[7]

A film meant to combine the talents of Larry Semon, Dorothy Dwan and Kathleen Clifford. Clifford was supposed to do her famous male characterization in the movie. Clifford was to imitate Larry, while Larry was to slip into her role. A one-act stage play was planned to open in Los Angeles and move to Europe three weeks later. Reportedly, Dorothy was intended for the movie, but not for the stage play; *scheduled for:* July–August 1926; *cast:* Larry Semon, Kathleen Clifford, Dorothy Dwan

Sunshine of Paradise Alley[8]

Larry was considered as director for Mabel Normand's screen comeback, but in the end neither Mabel nor he were part of the project.

release date: December 15, 1926; *director:* Jack Nelson; *writers:* Josephine Quirk, George W. Ryer, Denman Thompson; *produced by:* Chadwick; *cast:* Barbara Bedford

(Sunshine O'Day), Kenneth MacDonald (Jerry Sullivan), Max Davidson (Solomon Levy), Nigel Barrie (Stanley Douglas)

Larry Semon Films Available on 8mm, S8mm, and 9.5mm

Just like Laurel & Hardy pictures and Chaplin films, many Larry Semon comedies were available on 8mm, S8mm and even 9.5mm. The bulk of these releases are not too interesting for collectors, because they consist of heavily edited versions or more or less randomly compiled scenes. However, (nearly) uncut versions exist. Some releases contain scenes that are missing from other releases. Prints like these can occasionally be retrieved on the Internet, usually at various auction sites.

The following catalog is far from complete, as it only lists titles that are definitely available. The list is not only based on old sales lists, but also on details about missing scenes.

USA
(if not marked otherwise, released by Blackhawk)

Bathing Beauties and Big Boobs
Frauds and Frenzies
The Grocery Clerk
School Days: Missing: some scenes showing the school's director and the parents' council, Frank Hayes being pelted and the arrival of the groom.
The Bakery: Missing: opening sequence.
The Bell Hop
The Show: Missing: Most of Lucille's mirror performance, a bouquet acting as ink fountain and a few frames in the tunnel scene of the final chase.
The Saw Mill: Missing: Short scene on the roof, in which Larry takes a run-up.
Golf: Missing: bulk of a gopher scene.
The Perfect Clown
The Wizard of Oz (*released by:* Niles): Missing: opening scenes.
A Simple Sap
UK (Collector's Club releases are identical in content with the Blackhawk releases)
Dunces and Dangers (*released by:* Collector's Club)
The Saw Mill (*released by:* Collector's Club)
Golf (*released by:* Collector's Club; Vistapaks; identical content with Blackhawk release)
Kid Speed (*released by:* British Film Institute): Missing: a few seconds from *Smithy*.

Spain
Frauds and Frenzies (*released by:* Kinoluxe; *title:* Jaimito—Peligros a granel)
Bears and Bad Men (*released by:* Kinoluxe; *title:* Que viene el oso)
Pluck and Plotters (*released by:* Eurofilms; *title:* Jaimito—Espiando a los espías): offers a rare complete ending.
The Star Boarder (*released by:* cpa; *title:* Jaimito–El fresco numero uno): Offers a rare complete ending.
His Home Sweet Home (*released by:* Kinoluxe; *title:* Jaimito—Cocinero a la fuerza): Missing: scenes of Larry fighting with his mother-in-law (reel change in original?) and the last scene in which Larry takes revenge on her.
Dew Drop Inn (*released by:* cpa; *title:* Jaimito—Golpes y estrellas): Heavily edited; missing: beginning and end, but still worth viewing.
The Grocery Clerk (*released by:* Kinoluxe; *title:* Jaimito—Chico de colmado): Several minutes deleted.
The Sportsman (*released by:* Eurofilms; *title:* Jaimito—Delicias del harem; *released by:* cpa; *title:* Lluvia de golpes; *released by:* Aries; *title:* Jaimito Explorador): Rabbit hiding in his hole has slightly been shortened in all releases.
The Rent Collector (*released by:* Aries; *title:* Jaimito juez)
The Bakery (*released by:* Kinoluxe; *title:* Jaimito—Recibiendo tortas): Offers a rare opening sequence.
The Saw Mill (*released by:* Kinoluxe; 2 parts; *title part 1:* Troncos y tyros; *title part 2:* Suegro recalcitrante): Missing: final scene.
The Show (*released by:* Aries; *title:* Jaimito en el teatro): Lucille's performance, ink in bouquet and tunnel scene complete, although cut by several minutes otherwise.

A Pair of Kings (*released by:* cpa; *title: Jaimito—Cambiando a los papeles*; *released by:* Aries; *title: Jaimito—Camaradas a bordo*): Both Spanish releases lack the final fight with Oliver Hardy. Also missing: some attempted assassinations on King August I. Offers a rare complete checkerboard game in the opening sequence.

Golf (*released by:* Aries; *title: Jaimito jugador de Golf*): Offers a complete gopher scene and additional slightly "extended" scenes not available in any other releases. Omits some golf practicing by Lucille.

No Wedding Bells (*released by:* Aries; *title: Jaimito entre chinos*; *released by:* cpa; *title: Chinos a granel*)

The Barnyard (*released by:* cpa and Kinoluxe; *title of both releases: Jaimito—Bronca en la granja*)

Lightning Love (*released by:* cpa; *title: Jaimito contra viento y marea*)

Horseshoes (*released by:* cpa; two parts; *title part 1: El terror de la calle*; *title part 2: Jugando a carambolas*): Offers a rare complete scene of a policeman protecting Larry.

Trouble Brewing (*released by:* cpa; *title: Jaimito—Se bebe e se vive*)

Italy

8mm/S8mm-releases: Some releases did not content themselves with creating funny effects and dialogue when it came to the soundtrack. For example, the soundtrack of *A Pair of Kings* bestows on the film dramatic qualities thanks to thrilling music and the sounds of clashing swords in sync with the action, making it unnecessary for the viewer to know a word of Italian.

Bears and Bad Men (*released by:* SPF; *title: Ridolini e la belva nera*)

Frauds and Frenzies (*released by:* SPF; *title: Ridolini al bagno penale*)

Scamps and Scandals (*released by:* SPF; *title: Ridolini prende moglie*)

Between the Acts (*released by:* SPF; *title: Ridolini macchinista*)

Dull Care (*released by:* SPF; *title: Ridolini e i teppisti*)

The Fly Cop (*released by:* SPF; *title: Ridolini e il pericolo gialo*)

Solid Concrete (*released by:* Istituto Europa; *title: Ridolini in cantiere*): Offers an almost complete first reel, while the release of a second reel remains unconfirmed.

School Days (*released by:* SPF; *title: Ridolini scolaro*): Missing: all scenes of Larry being kicked by a donkey and the arrival of the groom.

The Bell Hop (*released by:* SPF; *title: Ridolini groom*)

The Saw Mill (*released by:* SPF; *title: Ridolini alla segheria*): Larry's run-up on the roof is included in this release.

The Show (*released by:* SPF; *title: Ridolini al varietà*)

A Pair of Kings (*released by:* SPF; *title: Ridolini granduca*): Complete ending included, but checkerboard deleted.

The Counter Jumper (*released by:* SPF; *title: Ridolini commesso di bazar*)

Horseshoes (*released by:* SPF; *title: Ridolini pugilista*): Missing: scenes of a policeman protecting Larry.

9.5mm-releases: (Pathé Baby, Roma. All releases are slightly cut)

Scamps and Scandals (*title: Ridolini prende moglie*)

Well, I'll Be... (*title: Ridolini sceriffo*)

The Star Boarder (*title: Ridolini prigoniero per amore*)

The Simple Life (*title: Ridolini e la figlia del fattore*)

Between the Act (*title: Ridolini macchinista*)

School Days (*title: Ridolini scolaro*)

Solid Concrete (*title: Ridolini nelle cave*)

The Stage Hand (*title: Ridolini inserviente teatrale*)

The Suitor (*title: Ridolini predendente*)

The Hick (2 parts; *title part 1: Ridolini deluso*; *title part 2: Ridolini e la fidanzata*)

The Fall Guy (*title: Ridolini ispettore*)

The Agent (*title: Ridolini agente segreto*)

No Wedding Bells (*title: Ridolini e i cinesi*)

The Gown Shop (*title: Ridolini nelle sartoria*)

Horseshoes (*title: Ridolini pugilista*)

Lightning Love (*title: Ridolini e il colpo di fulmine*)

Chapter Notes

Preface

1. Walter Kerr, "Some Imperfect Fools," in *The Silent Clowns* (New York: Anntess Enterprises, 1975), 151–156.
2. Petr Král, "Le Message de Larry Semon," *Positif*, 106 (1969): 28–33; Petr Král, *Larry, un pâle dans les ronces. Les Burlesques ou Parade des somnambules* (Paris: éditions Stock, 1986), 260–278.
3. Jean-Jacques Couderc, "Quatre Vedettes des 'Majors,' Larry Semon," in *Les petits maîtres du burlesque américain, 1909–1929* (Paris: CNRS Editions, 2001), 285–314.
4. Camillo Moscati, *Il re della risata* (Milano: Editoriale Lo Vecchio, 1987).
5. Phil Hall and Rory Leighton Aronsky, *What If They Lived?* (Duncan: BearManor Media, 2011), 40–47.
6. Rob Stone, *Laurel Or Hardy* (Temecula: Split Reel, 1996).
7. Richard M. Roberts, "Larry Semon, Part I, The Cartoonist as Comic," *Classic Images*, April 1999, 59–60; Richard M. Roberts, "Larry Semon, Part II, Heyday," *Classic Images*, October 1999, 13–16; Richard M. Roberts, "Larry Semon, Part III, Trouble Brewing," *Classic Images*, July 2000, 5–12.
8. Kalton C. Lahue and Sam Gill, *Clown Princes and Court Jesters* (South Brunswick: A. S. Barnes, 1970), 332–341.
9. Anthony Slide, *The Big V—A History of the Vitagraph Company* (Metuchen: Scarecrow Press, 1976), 89–93.
10. "Stripper's Guide on the History of the American Newspaper Comic Strip" last retrieved: September 8, 2013, http://www.strippersguide.blogspot.de/search?q=Marcus+the+Boarding+House+Goat.

Chapter 1

1. Herbert T. Ezekiel and Gaston Lichtenstein, *The History of the Jews of Richmond from 1769 to 1917* (Richmond: Herbert T. Ezekiel Publisher, 1917), 93.
2. "Obituary," *Illustrated New Age*, Philadelphia, November 24, 1865, 3.
3. "To Pay A Father's Debt," *Times*, Philadelphia, May 15, 1892, 4.
4. "Muchly Improved," *Daily State Journal*, November 18, 1871.
5. "The City," *Richmond Whig*, December 19, 1871, 3.
6. "A Southern Pardon," *Boston Herald*, May 30, 1885, Quarto Sheet.
7. Louella O. Parsons, "In and Out Of [illegible]," *Morning Telegraph*, June 20, 1920.
8. "Executors' Claim," *Philadelphia Inquirer*, February 25, 1898, 8.
9. Herbert C. Howe, "Cartooned into the Cinema," *Photoplay Journal*, October 1920, 24–25.
10. "Zera. An Address to the Public," *St. John's Evening Telegram*, October 21, 1879.
11. "The Mystery of the Sphinx," *Zera Semon's Journal of Wonders*, August 1881, Vol. 17, No. 501 Chestnut Street, Philadelphia; cf. Virginia Historical Society. General Collection o.s. BF1598. S38 Z3.
12. Unidentified paper, Denton, Maryland, October 26, 1878.
13. "Zera," *Wheeling Register*, March 9, 1876, 4.
14. "Amusements. Zera," *Indianapolis Sentinel*, April 8, 1876, 5–6.
15. *Williamsport Gazette And Bulletin*, September 30, 1875.
16. "State News," *Ogdensburg Advance and St. Lawrence Weekly Democrat*, January 31, 1878, 1.
17. "The Trick of an Illusionist," *Cincinnati Enquirer*, July 1, 1877, 1.
18. *Times Picayune*, May 25, 1880, 2.
19. "The Week's Gossip," *Chicago Sunday Times*, November 26, 1876, 13.
20. *Union and Recorder*, November 15, 1881, 4.
21. Douglas de Younge Silver, "Larry Semon Insisted on Double Measure of Success and He Got It," *Brooklyn Daily Eagle*, May 31, 1925, 4.
22. "Zera's Entertainment," *Wheeling Daily Intelligencer*, March 10, 1876, 4.
23. "Zera's Entertainment," *Wheeling Daily Intelligencer*, March 10, 1876, 4.
24. "What Wilkes Thinks of 'Zera,'" *Wilkes' Spirit*

of the Times cited in: *Wheeling Daily Intelligencer*, March 20, 1876, 4.
  25. "Amusement Notes," *Wheeling Daily Intelligencer*, March 13, 1876, 4.
  26. "The Last of Zera," *Wheeling Register*, March 16, 1878, 4.
  27. "Petit Thieving," *Wheeling Register*, March 4, 1878, 4.
  28. "Banner Sold Libby-Prison Museum," *Richmond Dispatch*, October 12, 1889.
  29. *Society of American Magicians Monthly Magazine*, 1918.
  30. "Prof. Zera's Entertainment," *St. Albans Daily Messenger*, October 9, 1874, 3.
  31. *Zera Semon's Journal of Wonders*, c August 1881, Vol. 17, No.501 Chestnut Street, Philadelphia; cf. Virginia Historical Society. General Collection o.s. BF1598.S38 Z3.
  32. "Wanted," *Reading Times*, April 7, 1880, 4.

Chapter 2

  1. Douglas de Younge Silver, "Larry Semon Insisted on Double Measure of Success and He Got It," *Brooklyn Daily Eagle*, May 31, 1925, 4.
  2. "Slick Tricks and Funny Things," *Wilmington Messenger*, April 4, 1894, 4.
  3. "Zera Semon Coming," *Ottawa Journal*, March 8, 1895, 7.
  4. "For Vicksburg," *New York Clipper*, November 26, 1887, 4.
  5. "Zera Semon and Royal Marionettes," *Clarion*, Jackson, MS, March 10, 1886, 3.
  6. "Children Dance at Atlantic, the Young People's Hop at the Mansion Largely Attended," *Philadelphia Inquirer* (Philadelphia, PA), August 1, 1889, 3.
  7. Al Fostell, "Harking Back," *Vaudeville News*, December 31, 1920, 2.
  8. "Austin & Stone's," *Boston Herald*, October 15, 1899, 14.
  9. *Fort Worth Daily Gazette*, Texas, April 1, 1887, 8.
  10. "Zera in Atlanta," *Charlotte Observer*, April 22, 1894, 6.
  11. "Fotosho," *Miami Herald*, February 3, 1925, 14.
  12. Carl Wilmore, "Larry Semon Wants to Quit," *Boston Post Sunday Magazine*, August 21, 1920, 7.
  13. "Slick Tricks and Funny Things," *Wilmington Messenger*, April 4, 1894, 4.
  14. "The Attraction at the Opera House," *Wilmington Messenger*, April 4, 1894, 5.
  15. Alice L. Tildesley, "My Best Remembered Christmas," *Springfield Republican*, December 25, 1927, 34.
  16. "Larry Semon at Rialto Sunday in Story of his Life," *Cedar Rapids Tribune*, July 29, 1927, 2.
  17. *New York Dramatic Mirror*, February 27, 1897, 7.
  18. "Oakland Theater," *Oakland Tribune*, January 16, 1897, 1.
  19. Károly Simonyi: *Kulturgeschichte der Physik* (Frankfurt a. M.: Urania, 1990), 393–497.
  20. "At the Chutes," *San Francisco Call*, June 27, 1897, 25.
  21. "And That's That!," *Film Daily*, July 4, 1927, 25.
  22. *Niagara Falls Gazette*, Saturday, July 28, 1923, 4.
  23. "A Crowded Hall," *St. John's Evening Telegram*, February 6, 1899.
  24. *Manitoba Morning Free Press*, December 13, 1897.
  25. Lawrence Semon, "Mysteries of Magic, Past and Present, Exposed," *San Francisco Chronicle*, August 8, 1909.
  26. Semon, "Mysteries of Magic, Past and Present, Exposed."
  27. "Got to Savannah All Right. Ten-Year-Old Boy Travels All the Way from Newfoundland," Savannah, September 27, cited in: *Atlanta Constitution*, September 28, 1900, 6.
  28. "Comedian Retains Cartooning Habit," *LA Times*, December 27, 1925, C35.
  29. Eduardo Guaitsel, "Larry Semon me jura que Su Papá Fué Brujo," *Cine-Mundial*, March 1923, 139.
  30. "Larry Semon Has Many Abilities," *State Times Advocate*, November 3, 1924, 4.
  31. de Younge Silver, "Larry Semon Insisted."
  32. "Savannah, GA," *Atlanta Constitution*, June 15, 1902, 29.

Chapter 3

  1. *Philadelphia Inquirer*, June 11, 1908.
  2. "The Call Boy's Chat," *Philadelphia Inquirer*, October 14, 1928.
  3. "Zera," *Watertown Re-Union*, April 30, 1874, 8.
  4. Carl Wilmore, "Larry Semon Wants to Quit," *Boston Post Sunday Magazine*, August 21, 1920, 7.
  5. Wedding invitation, courtesy of Joan Berschler.
  6. "'The Merry Kiddo' and 'Madame Flutterby,'" *Philadelphia Inquirer*, February 2, 1908, 7.
  7. "Balbazoo Club to Give New Comedy," *Philadelphia Inquirer*, January 25, 1909.
  8. Elizabeth Peltret, "On Location with Larry Semon," *Motion Picture Magazine*, November 1920.
  9. Douglas de Younge Silver, "Larry Semon Wanted Double Measure of Success and Got It," *Brooklyn Daily Eagle*, May 31, 1925, 4.
  10. Alexander Braun, *Winsor McCay. Comics, Filme, Träume*. (Bonn: Bocola Verlag, 2012).
  11. "'Larry' Semon 'Goat' in $35 Per Job Now Rivals Chaplin As Movie King," *New York Telegram*, 1919.
  12. Record of a Birth, Virginia Semon, Philadelphia, Department Of Public Health.
  13. Carl Wilmore, "Larry Semon Wants to Quit," *Boston Post Sunday Magazine*, August 21, 1920, 7.
  14. "The Argyle Case. They Bleach Real Money on the Stage But Don't Make It," *Springfield Union*, October 30, 1913, 10.
  15. *Variety*, November 14, 1913, 18.
  16. "Union Square," *Variety*, 1914.
  17. "Exhibitor Gets Inside View of Screen Capital," *Oregon Daily Journal*, December 12, 1920, 4.
  18. "Coleman's Baseball Player," *Variety*, May 1, 1914, 16.

19. Lyman Hardeman, "The Baseball Artwork of Larry Semon: A Prelude to Silent Movie Stardom," *Old Cardboard*, 28, Fall 2012, 26–33.
20. "Failure Now Gets Million," *Macon Telegraph*, December 14, 1919, 5.
21. Charles Carter, "I Knew Him When," *Picture-Play Magazine*, February 1920, 37.
22. "Screen Stars Go Hunting," *Detroit Free Press*, May 22, 1921, D10.
23. "Nation's Laughs Profitable to the Comic Artist," *New York Sun*, May 2, 1915, 6.
24. "Keeping Cool," *Bay City Times*, September 7, 1915, 10.
25. *Brooklyn Eagle*, August 7, 1940, 6.
26. "Billboards to Talk, Film Director Says," *Chronicle Telegram*, December 21, 1928, 2.
27. Damon Runyon, "The Brighter Side," *Idaho Statesman*, Boise, June 5, 1946, 4.
28. "Surprises at Golf Pool—Sid Mercer Defeated by Semon in Doyle's Billiard Academy," *New York Press*, January 19, 1916, BC7.
29. "Golf Pool Experts Clash: Newspaper Men Meet at the Doyle Country Club," *The Sun*, December 1, 1915, 8.

Chapter 4

1. *Cinémagazine*, April 11, 1922.
2. "Mutual Film Corporation," *Moving Picture World*, December 20, 1915.
3. "Albany," *Motion Picture News*, December 8, 1923.
4. "Sid Golden Back After Six Years," *Exhibitor's Trade Review*, October 24, 1925, 12.
5. "Screen Veteran Seen in 'Third Floor Back,'" *Motion Picture News*, April 20, 1918.
6. "Directors," *Motion Picture News*, January/February 1916, 9.
7. "In The Picture Studios," *New York Dramatic Mirror*, February 12, 1916, 32.
8. Rob Stone, *Laurel or Hardy* (Temecula: Split Reel, 1996), 102–103.
9. Anthony Slide, *The Big V—A History of the Vitagraph Company* (Metuchen: Scarecrow Press, 1976).
10. Jack W. Hoins, "All Around Town," *Brooklyn Standard Union*, October 9, 1928, 8.
11. "In New York," *The Wilmington Messenger*, August 31, 1916, 6.
12. Steve Rydzewski, *For Art's Sake, The Biography & Filmography of Ben Turpin* (Duncan: Bear-Manor, 2013), 42.
13. *The Vitagraph Bulletin*, January 1916, 14; *Ogden Standard*, January 5, 1916, 4.
14. *The Auburn Citizen*, August 14, 1916.
15. *Richmond Times Dispatch*, May 18, 1916.
16. Douglas de Younge Silver, "Larry Semon Wanted Double Measure of Success and Got It," *Brooklyn Daily Eagle*, May 31, 1925, 4.
17. H. C. Witver, "The Shooting Stars, Reel VII, Chapter XV," *The Brooklyn Daily Eagle*, January 12, 1923, A3.
18. "Comedian Whose Rise to Fame Has Been Meteoric," *Lincoln Evening Journal*, January 15, 1920, 2.
19. Graham Baker, "The Dancing Girl of the Movies," *Motion Picture Magazine*, January 1916, 100.
20. *The New York Dramatic Mirror*, June 17, 1916, 17.
21. "Dancer in "Big V" Comedies," *Motography*, September 15, 1917, 585.
22. Robert C. Duncan, "The Vitagraph Studio," *Picture Play Magazine*, October 1916, 232–233.
23. "Vitagraph Offers 'The Last Man,'" *Motography*, November 4, 1916, 1027.
24. Malcolm Oettinger, "The Heartbreaking Game of Being Funny," *New York Tribune*, November 27, 1921, 7.
25. "Director Gets Too Much Attention," *Motography*, June 9, 1917.
26. "Three 'Big V' Comedy Companies Working—Semon Signs New Contract with Vitagraph and Goes West," *Motography*, December 15, 1917, 1245.
27. Herbert C. Howe, "Cartooned Into The Cinema," *Photoplay*, October 1920, 25.
28. "Larry Gets Noisesome Welcome," *Motography*, December 22, 1917, 1286.
29. "New Comedy Company," *Motography*, June 30, 1917.
30. "Reservoir Built at Studio," *Motography*, June 1, 1918, 1068.
31. "Heavyweight Fighter Working in the Movies," *Richmond Times-Dispatch*, April 16, 1916, 9.
32. *Lima Daily News*, July 1, 1917.
33. "Film Flickers," *Oregonian*, Portland, March 11, 1917, 62.
34. "Who Would Want To Be A Movie Hero?," *New York Herald*, October 1, 1916, 5.
35. *Filmdom*, May 21, 1916.
36. "Movie Notes," *Atlanta Constitution*, November 11, 1917.
37. Elizabeth Peltret, "On Location with Larry Semon," *Motion Picture Magazine*, November 1920, 70.
38. *Motion Picture News*, April 24, 1920.
39. "Imitation Brick," *Riverside Independent Enterprise*, November 7, 1916, 3.
40. Maude Cheatham, "The Cinema Caricaturist," *Motion Picture Classic*, 1922.
41. Elizabeth Peltret, "On Location with Larry Semon," *Motion Picture Magazine*, November 1920.
42. Edwin Schallert, "Exploding the Comedy Plot," *Los Angeles Times*, June 6, 1920.
43. Bernard Rosenberg and Harry Silverstein, *The Real Tinsel* (New York: Macmillan, 1970), 50–51.

Chapter 5

1. "Gossip of the Photoplays and Photoplay People," *Williamsport Sun-Gazette*, May 5, 1917, 12.
2. "In the Movies," *Chicago Day Book*, March 15, 1917, 14.
3. Robert Florey, "Hollywood D'Hier et

D'Auhourd'Hui" (Paris: Editions Prisma, 1948), 236–37.

4. Hans F. Koenekamp, interviewed by Kevin Brownlow.

5. Clarke Irvine, "Doings in Studioland," *Philadelphia Inquirer*, March 12, 1922.

6. Pictures, *Variety*, May 5, 1922.

7. Rob Stone, *Laurel or Hardy* (Temecula: Split Reel, 1996), 419.

8. John McCabe in a letter to Chris Seguin, February 10, 1996.

9. Rob Stone, *Laurel or Hardy*.

10. John McCabe, *The Comedy World of Stan Laurel* (New York: Doubleday, 1974).

11. Edwin Schallert, "Exploding the Comedy Plot," *Los Angeles Times*, June 6, 1920.

12. "How They See Themselves," *Picture Play Magazine*, February 1921, 26–27.

13. "The Magic Men of the Movies," *Buffalo Courier-Express*, March 16, 1969, 14.

14. "Cartoons His Stunts in Comedy," *Los Angeles Times*, August 7, 1921.

15. Herbert C. Howe, "Cartooned into the Cinema," *Photoplay Journal*, October 1920, 25.

16. "Larry Semon Stars on Golf Course," *Los Angeles Times*, April 21, 1923.

17. "Pictorial Section," *Exhibitors Herald*, September 30, 1922, 31.

18. Grace Kingsley, "Tea-cup Tete-a-Tete with Stella, the Star-Gaze," *Los Angeles Times*, May 20, 1925.

19. "Larry Is Golf Bug," *Los Angeles Times*, October 22, 1922.

20. "Personalities of the Southland Golf Links," *Los Angeles Times*, May 3, 1922.

21. Hans F. Koenekamp, interviewed by Kevin Brownlow.

22. Anthony Slide, *The Big V—A History of the Vitagraph Company* (Metuchen: Scarecrow Press, 1976), 91.

23. Rob Foster, *When Silence was Golden. Legendary Laughter Series Vol. 2.* (Createspace, 2012).

24. Gerald Mast, *The Comic Mind*, (Chicago: University of Chicago Press, 1979), 194–95.

25. "Life Stories of Screen Heroes: Larry Semon," *Boys' Cinema*, June 5, 1920, 13.

26. Louella O. Parsons, "In and Out Of [illegible]," *Morning Telegraph*, June 20, 1920.

27. Rob Stone, *Laurel or Hardy*.

28. Leonard Maltin, *Leonard Maltin's Movie Crazy: For People Who Love Movies* (Dark Horse Comics 2008), 181.

29. "Pictures," *Variety*, July 14, 1922, 41.

30. Helen Louise Walker, "He Dug his Way in," *Picture Play Magazine,* November 1929, 47.

31. Argentina Brunetti, "Quel Terribile, Folle, Povero Ridolini," *GENTE*, 8 February 20, 1980, 67.

32. Coy Watson, personal communication, January 21, 2003.

33. Maude Cheatham, "The Cinema Caricaturist," *Motion Picture Classic*, 1922.

34. "Notes of the Industry in General," *Motography*, June 8, 1918, 1107.

35. *Motion Picture News*, October 6, 1917, 2384.

36. *Albany Evening Journal*, August 7, 1918, 7.

37. "$3,000,000 In Three Years for Larry Semon; Film Comedian's New Contract for Slapstick," *New York Times*, May 26, 1923.

38. *North Tonawanda Evening News*, March 22, 1920, 8.

39. "Acrobat Beats Monk," *Seattle Sunday Times*, July 27, 1919, 3.

40. "New Air Sport Thrills," *Seattle Daily Times*, February 26, 1922, 52.

41. Clarke Irvine, "Doings in Studioland," *Philadelphia Inquirer*, April 2, 1922, 14.

42. Paul H. Douglas, "Wages and Hours of Labor in 1919," *Journal of Political Economy*, Vol. 29, No. 1, 1921, 78.

43. "Chaplin Has a Pay Rival—New Contract Gives Larry Semon a Million Dollars Annually," *Kansas City Star*, November 23, 1919, 20.

44. "The Call Boy's Chat," *Philadelphia Inquirer*, November 23, 1919, 20.

45. "Production Schedule Fixed," *Exhibitors Herald*, June 12, 1920, 55.

46. "Failure Now Gets Million," *Macon Telegraph*, December 14, 1919, 5.

47. "'Nix,' Says Larry," *Seattle Daily Times*, November 23, 1919, 44.

48. "Anonians Hold Meeting To Discuss Convention," *Daily Illini*, November 1, 1922, 3.

49. *Exhibitor's Trade Review*, April 26, 1919, 1613.

50. "Italy Awards Merit Medal to Semon," *Exhibitors Herald*, September 30, 1922, 56.

51. "Vous avez la parole," *Mon Ciné*, March 30, 1922.

52. *Los Angeles Express*, June 30, 1919.

53. "Exhibitor Gets Inside View of Screen Capital," *Oregon Daily Journal*, December 12, 1920, 4.

Chapter 6

1. Malcolm Oettinger, "The Heartbreaking Game of Being Funny," *New York Tribune*, November 27, 1921, 7.

2. "To Limit Runs of Broadways Successes—Gossip of the Theater," *Trenton Evening Times*, October 15, 1922, 9.

3. "The Winners," *Photoplay Magazine*, July 1916, 14.

4. "'Beauty and Brains' Contest—Eleven Winners Chosen," *Photoplay Magazine*, June 1916, 101.

5. "Movie Beauty Fights Film Company," *State Times Advocate*, October 4, 1916, 2.

6. "Movie Men Fakers?," *Rockford Republic*, October 2, 1916, 5.

7. "Photoplay's Letter to Pharos-Reporter," *Logansport Pharos-Reporter*, March 29, 1915, 7.

8. Carl Wilmore, "Larry Semon Wants to Quit," *Boston Post Sunday Magazine*, August 21, 1920, 7.

9. "Silent Drama," September 9, 1917, *Oregonian*.

10. *Los Angeles Times*, April 15, 1919.

11. Edwin Schallert, "Even As Eve," *Los Angeles Times*, February 2, 1920.

12. "Even as Caesar," *Picture Play Magazine*, November 1920, 29.

13. Ed Roberts, *The Sins of Hollywood: An Expose of Movie Vice* (Los Angeles: Hollywood Publishing, 1922), 47.

14. "Pictorial Section," *Exhibitors Herald*, November 25, 1922, 43.

15. Personal communication Lynne Whitcopf, January 2001.

16. Personal communication Lynne Whitcopf, January 2001.

17. "Behind The Screen in Hollywood," *Philadelphia Inquirer*, August 15, 1926, 10.

18. P. Bardance, "Zigoto, L'homme qui fait rire," *Mon Ciné*, 17, 1920.

19. "Plays and Players," *Photoplay*, October 1920, 105.

20. "Lucille Carlisle Leading Woman for Larry Semon Again," *Saginaw News*, December 8, 1921, 16.

21. Kalton C. Lahue and Samuel Gill, *Clown Princes and Court Jesters* (South Brunswick: A. S. Barnes, 1970), 334–36.

22. Robert Florey, *Filmland* (Paris: Éditions de Cinémagazine, 1923).

23. Edwin Schallert, "Exploding the Comedy Plot," *Los Angeles Times*, June 6, 1920.

24. "Wee Bit Personal," *Oregon Daily Journal*, December 26, 1920, 38.

25. José Maria Sanchez García, "Larry Semon el Narizotas," *Prensa*, San Antonio, August 20, 1930, 33.

26. Grace Kingsley, "Semon to Enter King-Pin Ranks," *Los Angeles Times*, May 24, 1925, 19.

27. "Larry Semon Slightly Injured During Work," *Exhibitors Herald*, February 5, 1921, 68.

28. *Atlanta Constitution*, July 3, 1922.

29. "What the Movie Fan Wants to Know," *Boston Herald*, August 3, 1921, 17.

30. "Get in Line, Girls; Larry Semon Wants New Leading Woman," Wichita Beacon, September 4, 1921, 5.

31. "Beauty Quest Ends as Larry Signs Ann," *Salt Lake Telegram*, November 17, 1921.

32. "Stills between Shots," *Motion Picture Magazine*, March 1923, 112.

33. "When Larry's Lady Left," *Kansas City Star*, December 4, 1921.

34. Grace Kingsley, "Returns to Larry," *Los Angeles Times*, November 26, 1921.

35. "Lucille Carlisle Leading Woman for Larry Semon Again," *Saginaw News*, December 8, 1921, 16.

36. *San Diego Union*, December 18, 1921.

37. "Larry and Lucille Reunite," *Motion Picture Magazine*, March 1922, 114–115.

38. Ed Roberts, *The Sins of Hollywood: An Expose of Movie Vice* (Los Angeles: Hollywood Publishing, 1922), 49.

39. "Filmland," *San Diego Union*, December 18, 1921, 18.

40. "Answer Chap," *Brooklyn Standard Union*, March 18, 1923, 9.

41. "Friends Reveal Nose Operation," *Los Angeles Times*, March 8, 1924.

42. "Plastic Surgeon Fixes Nose for Miss Carlisle," *Los Angeles Times*, March 16, 1924, 5.

43. *Sunday Oregonian*, March 15, 1925, 2.

44. Personal communication, Jessie Salmon, Shirley Lagasse, 2001.

45. James A. Daniels, "The Trail of Tragedy That Haunted Paul Bern," *New Magazine*, December 1932.

Chapter 7

1. "Semon's Company Out; But Semon Remains," *Variety*, May 5, 1922, 38.

2. "The Observer," *Picture Play Magazine*, May 1920, 44.

3. "Public Notice and Warning to the Trade," *Film Daily*, August 20, 1920, 4–5.

4. "After Jumpers," *Wid's Daily*, September 11, 1920, 5.

5. "Larry Semon Sued by Vitagraph," *Utica Saturday Globe*, January 8, 1921, 7.

6. *IT*, September 11, 1920.

7. "Comedian Counters Heavily—Company Wants Four Hundred Thousand; He Asks Million for 'Hatred,'" *Los Angeles Times*, October 6, 1920, 17.

8. Helen Ogden, "The Wear and Tear in Comedies," *Picture Play Magazine*, April 1924, 89.

9. *Exhibitor's Trade Review*, January 20, 1923, 406.

10. "Hickville Police Patrol Destroyed," *Columbus Courier*, March 12, 1920, 7.

11. Denis Gifford, *Cine World*, September 15, 1966, 379.

12. *Atlanta Constitution*, August 28, 1921, 3.

13. "Studio Closeups and Gossip," *Wichita Beacon*, January 23, 1921, 4C.

14. "Daily Movie Service," *San Luis Obispo Daily Telegram*, July 7, 1921, 4.

15. Albert E. Smith in a letter to his brother Steve, October 26, 1921, Special Collections-URL, UCLA, California.

16. Hans F. Koenekamp, interviewed by Kevin Brownlow.

17. *Salt Lake Telegram*, September 12, 1921, 7.

18. "S. F. Grand Jury Holds Special Session On Probe," *Fresno Morning Republican*, September 14, 1921, 1.

19. "Larry Semon Wins in Suit with Vitagraph," *Syracuse New York Journal*, April 5, 1922, 22.

20. "Letter of Albert E. Smith to W. Steve Smith," May 22, 1922, Special Collections-URL, UCLA, California.

21. "Larry Semon Out. Arranges with Vitagraph to Finish Contract and Leave," *Variety*, May 26, 1922, 37.

22. "The Observer," *Picture Play Magazine*, May 1920, 44.

23. David Yallop, *The Day The Laughter Stopped* (New York: St. Martin's Press, 1976).

24. "Miss Kathleen Myers," *San Diego Evening Tribune*, February 14, 1922, 2.

25. "Semon on His Own," *Washington Times*, November 19, 1922.

26. "Myron Zobel's News of Picture People," *Oakland Tribune*, December 17, 1922.
27. "Screen Gossip," *Oregonian*, April 26, 1921, 20.
28. "Filmograms," *Duluth Evening Herald*, May 18, 1922, 11.
29. *Niagara Falls Gazette*, March 17, 1923, 9.
30. Grace Kingsley, "Semon to Enter King-Pin Ranks," *Los Angeles Times*, May 24, 1925, 19.
31. "Fine Arts Purchased by TruArt Pictures," *Exhibitor's Trade Review*, June 23, 1923, 157.
32. "TruArt Announces Its Sales Policy on Semon Features," *Moving Picture World*, September 13, 1923, 268.
33. "$3,000,000 in Three Years for Larry Semon; Film Comedian's New Contract for Slapstick," *New York Times*, May 26, 1923.
34. "Poor Artists!," *Omaha World Herald*, June 4, 1923, 5.
35. "Flashes out of Silence. Larry Semon May Take Flyer Into Vaudeville," *Los Angeles Times*, September 15, 1923, 17.
36. *Canton Sunday Repository*, November 11, 1923, 34.
37. "Semon Engagement Positively Denied," *Riverside Daily Press*, June 14, 1923, 6.
38. "Larry Semon in Chicago to Marry, Says Rumor," *Los Angeles Times*, July 10, 1923.
39. "Semon Here for Cast," *Film Daily*, October 23, 1923, 2.
40. "Over the Teacups," *Picture Play Magazine*, January 1924, 31.
41. "Larry Semon Returns to West Coast," *Moving Picture World*, June 16, 1923, 590.
42. "Inside Stuff on Pictures," *Variety*, June 7, 1923, 22.
43. "Semon Contract is All Signed Up. Gold Fountain Pen Does Work In New York Golden Sunlight," *New York Times*, reprinted in *Los Angeles Times*, May 26, 1923, I2.
44. "Semon Salary Sets Record," *Los Angeles Times*, May 23, 1923.
45. "A Statement to the Motion Picture Exhibitor," *Film Daily*, June 10, 1923, inside front cover.
46. "Work Begun on First Semon Feature Comedy," *Moving Picture World*, October 6, 1923, 507.
47. "Frisco Knows Wate," *Variety*, May 10, 1923, 4.
48. "Motion Picture Company Sold," *Charlotte Observer*, April 23, 1925, 1.
49. "Fate of Pepper Trees Arouses Film Comedian," *Los Angeles Times*, February 10, 1924, 20.

Chapter 8

1. "What the Fans Think," *Picture-Play Magazine*, April 1920, 77.
2. "Slapstick Is Popular," *Seattle Daily Times*, October 22, 1922, 30.
3. *Pantomime*, May 13, 1922, 30.
4. Lynde Denig, "Larry Semon Knows Why You Laugh," unidentified magazine, 1924(?), 68.
5. "Amusements," *Tampa Morning Tribune*, October 21, 1924, 4.
6. Denig, "Larry Semon Knows."
7. "Semon Rents Train by Day for New Film," *Santa Cruz News*, December 3, 1924, 4.
8. "Stacy—Larry Semon," *Trenton Evening Times*, August 20, 1924, 10.
9. Grace Kingsley, "Flashes: It's A Knockout," *Los Angeles Times*, September 8, 1924, A6.
10. "With the Procession in Los Angeles," *Exhibitors Herald*, January 27, 1923, 63.
11. "Pictures," *Variety*, October 8, 1924, 30.
12. "'Her Boy Friend—Semon—Educ'l First Rate Entertainment," *Film Daily*, September 28, 1924, 11.
13. "Forget Powder Puff," *Seattle Daily Times*, May 17, 1925, 39.
14. "Dorothy Dwan, Western Star, Hails From Sleepy Philly," *St. Petersburg Times*, January 6, 1929, 4.
15. "Is Mother a Pest?," *Picture Play Magazine*, May 1927, 16.
16. "19-Year-Old Note to Movie Star Held as Valid," *Moberly Weekly Monitor*, April 10, 1930, 2.
17. "Dorothy Dwan, Western Star."
18. "Dorothy Dwan Learns How To Take Cues in 'Lombardi, Ltd.,'" *Los Angeles Times*, July 29, 1928, 15.
19. "Picture of Dorothy Dwan in 'The Star,'" *Sedalia Democrat*, March 29, 1926, 10.
20. Ruth Tildesley, "Happy Though Married," unidentified magazine, 1926(?), 17.
21. Grace Kingsley, "Rumor Was Right about Larry Semon," *Chicago Daily Tribune*, August 31, 1924.
22. "Information, Please," *Picture-Play Magazine*, May 1925, 102.
23. Grace Kingsley, "Tea-Cup Tete-a-tete with Stella, the Star-Gazer," *Los Angeles Times*, May 20, 1925, C10.
24. Grace Kingsley, "Makes Fiancée His Business Partner," *Chicago Daily Tribune*, September 21, 1924, F1.
25. "The Rialto," *Hamilton Daily News*, March 3, 1927.
26. Richard M. Roberts, "Larry Semon, Part III, Trouble Brewing," *Classic Images*, July 2000, 10.
27. "Semon Intends to Make His Bride a Movie Star," *Sedalia Weekly Democrat*, January 30, 1925, 3.
28. "Inside Stuff," *Variety*, January 28, 1925, 9.
29. "Larry Semon," *Variety*, January 21, 1925, 12.
30. "Personal Appearance Shatters Illusions," *Oakland Tribune*, February 8, 1925, W-3.
31. Peggy Nye, "Sub Deb Rosa," *Los Angeles Times*, March 7, 1926.
32. "California, Like Tennessee, is Getting Too Many Laws and Meddlers, Making It a Very Good Place to 'Stay Away From,'" *Helena Daily Independent*, Montana, July 19, 1925, 9.
33. "Gossip Around Studios out Hollywood Way," *Philadelphia Inquirer*, July 8, 1928, 7.
34. Grace Kingsley, "Tea-Cup Tete-a-tete."
35. "Semon's Wit Makes No Hit: Gets Ticket," *Santa Ana Daily Evening Register*, March 21, 1925, 7.
36. "Movie Director for Larry Semon Gets 5-Day Term," *Santa Ana Daily Register*, March 25, 1925, 12.

37. "Motion Picture News," *Evening Tribune*, San Diego, April 8, 1922, 11.
38. Ruth Tildesley, "Happy," 32.
39. "Screen Life in Hollywood," *Scranton Republican*, September 26, 1928, 7.
40. "Studio News and Gossip—East and West," *Photoplay*, December 1926, 84.
41. Alice L. Tildesley, "Should Women Reveal Their Knees?," *Springfield Sunday Union and Republican*, December 11, 1927, 4D.
42. "Former Sedalian Holds Good Position in Movie Land," *Sedalia Democrat*, July 27, 1933, 5.
43. "Semon Uses School Kids," *Moving Picture World*, October 31, 1925, 710.
44. Elizabeth Greer and Milton Howe, "The Latest News of Social and Professional Circles," *Motion Picture Magazine*, October 1926, 70/85.
45. "Semon Has New Film," *Seattle Daily Times*, January 11, 1925, 55.
46. "'Wizard of Oz' Booked for Broadway Run," *Exhibitor's Trade Review*, April 11, 1925, 31.
47. "Bitter Court Fight Pending Over 'Wizard of Oz' Rights," *Variety*, February 4, 1925, 28.
48. "Home Town Lure for Dorothy Dwan," *Sedalia Weekly Democrat*, August 7, 1925, 3.
49. "Mr. Semon, How Could You?," *Photoplay*, December 1925, 12.
50. "In Lima Theaters," *Lima Daily News*, February 19, 1925, 7.
51. Grace Kingsley, "Semon's Big Ones," *Los Angeles Times*, 1925, A9.
52. "Playing Jokes on the Stars," *Modesto Bee and News-Herald*, April 1, 1928, 24.
53. *Daily Star*, April 17, 1925, 20.
54. "Simple Semon," *Pictures and Picturegoers*, May 1925, 25.
55. Mae Tinée, "This Is Called a Comedy; Why No One Knows." *Chicago Daily Tribune*, January 9, 1926, 11.
56. "Judgment Against Semon," *Variety*, February 18, 1925, 24.
57. *Los Angeles Times*, July 29, 1925, 50.

Chapter 9

1. "Semon's Pathe Agreement," *Variety*, July 29, 1925, 26.
2. "Some Good Numbers," *San Francisco Chronicle*, August 24, 1925, 7.
3. "Larry Semon and Wife In New York," *Miami Herald*, Florida, January 3, 1926.
4. "'Stop, Look And Listen!' Showing Here," *Lebanon Daily News*, December 18, 1926, 56.
5. "Semon Scores Gotham Shows," *Los Angeles Times*, December 20, 1925.
6. Eugene V. Brewster, "That Semon Chap," *Motion Picture Classic*, August 1926, 72.
7. "Spuds," *Photoplay*, November 1927, 16.
8. Eugene V. Brewster, "That Semon Chap," *Motion Picture Classic*, August 1926, 72, 85.
9. Margaret Reid, "What I Think of My Wife—or My Husband—on the Screen," *Picture Play Magazine*, May 1927, 98.
10. "Side-Saddle Habits for Women out of Date," *San Francisco Chronicle*, May 30, 1927, 37.
11. Argentina Brunetti, "Quel Terribile, Folle, Povero Ridolini," *GENTE*, 8 February 20, 1980, 67.
12. "Has Nervous Collapse," *Trenton Evening Times*, January 2, 1926, 12.
13. Robert Florey, *Hollywood D'Hier Et D'Aujourd'Hui* (Paris: Editions Prisma, 1948), 236–37.
14. Kingsley Grace, "Semon to Develop Comedy Directors, Produce," *Los Angeles Times*, October 25, 1925.
15. *Oregonian*, May 9, 1926, 60.
16. "Which Picture Do the Players Like Best?," *Picture-Play Magazine*, June 1925, 114.
17. Warren M. Sherk, compiler and editor, *The Films of Mack Sennett* (Metuchen: Scarecrow Press, 1998), 51.
18. "Vaudeville Wants Comedian," *Times-Picayune*, August 8, 1926, 62.
19. Elizabeth Lonergan, "Hollywood Screen Stars Recall Visits to Portland," *Oregonian*, September 19, 1926, 58.
20. "Cold Water for His Joke," *Zanesville Times Signal*, June 13, 1926.
21. "New Movie Firm Will Make Pageants Its Specialty," *Huntington Press*, August 1, 1926, 15.
22. Louella O. Parsons, "Filmettes," June 6, 1926, 8.
23. "Vaudeville Wants Comedian," *Times-Picayune*, August 8, 1926, 62.
24. "Behind the Screen in Hollywood," August 16, 1926, 10.
25. "Should Opposites Marry?," *Daily Argus*, Mount Vernon, February 12, 1927, 18.
26. "What They Don't Like About Husbands," *San Francisco Chronicle*, February 10, 1929, 15.
27. "Davis Would Be Producer of Film Comedies," *San Diego Union*, August 24, 1926, 1.
28. "'Underknee-Th,'" *Syracuse Herald*, February 14, 1926, 2.
29. "Larry Semon's Car Robbed," *Syracuse American Journal*, September 26, 1926.
30. "Larry Semon's Stolen Car Recovered After Wild Chase," *Van Nuys News*, January 7, 1927, 1.
31. "Wallace Beery to Make 'Taking the Air.'" *Motion Picture News*, January 28, 1927, 300.
32. "Semon 'Triples in Brass' for Paramount," *Moving Picture World*, December 11, 1926, 405.
33. "Twelve Beauties Arrive On Lots, Seeking Fame," *Times-Picayune*, March 27, 1927, 3.
34. "Crowd Finds 'Fatty' a Chastened Clown," *Chicago Daily Tribune*, June 6, 1923.
35. "Twelve Beauties."
36. W. Ward Marsh, "Comedian Talks About Screen Work; Tells of Remaking a Recent Film," *Cleveland Plain Dealer*, October 28, 1927, 21.
37. "Semon Wears Seven Suits in Picture," *San Francisco Chronicle*, April 24, 1927, 6D.
38. Doug Fetherling, *The Five Lives of Ben Hecht* (Lester and Orpen Limited, 1977), 93.
39. "C.M.D. Close Ups," *Boston Herald*, March 19, 1927.

40. "Bancroft Gets Bad Break in Filming of Underworld," *Chicago Daily Herald*, December 2, 1927, 13.
41. "What Makes Crooks Laugh Discovered by Larry Semon," *Oregonian*, May 15, 1927, 2.
42. "You Can't Get Away With It!," *Medina Daily Journal*, February 25, 1928, 3.
43. W. Ward Marsh, "Comedian Talks About Screen Work; Tells of Remaking a Recent Film," *Cleveland Plain Dealer*, October 28, 1927, 21.
44. Mordaunt Hall, "The Screen. The Strong and the Meek, Underworld," *New York Times*, undated; 382.
45. "Bancroft to Appear on Two Screens Next Week; Other Picture Comment," *Cleveland Plain Dealer*, October 27, 1927, 25.
46. "Cat Party-ing with Dorothy Dwan," *Los Angeles Times*, May 9, 1926.
47. *Photoplay*, November 1926, 121–22.
48. "Sidelights of Stage and Screen," *Joplin Globe*, April 24, 1927, 33.
49. "Behind Screen in Hollywood," *Cleveland Plain Dealer*, June 28, 1925, 5.
50. Louella O. Parsons, "Chaliapin for the Movies, Maybe," *Syracuse Journal*, August 26, 1927; *Oregonian*, Portland, August 28, 1927, 3.
51. "Death Fails To Halt Film Camera Work," *Santa Ana Register*, July 1, 1927, 16.
52. "Larry Semon Active," *Film Daily*, July 10, 1927, 8; Semon to Be Starred in Eight Comedies, *Daily Star*, Queens Borough, New York, July 19, 1927, 4.
53. "Comedy Actress Injured," *Seattle Daily Times*, July 21, 1927, 14.
54. "Larry Semon on the Air in News Hour Tonight," *Buffalo Evening News*, November 8, 1927, 19.
55. "Loew's State," *Los Angeles Examiner*, December 31, 1927.
56. "Three Stars Plan to Play Golf All Day," *San Francisco Chronicle*, December 25, 1927, D3.
57. Louella O. Parsons, "In and Out Of [illegible]," *Morning Telegraph*, June 20, 1920.

Chapter 10

1. *Sunday Oregonian*, February 19, 1928, 3.
2. "Larry Semon Goes 'Broke,'" *Fitchburg Sentinel*, March 14, 1928, 1.
3. "Larry Semon Bankrupt," *Macon Telegraph*, March 15, 1928, 5.
4. "Larry Semon's Income Taxes Harass Widow," *Los Angeles Examiner*, February 25, 1929.
5. "Screen Comedian in Poor Way Financially," *Riverside Daily Press*, March 14, 1928,1.
6. Douglas Hodges, "'Lilac Time' Breaks 2nd Week Record at Carthay Circle Theater," *Exhibitors Herald and Moving Picture World*, August 11, 1928, 44.
7. "Up and Down," *Tampa Tribune*, March 11, 1928.
8. "The Two-a-Day Racket," *Picture-Play Magazine*, April 1928, 119.
9. "Co-eds, Take Notice," *Emporia Gazette*, March 12, 1928, 1.
10. Cass Baer Hicks, "Film Stars to Be Enter Vaudeville—Many Movie Actors Eager to Make Real Money, Purses Becoming Flat," *Oregonian*, April 22, 1928, 47.
11. "Civic Repertory Season Ending," *Brooklyn Daily Eagle*, May 2, 1928, 38.
12. "Gossip of Vaudeville," *New York Times*, April 15, 1928.
13. *Davenport Democrat and Leader*, April 23, 1928, 5.
14. "Smart Audiences Demand Fast Action in Movie Comedies, Larry Semon Says," *Waterloo Evening Courier*, April 21, 1928, 3.
15. "Larry Semon Comedies," *Exhibitors Herald and Moving Picture World*, November 3, 1923, 76.
16. "Larry Semon to Appear Sunday in Rock Island," *Davenport Democrat and Leader*, April 20, 1928, 18.
17. "Mother of Dorothy Dwan Is a Bride," *Sedalia Democrat*, May 21, 1928, 1.
18. "Film Company Sued," *Los Angeles Times*, June 28, 1928; "$100,000 Suit Hits Larry Semon," *Los Angeles Examiner*, July 28, 1928.

Chapter 11

1. Claudia Sassen, "Larry Semon—Untersuchungen zur Möglichkeit eines vorgetäuschten Ablebens," *Two Tars Journal*, 30, December 1999; Claudia Sassen "Larry Semon—How Many Times Did He Die?," *Slapstick!*, July 2, 2000.
2. "Former Carman Girl In Featured Act At Proctor's," *Schenectady Gazette*, April 9, 1920, 13.
3. Grace Kingsley, "A Radio Party and a Shower," *Los Angeles Times*, August 26, 1928, J4.
4. "Dorothy Dwan to a Stage Career," *Sedalia Democrat*, August 1, 1928, 5.
5. "Larry Semon, Film Comedian, is Dying," *Montreal Gazette*, October 8, 1928, 10.
6. "Club is Being Pushed Ahead," *San Bernardino County Sun*, September 19, 1926, 26.
7. Richard M. Roberts, "Larry Semon, Part III, Trouble Brewing," *Classic Images*, 286, July 2000, 14.
8. "Larry Semon Dying on California Ranch," *New York Times*, October 7, 1928, 30.
9. *Oregonian*, November 4, 1928, 48.
10. "Larry Semon Of Movies is Ill," *San Jose Evening News*, August 22, 1928, 19.
11. "Semon Nearing Illness Crisis," *Los Angeles Times*, September 20, 1928.
12. "Comedian's Health Is In Serious Condition," *Riverside Daily Press*, September 20, 1928, 1.
13. "Party Given By Lois Wilson," *San Francisco Chronicle*, September 30, 1928.
14. "Larry Semon Continues as Very Sick Man," *Los Angeles Times*, September 28, 1928.
15. "Larry Semon near Death," *Waco News-Tribune*, September 29, 1928, 1.
16. *Buffalo Courier Express*, September 28, 1928, 24.

17. www.ebay.com/itm/1928-Movie-Star-Comedian-Larry-Semon-Mojave-Desert-Sanitarium-Original-Photo.
18. "Passing Of Larry Semon," *Brooklyn Standard Union*, October 9, 1928, 6.
19. "Long-Haired Women Soon to Be Rage in Hollywood," *Oregonian*, April 10, 1927, 2.
20. "What Makes Crooks Laugh Discovered by Larry Semon," *Oregonian*, May 15, 1927, 2.
21. "Secrets of 'Making-up' Movie Stars," *Dallas Morning News*, Dallas, February 26, 1928, 8.
22. John R. Finch and Paul A. Elby, *Close-Ups* (South Brunswick, New York: Barnes, 1978); *Blue Book of the Screen* (Hollywood: Pacific Gravure, 1924), 224.
23. *Trenton Evening Times*, September 30, 1928, 18.
24. Richard M. Roberts, "Larry Semon, Part III, Trouble Brewing," *Classic Images*, 286, July 2000, 14.
25. "Larry Semon, Screen Star, near Death," *San Luis Obispo Daily Telegram*, October 6, 1928, 1.
26. "Semon, Popular Film Comedian, Believed Dying," *Modesto Bee And News Herald*, October 6, 1928, 2.
27. "Larry Semon, Film Comedian, Dying in Mojave Sanitarium," *San Diego Union*, October 7 (6), 1928, 1.
28. "Larry Semon near Death," *Emporia Gazette*, October 6, 1928, 6.
29. "Larry Semon, Comedian, Dying near Victorville," *San Bernardino County Sun*, October 7, 1928, 1.
30. "Actor Rallies at Desert Hospital, then Sinks Again," *San Bernardino County Sun*, October 8, 1928, 9.
31. Richard M. Roberts, "Larry Semon, Part III, Trouble Brewing," *Classic Images*, 286, July 2000, 14.
32. "He Gave Us Merriment," *Rockford Republic*, October 9, 1928, 10.
33. "Hope Abandoned for Saving Life of Larry Semon," *Los Angeles Times*, October 8, 1928, 1.
34. "Death near for Semon, Film Actor," *Los Angeles Times*, October 7, 1928.
35. "Funeral is Held for Larry Semon," *Los Angeles Herald*, October 9, 1928.
36. "Semon Funeral Will Be Simple," *Los Angeles Times*, October 9, 1928.
37. "Simple Rites Mark Passing of Film Star," *San Bernardino County Sun*, October 10, 1928, 11.
38. "Only Six Persons at the Funeral of Larry Semon," *Danville Bee*, October 10, 1928, 7.
39. "Simple Rites."
40. "Funeral Services for Larry Semon," *Trenton Evening Times* October 9, 1928, 5.

Chapter 12

1. Louella O. Parsons, "Larry Semon's Income Taxes Harass Widow," *Los Angeles Examiner*, February 25, 1925.
2. Robert Florey in Jacques Chevallier, *Le cinéma burlesque américain au temps du muet (1912–1930)* (Paris: Institut pédagogique national, 1964), 47.
3. "The Call Boy's Chat," *Philadelphia Inquirer*, October 14, 1928.
4. P. Bardance, "Zigoto, L'homme qui fait rire," *Mon Ciné*, 17, 1920.
5. Argentina Brunetti, "Quel Terribile, Folle, Povero Ridolini," *GENTE*, 8, February 20, 1980, 67.
6. Alan Sylvester, "The Fatal Number Three," *Picture Play Magazine,* February 6, 1929, 111.
7. Jess Ranch, "Historical Points of Interest in Apple Valley. The Town of Apple Valley," pdf-document: www.applevalley.org, last retrieved May 13, 2014.
8. "Dorothy Dwan Injured," *Rockford Republic*, November 15, 1928, 2.
9. "$14,000 Lien Against Larry Semon Estate," *Post Crescent,* Appleton, May 30, 1929, 1.
10. Louella O. Parsons, "Larry Semon's Income Taxes Harass Widow," *Los Angeles Examiner*, February 25, 1925.
11. "Dorothy Dwan," *Sedalia Democrat*, December 3, 1935, 4.
12. Scott Hayden in a letter to the author, May 30, 2001.
13. Jack W. Hoins, "All Around Town," *Brooklyn Standard Union*, October 9, 1928, 8.
14. "Hughie Mack Dies at Santa Monica Home," *Riverside Daily Press*, October 14, 1927, 12.
15. Jack W. Hoins, "All Around Town," *Brooklyn Standard Union*, October 9, 1928, 8.
16. "Two Die after Pilot Faints," *Los Angeles Times*, July 18, 1929, A1.
17. "Norman Taurog, Director, Dies; Winner of an Oscar for 'Skippy,'" *New York Times*, January 12, 2007.
18. "Hans F. Koenekamp; Retired Cinematographer," *Los Angeles Times*, September 15, 1992, 6.
19. Uthai Vincent Wilcox, "The Clown Turns Ringmaster; Larry Semon Now a Director," unidentified magazine, c. 1926.
20. "Goldin Bankrupt," *Exhibitors Daily Review*, November 10, 1928, 2.
21. Hans F. Koenekamp, interviewed by Kevin Brownlow.

Filmography

1. "In Bunny's Footsteps," *Canton Repository*, March 26, 1925, 21.
2. "In the Picture Studios," *New York Dramatic Mirror*, February 12, 1916, 32.
3. Eugene V. Brewster, "That Semon Chap," *Motion Picture Classic*, August 1926, 72.
4. *Oregonian*, August 5, 1923, 2; "Semon Prepares to Film TruArt Picture," *Moving Picture World*, November 23, 1923, 249; "The Screen," *Indianapolis Star,* June 9, 1923, 7
5. "Gossip Around the Studios," *The Philadelphia Inquirer*, June 21, 1925, 9.
6. Hallet Abend, "Whispers from behind the Screen," *Idaho Statesman*, May 17, 1925, 3; *Exhibitor's Trade Review*, May 23, 1925, 43
7. Louella Parsons, "Filmettes," *The Idaho Statesman* June 18, 1926, 3.
8. "Mabel Normand back?," Variety, May 6, 1925, 35.

Bibliography

Abend, Hallet. "Whispers from behind the Screen." *Idaho Statesman*, May 17, 1925.
Atlanta Constitution. "Got to Savannah All Right: Ten-Year-Old Boy Travels All the Way from Newfoundland." September 28, 1900.
Baker, Graham. "The Dancing Girl of the Movies." *Motion Picture Magazine*, January 1916.
Bardance, P. "Zigoto, l'homme qui fait rire." *Mon Ciné*, 17, 1920.
Bay City Times. "Keeping Cool." September 7, 1915.
Blue Book of the Screen. Hollywood: Pacific Gravure Company, 1924.
Boston Herald. "Austin & Stone's." October 15, 1899.
———. "C.M.D. Close Ups." March 19, 1927.
———. "A Southern Pardon." May 30, 1885, Quarto Sheet.
———. "What the Movie Fan Wants to Know." August 3, 1921.
Boys' Cinema. "Life Stories of Screen Heroes: Larry Semon." June 5, 1920.
Braun, Alexander. *Winsor McCay: Comics, Filme, Träume*. Bonn: Bocola Verlag, 2012.
Brewster, Eugene V. "That Semon Chap." *Motion Picture Classic*, August 1926.
Brooklyn Daily Eagle. "Civic Repertory Season Ending." May 2, 1928.
Brooklyn Standard Union. "Answer Chap." March 18, 1923.
———. "Passing Of Larry Semon." October 9, 1928.
Brunetti, Argentina. "Quel Terribile, Folle, Povero Ridolini." *GENTE*, 8, February 20, 1980.
Buffalo Courier Express. "The Magic Men of the Movies." March 16, 1969.
Buffalo Evening News. "Larry Semon on the Air in News Hour Tonight." November 8, 1927.
Canton Repository. "In Bunny's Footsteps." March 26, 1925.
Carter, Charles. "I Knew Him When." *Picture Play Magazine*, February 1920.
Cedar Rapids Tribune. "Larry Semon at Rialto Sunday in Story of his Life." July 29, 1927.
Charlotte Observer. "Motion Picture Company Sold." April 23, 1925.
———. "Zera in Atlanta." April 22, 1894.

Cheatham, Maude. "The Cinema Caricaturist." *Motion Picture Classic*. 1922.
Chevallier, Jacques. *Le Cinéma Burlesque Américain au Temps du Muet (1912–1930)*. Paris: Institut pédagogique national, 1964.
Chicago Daily Herald. "Bancroft Gets Bad Break in Filming of Underworld." December 2, 1927.
Chicago Daily Tribune. "Crowd Finds 'Fatty' a Chastened Clown." June 6, 1923.
Chicago Sunday Times. "The Week's Gossip." November 26, 1876.
Chronicle Telegram. "Billboards to Talk, Film Director Says." December 21, 1928.
Cincinnati Enquirer. "The Trick of an Illusionist." July 1, 1877.
Clarion, Jackson, MS. "Zera Semon and Royal Marionettes." March 10, 1886.
Cleveland Plain Dealer. "Bancroft to Appear on Two Screens Next Week; Other Picture Comment." October 27, 1927.
———. "Behind Screen in Hollywood." June 28, 1925, 5.
Columbus Courier. "Hickville Police Patrol Destroyed." March 12, 1920.
Couderc, Jean-Jacques. *Les petits maîtres du burlesque américain. 1909–1929*. Paris: CNRS Editions, 2001.
Daily Argus. Mount Vernon. "Should Opposites Marry?" February 12, 1927.
Daily Illini. "Anonians Hold Meeting to Discuss Convention." November 1, 1922.
Daily Star. "Semon to Be Starred in Eight Comedies." July 19, 1927.
Daily State Journal. "Muchly Improved." November 18, 1871.
Dallas Morning News. "Secrets of 'Making-up' Movie Stars." February 26, 1928.
Daniels, James A. "The Trail of Tragedy That Haunted Paul Bern." *New Magazine*. December 1932.
Danville Bee. "Only Six Persons at the Funeral of Larry Semon." October 10, 1928.
Davenport Democrat and Leader. "Larry Semon to Appear Sunday in Rock Island." April 20, 1928.

The Day Book, Chicago, Ill., "In the Movies." March 15, 1917.
Denig, Lynde. "Larry Semon Knows Why You Laugh." Unidentified magazine, 1924(?).
Detroit Free Press. "Screen Stars Go Hunting." May 22, 1921, D10.
Douglas, Paul H. "Wages and Hours of Labor in 1919." *Journal of Political Economy* 29, no. 1 (1921): 78.
Duluth Evening Herald. "Filmograms." May 18, 1922.
Duncan, Robert C. "The Vitagraph Studio." *Picture Play Magazine*, October 1916.
Emporia Gazette. "Co-eds, Take Notice." March 12, 1928.
_____. "Larry Semon near Death." October 6, 1928.
Evening Tribune. San Diego. "Motion Picture News." April 8, 1922.
Exhibitors Daily Review. "Goldin Bankrupt." November 10, 1928.
Exhibitors Herald. "Italy Awards Merit Medal to Semon." September 30, 1922.
_____. "Larry Semon Comedies." November 3, 1923.
_____. "Larry Semon Slightly Injured During Work." February 5, 1921.
_____. "Production Schedule Fixed." June 12, 1920.
_____. "With the Procession in Los Angeles." January 27, 1923.
Exhibitor's Trade Review. "Fine Arts Purchased by TruArt Pictures." June 23, 1923.
_____. "Sid Golden Back after Six Years." October 24, 1925.
_____. "'Wizard of Oz' Booked for Broadway Run." April 11, 1925.
Ezekiel, Herbert T., and Gaston Lichtenstein. *The History of the Jews of Richmond from 1769 to 1917*. Richmond: Herbert T. Ezekiel Publisher, 1917.
Fetherling, Doug. *The Five Lives of Ben Hecht*. Toronto: Lester and Orpen Limited, 1977.
Film Daily. "After Jumpers." September 11, 1920.
_____. "And That's That!" July 4, 1927.
_____. "'Her Boy Friend': Semon—Educ'l First Rate Entertainment." September 28, 1924.
_____. "Larry Semon Active." July 10, 1927.
_____. "Public Notice and Warning to the Trade." August 20, 1920.
_____. "Semon Here for Cast." October 23, 1923.
_____. "A Statement to the Motion Picture Exhibitor." June 10, 1923.
Finch, John R., and Paul A. Elby. *Close-Ups*. South Brunswick, New York: Barnes, 1978.
Fitchburg Sentinel. "Larry Semon Goes 'Broke.'" March 14, 1928.
Florey, Robert. *Filmland*. Paris: Editions de ciné-magazine, 1923.
_____. *Hollywood d'hier et d'auhourd'hui*. Paris: Editions prisma, 1948.
Fostell, Al. "Harking Back." *Vaudeville News*, December 31, 1920.
Foster, Rob. *When Silence was Golden: Legendary Laughter Series Vol. 2*. Createspace, 2012.
Fresno Morning Republican. "S. F. Grand Jury Holds Special Session on Probe." September 14, 1921.
Gifford, Denis. *Cine World*. September 15, 1966.

Greer, Elizabeth, and Milton Howe. "The Latest News of Social and Professional Circles." *Motion Picture Magazine*, October 1926.
Guaitsel, Eduardo. "Larry Semon me jura que su papá fué brujo." *Cine-Mundial*, March 1923.
Hall, Mordaunt. "The Screen. The Strong and the Meek, Underworld." *New York Times*, undated.
Hall, Phil, and Rory Leighton Aronsky. *What If They Lived?* Duncan: BearManor Media, 2011.
Hamilton Daily News. "The Rialto." March 3, 1927.
Hardeman, Lyman. "The Baseball Artwork of Larry Semon: A Prelude to Silent Movie Stardom." *Old Cardboard*, 28, Fall 2012.
Helena Daily Independent. "California, Like Tennessee, is Getting Too Many Laws and Meddlers: Making It a Very Good Place to 'Stay Away from.'" Montana, July 19, 1925.
Hicks, Cass Baer. "Film Stars to Be Enter Vaudeville: Many Movie Actors Eager to Make Real Money, Purses Becoming Flat." April 22, 1928.
Hodges, Douglas. "'Lilac Time' Breaks 2nd Week Record at Carthay Circle Theater." *Moving Picture World*, August 11, 1928.
Hoins, Jack W. "All Around Town." *Brooklyn Standard Union*, October 9, 1928.
Howe, Herbert C. "Cartooned into the Cinema." *Photoplay*, October 1920.
Huntington Press. "New Movie Firm Will Make Pageants Its Specialty." August 1, 1926.
Illustrated New Age, Philadelphia. "Obituary." November 24, 1865.
Indianapolis Sentinel. "Amusements: Zera." April 8, 1876.
Indianapolis Star. "The Screen." June 9, 1923.
Irvine, Clarke. "Doings in Studioland." *Philadelphia Inquirer*, April 2, 1922.
Joplin Globe. "Sidelights of Stage and Screen." April 24, 1927.
Kansas City Star. "Chaplin Has a Pay Rival: New Contract Gives Larry Semon a Million Dollars Annually." November 23, 1919.
_____. "When Larry's Lady Left." December 4, 1921.
Kerr, Walter. *The Silent Clowns*. New York: Anntess Enterprises, 1975.
Kingsley, Grace. "Flashes: It's A Knockout." *Los Angeles Times*, September 8, 1924.
_____. "Makes Fiancee His Business Partner." *Chicago Daily Tribune*, September 21, 1924.
_____. "A Radio Party and a Shower." *Los Angeles Times*, August 26, 1928.
_____. "Returns to Larry." *Los Angeles Times*, November 26, 1921.
_____. "Rumor was Right about Larry Semon." *Chicago Daily Tribune*, August 31, 1924.
_____. "Semon to Develop Comedy Directors, Produce." *Los Angeles Times*, October 25, 1925.
_____. "Semon to Enter King-Pin Ranks." *Los Angeles Times*, May 24, 1925.
_____. "Semon's Big Ones." *Los Angeles Times*, 1925.
_____. "Tea-Cup Tete-a-tete with Stella, the Star-Gazer." *Los Angeles Times*, May 20, 1925.

Král, Petr. "Le message de Larry Semon." *Positif*, 106, 1969.

_____. *Les burlesques, ou parade des somnambules*. Paris: Editions Stock, 1986.

Lahue, Kalton C., and Sam Gill. *Clown Princes and Court Jesters*. South Brunswick: A. S. Barnes, 1970.

Lebanon Daily News. "'Stop, Look And Listen!' Showing Here." December 18, 1926.

Lima Daily News. "In Lima Theaters." February 19, 1925.

Lincoln Evening Journal. "Comedian Whose Rise to Fame Has Been Meteoric." January 15, 1920.

Logansport Pharos-Reporter. "Photoplay's Letter to Pharos-Reporter." March 29, 1915.

Lonergan, Elizabeth. "Hollywood Screen Stars Recall Visits to Portland." *Oregonian*, September 19, 1926.

Los Angeles Examiner. "Larry Semon's Income Taxes Harass Widow." February 25, 1929.

_____. "Loew's State." December 31, 1927.

_____. "$100,000 Suit Hits Larry Semon." July 28, 1928.

Los Angeles Herald. "Funeral is Held for Larry Semon." October 9, 1928.

Los Angeles Times. "Cartoons His Stunts in Comedy." August 7, 1921.

_____. "Cat Party-ing with Dorothy Dwan." May 9, 1926, H5.

_____. "Comedian Counters Heavily: Company Wants Four Hundred Thousand; He Asks Million for 'Hatred.'" October 6, 1920.

_____. "Comedian Retains Cartooning Habit." December 27, 1925.

_____. "Death Near for Semon, Film Actor." October 7, 1928.

_____. "Dorothy Dwan Learns How to Take Cues in 'Lombardi, Ltd.'" July 29, 1928.

_____. "Fate of Pepper Trees Arouses Film Comedian." February 10, 1924.

_____. "Film Company Sued." June 28, 1928.

_____. "Flashes out of Silence. Larry Semon May Take Flyer into Vaudeville." September 15, 1923.

_____. "Friends Reveal Nose Operation." March 8, 1924.

_____. "Hans F. Koenekamp; Retired Cinematographer." September 15, 1992.

_____. "Hope Abandoned for Saving Life of Larry Semon." October 8, 1928.

_____. "Larry Is Golf Bug." October 22, 1922.

_____. "Larry Semon in Chicago to Marry, Says Rumor." July 10, 1923.

_____. "Larry Semon Stars on Golf Course." April 21, 1923.

_____. "Personalities of the Southland Golf Links." May 3, 1922.

_____. "Plastic Surgeon Fixes Nose for Miss Carlisle." March 16, 1924.

_____. "Semon Contract is All Signed Up. Gold Fountain Pen Does Work in New York Golden Sunlight." May 26, 1923, I2.

_____. "Semon Funeral Will Be Simple." October 9, 1928.

_____. "Semon Nearing Illness Crisis." September 20, 1928.

_____. "Semon Salary Sets Record." May 23, 1923.

_____. "Semon Scores Gotham Shows." December 20, 1925.

Los Angeles Times. "Two Die after Pilot Faints." July 18, 1929.

Macon Telegraph. "Failure Now Gets Million." December 14, 1919.

_____. "Larry Semon Bankrupt." March 15, 1928.

Maltin, Leonard. *Leonard Maltin's Movie Crazy: For People Who Love Movies*. Milwaukie: Dark Horse Comics, 2008.

Marsh, W. Ward. "Comedian Talks about Screen Work; Tells of Remaking a Recent Film." *Cleveland Plain Dealer*, October 28, 1927.

Mast, Gerald. *The Comic Mind*. Chicago: University of Chicago Press, 1979.

McCabe, John. *The Comedy World of Stan Laurel*. New York: Doubleday, 1974.

Medina Daily Journal. "You Can't Get Away with It!" February 25, 1928.

Miami Herald. "Larry Semon and Wife in New York." Florida, January 3, 1926.

Mitchell, Glenn. *A-Z of Silent Film Comedy: An Illustrated Companion*. London: Batsford, 1998.

Moberly Weekly Monitor. "19-Year-Old Note to Movie Star Held as Valid." April 10, 1930.

Modesto Bee and News Herald. "Playing Jokes on the Stars." April 1, 1928.

_____. "Semon, Popular Film Comedian, Believed Dying." October 6, 1928.

Mon Ciné. "Vous avez la parole." March 30, 1922.

Montreal Gazette. "Larry Semon, Film Comedian, Is Dying." October 8, 1928.

Moscati, Camillo. *Ridolini: Il re della risata*. Milano: Editoriale Lo Vecchio, 1987.

Motion Picture Magazine. "Larry and Lucille Reunite." March 1922.

_____. "Stills between Shots." March 1923.

Motion Picture News. "Albany." December 8, 1923.

_____. "Directors." January/February 1916.

_____. "Screen Veteran Seen in 'Third Floor Back.'" April 20, 1918.

_____. "Wallace Beery to Make 'Taking the Air.'" January 28, 1927.

Motography. "Dancer in 'Big V' Comedies." September 15, 1917.

_____. "Director Gets Too Much Attention." June 9, 1917.

_____. "New Comedy Company." June 30, 1917.

_____. "Notes of the Industry in General." June 8, 1918.

_____. "Reservoir Built at Studio." June 1, 1918.

_____. "Three 'Big V' Comedy Companies Working: Semon Signs New Contract with Vitagraph and Goes West." December 15, 1917.

_____. "Vitagraph Offers 'The Last Man.'" November 4, 1916.

Moving Picture World. "Larry Semon Returns to West Coast." June 16, 1923.

_____. "Mutual Film Corporation." December 20, 1915.

_____. "Semon Prepares to Film TruArt Picture." November 23, 1923.
_____. "Semon 'Triples in Brass' for Paramount." December 11, 1926.
_____. "Semon Uses School Kids." October 31, 1925.
_____. "TruArt Announces Its Sales Policy on Semon Features." September 13, 1923.
_____. "Work Begun on First Semon Feature Comedy." October 6, 1923.
New York Clipper. "For Vicksburg." November 26, 1887.
New York Dramatic Mirror. "In the Picture Studios." February 12, 1916.
New York Herald. "Who Would Want To Be A Movie Hero?" October 1, 1916, 5.
New York Press. "Surprises at Golf Pool—Sid Mercer Defeated by Semon in Doyle's Billiard Academy." January 19, 1916, BC7.
New York Sun. "Nation's Laughs Profitable to the Comic Artist." May 2, 1915.
_____. "Golf Pool Experts Clash: Newspaper Men Meet at the Doyle Country Club." December 1, 1915.
New York Telegram. "'Larry' Semon 'Goat' in $35 per Job Now Rivals Chaplin As Movie King." 1919.
New York Times. "Gossip of Vaudeville." April 15, 1928.
_____. "Larry Semon Dying on California Ranch." October 7, 1928.
_____. "Norman Taurog, Director, Dies: Winner of an Oscar for 'Skippy.'" Reprint: January 12, 2007.
_____. "$3,000,000 in Three Years for Larry Semon: Film Comedian's New Contract for Slapstick." May 26, 1923.
Nye, Peggy. "Sub Deb Rosa." *Los Angeles Times*, March 7, 1926.
Oakland Tribune. "Myron Zobel's News of Picture People." December 17, 1922.
_____. "Oakland Theater." January 16, 1897.
_____. "Personal Appearance Shatters Illusions." February 8, 1925.
Oettinger, Malcolm. "The Heartbreaking Game of Being Funny." *New York Tribune*, November 27, 1921.
Ogden, Helen. "The Wear and Tear in Comedies." *Picture Play Magazine*, April 1924.
Ogdensburg Advance and St. Lawrence Weekly Democrat. "State News." January 31, 1878.
Omaha World Herald. "Poor Artists!" June 4, 1923.
Oregon Daily Journal. "Exhibitor Gets Inside View of Screen Capital." December 12, 1920.
_____. "Wee Bit Personal." December 26, 1920.
Oregonian. "Film Flickers." March 11, 1917.
"Long-Haired Women Soon to Be Rage in Hollywood." April 10, 1927.
_____. "Screen Gossip." April 26, 1921.
_____. "Silent Drama." September 9, 1917.
_____. "What Makes Crooks Laugh Discovered by Larry Semon." May 15, 1927.
Ottawa Journal. "Zera Semon Coming." March 8, 1895.
Parsons, Louella O. "Chaliapin for the Movies: Maybe." *Syracuse Journal*, August 26, 1927.

_____. "Filmettes." *The Idaho Statesman*, June 6, 1926.
_____. "In and out of [illegible]." *Morning Telegraph*, June 20, 1920.
_____. "Larry Semon's Income Taxes Harass Widow." *Los Angeles Examiner*, February 25, 1925.
Peltret, Elizabeth. "On Location with Larry Semon." *Motion Picture Magazine*, November 1920.
Philadelphia Inquirer. "Balbazoo Club to Give New Comedy." January 25, 1909.
_____. "Behind The Screen in Hollywood." August 15, 1926.
_____. "The Call Boy's Chat." November 23, 1919.
_____. "Children Dance at Atlantic: The Young People's Hop at the Mansion Largely Attended." August 1, 1889.
_____. "Executors' Claim." February 25, 1898.
_____. "Gossip around Studios out Hollywood Way." July 8, 1928.
_____. "Gossip around the Studios." June 21, 1925.
_____. "'The Merry Kiddo' and 'Madame Flutterby.'" February 2, 1908.
Photoplay. "'Beauty and Brains' Contest: Eleven Winners Chosen." June 1916.
_____. "Mr. Semon, How Could You?" December 1925.
_____. "Plays and Players." October 1920.
_____. "Spuds." November 1927.
_____. "Studio News and Gossip: East and West." December 1926.
Picture Play Magazine. "Even as Caesar." November 1920.
_____. "How They See Themselves." February 1921.
_____. "Information, Please." May 1925.
_____. "Is Mother a Pest?" May 1927.
_____. "The Observer." May 1920.
_____. "Over the Teacups." January 1924.
_____. "The Two-a-Day Racket." April 1928.
_____. "What the Fans Think." April 1920.
_____. "Which Picture Do the Players Like Best?" June 1925.
Pictures and the Picturegoer. "Simple Semon." May 1925.
Post Crescent, Appleton. "$14,000 Lien against Larry Semon Estate." May 30, 1929.
Ranch, Jess. "Historical Points of Interest in Apple Valley," *The Town of Apple Valley*, 2005, http://www.applevalley.org/gcsearch.aspx?q=garcelon.
Reading Times. "Wanted." April 7, 1880.
Reid, Margaret. "What I Think of My Wife—or My Husband—on the Screen." *Picture Play Magazine*, May 1927.
Richmond Dispatch. "Banner Sold Libby-Prison Museum." October 12, 1889.
Richmond Times Dispatch. "Heavyweight Fighter Working in the Movies." April 16, 1916.
Richmond Whig. "The City." December 19, 1871.
Riverside Daily Press. "Comedian's Health Is in Serious Condition." September 20, 1928.
_____. "Hughie Mack Dies at Santa Monica Home." October 14, 1927.
_____. "Screen Comedian in Poor Way Financially." March 14, 1928.

_____. "Semon Engagement Positively Denied." June 14, 1923.
Riverside Independent Enterprise. "Imitation Brick." November 7, 1916.
Roberts, Ed. *The Sins of Hollywood: An Expose of Movie Vice.* Los Angeles: Hollywood Publishing, 1922.
Roberts, Richard M. "Larry Semon, Part I: The Cartoonist as Comic." *Classic Images,* April 1999.
_____. "Larry Semon, Part II: Heyday," *Classic Images.* October 1999.
_____. "Larry Semon, Part III: Trouble Brewing." *Classic Images,* July 2000.
Rockford Republic. "Dorothy Dwan Injured." November 15, 1928.
_____. "He Gave Us Merriment." October 9, 1928.
_____. "Movie Men Fakers?" October 2, 1916.
Rosenberg, Bernard, and Harry Silverstein. *The Real Tinsel.* New York: Macmillan, 1970.
Runyon, Damon. "The Brighter Side." *Idaho Statesman,* Boise, June 5, 1946.
Rydzewski, Steve. *For Art's Sake: The Biography & Filmography of Ben Turpin.* Duncan: BearManor, 2013.
Saginaw News. "Lucille Carlisle Leading Woman for Larry Semon Again." December 8, 1921.
St. Albans Daily Messenger. "Prof. Zera's Entertainment." October 9, 1874.
St. John's Evening Telegram. "A Crowded Hall." February 6, 1899.
_____. "Zera: An Address to the Public." October 21, 1879.
St. Petersburg Times. "Dorothy Dawn, Western Star, Hails From Sleepy Philly." January 6, 1929.
Salt Lake Telegram. "Beauty Quest Ends as Larry Signs Ann." November 17, 1921.
San Bernardino County Sun. "Actor Rallies at Desert Hospital, Then Sinks Again." October 8, 1928.
_____. "Club is Being Pushed Ahead." September 19, 1926.
_____. "Larry Semon, Comedian, Dying Near Victorville." October 7, 1928.
_____. "Simple Rites Mark Passing of Film Star." October 10, 1928.
Sanchez García, José Maria. "Larry Semon el Narizota." *Prensa,* San Antonio, August 20, 1930.
San Diego Evening Tribune. "Miss Kathleen Myers." February 14, 1922.
San Diego Union. "Davis Would Be Producer of Film Comedies." August 24, 1926.
_____. "Filmland." December 18, 1921.
_____. "Larry Semon, Film Comedian, Dying in Mojave Sanitarium." October 7 (6), 1928.
San Francisco Call. "At the Chutes." June 27, 1897.
San Francisco Chronicle. "Party Given by Lois Wilson." September 30, 1928.
_____. "Semon Wears Seven Suits in Picture." April 24, 1927.
_____. "Some Good Numbers." August 24, 1925.
_____. "Side-Saddle Habits for Women out of Date." May 30, 1927.
_____. "Three Stars Plan to Play Golf All Day." December 25, 1927.
_____. "What They Don't Like About Husbands." February 10, 1929.
San Jose Evening News. "Larry Semon of Movies Is Ill." August 22, 1928.
San Luis Obispo Daily Telegram. "Daily Movie Service." July 7, 1921.
_____. "Larry Semon, Screen Star, Near Death." October 6, 1928.
Santa Ana Daily Evening Register. "Semon's Wit Makes No Hit: Gets Ticket." March 21, 1925.
Santa Ana Daily Register. "Movie Director for Larry Semon Gets 5-Day Term." March 25, 1925.
Santa Ana Register. "Death Fails to Halt Film Camera Work." July 1, 1927.
Santa Cruz News. "Semon Rents Train by Day for New Film." December 3, 1924.
Sassen, Claudia. "Larry Semon: How Many Times Did He Die?" *Slapstick!,* 2 July 2000.
_____. "Larry Semon: Untersuchungen zur Möglichkeit eines vorgetäuschten Ablebens." *Two Tars Journal,* 30, December 1999.
Schallert, Edwin. "Even as Eve." *Los Angeles Times,* February 2, 1920, II9.
_____. "Exploding the Comedy Plot." *Los Angeles Times,* June 6, 1920.
Schenectady Gazette. "Former Carman Girl in Featured Act at Proctor's." April 9, 1920.
Scranton Republican. "Screen Life in Hollywood." September 26, 1928.
Seattle Daily Times. "Acrobat Beats Monk." July 27, 1919.
_____. "Comedy Actress Injured." July 21, 1927.
_____. "Forget Powder Puff." May 17, 1925.
_____. "New Air Sport Thrills." February 26, 1922.
_____. "'Nix,' Says Larry." November 23, 1919.
_____. "Semon Has New Film." January 11, 1925.
_____. "Slapstick Is Popular." October 22, 1922.
Sedalia Democrat. "Dorothy Dwan." December 3, 1935.
_____. "Dorothy Dwan to a Stage Career." August 1, 1928.
_____. "Former Sedalian Holds Good Position in Movie Land." July 27, 1933.
_____. "Mother of Dorothy Dwan Is a Bride." May 21, 1928.
_____. "Picture of Dorothy Dwan in 'The Star.'" March 29, 1926.
Sedalia Weekly Democrat. "Home Town Lure for Dorothy Dwan." August 7, 1925.
_____. "Semon Intends to Make His Bride a Movie Star." January 30, 1925.
Semon, Lawrence. "Mysteries of Magic, Past and Present, Exposed." *San Francisco Chronicle,* August 8, 1909.
Sherk, Warren M. (comp., ed.). *The Films of Mack Sennett.* Metuchen: Scarecrow Press, 1998.
Slide, Anthony. *The Big V: A History of the Vitagraph Company.* Metuchen: Scarecrow Press, 1976.
Springfield Union. "The Argyle Case: They Bleach Real Money on the Stage but Don't Make It." October 30, 1913.
State Times Advocate. "Larry Semon Has Many Abilities." November 3, 1924.

_____. "Movie Beauty Fights Film Company." October 4, 1916.
Stone, Rob. *Laurel Or Hardy*: The Solo Films of Stan Laurel and Oliver "Babe" Hardy. Temecula: Split Reel, 1996.
Sylvester, Alan. "The Fatal Number Three." *Picture Play Magazine*, February 6, 1929.
Syracuse American Journal. "Larry Semon's Car Robbed." September 26, 1926.
Syracuse Herald. "'Underknee-Th.'" February 14, 1926.
Syracuse New York Journal. "Larry Semon Wins in Suit with Vitagraph." April 5, 1922.
Tampa Morning Tribune. "Amusements." October 21, 1924.
Tampa Tribune. "Up and Down." March 11, 1928.
Tildesley, Alice L. "My Best Remembered Christmas." *Springfield Republican*, December 25, 1927.
_____. "Should Women Reveal their Knees?" *Springfield Sunday Union and Republican*, December 11, 1927, 4D.
Tildesley, Ruth. "Happy Though Married." Unidentified magazine, 1926(?).
Times, Philadelphia. "To Pay a Father's Debt." May 15, 1892.
Times Picayune. "Twelve Beauties Arrive on Lot Seeking Fame." Section 4, March 27, 1927.
_____. "Vaudeville Wants Comedian." August 8, 1926.
Tinée, Mae. "This Is Called a Comedy; Why No One Knows." *Chicago Daily Tribune*, January 9, 1926.
Trenton Evening Times. "Has Nervous Collapse." January 2, 1926.
_____. "Funeral Services for Larry Semon." October 9, 1928.
_____. "Stacy—Larry Semon." August 20, 1924.
_____. "To Limit Runs of Broadways Successes: Gossip of the Theater." October 15, 1922.
Utica Saturday Globe. "Larry Semon Sued by Vitagraph." January 8, 1921.
Van Nuys News. "Larry Semon's Stolen Car Recovered after Wild Chase." January 7, 1927.
Variety. "Bitter Court Fight Pending Over 'Wizard of Oz' Rights." February 4, 1925.
_____. "Coleman's Baseball Player." May 1, 1914.
_____. "Inside Stuff on Pictures." June 7, 1923.
_____. "Judgment Against Semon." February 18, 1925.
_____. "Larry Semon." January 21, 1925.
_____. "Larry Semon Out. Arranges with Vitagraph to Finish Contract and Leave." May 26, 1922.
_____. "Mabel Normand back?" May 6, 1925.
_____. "Semon's Company out; But Semon Remains." May 5, 1922.
_____. "Semon's Pathe Agreement." July 29, 1925.
_____. "Union Square." 1914.
Waco News-Tribune. "Larry Semon near Death." September 29, 1928.
Walker, Helen Louise. "He Dug His Way in." *Picture Play Magazine*, November 1929.
Washington Times. "Semon on His Own." November 19, 1922.
Waterloo Evening Courier. "Smart Audiences Demand Fast Action in Movie Comedies, Larry Semon Says." April 21, 1928.
Watertown Re-Union. "Zera." April 30, 1874.
Wheeling Daily Intelligencer. "Amusement Notes." March 13, 1876.
_____. "Zera's Entertainment." March 10, 1876.
Wheeling Register. "The Last of Zera." March 16, 1878.
_____. "Petit Thieving." March 4, 1878.
Wichita Beacon. "Studio Closeups and Gossip." January 23, 1921, 4C.
_____. "Get in Line, Girls; Larry Semon Wants New Leading Woman." September 4, 1921.
Wilcox, Uthai Vincent. "The Clown Turns Ringmaster; Larry Semon Now a Director." Unidentified magazine, c. 1926.
Williamsport Gazette And Bulletin. September 30, 1875.
Williamsport Sun-Gazette. "Gossip of the Photoplays and Photoplay People." May 5, 1917.
Wilmington Messenger. "The Attraction at the Opera House." April 4, 1894.
_____. "Slick Tricks and Funny Things." April 4, 1894.
Wilmore, Carl. "Larry Semon Wants to Quit," *Boston Post Sunday Magazine*, August 21, 1920.
Witwer, H. C. "The Shooting Stars, Reel VII, Chapter XV." *The Brooklyn Daily Eagle*, January 12, 1923, A3.
Yallop, David. *The Day The Laughter Stopped*. New York: St. Martin's Press, 1976.
Zanesville Times Signal. "Cold Water for His Joke." June 13, 1926.
Zera. Unidentified paper, Denton, Maryland, October 26, 1878.
Zera Semon's Journal of Wonders 17, no. 501 Chestnut Street, Philadelphia, c. August 1881; cf. Virginia Historical Society. General Collection o.s. BF1598. S38 Z3.

Newspapers and Magazines

Albany Evening Journal
Atlanta Constitution
Auburn Citizen
Bay City Times
Boston Herald
Boys' Cinema
Brooklyn Daily Eagle
Brooklyn Eagle
Brooklyn Standard Union
Buffalo Courier Express
Buffalo Evening News
Canton Repository
Cedar Rapids Tribune
Charlotte Observer
Chicago Daily Herald
Chicago Daily Tribune
Chicago Sunday Times
Chronicle Telegram
Cincinnati Enquirer
Cinémagazine

Cine-Mundial
Cleveland Plain Dealer
Columbus Courier
Daily Argus
Daily Illini
Daily Star
Daily State Journal
Dallas Morning News
Danville Bee
Davenport Democrat and Leader
The Day Book, Chicago
Detroit Free Press
Duluth Evening Herald
Emporia Gazette
Evening Tribune
Exhibitors Herald
Exhibitor's Trade Review
Film Daily
Filmdom
Fitchburg Sentinel
Fort Worth Daily Gazette
Fresno Morning Republican
Helena Daily Independent
Huntington Press
The Idaho Statesman
Illustrated New Age, Philadelphia
Indianapolis Sentinel
Indianapolis Star
Kansas City Star
Lebanon Daily News
Lima Daily News
Lincoln Evening Journal
Los Angeles Examiner
Los Angeles Express
Los Angeles Herald
Los Angeles Times
Macon Telegraph
Manitoba Morning Free Press
Miami Herald
Moberly Weekly Monitor
Modesto Bee and News Herald
Mon Ciné
Montreal Gazette
Motion Picture Magazine
Motion Picture News
Motography
Moving Picture World
New York Clipper
New York Dramatic Mirror
New York Press
New York Sun
New York Telegram
New York Times
Niagara Falls Gazette
North Tonawanda Evening News
Oakland Tribune

Ogden Standard
Old Cardboard
Oregon Daily Journal
Oregonian
Pantomime
Philadelphia Inquirer
Photoplay
Pictures and the Picturegoer
Richmond Dispatch
Richmond Times Dispatch
Riverside Daily Press
Riverside Independent Enterprise
Rockford Republic Salt Lake Telegram
Saginaw News. San Diego Union
St. Albans Daily Messenger
St. John's Evening Telegram
St. Petersburg Times
Salt Lake Telegram
San Bernardino County Sun
San Francisco Call
San Francisco Chronicle
San Jose Evening News
San Luis Obispo Daily Telegram
Santa Ana Daily Evening Register
Santa Ana Daily Register
Santa Ana Register
Schenectady Gazette
Scranton Republican
Seattle Daily Times
Sedalia Democrat
Sedalia Weekly Democrat
Society of American Magicians Monthly Magazine
Springfield Union
State Times Advocate
Syracuse American Journal
Syracuse Herald
Syracuse New York Journal
Tampa Morning Tribune
Tampa Tribune
Times Picayune
Times, Philadelphia
Trenton Evening Times
Union and Recorder
Variety
Vitagraph Bulletin
Waco News-Tribune
Washington Times
Watertown Re-Union
Wheeling Daily Intelligencer
Wheeling Register
Wichita Beacon
Williamsport Gazette and Bulletin
Williamsport Sun-Gazette
Wilmington Messenger
Zanesville Times Signal

Index

Numbers in ***bold italics*** indicate pages with photographs.

accidents 7, 67–70, 98, 156, 168, 188
Ackermann, C.M. "Ackie" 54, 194
Adams, Claire 133, ***135***
Adams, Jimmie 125
Adams, John H. 152
Adorée, Renée 169
Adventure 112
The Agent 94
à Hiller, Lejaren 136, 137
Albee, E.F. 143
Alexander, Frank 71, 75, ***107***, ***115***, ***116***
Allen, Victoria 74
Amann, Philippine "Bee" 168, 169–171
Appleby, Dorothy 179
Aramondo, Pietro 65; *see also* Gordon, Pete
Arbuckle, Roscoe 93, 115, 122, 125, 161–162
The Argyle Case 42
Arnold, Helen 97
Aronsky, Rory 4
Astaire, Marie 168
Astor, Gertrude 127, 168, ***171***
Atwell, Roy 74
Aubrey, James "Jimmie" 54, ***63***, 64–65, 84, 131, 133, 155, 159, 177, 194
Austin and Stone's 21
automatons 11, 17, 44, 46
auto-ped craze 62; *see also* Conkwright, A.B. "Conky"
The Aviator 188
Aye, Marion 108
Ayres, Agnes 64
Ayres, Edward W. 10

The Baby and the Boss 194
Baker, C. Graham 56, 59, 70, 136

The Bakery 125, 126, 127
Balbazoo Club 32–33
Balboa (seaside resort) 69, 145
Balloon-Birds (contest) 90–91
Balshofer, Fred 122
Bancroft, George ***163***, 164, 168
bankruptcy 151, 154, 169, 172–174, 175, 185, 188
Bardine, Mabel 130
Barnes, Roy 74
Barnhill, Dr. Oliver 143
The Barnyard 119, 126, 127
baseball 26, 37, 39, 43–44, 46, 48–50, ***51***, 52, 89, 113
Basil, Joe ***60***, 64, 65, 69, 100, 136, 158
Basquette, Lina 169
Bathing Beauties and Big Boobs 16, 98
The Battler 39, 62, 66
Baum, L. Frank 148
Baum, L. Frank, Jr. 148
Baxter, Billy 60; *see also A Jealous Guy*
Bears and Bad Man 67, 74–75, ***90***
Beauties Brigade 66, ***68***
Beery, Wallace 161
Bell, Gus 17
The Bell Hop ***107***, ***118***, 120
Bell's Royal Marionettes ***16***, 17, 21
Bennett, Alma 165
Bern, Paul 112
Bernstein, Sam 44, 72
Between the Acts 21, 90, 126
Big Bluff and Bowling Balls 49
Black, G. Howe 149
Black, John 79
Blackton, James Stuart 54, 56, 59, 76, 98
Blackwell, Carlyle 96
blizzard (New York, 1910) 36

Blythe, Betty 142
Boggs, Paul H. 185
Bombs and Blunders 66, 69
Boodle and Bandits 66, 98
Booth, John Wilkes
Bow, Clara 163
Bowman, Rebecca 18, 26
Bradford (illustrator) 28, ***30***
Bradford, Edgar Nelton *see* Nelton, Nino
Bradley, George E. 159
Brady, Alice 96
Brady, William A. 96
Brains and Beauty (contest) 96–97
Brenon, Herbert 97, 148
Brent, Evelyn 164
Brewster, Eugene V. 154
Bringing Up Father 59
British Exhibitors' Films 149
Brook, Clive 164
Brooke, Tyler 173
Brown Faire, Virginia 174
Brownlow, Kevin 72, 79, 121
Brule, Frank ***60***, 186
Brunetti, Argentine 85, 156
Buckles, Dorothy *see* Dwan, Dorothy
Bunny, John ***55***, 56
Bunny's Suicide ***55***
Burns, Neal 79
Bushwick 143
Butler Lee, Claire Lois 96–97

Cagney, James 50
Cantor, Eddie 157, 161–163
The Canyon of Light 142
Carlisle, Helen 96, 97, 112–113
Carlisle, Lucille 3, 4, 94–101, ***94***, ***97***, ***98***, 103–113, ***105***, ***106***, ***109***, ***111***, ***114***, 120, 123, 125, ***126***, 127, 129, 141, 142

247

Index

Carr, Mary 149
carte blanche 92, 115, 129
casting 108, 112–113, 139–140; see also recruitment of players
The Cawthorne Boys 13–15
Century (film company) 125
Chadwick, I.E. 133, 142
Chadwick Picture Corporation 148, 149–151, 168, 169
Chaplin, Charlie 1, 2, 32, 92, 93, 99, 106, 115, 125, 133, 149, 154, 156
Chaplin, Sidney 72, 160
Cheatham, Maude 87, 89
Christie, Al 125
Chutes Amusement Park 23
Cinema Finance Corporation 172
Clarke, Kit 21
Clifford, Kathleen 157
Clinton, Bert 174
The Cloudhopper 125, 136
Coconut Grove 89, 141–142
Code, Rose 108, 121
Cohen, Phillip 117
Coleman's Baseball Player 44, 46
Conkwright, A.B. "Conky" 62; see also auto-ped craze
Cook, Clyde 169
Cortez, Ricardo 164
Couderc, Jean-Jacques 4
The Count of Luxembourg 151
The Counter Jumper 11, 125, **126**
counterfeiting 42–43, 64
Cox, Joe 62
Crawford, Joan 169
Cross, Harry 52
Crowe, Regine 151
Cruickshank, B.W. 182, 183
Cruze, James 141
Cryer, George E. (mayor) 123
Cummins, Irving 96
Cunningham, Elizabeth May see Semon, Elizabeth May
Cunningham, Elizabeth May "Bettie" 17
Cunningham, Howell Chestnut 17
Cunningham, Howell Chestnut, Jr. 17
Curtis, Florence 75
cut-out paper toys 28, *30*, *31*, *32*, 191–192, *191*

Daley, Lillian 176
Dana, Viola 169
Daniels, Bebe 108
Daniels, Frank 56, *57*, 194
Davenport's Spiritistic Canopy Act 31
Day, Alice *158*, 166
Dead Men Tell No Tales 117

Deane, Doris 125
De Forest, Patsy 60, *61*, *66*, 67, 72
de Garde, Adele 59
Demaree, Al *48*
DeMille, Cecil B. 98, 141, 157
Dempsey-Tunney boxing fight 166
De Silva, Fred ***124***, ***128***
Devore, Dorothy 168
Dew Drop Inn ***106***
Dexter, Elliott 99
Dick Turpin 125
Dill, Jack 65
The Dome Doctor 138
Donelly, James 131
Donohoe, "Doc" 60, *61*
Dorgan, "Tad" 49–50, *51*
Down on the Farm (1920) 125
A Dozen Socks ***158***
Dream of a Rarebit Fiend 40
Dressler, Marie 169
Drew, Mr. and Mrs. Sidney 133
Düsseldorfer Malerschule 26
Dull Care 77, 80, 84, ***105***
Dummies ***167***, 168
Duncan, Robert C. 62–63
Duncan, William 65
Dunham, Phil ***122***
Dunn, Bill 186
Dunn, Ed(die) "Needles" 64, 66
Dwan, Allan 141
Dwan, Dorothy 139–149, ***139***, ***140***, 151, 153, ***153***, ***154***, 155–156, 159–160, 165–166, 168, 169, 172, 173, ***173***, 174, 176–183, 185–186
dynamite 69, 76

Earle, Edward 64
Edington, Mae 146
Edison, Thomas A. 22
Educational Film Company 137–139, 142, 143, 166–171, 172, 175
Enoch Pickleweight 28
Es darf gelacht werden 1
Even as Eve ***100***

Factor, Max 69, 137, 179
Fairbanks, Douglas 106, 128
Faire, Elinor 146
The Fall Guy 107
Famous Players Lasky 98, 141
fan mail 93, 166
Farrar, Geraldine 129
Fatty's Fatal Fun 54
F.B.O. Studios 139, 154, 155, 168
The Fiddler 53, 194
Fields, W.C. 186
The Fighting Legion 185
Finch, Flora *55*

Fine Arts Studio 128
The Firefly of France 98
First National Exhibitor's Circuit 124
Flatow, John L. 67
Fleming, Victor 112
Florey, Robert 104, 157, 184
The Fly Cop 39, 67, 80
Ford, Jack 161
Fostell, Al 19–20
Foster, Robert 80
Fox Sunshine Comedies 82
Foxfilm 71, 125
Frauds and Frenzies 75–76, 80, ***182***
The Freshman 152
Frew, John 14
Friars Club 143
Frohman, Daniel 97
Fuller, Ida 23
Fuller, Loïe 22–23

gags, repetition and variation of 76–77, 125–127, 132, 134, 137
Gall and Golf 79
Garcelon, Dr. Harris S. 175, 176–178, 180–181, 185
Gaynor, William Jay (mayor) 37
Geraghty, Carmelita ***131***, 131
Gifford, Denis 120
gift shows 13, 19, 24
Gill, Sam 1, 4, 54, 104, 177, 194
The Girl in the Limousine 21, 129, 130, 131, 133, ***134***, ***135***, 135–137, 139
Go Straight 138
The Gob 157
Goldberg, Rube (Reub) 50, *51*
The Golden Age of Comedy 1
Goldin, Sidney 54, 188
golf 17, 79, 89–90, 125, 160, 169, 175, 177
Golf 85, 107, 123, 127
Gone with the Wind 112
Goodrich, Will H. see Arbuckle, Roscoe
The Gown Shop 126, ***128***
Gordon, Pete 131; see also Aramondo, Pietro
Gottschalk, Louis Moreau 12
Grauman, Sid 127
greasepaint 58, 69, 80, 89, 161
The Great K and A Train Robbery 159–160
Greed 123
Grif (illustrator) 28
Griffith, David W. 71, 133, 164
The Grocery Clerk 77, 90, 119, 126

Halifax, Nova Scotia 19, 20, 24–25

Index

Hall (Draper), Ethel 166
Hall, Phil 4
Hammons, Earle W. 143, 169, **170**
Hardy, Oliver Norvell 4, 54, 75, 84, 107, **118, 126**, 127, **128**, 131, 147, 149, 169, 177
Harms, Clyde 152
Hart, William S. 185
Hartz, Joseph 13
Hastings, Ann 108–110
Hauber, William "Bill" 67, 71, 75, 188
Hayden, Scott 186
Hays and Wiedersheim (illustrators) 28
He Laughs Last 63
The Head Waiter 84
Hearst, William Randolph 43
Heidelberg, Germany 11
Heller, Robert 13, 17
Henley House 18
Henry Duffy Players 178
Her Boy Friend 120, 137, **138**, 139, 141, 165
Hermann the Great 7, 11, 30
Heywood, Bessie 26
The Hick 84, 101, 104, 106
Hicksville, NY 119–120
Hilliard, Robert 42
Hindoos and Hazards 78–79
His Little Widows 98
Ho Fans! (column) 42
Hoffman, M.H. 128, 129, 130
Hoins, Jack W. 186
Holloway, Carol 65
Holt, Jack 169
Horseshoes 11, 125, 127, 131
Horton, Aida 101
Howard, Willie 162
Howe, J.A. 65
Hughes, Charles Evans 37
Humbugs and Husbands 78, 107
Hume Lake 121
Humpty Dumpty Pantomime 17
The Hunchback of Notre Dame 112
Huns and Hyphens 11, 74, 92
Hunt, Jewell 60

I Knew Him When Club 49, 92
Ilgenfritz, Dorothy Belle *see* Dorothy Dwan
Ilgenfritz, Melvin 140
I'm Looking for the Man Who Invented Work (song) 99
Ince, Thomas 133
It's Only Ethelinda 28, **33**, 192

A Jealous Guy 16, 59; *see also* Baxter, Billy
Jeffries of the Dodgers 39, **40**

Jenks, Si 74
Jeritza, Maria 129
Jordan, A.A. 131
Joyce, Alice 62
J.R. Rich Company 183
Jumps and Jealousy 67

Kaptin Kiddo 28, **191**, 192
Keaton, Buster 1, 4, 154
Keith-Albee Orpheum 174
Keith's Riverside 142
Kelly, Kitty 152
Kendig, Walter 54
Kennedy, Madge 62
Kenyon, Doris 130
Keystone 72
Keystone Kid *see* Watson, Coy
Kid Boots 163
Kid Speed 138, **139**
King Vidor 141
Kingsley, Grace 149, 176
Kirby, Audrey 71
Kirby, Madge 71, 76, 98
Kirby, Morris 71
Klamottenkiste 1
Koenekamp, Hans F. 72, 77–78, 79, 121–122, 188, 189
Kohler, Fred 164
Knapp, Ruth 103
Knechtel, Alvin 188

Laemmle, Carl 176
Lahue, Kalton C. 1, 4
La Marr, Barbara 112
Lamont, Dixie **63**
Langdon, Harry 157, 175, 186
LaPlante, William 147–148
Larry Semon Athletics **74**
Larry Semon Polka 93
Larry Semon Productions Inc. 142, 152, 153, 154, 161, 172, 175, 184
Larry Semon Studio *see* Larry Semon Productions Inc.
L.A.S.M. (Los Angeles Society of Magicians) 25
Laurel, Mae 76
Laurel and Hardy 1, 4, 75, 169, 177, 186
Lee, Leon 52, 133
Lee, Mildred *see* Moore, Mildred
Lee Corbin, Virginia 174
Lee Worting, Helen 174
Lehrman, Henry 64, 82, 84, 122, 162
Leonard, Babs 168
Leonard, Robert 144
Let's Go 129
Levy, Henry 101
Levy, Maxine 101
Lewis, Jane 58
Lewis, Jerry 87

Lightning Love 11, 127, 129
Lil' Artha **44**
Linderman, J.C. 23
Lippman, Emma 25–26
Lippman, Leonard 26
Lippman, Lewis 25–26
Lippman, Marie 26
Livingston, Margaret 146
Lloyd, Harold 1, 59, 93, 106, 115, 133, 148–149, 152, 154, 157, 175
Lloyd, Mildred Davis 157
Loescher, Madge *see* Kirby, Madge
Loew, Marcus 110, 143, 166, 169
Lombardi Ltd. (stage play) 176–178, 185
London, Jack 112
Lonergan, Elizabeth 158
Loomis, Frank 56
The Luck of the Irish 122
A Lucky Dog 84
Lyons, Eddie 97

M., Aloysius 144
MacAllister, Mary 159
Mack, Hughie 59–60, 62–64, 66–67, 71, 133, 155, 186, 195–201, 246
MacLean, Douglas "Doug" 136, 149
Mad Movies 1, 156
Madame Flutterby 33
Maddox, Dr. C. Sidney 159
makeup 58, 60, 63, 65, 69–70, 71, 80, **124**, 137–138, 164, 179, 183, 186
Maltin, Leonard 84
The Man from Egypt 59
Manitoba, Winnipeg
Männer ohne Nerven 1
Manufacturers and Wholesalers Credit Corporation 152
Marcus, Edythe **36**
Marcus, Rebecca **36**
Marcus, Simon **36**
Marcus, the Boarding House Goat 50
Marton, Alatia 97
Mask and Wig Club 33, **35**
Masons 1, 17, 74
Mast, Gerald 80
Matzkin, Reuben 101
Maynard, Ken 185
McCabe, John 75
McCay, Winsor 30, 40, 50
McClure Newspaper Syndicate 139
McCoy, Tim **173**
McGillicuddy, Cornelius (Connie Mack) **49**
McGowan, Hugh R. *see* Mack, Hughie

Index

McManus, George 59
Meighan, Thomas 99
Menjou, Adolphe 169, 174
Mercer, Sid 52
Merely a Monarch **35**
The Merry Kiddo 33
metalepsis 119
Metro Pictures 143
Metropolitan, New York 127, 174
Meyer Both Company 62
The Midnight Cabaret 125
Millikin, Leland H. 113
million dollar contracts 3, 49, 91–93, 129–130, 173
Mills, B.H. 53
Mills, Florence 175
Missing 98
Mr. and Mrs. Sidney Drew 133
Mr. Wood B. Sport 37, **37**, **38**
Mittenthal Brothers 54, 194
Mix, Tom 125, 139, 142, 156, 159–160, 166, 175, 185
Moby Dick 188
Mojave Lake Club 177
Monkhouse, Bob 1, 156
Montana, Bull **153**
Montgomery, Earl **61**, 64, 65, 67, 70, 145–146
Montgomery and Rock 67, 76
Moonshines see *Trouble Brewing*
Moore, Mildred 97
Moran, Lee 97
Moreno, Antonio 75
Morrison, Charles 174
Moscati, Camillo 4
Mothers of America 113
Motion Picture Capital Corporation 175
Murphy, Charley 37
Murphy, Tommy 62
Murray, Charlie 21, 136
Murray, Mae 120
Murray and Mack 21
Musketeers of Pig Alley 164
Mutual Film Corporation 54, 194
My Best Girl 151
Myers, Kathleen 125
Mysteries of Magic, Past and Present, Exposed 20, 30–31, **34**

Napoleon III 11
National Film Corporation 147
Nazimova, Alla 97
Needling, Edward A. 21
Negri, Pola 141
Nelson, Nino see Nelton, Nino
Nelton, Nino 21, 24
New York Evening Sun 50, 54, 56, 60, 77, 187

New York Evening Telegram 35–37, 49, 92, 187
New York Giants 37, 46, 48, **49**, **50**, 52
New York Herald 37
New York Morning Telegraph 41
New York Times 54, 56, 59
Newmeyer, Fred 149
Newspapermen's Pocket Billiard Tournament 52
Nichols, Norma **107**, 108
No Wedding Bells 112, 127, 138
Normand, Mabel 151
The North American 20, 28–36, **29**, 131–132
novelty film 53–54, 194

O'Connor, Kathleen 108, 121
Oettinger, Malcolm 94
Oh, What a Man 16, 127, 168, **171**
O'Hara, John 60, **61**
Olga Steeb School 160
Ordley, Karoly 21
Orr, Getrude 146
orthochromatic film 23, 58, 80
Osborne, Frank C. 12
O'Shea, Danny **158**
Our Gang 169
Out Again, In Again 59, 60
outtakes 131

Pagliacci, Semon 136, **137**
A Pair of Kings 76, 87, 114–115, **114**, **122**, 123, **124**, 145
Palace Players Film Corporation 54, 59, 194
Palace Theater 44, 143–144
Palmer, A.H. 175
Papa Roujoul's magic store 11
Paramount Pictures 112, 149, 152, 157, 161–162, 164–165, 168, 172, 184
Paris, France 11, 93, 108
Parsons, Louella 80, 82, 157
Parsons, "Smiling Billy" 147
Passing the Buck 69
Pathé 54, 108, 152, 153, 154, 156, 158, 163
Peiken, Evelyn **36**
Peiken, Max **36**
Peltret, Elizabeth 67
Pennington, Ethel 56
Pepper Pot 20
The Perfect Clown 149, **150**
Perils of the Coast Guard 159–160
Peter Pan 148
The Phantom Melody 97
Photoplay Magazine 96–97, 100, 103, 113
Pickford, Mary 128
Pickles and Peanuts 33

Plagues and Puppy Love 75
Pluck and Plotters 16, **74**, 76, 80, **82**
Pollard, Harry "Snub" 121, 183
Presley, Elvis 188
The Prisoner of Zenda 123
Proctor's Theater 44
Professor and Madam Zera see Osborne, Frank C.
Publix Theaters Corporation 174

The Queen Mother 97

Ralston, Jobyna 146, 163
Rankin, Caroline 65
Rappé, Virginia 122, 161, 162
Rayart Pictures Corporation 159
Raynor, Dorothea **167**, 168
Rea, Irene see Semon, Irene
Rea, Jane Elizabeth 17
Rea, Samuel M. 17
recruitment of players 84–85, 129–130; see also casting
The Red Mill 162
Reed, Florence 97
The Rent Collector 39, **107**
retakes 85, 94, 135, 162
Reynolds, Vera 146
Richardson, Jazz "Lips" 175
Riders of the Dark **173**
Rinaudo, Joe 188
Roach, Hal 157, 169
Robert-Houdin, Jean Eugène 11, 20, 122, 161
Roberts, Ed 100–101, 104–105, 110
Roberts, Richard M. 176, 179, 182
Rock, Joe 74
Roentgen Rays 21
Rogers, Will 130
Rohauer, Raymond 188
Roomberg, Dorothy **36**
Roomberg (née Rosenbaum), Hannah **36**
Roomberg, Nathan 32, **36**
Roosevelt, A. 58
Rosenbaum, Augusta "Gussie" 32–35, **36**, 38, **39**, 41, 52, 99–103, **102**, 105
Rosenbaum, Ethel 32, **36**
Rosenbaum, Dr. George 32, **36**
Rosenbaum, Matilda **36**
Rosenbaum, William "Bill" **36**
Ross, Bobby 79
Rubey, Harry M. 152
Ruth, Babe 48
Ryan, Coletta 129, 130
Rydzewski, Steve 176

St. John's, Newfoundland 24
Salvage 159

San Bernardino 175, 179, 181–183
San Francisco 22–25, 91
Savannah 25–26, 28
The Sawmill 123
Sawyer-Lubin Company 143
Scamps and Scandals 3, 99
Schallert, Edwin 76, 99, 134
Schenck, Joseph 87, 132
Schipa, Tito *137*
School Days **109**, *182*
Schulberg, B.P. 161
Scotti, Tino *182*
Sebastian, Dorothy 144
Selznick, Lewis J. 97
Semon, Benjamin 7
Semon, Elizabeth May 17, 182
Semon, Emanuel 7–9, 10, 11, 15
Semon, Emma 16
Semon, Irene 13, *16*, 17
Semon, Jacob "Jake" S. 8–10, 93
Semon, Judah C. 8, 182
Semon, Rachael 15–16
Semon, Rebecca *see* Bowman, Rebecca
Semon, Rosa Belle 28, 93
Semon, Virginia 18, 41, 99–101, 103, *104*, 178, 179–180, 181
Semon, William Zera 17
Semon, Zera 8, 10–17, 18–26, 30–32, 80, 136, 138, 182
Semon, Zera, Jr. 17
Semon and Laurel comedy team 75
Semon's Sea Lions 60, *61*, 63
Sennett, Mack 125
Señor Wences 12
seriality 125–127
Service, Robert W. 143
Shadows of Paris 141
Shanks and Chivalry 60
Shea, William "Bill" 60, *61*
Shipman, Nell 65
The Shooting of Dan McGrew 143
The Show 108–110, 126, 152
Shubert Show 98, 129
Sidle, Karl 74
The Silent Vow 140
Simberg, Joseph *see* Rock, Joe
The Simple Life 16, **83**, 99
A Simple Sap 157, 169, 171, 179
Simple Simon *32*
sleight-of-hand tricks 12, 17, 27, 30–32, 160, 165
Slide, Anthony 4, 80
Smith, Albert Edward 56, 64–65, 76–77, 84, 91–92, 99, 108, 115–117, 121, 123–125, 131–132
Smith, Dorothy *see* Dwan, Dorothy
Smith, Frank 131
Smith, George Hughes Lieutenant 140–141

Smith, Leonard "Len" 60, *61*
Smith, Nancy 141–142, 146, 175–177, 180–181, 183
Smith, W. Steve 65, 123
Snellenburg (department store warehouse) 28
Solid Concrete 78, **98**, 99
Sollars, Charles 175, 182, 183, 185
Sollars, Nancy *see* Smith, Nancy
Special Delivery 161–163
Spencer, Fred *138*
Spies and Spills 76, 80
The Sportsman 103–104, *116*, 118–119, 156
Spuds 32, 40, 142, 154–158, *154*
Square Crooks 179
The Stage Hand 78, 84, *97*, 126
Stageland and Society 33, *35*
Standard Pictures Corporation 159
The Star Boarder 76, **91**, *182*
Steadman, Vera *72*, 99
Sterling, Marta *128*
Stone, Fred 147
Stone, Rob 4, 76, 84, 126
Stop, Look and Listen 147, 151–153, *153*
storyboard 78
strength tester 66
Stripes and Stumbles 76
Stroheim, Erich von 123
The Stunt Man 3, 168
stunts (thrills) 1, 20–21, 66–70, 71, 77, 87, 107, 115, 121, 123, 125, 129, 134, 136, 138, 155, 188
The Suitor 16, 103, 107, 115–117, *115*
Sunshine of Paradise Alley 151
Swain, Mack 72
Swanson, Gloria 144
Sweetwater Waltz 12
Swickard, Joseph 151

Taft, William Howard 33
Taking the Air 161
Takushi, James 89
The Talking Hand 12
Talmadge, Richard 71, 87, 107, *105*
Tanabe, John 89
Taurog, Norman 122
Telly *see* New York Telegram
Terry, Paul 161
Terry's Tea Party 59
Thanhouser-Mutual Company 194
Thompson, Al **97**, *115*
Tiffany Productions 128
Tildesley, Ruth 146
Tiny Doll 162
Tourneur, Maurice 96, 133

Traps and Tangles 3, *72*
trick photography 11–12, 59, 77–78, 118–119, 126, 156, 188
Triumph 141
Trouble Brewing **131**
TruArt Film Corporation 128–132
Tubby Turns the Tables 59
Tumbling River 166
Turks and Troubles 66
Turnbull, Hector *163*
Turpin, Ben 58, 158–159
Tuxedo tobacco 50

Underworld 161, **163**, 164–165
Universal Pictures 54, 97, 141, 194
Uyeda, Frank 89

Vanciel, Clifford 161
vaudeville 12, 18–26, 43–44, 46, 59, 76, 84, 99, 112, 129–130, 143–144, 151, 158–159, 162, 168–169, *170*, 174–175, 176, 177
ventriloquism 12
Victorville 175–179, 181, 183
A Villainous Villain 66
The Violinist see The Fiddler
The Virgin Queen 174
Vitagraph 3–4, 44, 49, 54–73, 76, 79–94, 97, 98, 100, 101, 103, 105, 106, 107, 109, 114–118, 120–123, 126–132, 134, 137, 173, 175, 177, 182, 186, 188, 193–194
V-L-S-E (Vitagraph-Lubin-Selig-Essanay) 60
Vogue comedies 71
von Eltz, Theodore 174
von Sternberg, Josef 161, 164–165

Waldron, D.G. 23
Wallace, Dorothy W. *see* Smith, Nancy
Wallace, Sir William 140
Walls and Wallops 62
Walsh, George 149
Walska, Ganna 144
WAMPAS (Western Association of Motion Picture Advertisers) baby 131
War Brides 97
Warner Brothers Inc. 132, 159, 188
Warren, Edward 54, 194
WASPS (Women's Association of Screen Publicists) 140
Watson, Coy, Jr. 87
Webster, Daniel
Welch, Galen H. 185
West Montok 123
West Point, Mississippi 18–19

Westford, Suzanne 54, 194
Wheeling Intelligencer 13–15
When Comedy Was King 1
Whistles and Windows 39
Whitcopf, Lynne 103
White, Edna Ellen "Helen" *see* Carlisle, Helen
White, Frank 104, 131
White, Ida Lucille *see* Carlisle, Lucille
Williams, C. Jay 56
Williams, Earl 159
Williams, Guinn "Big Boy" 84–85

Wilson, Lois 178
Wine of Youth 141
Wistar, Richard 10
Witwer, Harry Charles 50
Witzel, Albert 75, 79, 81, 88
The Wizard of Oz 3, 21, 129, 133, 141, 142–143, 147–149, *148*, 151
Wolff, Rube 169
Wong, Anna May 127
World Film Corporation 96
Writer's Club, Hollywood 147
Wynn, Ed 32, 144

x-rays *see* Roentgen Rays

Yankee Doodle Dandy 129
Young, Jordan 177, 194
Young Men's Hebrew Association (YMHA) 32
Youth Is Youth see *My Best Girl*

Zintheo, Lucille *see* Carlisle, Lucille
Zinther, Lucille *see* Carlisle, Lucille

www.ingramcontent.com/pod-product-compliance
Lightning Source LLC
Chambersburg PA
CBHW081548300426
44116CB00015B/2795